Actively Caring for People

Cultivating a Culture of Compassion

Fourth Edition

E. Scott Geller, Ph.D.

Published by
Make-A-Difference, LLC.
Newport, Virginia

Actively Caring for People™: *Cultivating a Culture of Compassion*

Copyright © 2014 by E. Scott Geller, Ph.D.
Text processing: Jenna McCutchen
Editorial assistance: Dave Johnson
Illustrations: George V. Wills
Cover design: Nancy Poes

Make-A-Difference, LLC.
161 Make-A-DiffRanch Drive
P. O. Box 73 • Newport, Virginia 24128-0073
www.ac4p.org • www.safetyperformance.com

ISBN 0-926487-65-5

Library of Congress Control Number is available upon request

Printed in the United States of America

Praise for
Actively Caring for People ™

*T*HIS NEW BOOK *by Dr. E. Scott Geller and colleagues pro-*
vides an inspiring example of how theory and practice can
come together to change lives. The Actively Caring for People
Movement builds upon the spirit of service that defines Virginia
Tech through its motto Ut Prosim (That I May Serve). As Provost,
I have seen firsthand how our students have embraced and used
actively caring in many different situations. Under the leadership
of Scott Geller, this Movement has the potential to benefit the
lives of millions of individuals and groups. This book provides
the research-based principles and real-life stories that will help
advance the Actively Caring for People Movement.

Mark McNamee
Senior Vice President and Provost
Virginia Tech
Blacksburg, Virginia

SCOTT GELLER'S CONCEPT of Actively Caring for People (AC4P) has been fundamental to keeping our employees safe for over ten years. Regardless of the type of work, reaching people is what makes the difference. Many might think Actively Caring is not a comfortable fit for rough necks in the oil-drilling business, but that's simply not true. With AC4P we have achieved "Best in Class" in our industry. The AC4P principles and applications have benefitted the lives of our employees at work and at home.

Dave Werner
Vice President and General Manager for California Operations
Nabors Completion and Production Services

ON THEIR RECENT speaking tour in Western Australia, Scott and Joanne Geller touched the hearts and minds of nearly 600 workers engaged in the "pointy end" of organizational safety and improvement efforts. One might think with our geographically dispersed workplaces, remote lifestyles and harsh outback working environments, the average West Aussie is a rough and tumble type who could care less about the welfare of fellow employees and the well-being of their community. But this stereotype was destroyed by the manner in which the Actively Caring for People concept was embraced by those fortunate enough to see Scott and Joanne in action. We now have researchers, school and community groups queuing up to explore how AC4P can make a difference in their lives. This is a long and no doubt challenging road we set upon, but Scott and Joanne inspired us to take the first step.

Martin Ralph
Managing Director
Industrial Foundation for Accident Prevention (IFAP)
Perth, Western Australia

This book is dedicated to the families and friends of the thirty-three Hokies who lost their lives on April 16th, 2007.

Ross A. Alameddine

Christopher James Bishop

Brian R. Bluhm

Ryan Christopher Clark

Austin Michelle Cloyd

Jocelyne Couture-Nowak

Kevin P. Granata

Matthew Gregory Gwaltney

Caitlin Millar Hammaren

Jeremy Michael Herbstritt

Rachael Elizabeth Hill

Emily Jane Hilscher

Jarrett Lee Lane

Matthew Joseph La Porte

Henry J. Lee

Liviu Librescu

G.V. Loganathan

Lauren Ashley McCain

Partahi Mamora Halomoan Lumbantoruan

Daniel Patrick O'Neil

Juan Ramon Ortiz-Ortiz

Minal Hiralal Panchal

Daniel Alejandro Perez Cueva

Erin Nicole Peterson

Michael Steven Pohle, Jr.

Julia Kathleen Pryde

Mary Karen Read

Reema Joseph Samaha

Waleed Mohamed Shaalan

Leslie Geraldine Sherman

Maxine Shelly Turner

Nicole Regina White

**All book proceeds support the
Actively Caring for People Foundation, Inc.**

The Actively Caring for People Foundation, Inc. is
dedicated to researching and teaching principles and
procedures to cultivate a worldwide
Actively Caring for People Culture of Compassion.

The preparation of this book was supported by the

American Psychological Foundation

750 First Street NE, Washington, DC, USA

Contents

Foreword

Dave Johnson

IT WAS THE ANNUAL MEETING of the National Safety Congress back in 1987 when I first came across Dr. E. Scott Geller. All that separated us was a standing-room-only crowd of six- or seven-hundred safety pros at a session where Dr. Geller paced up and down aisles and across the speaker's platform. Actually, I couldn't even get into the room at first; the audience spilled out into the hallway.

So I listened from outside and soon realized I'd never heard anyone talk about safety like this guy. His voice boomed like a football coach as he told jokes and stories and ripped through a stack of overhead transparencies. The man was seriously pumped and passionate, and his vitality was contagious. Laughs rolled through the large room and echoed out into the hall, where a group of us stood on our toes peeking through the door, trying to figure out this wiry professor with the energy of a rock-and-roll drummer.

But this was not another motivational speaker. What separated Scott was his message, his substance. He's always had this knack for making ivory-tower research somehow interesting. Scott's research is all about why we do the things we do, and how to help people do better, and how to help people actively care for one another. "I've got to get him to write articles for *Industrial Safety & Hygiene News (ISHN),*" I thought after listening for maybe five minutes.

As it turned out, Scott wrote a monthly *ISHN* article for a *Psychology of Safety* column for 19 years. Many of his articles focused on topics you'll read about in the following pages: systems thinking, culture, servant leadership, actively caring, self-motivation, observation and feedback, coaching, courage, interpersonal recognition, empowerment, self-esteem, employee engagement, seeking success vs. avoiding failure, fixed vs. growth mindset, personality traits vs. states, bystander intervention, commitment, reciprocity, pro-social behavior, intrinsic vs. extrinsic reinforcement, and the do's and don'ts of incentive/reward programs.

They say a preacher has maybe ten good sermons in him – after that it's all recycling and repackaging. With a microphone in his hand, Scott works the room with a missionary's zeal, but his mission is to always give his audience and readers something new. New research, insights, and ideas are delivered to reach his vision of an Actively Caring for People (AC4P) culture.

The ultimate humane behavior, believes Scott, is to go above and beyond what is asked of us in our daily lives. Beyond the call of duty, he says, which infers that to actively care is an obligation to be met, certainly not ignored. We are obliged to actively care because we have it within us to do so. We can learn how to actively care through books such as this, and through related workshops and group discussions. Armed with this profound knowledge, how can we fail to act on our caring and our empathy?

Scott is a distinguished expert on the foibles of human nature, and he'll tell you right off that AC4P is a tall order. For any number of reasons. We fear our good intentions will be misinterpreted or rejected. We don't believe ourselves capable. "I'm just not feelin' it, dude." "I just don't want to take the time or expend the energy." "Someone else will do it." "Don't you see, I'm really an introvert, timid, and tend to veer to pessimistic thinking." "Actively caring is not in our DNA."

But this book challenges the excuses and provides evidence that thousands of people have upped their game to actively care. They have risen above their more hesitant, uncertain selves. Most of the time they have had help: friends, family, teachers, peers and strangers who have given them face-to face-encouragement, role modeling, and positive reinforcement.

Today, sufficient numbers of people are engaged in AC4P to call it a "Movement". This is really no surprise; AC4P behavior is viral, it's contagious, it's rewarding and fun. It's a cultural value around which communities of like-minded AC4P participants gravitate and reinforce one another.

Scott and his team at Virginia Tech have, through technology and creative thinking, constructed a global infrastructure to support AC4P. Their Movement is ambitious, idealistic, bold and grounded. It's based on psychological science and field research, not high hopes and do-gooder intentions. It aspires to increase the competence, commitment, and courage needed to sustain AC4P behavior in all the nooks and crannies of daily life: our workplaces, schools, the military, communities, families, heath care, and counseling. The book you are holding is Exhibit A.

Anything less aspiring would disappoint one of Dr. Geller's life-long inspirations, B.F. Skinner. Skinner, the Harvard psychologist and founder of behavior analysis, was preoccupied not with the manipulation of rats and mice in mazes, as his critics would have it, but to help people lead more satisfying and more productive lives. Skinner was convinced communities should actively shape human behavior to promote social justice and harmony. Scott and his team have done just that with the AC4P Movement.

Care to join them?

Preface: Why Read This Book?

E. Scott Geller

I coined the term "actively caring" in 1990 when working with a team of safety leaders at Exxon Chemical in Baytown, Texas.[1] Our vision was to cultivate a brother's/sister's keepers culture. Everyone would look out for each other's safety. People would routinely go above and beyond the call of duty to benefit the health, safety, and well-being of others.

We agreed "actively caring for people" (AC4P) was an ideal description for this company-wide paradigm shift.[2] Everyone naturally cares about the well-being of others. But certainly not everyone "acts" on their feelings of caring. Our challenge was to get everyone to *actively* care – to take effective action based on their caring.

This marked the beginning of systematic research in our Center for Applied Behavior Systems (CABS) at Virginia Tech (VT) to develop, evaluate, and continuously improve intervention techniques to increase the frequency and quality of person-to-person and group-to-group AC4P throughout a culture. For more than three decades we have continued this research, up to the present and into the future.

Applications have been tested in educational and work settings and throughout communities. A variety of behaviors affecting human and community welfare have been targeted. This book presents evidence-based interventions we developed to increase occurrences of AC4P behavior.

Following the VT campus shooting rampage on April 16, 2007 that took the lives of 33 people and injured 15 others, the mission of AC4P took on a new focus and prominence for my students and me. In a time of great uncertainty and reflection, those most affected by the tragedy did not think about themselves, but rather acted to help classmates, friends, and even strangers. This collective effort was manifested in an AC4P Movement for culture change (see www.ac4p.org).

My current and former students helped me compile this book to provide: a) the behavioral and psychological science behind the AC4P Movement, b) practical and successful applications of the evidence-based AC4P principles, and c) inspirational evidence of the beneficial consequences from the AC4P approach.

We hope this book empowers and motivates you to join the Movement and spread AC4P among your friends, family, co-workers, peers, and even strangers in schools, workplaces, organizations, and throughout communities.

The AC4P Approach for Behavior Change

We are besieged by daunting societal problems. Thanks to the 24/7 news cycle and the Internet, smartphones and tablet devices, we know more than perhaps we'd like about the nation's obesity epidemic, millions of medical errors, Wall-Street greed, online scams, cyberbullying, violence and drugs in schools, bankrupt cities, terrorism, political gridlock, and alcohol abuse. This is a time of significant adversity. Since human behavior contributes to each of these societal problems; it must also be part of the solutions.

What if people were only more considerate and empathic to the circumstances, opinions, and behaviors of others? Imagine the beneficial impact of a world with more interpersonal compassion and AC4P – more empathy and kindness. The practical research-based AC4P interventions described in this book illustrate how such a culture can be achieved. The AC4P Movement combines humanism and behaviorism (i.e., *humanistic behaviorism*) to improve behaviors related to the health, safety, and well-being of people worldwide.

In 1971, B.F. Skinner told us, "Our culture has provided the science and technology to save itself".[3] The AC4P Movement reflects this assertion. It empowers individuals to be self-motivated to actively care and to increase the occurrence of AC4P behaviors from others as well. AC4P cultures empower people to improve their own school, work, and home environments, and as they do we will see AC4P cultures begin to flourish in organizations and communities worldwide.

Chapters 1 to 6 define evidence-based strategies for increasing AC4P behavior in various settings, while reviewing the supportive theory and research for each intervention approach. We aren't talking about common-sense solutions here; we're sharing practical techniques verified through empirical research.

The lead authors of the remaining chapters in this book are change agents who have successfully applied the AC4P principles and procedures for diverse environments and circumstances. They have experienced firsthand the beneficial impact of applying the AC4P approach to critical large-scale problems, particularly personal injuries and fatalities in the workplace (Part II). The chapters in Part III illustrate community applications of AC4P to address the societal issues of traffic safety, alcohol abuse, and identity theft.

My students and I regularly hear many heartwarming personal stories of the profound positive effects of AC4P applications. A sample of those stories that teach practical AC4P lessons are included in Part IV of this book. Each personal story illustrates how the benefits of AC4P behavior far outweigh the costs.

In every case, the mutual rewards from the AC4P exchange exceed any inconvenience of the AC4P behavior. Many stories show how one simple AC4P act can go viral, in effect be transmitted to other people and contribute to cultivating an AC4P culture of compassion. We call this "the AC4P ripple effect."

The Quality and Quantity of AC4P Behavior

Why isn't AC4P behavior more frequent? After all, the consequences of AC4P behavior are typically positive for both the giver and the receiver. And the beneficial impact of an AC4P interaction can serve as an activator and vicarious reinforcer for observers (see Chapter 5).

First, consider that AC4P behavior is more common than we realize. Daily occurrences of behavior opposite to AC4P make the news, but there are many untold stories of people worldwide reaching out daily to help others deal with unfortunate situational and/or dispositional factors.

Thousands of these people are professionals – fire fighters, police officers, doctors, nurses, home health aides, social workers, ministers, teachers, and personnel in the safety and human-relations departments of organizations. These AC4P professionals look out for the safety, health, and well-being of others morning, noon and night, every day and every shift.

Consider too the vast number of ordinary people who volunteer their time daily on behalf of the health and well-being of others, or who step out of themselves without forethought to instantaneously actively care for another person.

Quality of AC4P Behavior

I am actually more concerned about the quality of AC4P behavior than the quantity. Our behaviors at work, school, on the road, and at home with our families often come across as self-serving and non-caring. Sure, most of our interpersonal behaviors might be well-intentioned, but too often they are not executed well. We may be well-intended, but for a variety of reasons, including "unconscious incompetence," the behavior performed to help another person (e.g., like offering feedback to improve someone's performance) is not viewed as AC4P behavior.

Our society, thanks to our legal system, is overly focused on using punitive consequences to stop peoples' undesirable behaviors, with limited attention to applying positive consequences to motivate desirable behavior.

Our pop culture can be a detriment. Hundreds of self-help books and many TV and radio talk shows make behavior and attitudinal change seem easier than it is.

Misinformed but popular authors proclaim that using incentives and rewards to increase the occurrence of desirable behavior does more harm than good.[4] The success of many positive AC4P interventions explicated in this book show the flaw in this silly assertion.

More importantly, the AC4P applications in Parts II, III, and IV illustrate practical ways to improve any attempt to actively care by incorporating evidence-based principles of behavioral and psychological science. The quality of AC4P behavior can often be readily enhanced, and this book shows you how to do that.

Quantity of AC4P Behavior

The quantity of AC4P behavior can be increased by considering the variety of successful applications of the AC4P principles and procedures illustrated throughout this book. Most influential, for me, are the personal stories of individuals who experienced the rewards of performing and receiving a simple AC4P behavior (i.e., Parts IV and V).

Part V includes a sample of the numerous AC4P stories posted on our website. Since January 2011, more than 2,000 individuals have posted brief AC4P stories, illustrating the positive consequences of actively caring for both those performing and those receiving AC4P behavior. These stories simply inspire me. Sharing their occurrence will contribute to making AC4P behavior a social norm.

Posting an AC4P story on our website connects immediately to your Facebook, and communicates to your friends the occasion of one more AC4P behavior, and its positive consequences. As more and more people post their AC4P tales, people will begin to accept AC4P behavior as the norm. Successive approximations of a worldwide culture of compassion will follow. So we hope you will, "Think globally and act locally".

Read this book and learn what you can do to increase the quantity and improve the quality of AC4P behavior in your life. Make your learning practical. Commit to being more intentional at actively caring for others and at rewarding people for their AC4P behaviors. When you share your AC4P story on our website, others see your kind act and consider modeling your AC4P behavior. Your story may in fact find its way into the next edition of this book.

Our world brims with caring and compassion that goes untapped. A world filled with interpersonal compassion! This vision will become reality if more people reach out to help others more effectively and more often. This book shows you how to make that happen, and thereby live an AC4P lifestyle and help lead the AC4P Movement.

Notes

1. Geller, E.S. (1991). If only more would actively care. *Journal of Applied Behavior Analysis, 24,* 763-764.

2. Geller, E.S., (1994) . *Actively caring for safety*. Dallas, TX: Westcott Communications [Three 25-min. instructional videotapes with workbooks on the psychology of safety. One videotape teaches techniques to motivate safe work practices, another teaches a behavior-based process for addressing the human dimension of safety problems, and the third videotape teaches strategies for interpersonal coaching to improve industrial safety]; Geller, E.S. (1997). *Actively caring for safety: The psychology of injury prevention*. Blacksburg, VA: Safety Performance Solutions [Twelve 30-min. audiotapes with a workbook to teach principles and procedures for preventing unintentional injury at work, at home, and on the road.]

3. Skinner, B.F. (1971). *Beyond freedom and dignity*. New York, NY: Knopf.

4. Kohn, A. (1993). *Punished by rewards: The trouble with gold stars, incentive plans A's, praise, and other bribes*. Boston, MA: Houghton Mifflin; Pink, D.H. (2009). Drive: *The surprising truth about what motivates us*. New York, NY: Penguin Group.

Actively Caring for People™

Cultivating a Culture of Compassion

Fourth Edition

E. Scott Geller, Ph.D.

Part I: Evidence-Based Principles of AC4P

E. Scott Geller

THE FIRST SIX CHAPTERS of this book define principles on which the AC4P applications illustrated throughout this book were based, from popular people-based safety (PBS) procedures implemented worldwide in industry to reduce the frequency and severity of workplace injuries (Part II) to applications of AC4P principles to address traffic safety, alcohol abuse among college students, and the all-too-common problem of identity theft and credit-card fraud (Part III). Moreover, this book includes a number of personal stories by individuals who applied one or more of the AC4P principles delineated and illustrated in these first six chapters.

Throughout this book, authors refer to particular AC4P principles they applied to address the human dynamics of a certain social problem. So what's a "principle" anyway?

The first definition in my *American Heritage Dictionary* is "a basic truth, law, or assumption".[1] How does this definition connect to the behavioral and psychological science referenced in the following six chapters?

Note we use the adjective "evidence-based" when referring to the AC4P principles. This means the principles are based on objective research that demonstrates the validity of the principle. Does this mean an AC4P principle is a basic truth or fact?

I think it's risky to consider these principles immutable or changeless, like the Law of Gravity. However, the AC4P principles are as close to valid as any other principle in psychological science.

In contrast to evidence-based principles, consider statements used to explain or influence human behavior which are not evidence-based, but are quite popular. In fact, some of these are themes of self-help books and pop-psychology seminars. I hope my comments make you skeptical of these so-called "principles" of human behavior.

1. **We learn more from our mistakes.** This popular myth, along with the popular slogan "trial-and error" learning, influences more emphasis on failure than success, and this can be detrimental to learning. Think about it. Animals, including humans, learn more when a consequence indicates their behavior was correct than incorrect.

2. **After 21 times, behavior becomes habit.** There's no empirical evidence for this popular but overly simplistic and silly statement. Many factors determine habit formation, especially the nature of the behavior. Plus, many behaviors require mindful attention to be effective, and should not become habitual.

3. **The "secret" to success is self-affirmation.** Telling yourself you can do something is the surest way to accomplishment. This popular myth may sound good, but it's wrong. Chapter 1 explains why the secret to achievement resides in behavioral consequences, not the self-talk preceding behavior.

4. **Live by the "Golden Rule," meaning treat others the way you want to be treated.** We've heard this rule all our lives, yet in Chapter 2 you'll learn why this principle is

not optimal. For now, consider the value of treating others the way *they* want to be treated.

5. **Incentive and rewards are detrimental to self-motivation.** This pop-psychology statement is rarely supported by research; you'll learn evidence-based ways to increase self-motivation in Chapter 3. For example, behavior-based rewards and supportive feedback (e.g., recognition) are more likely to increase than decrease self-motivation.

6. **Reprimand privately and recognize publically.** Never recognize people publically without their permission. Some people are embarrassed in these situations, especially if others on their teams think they deserve recognition. Furthermore, public recognition of individuals on a team can promote win-lose independency over win-win interdependency. Chapter 3 details evidence-based ways to recognize teams, and Chapter 4 delineates strategies for rewarding individuals for their achievements.

7. **Practice makes perfect.** Practice without proper feedback can lead to permanence but certainly not perfection. Evidence-based principles for improving behavior through feedback are detailed in Chapter 4.

I could list many more assumptions people make about human dynamics which are not supported by research. And, some of these are incorrectly considered "principles" of human behavior. But, these seven make my point. What's my point? First, be skeptical about the pop-psychology "principles" you hear. My main point, however, is the AC4P principles illustrated in the next six chapters are founded on research.

One final point, the evidence-based principles explained in the following six chapters were selected from literally hundreds of verifiable principles related to understanding, predicting, and influencing the psychology of human experience. Those discussed in Chapters 1 to 6 were selected because at this point in our understanding of AC4P they are most relevant.

As we learn more about ways to enhance quality AC4P behavior in various situations, additional principles of behavioral science will become relevant. Plus, additional research and continuous learning could influence refinements or extensions of the AC4P principles defined and illustrated in Part I of this book.

These chapters offer state-of-the-art AC4P principles from humanism and behavioral science relevant to cultivating a culture of compassion.

Note

1. *The American Heritage Dictionary.* (1985) (2nd College Edition), p. 985.

CHAPTER 1

The Foundation:
Applied Behavioral Science

E. Scott Geller

COUNTLESS SOCIETAL PROBLEMS are brought to our attention every day by the news media. Violence and drug abuse, highway crashes, epidemics such as obesity and bullying, untold numbers of medical errors, conflicts both geopolitical and intensely personal, and environmental degradation – particularly climate change – carry significant economic burdens. They pose dehumanizing costs in terms of individual suffering and loss of life.

Human behavior contributes to each of these perplexing problems – but human behavior is also a critical part of the solution. For more than 50 years, applied behavioral scientists have helped people by developing, implementing, and evaluating interventions to increase the occurrence of positive acts of caring and decrease the frequency of undesirable behaviors.

Effective applications of Applied Behavioral Science (ABS) generally follow the seven key principles described below. Each principle is broad enough to include a wide range of practical operations, but narrow enough to define the ABS approach to managing behaviors relevant for promoting AC4P behavior (e.g., for benefitting safety, health, work productivity, parenting, coaching and environmental conservation, and for optimizing teaching and learning).[1]

1. Target Observable Behavior.

B. F. Skinner conceptualized and researched the behavioral science upon which the ABS approach is founded.[2] Experimental behavior analysis, and later ABS,[3] emerged from Skinner's research and teaching, and laid the groundwork for numerous therapies and interventions designed to improve the quality of life among individuals, groups, and entire communities.[4]

Whether working one-on-one in a clinical setting or with work teams throughout an organization, the intervention procedures always target specific behaviors relevant to promoting constructive change. ABS focuses on what people do, analyzes *why* they do it, and then applies an evidence-based intervention to *improve* what people do.

Acting people into thinking differently is the focus. This contrasts with *thinking people to act differently*, which targets internal awareness, intentions, or attitudes. Many clinical psychologists use this latter approach successfully in professional therapy sessions. But in group, organizational, or community-wide settings it's not cost-effective. To be effective, thinking-focused intervention requires extensive one-on-one interaction between a client and a specially-trained intervention specialist.

Few intervention agents in the real world (e.g., teachers, parents, coaches, healthcare workers, and safety professionals) possess the educational background, training, and experience to implement an intervention focused on internal and unobservable person states. A basic tenet of ABS is that interventions should occur at the natural site of the behavioral issue (e.g., corporation, school, home, or athletic field) and be administered by an indigenous change agent (e.g., work supervisor, teacher, parent, or coach).

2. Focus on External Factors to Explain and Improve Behavior.

Skinner did not deny the existence of internal determinants of behavior (such as personality characteristics, perceptions, attitudes, and values). These unobservable inferred constructs were rejected by Skinner for *scientific study* as causes or consequences of behavior. Factors in both our external and internal worlds obviously influence what we do – how we act.

But it's difficult to objectively define internal traits or states. It's simply more cost-effective to identify environmental conditions that influence behavior, and then change these factors when behavior change is called for.

Examining external factors to explain and improve behavior is a primary focus of organizational behavior management.[5] The ABS principles are used to develop interventions to improve work quality, productivity, and safety. "Behavior-based safety (BBS)" is the term for applying the ABS approach to occupational safety. BBS is currently used worldwide to increase safety-related behaviors, decrease at-risk behaviors, and prevent workplace injuries and fatalities.[6] In the past decade, the ABS approach to organizational safety has been customized and applied in health care facilities to prevent medical error and improve patient safety.[7]

The pertinent point here is that ABS focuses on the external environmental conditions and contingencies influencing a target behavior. A careful analysis is conducted of the situation before deciding on an intervention approach. The target behavior(s) and the individual(s) involved in any observed discrepancy between the behavior observed and the behavior desired (i.e., real vs. ideal behavior) are studied.

A behavior-focused intervention is designed and implemented if the gap between the actual and the desired behavior warrants change. This is accomplished by adhering to the next three principles.

3. Direct with Activators and Motivate with Consequences.

This principle enables us to understand why behavior occurs, and guides the design of interventions to improve behavior. It runs counter to common sense or "pop psychology." When people are asked why they did something, they make statements such as, "Because I wanted to do it," "Because I needed to do it," or "Because I was told to do it." Such explanations sound as if the cause of behavior precedes it. A multitude of "pop psychology" self-help books, audiotapes and DVDs support the belief we motivate our behavior with self-affirmations, positive thinking, optimistic expectations, or enthusiastic intentions.

The fact is, as Dale Carnegie put it, "Every act you have ever performed since the day you were born was performed because you wanted something."[8] We do what we do because of the consequences we expect to get, or avoid, or escape by doing it. Carnegie cited Skinner's research and scholarship as the foundation for this basic principle of motivation.

Activators (or signals preceding behavior) are only as influential as the consequences supporting them. Activators tell us what to do in order to receive a positive, reinforcing consequence. Or they tell us what not to do to avoid an unpleasant consequence.

Take a ringing telephone. If we see from the "call waiting" phone number the call is from a friend we haven't spoken with in a long time, we pick up the receiver and begin a rewarding conversation. But if the "call waiting" number is unknown to us, we might not pick up the receiver. We just let the call go to voicemail.

How about the ringing of a doorbell? Years ago, people always answered the door. Now, due to fears of unknown strangers and a plethora of visitors who want something from us ("Would you sign this petition?," "Can I count on your vote?," "Do you need your driveway blacktopped?"), we are more likely to peer through a window to see who it is, and note whether the consequence of opening the door will be pleasant or unpleasant.

We follow through with the particular behavior activated (from answering or ignoring a telephone to opening or refusing to open a door) based on whether we expect a pleasant consequence or can avoid an unpleasant consequence.

This principle is typically referred to as the ABC model or three-term contingency, with A for Activator (or antecedent), B for Behavior, and C for Consequence. Applied behavioral scientists use this ABC principle to design interventions for improving behavior at individual, group, organizational, and community levels. More than 50 years of behavioral-science research has demonstrated the efficacy of this general approach to directing and motivating behavior change. The ABC (Activator – Behavior – Consequence) contingency is reflected in the illustration on the next page.

The dog will move if he expects to receive food after hearing the sound of the can opener. The direction provided by an activator is likely to be followed when it is backed by a soon, certain, and significant consequence. This operation is termed operant or instrumental conditioning. The consequence is a positive reinforcer when behavior is emitted to obtain it. When behavior occurs to avoid or escape a consequence, the consequence is a *negative* reinforcer.

If the sound of the can opener elicits a salivation reflex in the dog, we have an example of classical or respondent conditioning. The can-opener sound is a conditioned stimulus (CS) and the salivation is a conditioned response (CR). The food that follows the sound of the electric can opener is the unconditioned stimulus (UCS), which elicits the unconditioned response of salivating without any prior learning experience. This UCS – UCR reflex is natural or "wired in" the organism.

Perhaps you recall this terminology from a basic learning course in psychology. We review it here because ABS is founded on these learning principles, especially operant conditioning. People choose behavior to obtain a pleasant consequence or to escape or avoid an unpleasant consequence. But as shown in the illustration, operant (instrumental) and respondent (classical) conditioning often occur simultaneously.

Although we operate on the environment to achieve a desired consequence or avoid an unwanted consequence, emotional reactions are often classically conditioned to specific stimulus events in the situation. We learn to like or dislike the environmental context and/or the people involved in administrating the ABC contingency. This is how the type of behavioral consequence influences attitude, and why ABS interventions focus on positive consequences.

4. Focus on Positive Consequences to Motivate Behavior.

Skinner's concern for people's feelings and attitudes is reflected in his antipathy toward the use of punishment (or negative consequences) to motivate behavior. "The problem is to free men, not from control, but from certain kinds of control."[9] Skinner proceeds to explain that control by negative consequences must be reduced to increase perceptions of personal freedom.

The same situation can often be viewed both ways: control by punishment of unwanted behavior or control by positive reinforcement of desired behavior. Some students in my university classes, for example, are motivated to avoid failure (e.g., a poor grade). Other students are motivated to achieve success (e.g., a good grade or increased knowledge).

Which of these groups of students feel more empowered and in control of their class grade? Which have a better attitude toward my classes? Of course, you know the answer. Reflect on your own feelings or attitude in similar situations where you perceived your behavior as influenced by positive or negative consequences.

Achieving Success vs. Avoiding Failure

Years ago, John W. Atkinson and his associates[10] found dramatic differences when comparing the decision-making of individuals with a high need to avoid failure and those with a high need to achieve success. Those motivated to achieve positive consequences set challenging but attainable goals. Participants with a high need to avoid failure were apt to set goals either overly easy or overly difficult.

Setting easy goals assures avoidance of failure; setting unrealistic goals provides an excuse for failure – termed self-handicapping by more recent researchers.[11] Thus, a substantial amount of behavioral research and motivational theory justifies advocacy of positive reinforcement over punishment contingencies. This is the case whether an ABC contingency is contrived to improve someone else's behavior or imagined to motivate personal rule-following behavior.

Figure 1.1 depicts four distinct achievement typologies initially defined by Covington.[12] These four classifications have been researched to explain differences in how people approach success and/or avoid failure.

It's most desirable to be a *success seeker*. These are the optimists, responding to setbacks (e.g., corrective feedback) in a positive and adaptive manner. They are self-confident and willing to take risks as opposed to avoiding challenges in order to avoid failure. They wake up each day to an *opportunity* clock rather than an *alarm* clock.

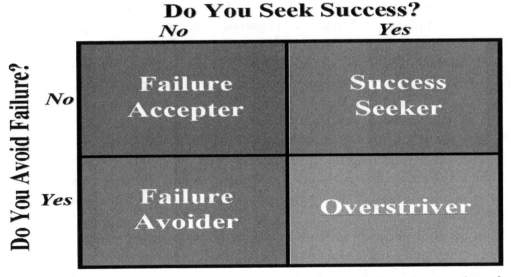

Figure 1.1. Achieving success vs. avoiding failure define four motivational typologies.

It's a mindset or attitude toward life you can influence in yourselves and others. This book teaches you how to do that.

Overstrivers are diligent, successful, meticulous, and at times optimistic. But they have self-doubt about their abilities and experience substantial evaluation anxiety. This drives them to avoid failure by working hard to succeed. Covington and Roberts[13] found overstrivers are preoccupied with perfection, often over-preparing for a challenge (e.g., a test of knowledge or ability).

Failure avoiders have a low expectancy for success and a high fear of failure. They do whatever it takes to protect themselves from appearing incompetent. They often use self-handicapping and defensive pessimism to shield themselves from potential failure.[14] These individuals are motivated but are not "happy campers." They are the students who say, "I've *got* to go to class; it's a requirement", rather than "I *get* to go to class; it's an opportunity."

Finally, the *failure accepters* score low in terms of both expecting success and fearing failure. Failure is merely accepted as indicative of low ability. Unlike failure avoiders, though, these individuals don't worry about failure or their inability to succeed. They have given up. Their behavior is analogous to learned helplessness.[15]

Interestingly failure accepters are better adjusted psychologically than the failure avoiders and overstrivers, according to Covington and Roberts.[13] They score relatively high on well-being, tolerance, self-control, and social presence. They report being relatively self-assured and self-disciplined. Theirs is a passive lifestyle relatively free of worry. Why? Perhaps because they've abandoned achievement, and in so doing they experience relatively few stressors throughout their days.

Personality Traits vs. States

Much of the research literature addressing these four achievement typologies seem to imply they reflect relatively stable and persistent qualities of individuals. They represent personality traits rather than states.[16] However, other researchers and practitioners, especially proponents of ABS, view these characteristics as fluctuating states. They exist under the influence of the environment and the three-term (ABC) contingency.

Environmental conditions and contingencies set the stage for success seeking, overstriving, failure avoiding, or failure accepting. The results or consequences of one's efforts can maintain or change one's perspective.

Success seeking is cultivated through positive reinforcement. Overstriving and failure avoiding result from negative reinforcement and punishment. A failure accepter might simply surrender after a history of consistent failure. Passive failure accepters who have "accepted their fate" are apparently "happier campers" than failure avoiders and overstrivers.

But in their surrendering they are not motivated to even try a challenging task. Wouldn't you rather have a failure avoider or overstriver on your team, and attempt to move their state toward success seeking?

The Contingency for Success Seeking

The ABS approach to promoting success seeking is to apply positive reinforcement contingencies strategically instead of negative reinforcement or punishment. Still, punishment contingencies are relatively easy to implement on a large scale. That's why our government selects this approach to behavior management. Simply pass a law and enforce it. And when monetary fines are paid for transgressions, the controlling agency obtains financial support for continuing its enforcement efforts. And punishment often seems to work, as the illustration shows.

Control by negative consequences is seemingly the only feasible approach in many areas of large-scale behavior management, especially transportation safety. Consequently, the side-effects of aggressive driving and road rage are relatively common and observed by anyone who drives.

Most of us have experienced the anxious emotional reaction of seeing the flashing blue light of a police vehicle in our rear-view mirror—another example of classical conditioning. You've probably witnessed the temporary impact produced by this enforcement threat.

Classic research in experimental behavior analysis teaches us to expect only temporary suppression of a punished behavior,[17] and to predict that some drivers in their "Skinner box on wheels" will speed up to compensate for the time they lost when slowing down in an "enforcement zone".[18]

Practical ways to apply positive reinforcement contingencies to driving are available,[19] but much more long-term research is needed in this domain. Various positive reinforcement contingencies need to be applied and evaluated to judge their ability to offset the negative side-effects of the existing negative reinforcement contingencies.[20]

Regardless of the situation, managers, teachers, work supervisors, and parents can often intervene to increase people's perceptions they are working to achieve success rather than avoid failure. Even our verbal behavior directed toward another person, perhaps as a statement of genuine approval or appreciation for a task well done, can increase perceptions of personal freedom, empowerment, and self-motivation (see Chapter 3).

Words of approval, though, are not as common as words of disapproval. So while ABS change agents focus their interventions on observable behavior, they are also concerned about attitude, as reflected in the next principle.

5. Design Interventions with Consideration of Internal Feelings and Attitudes.

Skinner was certainly concerned about unobservable attitudes or feeling states. This is evidenced by his criticism of punishment's impact on people's feelings and perceptions. This perspective also reflects a realization: Intervention procedures influence feeling states, and these can be pleasant or unpleasant, desirable or undesirable. Internal feelings or attitudes are influenced indirectly by the type of behavior-focused intervention procedure implemented, and this relationship must be carefully considered by developers and managers of a behavior-change process.

The differential feeling states provoked by positive reinforcement versus punishment procedures is the rationale for using more positive than negative consequences to motivate behavior. Similarly, the way we implement an intervention process can increase or decrease feelings of empowerment, build or destroy trust, and cultivate or inhibit a sense of teamwork or belonging.[21]

Thus, it's important to assess feeling states or perceptions occurring concomitantly with an intervention process. This can be accomplished informally through one-on-one interviews and group discussions, or formally with a perception survey.[22] However, surveys with few response alternatives have obvious limitations when it comes to assessing feelings or attitudes, as the illustration shows.

Social Validity

Decisions regarding which ABS intervention to implement, and how to refine existing intervention procedures, should be based on both objective behavioral observations and subjective evaluations of feeling states. Often, it's possible to employ empathy to evaluate the indirect internal impact of an intervention. Imagine yourself going through a particular set of intervention procedures. Then, ask the question, "How would I feel?"

Almost two decades ago

when my daughter wanted to drive my car to her high school I installed a sign on the back, as shown in the illustration. I bolted the sign to the vehicle after she achieved 100 percent safe on three consecutive coaching sessions with a Critical Behavior Checklist (CBC), as described later in this chapter. We had this "if-then" contingency: "Achieve a perfect score on three consecutive trips with the CBC, and you may drive my car to school."

I was sure she'd accept the addition of the sign on my vehicle. Note how this activator is more than an awareness prompt; it implies a consequence. We talked about the value of positive or supportive consequences, so I thought Krista would view this sign as a "fun" and positive approach to promote safe driving. "Let's be optimistic about this," I said to her, "and see how many positive phone calls I get about your safe and courteous driving behavior."

"Are you kidding me, Dad, there's no way I'd park that car and sign at my high-school," was Krista's reply. "I'd be the laughing stock of the whole school. I'll talk to mom about this." My lesson: Don't assume you know how a well-intentioned intervention will be received by the participant(s); ask first.

Assessment of social validity is a more comprehensive and systematic approach advocated by ABS researchers and practitioners.[23] Social validity assessment includes the use of rating scales, interviews, and focus-group discussions to assess: (a) the societal significance of the intervention goals, (b) the social appropriateness of the procedures, and (c) the societal importance or clinical significance of the intervention effects.[24]

The Four Components of ABS Intervention

The four basic components of an ABS intervention process – selection, implementation, evaluation, and dissemination – are addressed in a comprehensive social validity evaluation.

Selection refers to the importance or priority of the behavioral problem and the people targeted for change. Addressing the large-scale problems of transportation safety, climate change, prison management, identity theft, child abuse, interpersonal bullying, and medical errors is clearly important, but given limited resources, which issue should receive priority? The answer to this question depends partly on the availability of a cost-effective intervention.

Assessing the social validity of the *implementation* stage of ABS intervention includes evaluating the behavior-change goals and procedures of the behavior-change process. How acceptable is the plan to potential participants and other parties, even those tangentially associated with the intervention?[25]

In the case of a bullying-prevention program, answering this question entails obtaining acceptability ratings not only from teachers, students, and school administrators, but also from the students' family members and the community members whose tax dollars support the intervention.

Are the intervention procedures consistent with the school's values and mission statement, and do they reach the most appropriate audience?   And, it's recommended to consult with the recipients of an intervention regarding acceptability and methodology, as depicted in the illustration.

The social validity of the *evaluation* stage refers, of course, to the impact of the intervention process. This includes estimates of the costs and benefits of an intervention as well as measures of participant or consumer satisfaction.

The numbers or scores obtained from various measurement devices (e.g., environmental audits, behavioral checklists, interview forms, output records, and attitude questionnaires) need to be reliable and valid. But they also need to be understood by the people who use them. If they are not, the evaluation scheme does not provide useful feedback and cannot lead to continuous improvement.

Meaningless or misunderstood evaluation numbers also limit the *dissemination* potential and large-scale applicability of an intervention. Now we're talking about the social validity of the *dissemination* stage of the ABS intervention process. This is the weakest aspect of ABS intervention, and perhaps applied psychology in general.

Intervention researchers and scholars justify their efforts and obtain financial support based on the scientific rigor of their methods and the statistical significance of their results. Rarely do these scholars address the real-world dissemination challenges of their findings.

Unfortunately, dissemination and marketability are left to corporations, consulting firms, and "pop psychologists." As a result, there are often disconnects between the science of ABS (and other psychological processes) and behavior-change intervention in the real world. One solution to this dilemma is to teach the real-world users of ABS how to conduct their own evaluations of intervention impact. This brings us to the next ABS principle.

6. Apply the Scientific Method to Improve Intervention.

Some people believe dealing with the human dynamics of behavior change requires only "good common sense".[26] Surely you realize the absurdity of such a premise. Common sense is based on people's selective listening and interpretation, and is usually founded on what sounds good to the individual listener, not necessarily on what works.[27] In contrast, systematic and scientific observation enables the kind of objective feedback needed to know what works and what doesn't work to improve behavior.

The occurrence of specific behaviors can be objectively observed and measured before and after the implementation of an intervention process. This application of the scientific method provides feedback with which behavioral improvement can be shaped.

I use the acronym "DO IT," as depicted in Figure 1.2, to teach this principle of ABS to change agents (e.g., coaches, teachers, parents, work supervisors, and hourly workers) empowered to improve the behavior of others, and who want to continuously improve their intervention skills. This process represents the scientific method ABS practi-

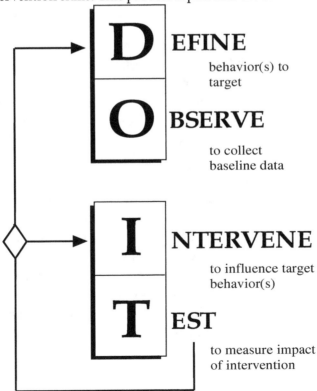

DEFINE behavior(s) to target

OBSERVE to collect baseline data

INTERVENE to influence target behavior(s)

TEST to measure impact of intervention

Figure 1.2 The scientific method of ABS is represented by DO IT.

tioners have used for decades to demonstrate the impact of particular behavior-change techniques.

"D" for Define

The process begins by defining specific behaviors to target, which are undesirable behaviors that need to decrease in frequency and/or desirable behaviors that need to occur more often. Avoiding certain unwanted behaviors often requires the occurrence of alternative behaviors, and so target behaviors might be behaviors to substitute for particular undesirable behaviors. On the other hand, a desirable target behavior can be defined independently of undesired behavior.

An AC4P approach to prevent interpersonal bullying applied reward techniques to increase interpersonal caring and sharing behaviors, and resulted in a decrease in bullying behavior without ever mentioning bullying as a target.[28] An undesirable behavior can be decreased in frequency by targeting desirable behavior(s) incompatible with the unwanted behavior.

Defining and evaluating ongoing behavior is often facilitated by the development of a behavioral checklist to use during observations. The development of behavioral definitions invoke an invaluable learning experience. When people get involved in deriving a behavioral checklist, they own a training process that can improve human dynamics on both the outside (behaviors) and the inside (feelings and attitudes) of people.

"O" for Observe

When people observe each other for certain desirable or undesirable behaviors, they realize everyone performs undesirable behavior, sometimes without even realizing it. The observation stage is not a fault-finding procedure. It's a fact-finding learning process to discover behaviors and conditions that need to be changed or continued in order to be competent at a task. No behavioral observation needs to be made without awareness and explicit permission from the person being observed. Observers should be open to learning as much (if not more) from the process as they expect to teach from completing the behavioral checklist.

The Critical Behavioral Checklist. There's not one generic observation procedure for every situation. Customization and refinement of a process for a particular setting never stops. You might begin the observation process with a limited number of behaviors and a relatively simple checklist. This reduces the possibility of people feeling overwhelmed at the beginning. Starting small also enables the broadest range of voluntary participation, and provides numerous opportunities to improve the process successively by expanding coverage of both behaviors and environmental settings.

I used the critical behavioral checklist (CBC) depicted in Figure 1.3 to teach my daughter safe-driving practices. She actually thought the "driver's ed program" she had in high school was sufficient. I knew better. We needed to develop and apply a CBC. Through one-on-one discussion, Krista and I derived a list of critical driving behaviors and then agreed on

Critical Behavior Checklist for Driving

Driver:	Date:	Day:
Observer 1:	Origin:	Start Time:
Observer 2:	Destination:	End Time:

Weather:

Road Conditions:

Behavior	Safe	At-Risk	Comments
Safety Belt Use:			
Turn Signal Use:			
Left turn			
Right turn			
Lane change			
Intersection Stop:			
Stop sign			
Red light			
Yellow light			
No activator			
Speed Limits:			
25 mph and under			
25 mph- 35 mph			
35 mph- 45 mph			
45mph- 55 mph			
55mph- 65 mph			
Passing:			
Lane Use:			
Following Distance (2 sec):			
Totals:			

$$\% \text{ Safe} = \frac{\text{Total Safe Observations}}{\text{Total Safe + At-Risk Obs.}} = \underline{\hspace{3cm}} \%$$

Figure 1.3. A critical behavior checklist can improve driving.

specific definitions for each item. My university students practiced using this CBC a few times with various drivers, resulting in a refined list of behavioral definitions.

After discussing the revised list of behaviors and their definitions with Krista, I was ready to implement the second stage of DO IT – observation. I asked my daughter to drive me to the university – about nine miles from home – to pick up some papers. I overtly recorded observations on the CBC during both legs of this roundtrip. When returning home, I totaled the safe and at-risk check marks and calculated the percentage of safe behaviors. Her percentage of safe driving was 85%. I considered this quite good for our first time. (Note my emphasis on achieving safe rather than avoiding at-risk.)

I told Krista her "percent safe" score and proceeded to show her the list of safe checkmarks, while avoiding the few checks in the at-risk column. To my surprise, she was not impressed with her percent-safe score. Rather she pushed me to tell her what she did wrong. "Get to the bottom line, Dad," she asserted, "Where did I screw up?"

This reaction was enlightening in two aspects. First, it illustrated the unfortunate reality that the "bottom line" for many people is, "Where did I go wrong?" My daughter, at age 15, had already absorbed that people evaluating her performance are more interested in mistakes than successes. This perspective activates failure-avoiding over success-seeking, an undesirable mindset I introduced earlier.

The realization people can be unaware of their at-risk behavior was a second important outcome from this CBC experience. Only through objective behavior-based feedback can we improve. Krista did not readily accept my corrective feedback regarding her four at-risk behaviors. She emphatically denied she did not always come to a complete stop at intersections with stop signs. However, she became convinced of her error when I showed her my data sheet and my comments regarding the particular intersection where there was no traffic and she made only a rolling stop before turning right.

Obviously, we are now in the *intervention* phase of DO IT, with interpersonal feedback being the ABS intervention tactic. I reminded Krista she used her turn signal at every intersection, and she should be proud of that behavior. To make this behavior-based coaching process a positive, success-seeking experience, I emphasized the behaviors I observed her do correctly.

"I" for Intervene

During this stage, interventions are designed and implemented in an attempt to increase the occurrence of desired behavior and/or decrease the frequency of undesired behavior. As reflected in Principle 2, intervention means changing external conditions of the behavioral context or system in order to make desirable behavior more likely than undesirable behavior.

When designing interventions, Principles 3 and 4 are critical: The most motivating consequences are soon, certain, and sizable (Principle 3); and positive consequences are preferable to negative consequences (Principle 4).

The process of observing and recording the frequency of desirable and undesirable behavior on a checklist is an opportunity to give individuals and groups valuable behavior-based feedback. When the results of a behavioral observation are shown to individuals or groups, they receive the kind of information that enables practice to improve performance.

Considerable research has shown that providing people feedback regarding their ongoing behavior is a very cost-effective intervention approach.[29] Chapter 3 details techniques for giving AC4P feedback effectively.

The Hawthorne Effect. Have you heard about "The Hawthorne Effect"? The classic Hawthorne Effect is characterized as demonstrating people change their behavior in desired directions when they know their behavior is being observed.[30]

The fact is, however, the Hawthorne Effect was not due to observation but to feedback. Mcilvaine Parsons[31] conducted a careful re-examination of the Hawthorne data (originally obtained at the Western Electric plant in the Hawthorne community near Chicago) and interviewed eyewitness observers, including one of the five female relay assemblers who were the primary targets of the Hawthorne studies. Here's what he found:

During the intervention phase, the five women observed systematically in the Relay Assembly Test Room received regular *feedback* about the number of relays each had assembled. Feedback was especially important to these workers because their salaries were influenced by an individual piecework plan. In ABS terminology this was a *fixed ratio reinforcement schedule*. The more relays each employee assembled, the more money each earned.

In addition to behavioral feedback, ABS researchers have found a number of other intervention strategies to be effective at increasing desirable behaviors, including behavioral prompts, interpersonal coaching, behavior-change promise cards, individual and group goal-setting, AC4P thank-you cards, individual and group celebrations, as well as incentive/reward programs for individuals or groups. These intervention strategies are described throughout this book, customized to target certain AC4P behaviors in particular situations.

"T" for Test

The *test* phase of DO IT provides work teams or change agents with information they need in order to refine or replace an ABS intervention, and so improve the process. If observations indicate significant improvement in the target behavior has not occurred, the change agents analyze and discuss the situation, and refine the intervention or choose another intervention approach.

On the other hand, if the target reaches the desired frequency level, the change agents can turn their attention to another set of behaviors. They might add new critical behaviors to their checklist, expanding the domain of their behavioral observations. Alternatively, they might design a new intervention procedure to focus on new target behaviors.

Every time participants evaluate an intervention approach, they learn more about how to improve targeted behaviors. They have essentially become AC4P behavioral scientists, using the DO IT process to: (a) diagnose a problem involving human behavior, (b) monitor the impact of a behavior-change intervention, and (c) refine interventions for continuous improvement. The results from such testing provide motivating consequences to sustain this learning process and keep the change agents and their participants involved.

7. Use Theory to Integrate Information, Not to Limit Possibilities.

B.F. Skinner was critical of designing research projects to test theory.[32] This despite much, if not most, research is theory driven. Theory-driven research can narrow the perspective of the investigator and limit the extent of findings with the scientific method. Applying the DO IT process merely to test a theory can be like putting blinders on a horse. It can limit the amount of input gained from systematic observation.

Exploratory ABS investigation has resulted in many important findings. Systematic observations of behavior before and after an intervention or treatment procedure attempt to answer the question, "I wonder what will happen if…?," rather than "Is my theory correct?"

ABS researchers are not expecting a particular result, but are open to finding anything relevant to influencing behavior. Then they modify their research design or observation process according to their behavioral observations, not a particular theory. Their innovative research has been data driven rather than theory driven, which is an important perspective for behavior-change agents, especially when applying the DO IT process.

It's often better to be open to many possibilities for improving performance than to be motivated to support a certain process. Numerous intervention procedures are consistent with the ABS approach, and an intervention process that works well in one situation will not necessarily be effective in another setting.

Thus, it's usually advantageous to teach change agents to make an educated guess about what intervention procedure to use at the start of a behavior-change process, while being open to intervention refinement as a result of the DO IT process. Of course, Principles 1 to 4 should always be used as guidelines when designing intervention procedures.

Distinct consistencies will be observed after many systematic applications of the DO IT process. Certain procedures will work better in some situations than others, with some individuals than others, or with some behaviors than others. Summarizing functional relationships between intervention impact and specific situational or interpersonal characteristics can lead to developing a research-based theory of what works best under particular circumstances.

In this case, theory is used to integrate information gained from systematic behavioral observation. Skinner approved of this use of theory, but cautioned that premature theory development can lead to premature theory testing and limited profound knowledge.[32]

Examples of ABS Intervention

Most large-scale ABS interventions designed to improve behavior can be classified as either activator or consequence strategies. This section reviews four activator (or antecedent) strategies and three consequence strategies ABS change agents have applied effectively to change socially important behaviors. The success of these ABS interventions was evaluated with a DO IT scheme.

Activators

Activators or antecedent interventions include: (a) education, (b) verbal and written prompts, (c) modeling and demonstrations, and (d) commitment procedures.

Education. Before attempting to improve a behavior, it's often important to provide a strong rationale for the requested change. Sometimes this process involves making remote, uncertain, or unknown consequences more salient to the relevant audience. For example, an intervention designed to increase recycling could provide information about the negative consequences of throwing aluminum cans in the trash (e.g., wasted resources, unnecessary energy consumption and overflowing landfills), as well as the positive consequences associated with recycling behavior (e.g., energy savings, decreased pollution, reduced-use of landfill space).

Educational antecedents can be disseminated through print or electronic media, or delivered personally in individual or group settings. Researchers have shown that education presented interpersonally is more effective when it's done in small, rather than large groups, and when it actively involves participants in relevant activities and demonstrations.[33]

Providing information and activating awareness of a problem are often important components of ABS intervention, but keep in mind information alone is seldom sufficient to change behavior, especially when the desired behavior is inconvenient.[34] Education or awareness antecedents are often combined with other intervention components, as discussed below.

Prompts. Prompting strategies are verbal or written messages strategically delivered to promote the occurrence of a target behavior. These activators are reminders to perform the target behaviors.

Geller, Winett, and Everett[35] identified several favorable conditions for the effectiveness of prompting antecedents. Prompts work best when: a) the target behavior is specifically defined by the prompt (e.g., "Buckle your safety belt" rather than "Drive safely"), b) the target behavior is relatively easy to perform (e.g., using a designated trash receptacle vs. collecting and delivering recyclables), c) the message is displayed where the target behavior can be performed (e.g., at the store where "green" commodities are sold vs. on the local news), d) when the message is stated politely (e.g., "Please buckle up" vs. "You must buckle up"), and e) when the activator implies a consequence, as discussed above.

Prompts are popular. They are simple to implement, cost relatively little, and can have considerable impact if used properly. Werner, Rhodes, and Partain increased dramatically the amount of polystyrene recycling in a university cafeteria by increasing the size of signs designed to prompt recycling, and placing them next to recycling bins.[36]

Geller, Kalsher, Rudd, and Lehman designed safety-belt reminders to be hung from the rear-view mirrors of personal vehicles.[37] In both of these successful applications, the prompts were displayed in close proximity to where the target behavior could be performed, and the behavior requested was relatively convenient to perform.

Modeling. Prompts can be effective for simple, convenient behaviors. Modeling is the more appropriate approach when the desired behavior is complex. Modeling involves demonstrating specific target behaviors to a relevant audience. This activator is more effective when the model receives a rewarding consequence immediately after the target behavior is performed.[38]

Modeling can be accomplished via an interpersonal demonstration, but reaches a broader audience through electronic media. However, as the illustration shows, we sometimes model and thus teach undesirable behavior.

A large-scale modeling intervention to increase energy conservation behaviors was evaluated by Winett and colleagues.[39] Participants who viewed a 20-minute videotaped presentation of relevant conservation behaviors significantly decreased their residential energy use over a nine-week period. It's noteworthy the video specified the positive financial consequences of performing the conservation behaviors.

Behavioral Commitment. Behavioral commitment is straightforward and easy to implement, and it can be very effective. Although all ABS interventions request behavior change, a behavioral commitment takes this process a step further.

Individuals are asked to agree formally to change their behavior. They make a behavioral commitment. Asking individuals to make a written or verbal commitment to perform a target behavior increases the likelihood that behavior will be performed.[40]

When individuals sign a pledge or promise card to increase the frequency of a desirable behavior (e.g., buckle-up, recycle, exercise) or cease occurrences of an undesirable behavior (e.g., drive while impaired, smoke cigarettes, litter) they feel obligated to honor their commitment, and often do.[41] More examples of successful applications of this intervention strategy are explained in Chapters 4 and 5.

Commitment-compliant behavior is explained by ABS professionals with the notion of *rule-governed behavior*. People learn rules for performance and through their experiences they learn that following the rule is linked to positive social and personal consequences (e.g., interpersonal approval), and breaking the rule can lead to the negative consequences of disapproval or legal penalties.

This tendency to follow through on a behavioral commitment is attributed by social psychologists to the social norm of *consistency*. This norm creates pressure to be internally and externally consistent.[41] You'll read more about this in Chapter 5.

This behavioral commitment strategy can be conveniently added to many ABS interventions. At a time when vehicle safety-belt use was not the norm, my students and I combined commitment and prompting strategies by asking university students, faculty, and staff to sign a card promising to use their vehicle safety belts. Participants also agreed to hang the *Promise Card* on the rear-view mirror of their vehicles, which served as a proximal prompt to buckle up.

As you may have guessed, individuals who signed the *Buckle-Up Promise Card* were already using their vehicle safety belt more often than those individuals who did not make the buckle-up pledge; but after signing the pledge, these individuals increased their belt use significantly.[42]

Consequence Strategies

Consequences are the primary determinant of voluntary behavior, according to ABS researchers and practitioners. The most effective activators make recipients aware of potential consequences, either explicitly or implicitly. Let's consider three basic consequence strategies: penalties, rewards, and feedback.

Penalties. These interventions identify undesirable behaviors and administer negative consequences to those who perform them. Although favored by governments, ABS practitioners typically avoid this approach in community interventions for a variety of reasons. One practical reason: It usually requires extensive enforcement to be effective, and enforcement requires backing by the proper authority. An ordinance that fined residents for throwing soda cans in the garbage would need some reliable way to observe this unwanted behavior, which obviously, would not be easy.

The negative impact of the penalty approach on the attitudes of the target audience is the main reason ABS practitioners have opposed use of behavioral penalties. Most individuals react to punishment with negative emotions and attitudes.[43] Instead of performing a behavior because of its positive impact, they simply do it to avoid negative consequences. And when enforcement is not consistent, behaviors are likely to return to their previous state.

Astute readers will note the label "penalty approach" rather than "punishment." And next, the term "reward" is used instead of "positive reinforcement." This differentiates the technical and application meanings of these consequence strategies. Reinforcement and punishment imply the consequence changed the target behavior. If punishment does not decrease behavior or reinforcement (positive or negative) does not increase behavior, the relevant consequences were not punishers or reinforcers, respectively.

Punishment and reinforcement procedures are defined by the effects of the consequence on the target behavior. Because large-scale or community-based applications of consequence strategies rarely identify the behavioral impact per individual, the terms penalty and reward are more appropriate. Regardless of their behavioral impact, penalties are negative consequences and rewards are positive consequences.

Rewards. Because of the negative side-effects associated with punishment, ABS practitioners favor following a desirable behavior with a positive consequence or reward. Rewards include money, merchandise, verbal praise, or special privileges, given as a consequence of the desired target behavior.

Reward strategies have some problems of their own. Still, many community-based reward interventions have produced dramatic increases in targeted behaviors.

Because rewards follow behaviors, they are included in the consequence section of this chapter. However, as the illustration shows, rewards are often preceded by antecedents announcing the availability of the reward following a designated behavior.

This activator is termed an *incentive*. An activator announcing punitive consequences for unwanted behavior is termed a *disincentive*.

Sometimes rewards or penalties are used without incentives or disincentives. In these cases, the positive or negative consequence follows the behavior without an advanced announcement of the response-consequence contingency.

A wide range of behaviors have been targeted with incentive/reward programs. Studies have shown significant beneficial impact of incentive/reward programs at increasing vehicle safety-belt use,[44] medication compliance,[45] commitment to organ donation,[46] and decreasing drug use,[46] environmental degradation,[47] alcohol abuse,[48] and interpersonal bullying.[28]

In addition, incentives and rewards are used frequently and effectively by employers to increase worker productivity and safety. A meta-analysis of 39 studies using financial incentives to increase performance quantity found that, averaged across all studies, workers offered financial compensation for increased production increased their productivity by 34% over those who were not offered behavior-based rewards.[49]

Behavior-based incentive-reward strategies are also effective at increasing safety-related behaviors and preventing personal injury.[50] Given the consistent effectiveness of incentive/reward strategies, one might ask, "Why use anything else?" Unfortunately, incentive/reward interventions have a few disadvantages. An obvious practical disadvantage of using rewards is they can be expensive to implement from both a financial and administrative perspective.

A second limitation: Target behaviors tend to decrease when the rewards are removed, almost as dramatically as they increase when the rewards are introduced. In fact, this effect is so reliable ABS researchers often use this effect to evaluate intervention impact. They first measure the pre-intervention (baseline) rate of a target behavior, then assess the increase in the frequency of the behavior while rewards are in place, and finally document a decrease in behavioral frequency when the rewards are removed.

When a target behavior occurs more often while an intervention is in place and returns to near baseline levels when the intervention is withdrawn, ABS researchers demonstrate *functional control* of the target behavior. The intervention caused the behavior change. An obvious solution to this reversal problem is to keep a reward strategy in place indefinitely. Bottle bills, which provide a refund of 5-10 cents when bottles and cans are returned, illustrate an effective long-term incentive/reward strategy.

Finally, some researchers criticize reward interventions by contending rewards diminish *intrinsic motivation*.[51] Instead of focusing on the positive aspects of completing a task for its own sake, individual's become *extrinsically motivated* to perform the behavior. In essence individuals reason, "If someone is paying me to perform a behavior, the activity must be unpleasant and not worth performing when the opportunity for reward is removed."

The overjustification effect, as this perspective of extrinsic rewards is termed, is depicted in the illustration.[52] The prior extrinsic reward for solving a math problem takes

the student's attention away from intrinsic or natural consequences of the behavior – solving an important problem.

Effective interpersonal recognition and feedback interventions call attention to the target behavior and can enhance intrinsic motivation. This issue is entertained further in Chapter 3, including a rationale and intervention techniques for using behavior-based rewards and interpersonal recognition to increase self-motivation and improve performance.

Feedback. Feedback strategies provide information to participants about their behavior. They can make the consequences of desirable behaviors more salient (e.g., money saved from carpooling, amount of weight lost from an exercise program), and increase the frequency of behaviors consistent with desired outcomes.

Many early environmental-conservation interventions targeting home-energy consumption used feedback strategies, and most of these interventions showed modest but consistent energy savings.[53] Feedback has been an effective strategy for addressing unsafe driving,[54] smoking cessation,[55] and depression.[56] Chapter 3 details communication techniques for giving supportive and corrective behavior-based feedback effectively in order to improve performance.

Although I reviewed these six non-punitive ABS intervention techniques (education, prompts, modeling, commitment, rewards, and feedback) separately, in practice several are often combined in a single intervention process. Most interventions combine some sort of antecedent information component with a behavior-based consequence (e.g., reward and/or feedback). The reward or feedback can be based on participants' behavior (i.e., process-based) or based on the cumulative results of several behaviors from one individual or a team of individuals (i.e., outcome-based).

It's important to apply behavior-based and outcome-based consequences strategically. The behavior-consequence contingency defines an accountability system which in turn influences the participant's behavior.

Outcome-based feedback and reward programs to promote industrial safety are popular worldwide, because they are easy to implement and they decrease the reports of injuries. Employees receive rewards (e.g., gift certificates, lottery tickets, or financial bonuses) when the company-wide injury rate is reduced to a certain level. The result: Rewards are received because the frequency of *reported* injuries decrease.

However, most of these outcome-based incentive/reward programs do more harm than good. Why? Because actual safety-related behaviors do not necessarily change – just the *reporting* of injuries.

When the factual reporting of injuries is stifled by outcome-based incentives and rewards, the opportunity for critical conversations about injury prevention is lost. The illustration shows how rewards for outcomes can have a detrimental effect on behavior. Managers get what they reward.

"JOE GETS THE SAFETY PRIZE AGAIN. HE WENT ANOTHER 30 DAYS WITHOUT AN ERROR."

The Challenge of Sustaining Behavior Change

The intervention approaches reviewed above will change behavior, but will the target behavior continue when the intervention is removed?

This is primarily a challenge of institutionalizing the ABC contingencies of the intervention process, contend some ABS professionals.[57] External and extrinsic activators and consequences need to be transferred from the behavioral scientist or intervention agent to the indigenous personnel of the organizational setting in which the target behavior occurs. The intervention is not removed; rather those who deliver the intervention contingencies are changed.

Other behavioral scientists claim this maintenance challenge is about behavior continuing in the absence of the extrinsic intervention.[58] Some presume the objectives of the intervention need to be internalized. As indicated earlier, people act themselves into thought processes consistent with the new behavior.[59] As such, personal change is viewed as a continuous spiral of behavior causing thinking, thinking inducing more behavior, and then this additional behavior influencing more thinking consistent with the behavior, and so on.

However, programmatic research indicates that some interventions do not facilitate an attendant change in thinking. This is reflected profoundly in Daryl Bem's classic theory of self-perception.

Behavioral Self-Perception

Bem prefaced his behavioral presentation of self-perception theory with " . . . individuals come to 'know' their own attitudes, emotions, and other internal states by inferring them from observations of their own overt behavior and/or the circumstances in which this behavior occurs".[60] We write mental scripts or make internal attributions about ourselves from our observations and interpretations of the various three-term or ABC contingencies that enter our life space.

And, " . . . if external contingencies seem sufficient to account for the behavior, then the individual will not be led into using the behavior as a source of evidence for his self-attributions".[61]

Children who had the excuse of a severe threat for not playing with a "forbidden toy" did not internalize a rule, and played with the forbidden toy when the threat contingency was removed.[62] Similarly, college students paid $20 for telling other students a boring task was fun did not develop a personal view that the task was enjoyable.[63] The reinforcement contingency made their behavior incredible as a reflection of their personal belief or self-perception.

In contrast, participants who received a mild threat or low compensation (only $1) to motivate their behavior developed a self-perception consistent with their behavior. The children avoided playing with the forbidden toy in a subsequent situation with no threat, and the college students who lied for low compensation decided they must have liked the boring task. In theory, these participants viewed their behavior as a valid guide for inferring their private views, since their behavior was not under strong contingency control. This theory and its practical implications are explained further and illustrated in Chapter 5 as the *Consistency Principle* of social influence.

The More Outside Control, the Less Self-Persuasion

According to substantial research, self-persuasion is more likely when the extrinsic control of the three-term contingency is less obvious or perhaps indirect. When there are sufficient external consequences to justify the amount of effort required for a particular behavior, the performer does not develop an internal justification for the behavior. There is no self-persuasion and performing the behavior does not alter self-perception.[64] Under these circumstances maintenance of the behavior is unlikely, unless it's possible to keep a sufficient accountability system (e.g., incentives or disincentives) in place over the long term, as was the case for a 13-year incentive process that successfully reduced injuries in an open-pit mine.[65]

Intervening to improve behavior over the long term is more complex than applying the three-term contingency. Not only is it necessary to consider whether the performer needs instruction, motivation, or only support to improve or maintain behavior,[66] it seems internal cognitive factors are important whenever external contingencies cannot remain in place to hold people accountable. This implicates self-persuasion and self-directed behavior, topics not typically considered in ABS. These concepts imply that indirect influence is more likely to lead to sustained behavior change than direct persuasion.

Direct Persuasion. Advertisers use direct persuasion. They show us actors enjoying positive consequences or avoiding negative consequences by using their products. They apply the three-term contingency or ABC paradigm to sell their goods and services. The activator announces the availability of a reinforcing consequence if the purchasing behavior is performed.

Advertisers also apply research-based principles from social psychology to make their messages more persuasive. Specifically, social scientists have shown advantages of using highly credible communicators, and of arousing their audience's emotions.[67] Sales pitches are often delivered by authority figures (celebrities, chief executives) who attempt to get viewers emotionally involved with product-related issues. In today's social-media world, one's friends can be influential if they indicate on Facebook they "like" a certain product. Advertisers are spending more and more money on this "peer persuasion" tactic.

These attempts at direct persuasion are not asking for behavior that is inconvenient or difficult to execute. Normally, the purpose of an advertisement is to persuade a consumer to select a certain brand of merchandise they already use. This boils down to merely choosing one commodity over another at the retail store. This is hardly a burdensome change in lifestyle.

AC4P behavior is usually more inconvenient and requires more effort than switching brands at a supermarket. Long-term participation in the AC4P Movement is far more cumbersome and lifestyle-changing than the consumer behavior targeted by advertisers.

In fact, direct attempts to persuade people to make inconvenient changes in their lifestyle have often yielded disappointing results. Communication strategies have generally been unsuccessful at persuading smokers to quit smoking[68] drivers to stop speeding,[69] homeowners to conserve water[70] or insulate their water heaters,[71] bigoted individuals to cease prejudicial behavior, or sexually active people to use condoms.[64] Similarly, the "Just Say No to Drugs" campaigns have not influenced significant behavior change.

The direct approach can give the impression the target behavior is accomplished for someone else's benefit. This can cause a disconnection between the behavior and self-perception. Then there's no self-persuasion – and self-perception is the mindset needed for lasting change in the absence of incentives/rewards, disincentives/penalties, or another type of extrinsic and external accountability system.

The Indirect Approach. Self-persuasion is more likely to occur when the motivational strategy is less obvious. Compliments regarding a person's performance are often more powerful when they are more indirect than direct.[72] Imagine you overhear a person tell someone else about your superb achievement on a particular assignment. Or suppose a friend gives you secondhand recognition by sharing what another person said about your AC4P behavior.

Both of these situations reflect indirect commendation, and will likely have more influence on your self-perception than a direct statement of praise. Why? Because the direct approach is tainted by the possibility flattery is given for an ulterior motive.

Indirect persuasion deviates significantly from the standard "command and control" method of promoting compliance. Both approaches might be equally effective at motivating behavior change, but an indirect approach will be far more successful at enhancing the kind of internal dialogue needed to sustain behavior in the absence of an external motivator or accountability system.

Defining intervention conditions to make this happen is not easy. Start by asking, "Does the situation promote individual choice, ownership, and personal accountability?" "Does the context in which AC4P behavior is desired contribute to connecting or disconnecting the link between what people do and what they think of themselves?" "Are the AC4P activities only behaviors or do they stimulate supportive cognitive activity or self-persuasion?"

The role of psychological states or expectancies in facilitating AC4P behavior are reflected in these questions. If certain feelings or beliefs affect people's participation in the AC4P Movement, then enhancing these states can be a powerful indirect way to cultivate an AC4P culture of compassion. The next chapter explains this further by specifying both direct and indirect ways to increase the frequency and improve the quality of AC4P behavior.

In Conclusion

This initial chapter reviewed seven fundamental principles and related applications of ABS. These serve as the foundation of the AC4P Movement, from analyzing the behavioral components of social issues to implementing and disseminating practical, evidence-based strategies for large-scale behavior change. Some research-based examples of effective ABS interventions were presented, but the following chapters offer many more.

The need to consider self-talk and person-states when designing and implementing AC4P interventions was explained. This domain of self-persuasion or self-motivation (see Chapter 3) justifies the label *humanistic behaviorism,* as introduced in the Preface. It takes us beyond traditional ABS.

The principles and applications in this book illustrate ways to make ABS methods more effective and durable by incorporating concepts from humanistic theory and therapy. Still, when all is said and done, we have only scratched the surface regarding the potential of ABS and the AC4P Movement to mitigate numerous negative consequences resulting from the intimidating social and environmental problems we face every day.

Notes

1. Geller, E. S. (1998). *Understanding behavior-based safety: Step-by-step methods to improve your workplace* (2nd Edition). Neenah, WI: J. J. Keller & Associates, Inc; Geller, E. S., & Williams, J. (Eds.). (2001). *Keys to behavior-based safety from Safety Performance Solutions.* Rockville, MD: Government Institutes; Geller, E. S. (2005). *People-based safety: The source.* Virginia Beach, VA: Coastal training and Technologies Corporation; Geller, E. S., & Johnson, D. J. (2007). *People-based patient safety: Enriching your culture to prevent medical error.* Virginia Beach, VA: Coastal Training and Technologies Corporation.

2. Skinner, B. F. (1938). *The behavior of organisms: An experimental analysis.* Acton, MA: Copley Publishing Group; Skinner, B. F. (1953). *Science and human behavior.* New York, NY: Macmillan; Skinner, B. F. (1974). *About behaviorism.* New York, NY: Alfred A. Knopf.

3. Actually, the intial term was *applied behavior analysis,* but since behavior-based intervention is founded on the scientific-method and involves more than *analysis,* the more relevant term is *applied behavioral science.*

4. Goldstein, A. P., & Krasner, L. (1987). *Modern applied psychology.* New York: Pergamon Press; Greene, B. F., Winett, R. A., Van Houten, R., Geller, E. S., & Iwata, B. A. (Eds.) (1987). *Behavior analysis in the community: Readings from the Journal of Applied Behavior Analysis.* Lawrence, KS: Society for the Experimental Analysis of Behavior, Inc.

5. Austin, J. (2000). Performance analysis and performance diagnostics. In J. Austin & J. E. Carr (Eds.) *Handbook of applied behavior analysis* (pp. 321-349). Reno, NV: Context Press; Austin, J., Carr, J. E., & Agnew, J. (1999). The need for assessing maintaining variables in OBM. *Journal of Organizational Behavior Management, 19,* 59-87; Bailey, J. S., & Austin, J. (1996). Evaluating and improving productivity in the workplace. In B. Thyer & M. Mattaini (Eds.) *Behavior analysis and social work* (pp. 179-200). Washington, DC: American Psychological Association.

6. Geller, E. S. (2001). *The psychology of safety handbook.* Boca Raton, FL: CRC Press; McSween, T. E. (2003). *The values-based safety process: Improving your safety culture with a behavioral*

approach (2nd Edition). New York, NY: Van Nostrand Reinhold; Sulzer-Azaroff, B., & Austin, J. (2000). Does BBS Work? Behavior-based safety and injury reduction: A survey of the evidence. *Professional Safety, 45*, 19-24.

7. Geller, E. S., & Johnson, D. J. (2007). *People-based patient safety: Enriching your culture to prevent medical error.* Virginia Beach, VA: Coastal Training and Technologies Corporation.

8. Carnegie, D. (1936). *How to win friends and influence people.* New York, NY: Simon and Schuster.

9. Skinner, B. F. (1971). *Beyond freedom and dignity.* New York, NY: Alfred A. Knopf.

10. Atkinson, J. W. (1957). Motivational determinants of risk-taking behavior. *Psychological Review, 64*, 359-372; Atkinson, J. W. (1964). *An introduction to motivation.* Princeton, NJ: Van Nostrand; Atkinson, J. W., & Litwin, G. F. (1960). Achievement motive and test anxiety conceived as motive to approach success and motive to avoid failure. *Journal of Abnormal and Social Psychology, 60*, 52-63.

11. Berglas, S., & Jones, E. E. (1978). Drug choice as a self-handicapping strategy in response to non-contingent success. *Journal of Personality and Social Psychology, 36*, 405-417; Rhodewalt, F. (1994). Conceptions of ability achievement goals, and individual differences in self-handicapping behavior: On the application of implicit theories, *Journal of Personality, 62*, 67-85; Rhodewalt, F., & Fairfield, M. (1991). Claimed self-handicaps and the self-handicapper: The relations of reduction in intended effort to performance. *Journal of Research in Personality, 25*, 402-417.

12. Covington, M.V. (1992). *Making the grade: A self-worth perspective on motivation and school reform.* Cambridge, MA: Cambridge University Press; Martin, A. J., & Marsh, H. W. (2003). Fear of failure: Friend or foe? *Australian Psychologist, 38*, 31-38.

13. Covington, M. V., & Roberts, B. W. (1994). Self-worth and college achievement: Motivational and personality correlates. In P. R. Pintrich, D. R. Brown, & C. E. Weinstein (Eds.). *Student motivation, cognition, and learning: Essays in honor of Wilbert J. McKeachie.* Hillsdale, NJ: Earlbaum.

14. Covington, M.V. (1992). *Making the grade: A self-worth perspective on motivation and school reform.* Cambridge, MA: Cambridge University Press.

15. Maier, S. F., & Seligman, M. E. P. (1976). Learned helplessness: Theory and evidence. *Journal of Experimental Psychology: General, 105*, 3-46.

16. Wiegand, D.M., & Geller, E.S. (2005). Connecting positive psychology and organizational behavior management: Achievement motivation and the power of positive reinforcement. *Journal of Organizational Behavior Management, Vol. 24*, 3-25.

17. Azrin, N. H., & Holz, W. C. (1996). Punishment. In W. K. Honig (Ed.), *Operant behavior: Areas of research and application* (pp. 380-447). New York, NY: Appleton-Century-Crofts.

18. Estes, W. K., & Skinner, B. F. (1941). Some quantitative properties of anxiety. *Journal of Experimental Psychology, 29*, 390-400.

19. Everett, P. B., Haywood, S. C., & Meyers, A. W. (1974). Effects of a token reinforcement procedure on bus ridership. *Journal of Applied Behavior Analysis, 7*, 1-9; Geller, E. S., Kalsher, M. J., Rudd, J. R., & Lehman, G. (1989). Promoting safety belt use on a university campus: An integration of commitment and incentive strategies. *Journal of Applied Social Psychology, 19*, 3-19; Geller, E. S. (1992). Solving environmental problems: A behavior change perspective. In S. Staub & P. Green (Eds.). *Psychology and social responsibility: Facing global challenges* (pp. 248-270). New York, NY: New York University Press; Hagenzieker, M. P. (1991). Enforcement or incentive? Promoting safety belt use among military personnel in the Netherlands. *Journal of Applied Behavior Analysis, 24*, 23-30; Rudd, J. R., & Geller, E. S. (1985). A university-based incentive program to increase safety-belt use: Toward cost-effective institutionalization. *Journal of Applied Behavior Analysis, 18*, 215-226.

20. Geller, E. S. (2001). Sustaining participation in a safety improvement process: Ten relevant principles from behavioral science. *Professional Safety, 46*, 24-29.

21. Geller, E. S. (2001). *The psychology of safety handbook.* Boca Raton, FL: CRC Press; Geller, E. S. (2002). *The participation factor: How to get more people involved in occupational safety.* Des Plaines, IL: American Society of Safety Engineers; Geller, E. S. (2005). *People-based safety: The source.* Virginia Beach, VA: Coastal Training and Technologies Corporation.

22. O'Brien, D. P. (2000) *Business measurements for safety performance.* New York, NY: Lewis Publishers; Petersen, D. (2001). *Authentic involvement.* Itasca, IL: National Safety Council.

23. Geller, E. S. (1991) (Ed.). *Social validity: Multiple perspectives.* Monograph Number 5. Lawrence, KS: Society for the Experimental Analysis of Behavior, Inc.

24. Wolf, M.M. (1978). Social validity: The case of subjective measurement or how behavior analysis is finding its heart. *Journal of Applied Behavior Analysis, 11*, 203-213.

25. Schwartz, I. S., & Baer, D. M. (1991). Social validity assessments: Is current practice state of the art? *Journal of Applied Behavior Analysis, 24*, 189-197.

26. Eckenfelder, D. J. (1996). *Values-driven safety.* Rockville, MD: Government Institutes, Inc.

27. Daniels, A. C. (2000). *Bringing out the best in people: How to apply the astonishing power of positive reinforcement* (2nd Edition). New York, NY: McGraw-Hill, Inc.

28. McCarty, S. M., & Geller, E. S. (2014). Actively caring to prevent bullying: Prompting and rewarding prosocial behavior in elementary schools. In E.S. Geller (Ed.). *Actively caring at your school: How to make it happen* (pp. 153-173). Newport, VA: Make-A-Difference, LLC.

29. Alvero, A. M., Bucklin, B. R., & Austin, J. (2001). An objective review of the effectiveness and characteristics of performance feedback in organizational settings. *Journal of Organizational Behavior Management, 21*, 3-29; Balcazar, F., Hopkins, B. L., & Suarez, I. (1986). A critical, objective review of performance feedback. *Journal of Organizational Behavior Management, 7*, 65-89.

30. Mayo, E. (1933). *The human problems of an industrialized civilization.* Boston, MA: Harvard university Graduate School of Business Administration; Rothlisberger, R. J., & Dickson, W. J. (1939). *Management and the worker.* Cambridge, MA: Harvard University Press; Whitehead, T. N. (1938). *The industrial worker.* Ambridge, MA: Howard University press.

31. Parsons, H. M. (1974). What happened at Hawthorne? *Science, 183*, 922-932.

32. Skinner, B. F. (1974). *About behaviorism.* New York, NY: Alfred A. Knopf.

33. Geller, E. S., & Hahn, H. A. (1984). Promoting safety-belt use at industrial sites: An effective program for blue-collar employees. *Professional Psychology: Research and Practice, 15*, 533-564; Lewin, K. (1958). Group decision and social change. In E. E. Maccoby, T. M. Newcomb, & E. L. Hartley (Eds.). *Readings in social psychology* (pp. 197-211). New York, NY: Holt, Rinehart & Winston.

34. Geller, E. S. (1992). Solving environmental problems: A behavior change perspective. In S. Staub & P. Green (Eds.). *Psychology and social responsibility: Facing global challenges* (pp. 248-270). New York, NY: New York University Press.

35. Geller, E. S., Winett, R. A., & Everett, P. B. (1982). *Environmental preservation: New strategies for behavior change.* New York, NY: Pergamon Press.

36. Werner, C. M., Rhodes, M. U., & Partain, K. K. (1998). Designing effective instructional signs with schema theory: Case studies of polystyrene recycling. *Environment and Behavior, 30*, 709-735.

37. Geller, E. S., Kalsher, M. J., Rudd, J. R., & Lehman, G. (1989). Promoting safety belt use on a university campus: An integration of commitment and incentive strategies. *Journal of Applied Social Psychology, 19*, 3-19.

38. Bandura, A. (1977). *Social learning theory*. Englewood Cliffs, NJ: Prentice Hall.

39. Winett, R. A., Leckliter, I. N., Chinn, D. E., Stahl, B., & Love, S. Q. (1985). Effects of television modeling on residential energy conservation. *Journal of Applied Behavior Analysis, 18*, 33-44.

40. Geller, E. S., & Lehman, G. R. (1991). The buckle-up promise card: A versatile intervention for large-scale behavior change. *Journal of Applied Behavior Analysis, 24*, 91-94.

41. Cialdini, R. B., & Goldstein, N. J. (2004). Social influence: Compliance and conformity. *Annual Review of Psychology, 55*, 591-621.

42. Geller, E. S., Kalsher, M. J., Rudd, J. R., & Lehman, G. (1989). Promoting safety belt use on a university campus: An integration of commitment and incentive strategies. *Journal of Applied Social Psychology, 19*, 3-19.

43. Sidman, M. (1989). *Coercion and its fallout*. Boston, MA: Authors Cooperative, Inc., Publishers.

44. Geller, E. S. (1983). Rewarding safety belt usage at an industrial setting: Tests of treatment generality and response maintenance. *Journal of Applied Behavior Analysis, 16*, 189-202.

45. Bamberger, J. D., Unick, J., Klein, P., Fraser, M., Chesney M., & Katz, M. H. (2000). Helping the urban poor stay with antiretroviral HIV drug therapy. *American Journal of Public Health. 90*, 699-701.

46. Silverman, K., Chutuape, M., Bigelow, G. E., & Stitzer, M. L. (1999). Voucher-based reinforcement of cocaine abstinence in treatment resistant methadone patients: Effects of reinforcement magnitude. *Outcomes Management, 146*, 128-138.

47. Lehman, P.K., & Geller, E. S. (2004). Behavior analysis and environmental protection: Accomplishments and potential for more. *Behavior and Social Issues, 13*, 13-32.

48. Fournier, A. K., Ehrhart, I. J., Glindemann,K.E., & Geller, E. S. (2004). Intervening to decrease alcohol abuse at university parties: Differential reinforcement of intoxication level. *Behavior Modification, 28*, 167-181; Glindeman, K. E., Ehrhart, I. J., Drake, E. A., & Geller, E. S. (2006). Reducing excessive alcohol consumption at university fraternity parties: A cost-effective incentive/reward intervention. *Addictive Behaviors, 32*(1), 39-48.

49. Jenkins, G. D., Mitra, A., Gupta, N., & Shaw, J. D. (1998). Are financial incentives related to performance? A meta-analytic review of empirical research. *Journal of Applied Psychology, 83*, 777-787.

50. Geller, E. S. (2001). *The psychology of safety handbook*. Boca Raton, FL: CRC Press; Geller, E. S. (2001). *Working safe: How to help people actively care for health and safety* (2nd Edition). New York, NY: Lewis Publishers; McSween, T. E. (2003). *The values-based safety process: Improving your safety culture with a behavioral approach* (2nd Edition). New York, NY: Van Nostrand Reinhold.

51. Deci, E. L., & Ryan, R. M. (1985). *Intrinsic motivation and self-determination in human behavior*. New York: Plenum Publishers; Kohn, A. (1993). *Punished by rewards: The trouble with gold stars, incentive plans, A's, praise, and other bribes*. Boston, MA: Houghton Mifflin; Pink, D. H. (2009). *Drive: The surprising truth about what motivates us*. New York, NY: Penguin Group.

52. Lepper, M., & Green, D. (1978). (Eds.). *The hidden cost of reward*. Hillsdale, NJ: Erlbaum.

53. Dwyer, W. O., Leeming, F. C., Cobern, M. K., Porter, B. E., & Jackson, J. M. (1993). Critical review of behavioral interventions to preserve the environment: Research since 1980. *Environment and Behavior, 25*, 485-505; Geller, E. S., Winett, R. A., & Everett, P. B. (1982). *Environmental preservation: New strategies for behavior change*. New York, NY: Pergamon Press.

54. Ludwig, T. D., & Geller, E. S. (2000). Intervening to improve the safety of delivery drivers: A systematic, behavioral approach. *Journal of Organizational Behavior Management, 19*, 1-124.

55. Walters, S. T., Wright, J., & Shegog, R. (2006). A review of computer and internet-based interventions for smoking behavior. *Addictive Behaviors, 31*, 264-277.

56. Geisner, I. M., Neighbors, C., & Larimer, M. E. (2006). A randomized clinical trial of a brief, mailed intervention for symptoms of depression. *Journal of Consulting and Clinical Psychology, 74*, 393-399.

57. Malott, R. W. (2001). Occupational safety and response maintenance: An alternative view. *Journal of Organizational Behavior Management, 21*(1), 85-102; McSween, T., & Matthews, G. A. (2001). Maintenance in organizational safety management. *Journal of Organizational Behavior Management, 21*(1), 75-83.

58. Baer, D. M. (2001). Since safety maintains our lives, we need to maintain maintaining. *Journal of Organizational Behavior Management, 21*(1), 61-64; Boyce, T. E., & Geller, E. S. (2001). Applied behavior analysis and occupational safety: The challenge of response maintenance. *Journal of Organizational Behavior Management, 21*(1), 31-60; Geller, E. S. (2001). Dream – Operationalize – Intervene – Test: If you want to make a difference – Just DO IT. *Journal of Organizational Behavior Management, 21*(1), 109-121; Stokes, T. F., & Baer, D. M. (1977). An implicit technology of generalization. *Journal of Applied Behavior Analysis, 10,* 349-367.

59. Geller, E. S. (2001). Sustaining participation in a safety improvement process: Ten relevant principles from behavioral science. *Professional Safety, 46*(9), 24-29.

60. Bem, D. J. (1972). Self-perception theory. In L. Berkowitz (Ed.). *Advances in experimental social psychology,* Vol. 6 (pp. 1-60). New York, NY: Academic Press, p.2.

61. Bem, D. J. (1972). Self-perception theory. In L. Berkowitz (Ed.), *Advances in experimental social psychology,* Vol. 6 (pp. 1-60). New York, NY: Academic Press, p.3.

62. Lepper, M., & Green, D. (1978). *The hidden cost of reward.* Hillsdale, NJ: Erlbaum.

63. Festinger, L., & Carlsmith, J. M. (1959). Cognitive consequences of forced compliance. *Journal of Abnormal and Social Psychology, 58,* 203-210.

64. Aronson, E. (1999). The power of self-persuasion. *American Psychologist, 54,* 875-884.

65. Fox, D. K., Hopkins, B. L., & Anger, W. K. (1987). The long-term effects of a token economy on safety performance in open-pit mining. *Journal of Applied Behavior Analysis, 20,* 215-224.

66. Geller, E. S. (2001). Dream – Operationalize – Intervene – Test: If you want to make a difference – Just DO IT. *Journal of Organizational Behavior Management, 21*(1), 109-121.

67. Aronson, E. (1999). The power of self-persuasion. *American Psychologist, 54,* 875-884; Hovland, C., & Weiss, W. (1951). The influence of source credibility on communication effectiveness. *Public Opinion Quarterly, 15,* 635-650.

68. Elder, J. P., Geller, E. S., Hovell, M. F., & Mayer, J. A. (1994). *Motivating health behavior.* New York, NY: Delmar Publishers.

69. Geller, E. S. (1998). *Applications of behavior analysis to prevent injury from vehicle crashes* (2nd Edition). Monograph published by the Cambridge Center for Behavioral Studies, Cambridge, MA.

70. Geller, E. S., Erickson, J. B., & Buttram, B. A. (1983). Attempts to promote residential water conservation with educational, behavioral, and engineering strategies. *Population and Environment, 6,* 96-112.

71. Geller, E. S. (1981). Evaluating energy conservation programs: Is verbal report enough? *Journal of Consumer Behavior, 8,* 331-334.

72. Allen, J. (1990). *I saw what you did and I know who you are: Bloopers, blunders and success stories in giving and receiving recognition.* Tucker, GA: Performance Management Publications; Geller, E. S. (1997). Key processes for continuous safety improvement: Behavior-based recognition and celebration. *Professional Safety, 42*(10), 40-44.

CHAPTER 2

The Psychology of AC4P Behavior

E. Scott Geller

THE LARGE-SCALE, LONG-TERM health, safety, and welfare of people require us to routinely go beyond the call of duty on behalf of others. We call this Actively Caring for People or AC4P – the theme of this book. Usually actively caring involves *self-motivation*, as I explain in the next chapter. Often AC4P behavior requires a certain amount of *courage*, and this is clarified in Chapter 4.

What is AC4P Behavior?

Figure 2.1 presents a simple flow chart summarizing a basic approach to culture change. We start a culture-change mission with a vision or ultimate purpose – for example, to achieve an AC4P culture of compassion. With group consensus supporting the vision, we develop procedures or action plans to accomplish our mission. These are reflected in process-oriented goals which denote goal-related behaviors.

The popular writings of Covey,[4] Peale,[5] Kohn,[6] and Deming[7] suggest behavior is activated and maintained by self-affirmations, internal motivation and personal principles or values. But, these authors as well as many motivational consultants miss a key component of human dynamics – the power of consequences.

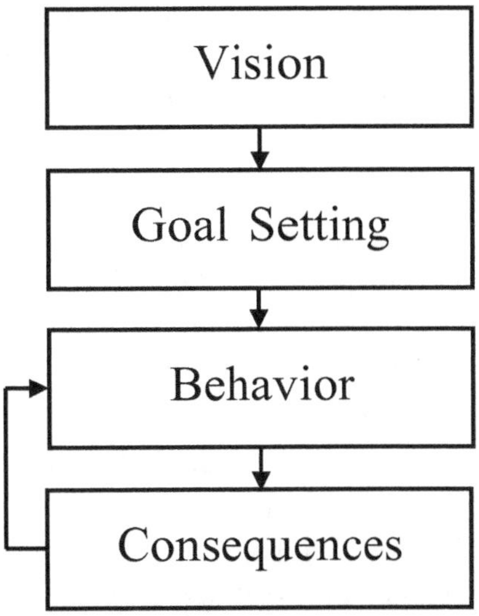

Figure 2.1. An AC4P culture requires vision and behavior management.

Consequences are Critical

Appropriate goal setting, self-affirmations, and a positive attitude can indeed activate behaviors to achieve goals and visions. But we must not forget one of B.F. Skinner's most important legacies – *selection by consequences*.[8] As depicted in Figure 2.1, consequences follow behavior and are needed to support the right behaviors and correct wrong ones.

Without support for the "right stuff," good intentions and initial efforts fade away. How long does a weight-loss plan as a New Year's resolution (vision) last if one cannot see initial weight loss (consequence) after the first few weeks of exercise (behavior) in an effort to lose 15 pounds (an outcome goal)?

In *How to Win Friends and Influence People*, Dale Carnegie affirms, "Every act you have ever performed since the day you were born was performed because you wanted something".[9] Sometimes natural consequences are available to motivate desired behaviors, but often extrinsic consequences (or external accountabilities) need to be managed to motivate the behavior needed to achieve our goals.

For example, I presume my students often have visions of earning an "A" in my university classes, and they set relevant process goals to study regularly in order to achieve that ultimate "A" grade (an outcome goal). I hold them accountable to study the material by giving exams periodically throughout the semester.

When the days for exams are announced in the course syllabus, students typically adjust their study behavior according to this accountability scheme. They increase their frequency of studying successively as the day of the exam approaches, performing most of their studying behaviors the night before an exam.

But when my assessment protocol is changed from announced to unannounced exams, most students change their study behavior dramatically. Under this accountability system, students feel compelled to prepare for every class, anticipating a possible exam on any class day. Although students uniformly dislike this second approach, they are substantially more prepared for class when the occurrence of an exam cannot be predicted.

Some students study the course material consistently to reach their learning goals, regardless of the external accountability agenda set by their teacher. These individuals are self-motivated and implement their own self-management procedures to keep them on track. I cover this special type of motivation in the next chapter, as well as ways to achieve this quality of personal responsibility.

Students' post-exam, course-related behaviors are usually affected by their test scores – the consequences of their test-taking behavior. But for a number of reasons, it's difficult to predict how a particular exam grade will influence an individual's goal-setting or study behavior.

A high grade does not always motivate a higher rate of course-related studying, as expected from the principle of positive reinforcement; and a low grade does not lead to less studying as could be predicted from punishment theory. A sense of competence or confidence from a high grade could influence less study behavior; and fear of failure after receiving a low grade might affect more study behavior, including some self-management goal-setting and feedback strategies.

As you can see, the driving motivators are consequences. This is a key lesson to learn and use. The "pop psychology" notion that people can overcome their challenges and achieve whatever they want through positive thinking, self-affirmations, and relevant goal-setting before their behavior is just not true.

Without appropriate consequences to support the right behavior and correct the wrong behavior, goal-directed behavior will simply stop. People cannot reach their behavior-specific process goals unless they receive relevant feedback to keep them on track. I'm talking about behavior-based feedback to support desirable behavior and correct undesirable behavior.

Actively Caring is Critical

In Figure 2.2, a new box is added to the basic flow diagram in Figure 2.1. The point is simple but extremely important: Vision, goals and consequences are not sufficient for culture change. People need to *actively care* about the goals, action plans, and consequences. They need to believe in and own the vision.

They need to feel empowered and encouraged from peers to attain process goals that support the vision. And peers need to give them supportive and corrective feedback to increase the quantity and quality of behaviors consistent with vision-relevant goals.

Corrective feedback is critical for individuals to improve their future behavior. Supportive feedback is a powerful consequence for the maintenance of behavior, because it tells individuals what they are doing right.

In most relationships, supportive feedback is rare; so special attention is needed to increase this important feedback process. Corrective feedback and supportive feedback are essential for continuous improvement and for achieving an AC4P culture of people contributing to the well-being of each other.

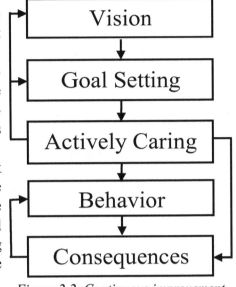

Figure 2.2. Continuous improvement requires actively caring.

Three Ways to Actively Care

When individuals perform AC4P behaviors, they can improve environment factors, enhance person factors, or increase the frequency of others' AC4P behaviors. When people alter environmental conditions, or reorganize resources in an attempt to benefit others, they are AC4P from an environmental perspective. Examples of AC4P behaviors in this category include: attending to a housekeeping detail, posting a warning sign near an environmental hazard, shoveling snow from a neighbor's sidewalk, washing another person's vehicle, organizing a colleague's desk, helping a party host collect recyclables, and cleaning up a spill or removing a trip hazard.

Person-based AC4P occurs when people attempt to make others feel better. Often, it doesn't take much to improve an individual's emotions, attitudes, or mood states. Examples of person-based AC4P include: listening proactively to others, expressing concern for another person's difficulties, complimenting an individual's academic or work performance, sending a get-well card, and posting birthday wishes on a person's Facebook. These types of AC4P behavior will likely boost people's self-esteem, self-efficacy, personal control, optimism, and/or sense of belonging – increasing their propensity to actively care.

Also included here are *reactive* AC4P behaviors performed in crisis situations. For example, if you save someone from drowning, administer cardiopulmonary resuscitation (CPR), or give a drunk driver a ride home you're AC4P from a person-based perspective.

From a proactive perspective, behavior-focused AC4P is most beneficial, but is also the most challenging. This happens when people apply an instructive, supportive, or motivational intervention to improve another person's desirable behavior.

When we teach others how to promote AC4P behavior or provide supportive comments or possible improvements regarding observed behavior, we are actively caring from a behavioral focus. Teachers and athletic coaches do this when they help another person achieve a desired performance goal. Plus, recognizing the desirable AC4P behavior of others in a one-to-one conversation is also AC4P with a behavior focus.

Why Categorize AC4P Behaviors

Why go to the trouble of categorizing AC4P behaviors? Good question! Consider what these behaviors are trying to accomplish, and realize the relative difficulty in performing each of them. Environment-focused AC4P behavior might be the easiest approach for some people because it usually does not involve interpersonal interaction.

When people contribute financially to a charity, donate blood, or complete an organ donor card, they do not interact personally with the recipient of the contribution. These AC4P behaviors are certainly commendable and may represent significant commitment and effort, but the absence of personal encounters between giver and receiver is separate from other types of AC4P behavior.

Certain situations and dispositions might facilitate or inhibit one type of AC4P behavior and not the other. For example, communication skills are needed for AC4P on the personal or behavioral level. And different aspects of those communication skills usually come into play. Behavior-focused AC4P is more direct and usually more intrusive than person-focused AC4P.

It's more risky and potentially confrontational to attempt to direct or motivate another person's behavior, in contrast to demonstrating concern, respect, or empathy for someone. Just consider the connotations of *intervention*. It's usually thought of as a form of confrontation, a negative interaction due to the frequent resistance of the person whose behavior is in question.

Helping someone in a crisis situation certainly takes effort and requires special skills, but there is rarely a possibility of rejection. On the other hand, attempting to step in to correct someone's behavior could lead to negative, even hostile, reaction. Effective behavior-based AC4P, as in interpersonal coaching, usually requires both interpersonal skills to gain the individual's trust, along with behavior-based skills to support desired behavior and/or correct undesired behavior.

Behavior-focused AC4P is actually expected from parents, teachers, supervisors, and coaches who are in charge of improving the behavior of individuals in certain situations. Thus, some behavior-focused AC4P is part of one's job and is expected. But here the question is whether you apply the best AC4P methods (e.g., supportive and corrective feedback that improve both behavior and attitude).

Suppose you observe a stranger not using a vehicle safety belt or driving while talking on a cell phone. Would you say something to keep this person safe? Some people even hesitate to offer such proactive AC4P feedback for a friend, co-worker, or colleague.

Is it beyond the call of duty to look out for the well-being of a family member or friend? Most readers would say "No". But when AC4P becomes a social norm or the expected behavior in a culture, actively caring for a stranger will not stretch beyond one's normal routine.

As legislated in Australia, it's your "duty to care". AC4P behavior occurs whenever you look out for the well-being of another, but the degree of self-motivation and courage needed to actively care varies dramatically as a function of situational and dispositional factors.

A Hierarchy of Needs

Probably the most popular theory of human motivation is the hierarchy of needs proposed by humanist Abraham Maslow.[10] Categories of needs are arranged hierarchically, and it's presumed people don't attempt to satisfy needs at one stage or level until the needs at the lower stages are satisfied.

First, we are motivated to fulfill physiological needs. This includes basic survival requirements for food, water, shelter, and sleep. After these needs are under control, we are motivated by the desire to feel secure and safe from future dangers. When we prepare for future physiological needs, we are proactively working to satisfy our need for safety and security.

Next we have our social-acceptance needs – the need to have friends and feel like we belong. When these needs are gratified, our concern focuses on self-esteem, the development of self-respect and feeling worthwhile.

When I ask audiences to tell me the highest level of Maslow's Hierarchy of Needs, several people usually shout "self-actualization". When I ask for the meaning of "self-actualization," however, I receive limited or no reaction. You see, the concept of being self-actualized is rather vague and ambiguous.

In general terms, we reach a level of self-actualization when we believe we have become the best we can be, taking the fullest advantage of our potential as human beings. We labor to reach this level when striving to be as productive and creative as possible. Once accomplished, we feel a sense of brotherhood and affection for all human beings. We desire to help humanity as members of a single family – the human race.[11] Perhaps it's fair to say these individuals are most ready to perform AC4P behavior.

Maslow's Hierarchy of Needs is illustrated in Figure 2.3. Note self-actualization is *not* at the top. Maslow[12] revised his renowned hierarchy shortly before his death in 1970, placing self-transcendence above self-actualization. Transcending the self means going beyond self-interest and is quite analogous to the AC4P concept.

According to Viktor Frankl,[13] self-transcendence includes giving ourselves to a cause or to another person and is the ultimate state of existence for the healthy individual. After satisfying our physiological needs, safety and security, acceptance, self-esteem, and self-actualization, people can be motivated to reach self-transcendence by reaching out to help others – to perform AC4P behavior.

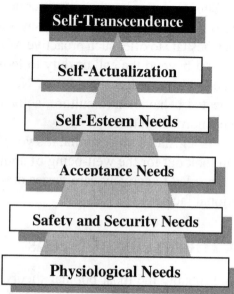

It seems intuitive that various self-needs require satisfaction before self-transcendent or AC4P behavior is likely to occur. But scant research supports ranking needs in a hierarchy. It's possible to think of many examples where individuals perform many AC4P behaviors before satisfying all their own needs. Mahatma Gandhi is a prime example of a leader who put the concerns of others before his own. He suffered imprisonment, extensive fasts, and eventually assassination in his 50-year struggle to help his poor and downtrodden compatriots.

Figure 2.3. The highest need in Maslow's revised hierarchy relfects AC4P.

I'm sure you can think of individuals in your life, including yourself perhaps, who reached the top level of self-transcendence before satisfying needs in the lower stages. Later in this chapter I'll show that satisfying lower-level needs might not be *necessary* for AC4P behavior, but people are generally more willing to actively care after satisfying the lower need levels in Maslow's hierarchy.

Psychological Science and AC4P

Walking home on March 13, 1964, Catherine (Kitty) Genovese reached her apartment in Queens, New York, at 3:30 A.M. Suddenly, a man approached her with a knife, stabbing her repeatedly, and then raped her. Kitty screamed, "Oh my God, he stabbed me! Please help me!" into the early morning stillness. Lights went on and windows opened in nearby buildings. Seeing the lights, the attacker fled. When he saw no one come to the victim's aid, he returned to stab her eight more times and rape her again.

The murder and rape of Kitty Genovese lasted more than 30 minutes, and was witnessed by 38 neighbors. One couple pulled up chairs to their window and turned off the lights so they could get a better view. Only after the murderer and rapist departed for good did anyone phone the police. When the neighbors were questioned about their lack of intervention, they couldn't explain it.

The reporter who first publicized the Kitty Genovese story, and later made it the subject of a book,[14] assumed *bystander apathy* was caused by big-city life. People's indifference to their neighbors' troubles was a conditioned reflex in crowded cities like New York, he reasoned.

After this horrific incident, hundreds of experiments were conducted by social psychologists to determine causes of this so-called *bystander apathy*.[15] This research discredited the reporter's common-sense conclusion. Several factors other than big-city alienation contribute to bystander apathy.

Lessons from Research

Professors Bibb Latané, John Darley, and their colleagues studied bystander apathy by staging emergency events observed by varying numbers of individuals. Then they systematically recorded the speed at which one or more persons came to the victim's rescue. In the most controlled experiments, the observers sat in separate cubicles and could not be influenced by the body language of other subjects. In the first study of this type, the participants introduced themselves and discussed problems associated with living in an urban environment.

In each condition, the first individual introduced himself and then casually mentioned he had epilepsy and the pressures of city life made him prone to seizures. During the course of the discussion over the intercom, he became increasingly loud and incoherent, choking, gasping, and crying out before lapsing into silence. The experimenters measured how quickly the participants left their cubes to help him.

When participants believed they were the only witness, 85 percent left their cubicles within three minutes to intervene. But only 62 percent of the participants who believed one other witness was present left their cubicle to intervene, and only 31 percent of those who thought five other witnesses were available attempted to intervene. Within three to six minutes after the seizure began, 100 percent of the lone participants, 81 percent of the participants with one presumed witness, and 62 percent of the participants with five other bystanders left their cubes to intervene.

The hesitancy of observers of an emergency to intervene and help a victim when they believe other potential helpers are available has been termed the *bystander effect*. It has been replicated in several situations.[16] Some researchers suggest ways to prevent bystander apathy – a critical barrier to achieving an AC4P culture.

Keep in mind this research only studied reactions in crisis situations; behaviors we categorize as reactive, person-focused AC4P behavior. It seems intuitive, though, the findings are relevant for both environment-focused and behavior-focused AC4P behaviors in proactive situations.

Diffusion of Responsibility. A key contributor to the bystander effect is the assumption that someone else should or could assume the responsibility. For example, many observers of the Kitty Genovese rape and murder assumed another witness would call the police, or attempt to scare away the assailant. Perhaps some observers waited for a witness more capable than they to rescue Kitty.

Does this factor contribute to lack of intervention when someone needs help? Do people ignore or deny opportunities to actively care for another person (i.e., a stranger) because they presume someone else will help? Perhaps some people assume, "If those who know the person seeking assistance don't care enough to help, why should I?"

Social psychology research suggests teaching people about the bystander effect can make them less likely to fall prey to it themselves.[17] Often, people have a "we-they" attitude or a territorial perspective ("I'm responsible for the people in this area; you're responsible for those in that area"). Eliminating this "we-they" perspective increases people's willingness to actively care for others.[18]

An AC4P Norm. Many, if not most, U.S. citizens are raised to be independent rather than interdependent. However, intervening for the benefit of others, whether reactively in a crisis situation or proactively to prevent potential crises, requires a sincere commitment toward interdependence.

Social psychologists refer to a *social responsibility norm* as the belief people should help those who need help. Subjects who scored high on a measure of this norm, as a result of upbringing during childhood or special training sessions, were more likely to intervene in a bystander intervention situation, regardless of the number of other witnesses.[16]

Knowing What to Do. When people know what to do in a crisis, they do not fear appearing foolish and do not wait for another, more skilled person to intervene. The bystander effect was eliminated when observers had certain competencies, such as training in first-aid treatment, which enabled them to take charge of the situation.[19] When observers believe they possess the appropriate tools to help, bystander apathy is decreased or eliminated.

Recognizing others for performing AC4P behaviors is critical for the development of an AC4P norm and an AC4P culture. But our field studies have shown this is easier said than done. Participants in these studies agreed with the mission to recognize others for their AC4P behaviors. Still, the percentage who delivered such recognition in prescribed ways was always much lower than expected and desired. These percentages increased dramatically following role playing to develop relevant interpersonal skills, accompanied by meetings of AC4P support groups.[20]

Most proactive AC4P action requires self-motivation (Chapter 3) and moral courage (Chapter 4) in addition to relevant interpersonal skills. Much of our AC4P research, some of which is reviewed in this book, addresses ways to facilitate the occurrence and improve the effectiveness of AC4P behaviors and remove barriers that hold us back from thanking people for their AC4P behavior.

It's Important to Belong. Bystander apathy is reduced, according to research, when observers know one another and have developed a sense of belonging or mutual respect from prior interactions.[21] Most, if not all, of the witnesses to Kitty Genovese's murder did not know her personally. It's likely the neighbors did not feel a sense of community with one another. Situations and interactions that reduce a "we-they" or territorial perspective and increase feelings of relatedness or community will increase the likelihood people will actively care for each other.

Mood States. Several social psychology studies have found people are more likely to offer help when they are in a good mood.[22] And the mood states that facilitated helping behavior were created very easily, for example, by arranging for potential helpers to find a dime in a phone booth, giving them a cookie, showing them a comedy film, or providing pleasant aromas. Are these findings relevant for cultivating an AC4P culture?

Daily events can elevate or depress our moods. Some events are controllable, while others are not. Clearly, the nature of our interactions with others can have a dramatic impact on the mood of everyone involved. The research on mood and its effects on helping behavior might motivate those of us who want to facilitate an AC4P culture to interject more positivity and optimism into our interpersonal conversations with others.

Beliefs and Expectancies. Social psychologists have shown that certain dispositional characteristics or beliefs influence one's inclination to help a person in an emergency. Specifically, individuals who believe their world is fair and predictable, a place where good behavior is rewarded and bad behavior is punished, are more likely to help others in a crisis.[23] Also, people with a higher sense of social responsibility and the general expectancy that people control their own destinies showed a greater willingness to actively care.[24]

The beliefs and expectancies that influence AC4P behaviors are not developed overnight and obviously cannot be changed overnight. But a particular culture, including its policies, appraisal and recognition procedures, educational opportunities and approaches to discipline, can certainly increase or decrease perceptions or beliefs in a just world, social responsibility, and personal control, and in turn influence people's willingness to perform AC4P behavior.[25]

Deciding to Actively Care

As a result of their seminal research, Latané and Darley[26] proposed that an observer makes four sequential decisions before helping a victim. These four decisions (depicted in Figure 2.4) are influenced by the situation or environmental context in which an AC4P opportunity occurs, the nature of the crisis, the presence of other bystanders and their reactions, and relevant social norms and rules.

Although the model was developed to evaluate intervention in emergency situations – where there's a need for direct, reactive, person-focused AC4P behavior – it's quite relevant for the other types of AC4P, as well.

Step 1: Is Something Wrong? The first step in deciding whether to intervene is simply perceiving something is wrong. Some situations or events naturally attract more attention than others. Most emergencies are novel and upset the normal flow of life. However, as shown by Piliavin et al.,[27] the onset of an emergency, such as a person

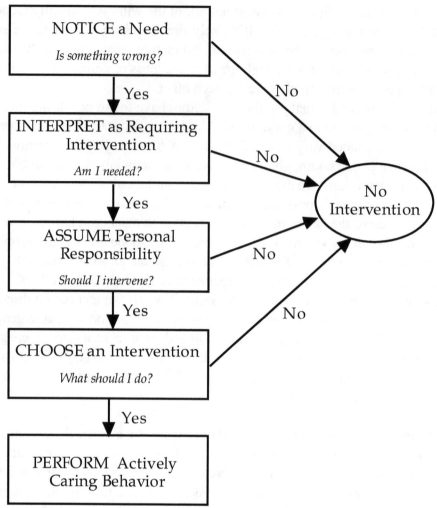

Figure 2.4. AC4P behavior requires four sequential decisions.

slipping on ice or falling down a flight of stairs, will attract more attention and helping behavior than the aftermath of an "injury," as when a victim is regaining consciousness or rubbing an ankle after a fall. Of course, we should expect much less attention to potential problems in daily, nonemergency situations at work, in school, and at home.

In active and noisy work environments, people narrow their focus to what is personally relevant. We learn to tune out irrelevant stimuli. In these situations, environmental hazards are easy to overlook. Even less noticeable and attention-getting are the ongoing behaviors of people around us. Yet these behaviors need proactive AC4P support or correction.

But, even if the need for proactive participation is noticed, AC4P behavior will not necessarily occur. The observer must interpret the situation as requiring intervention. This leads us to the next question requiring a "Yes" answer for AC4P behavior to occur.

Step 2: Am I Needed? Of course we can come up with a variety of excuses for not helping. Distress cues, such as cries for help, and the actions of other observers can clarify an event as an emergency. When we are confused, we look to other people for information and guidance.

In other words, by watching what others are doing, we figure out how to interpret an ambiguous event and how to react accordingly. The behavior of others is especially important when stimulus cues are not present.[28]

In situations where the need for intervention or corrective action is not obvious, we usually seek information from others to understand what's going on and to receive direction. This is the typical state of affairs when it comes to noticing a need for AC4P behavior or recognizing another person's AC4P behavior. In fact, the need for *proactive* AC4P behavior is rarely obvious.

When I ask my students to look for AC4P behavior around them and then recognize the person with an "AC4P Thank-You Card" (see p. 47), I typically receive less than 10% compliance. The most frequent excuse for not recognizing AC4P behavior is, "I didn't see actively caring worthy of a thank-you card."

Step 3: Should I Intervene?

"Is it my responsibility to intervene?" The answer is clear if you are the only witness to a situation you perceive as an emergency. But you might not answer "Yes" to this question when you know other people are also observing the same emergency, or cry for help. You have reason to believe someone else will intervene, perhaps a person more capable than you. This perception relieves you of personal responsibility. But what happens when everyone believes the other guy will take care of it? This is likely what happened in the Kitty Genovese incident.

A breakdown at this stage of the decision model doesn't mean the observers don't care about the welfare of the victim. Actually, it's probably incorrect to call lack of intervention *bystander apathy*.[29] The bystanders might care very much about the victim, but defer responsibility to others because they believe other observers are more likely or better qualified to intervene.

Similarly, employees might care a great deal about the safety and health of their co-workers, but feel relatively incapable of acting on their caring. People might resist taking personal responsibility to actively care because they don't believe they have the most effective tools to make a difference.

In addition to a "can do" attitude, people need to believe it's their personal responsibility to actively care for others. The challenge in achieving an AC4P culture is to convince everyone they have a responsibility to actively care for others. A social norm or expectancy needs to be established: That all participants share equally in a daily assignment to keep everyone healthy and productive.

Plus, AC4P leaders need to accept the special responsibility of teaching others any techniques they learn at conferences or group meetings that could increase a person's perceived competence (or self-efficacy) to actively care more effectively. If we don't meet this challenge, many people are apt to decide AC4P is not for them.

Step 4: What Should I Do? This last step of the Latané and Darley decision model pinpoints the importance of education and training. Education gives people the rationale and principles behind a particular intervention approach. It gives people information to design or refine intervention strategies, leading to a sense of ownership for the particular tools they help to develop. Through training, people learn how to translate principles and rules into specific behaviors or intervention strategies.

Bottom line: People who learn how to intervene effectively through relevant education and training are more likely to be successful agents of an AC4P intervention.

This decision logic suggests certain methods for increasing the likelihood people will actively care. Specifically, the model supports the need to teach people how to recognize a need for AC4P behavior at the environment, person, and behavior levels and then determine what intervention strategies are available and most effective in each case. Plus, people need to learn how to give supportive feedback and genuine recognition for those who emit AC4P behavior.

It's also imperative to promote AC4P as a core value of the particular culture. This means everyone assumes responsibility for the health, safety, and well-being of others in their culture and never waits for someone else to act.

Cultivating an AC4P Culture

Culture influences and sustains one's propensity to actively care. A work culture, for example, can incorporate an accountability system that encourages interpersonal helping. Plus, the daily interactions of people influence certain person-states that affect one's propensity to go beyond the call of duty for another person's well-being. The frequency of AC4P behavior varies *directly* with extrinsic-response contingencies and *indirectly* as a function of certain dispositional person-states.

The Direct Approach

For almost 30 years, I have promoted the use of a special "Actively-Caring Thank-You Card" at my University to recognize individuals for their AC4P behavior. The front of this brightly-colored card includes the mascot of our University and two University sponsors. The definition of AC4P behavior is given on the back of the card, along with specific examples of actively caring.

Several organizations have customized this thank-you card for their culture. I have seen this simple thank-you-card cultivate a sense of interdependence and belongingness throughout a work group, as well as help people feel good about their own AC4P behavior.

In their book, *Measure of a Leader*, Aubrey and James Daniels describe a cre-

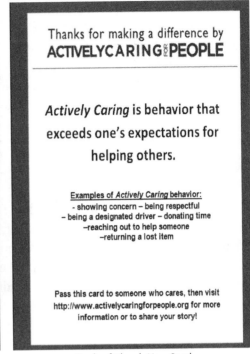

Front of Thank-You Card   Back of Thank-You Card

ative device they have used successfully for years to motivate discretionary behaviors throughout an organization. Specifically, managers hang a chart in a conspicuous location that lists the names of all employees in a certain work area. Then they give each person a sticker identifying that individual. Whenever a worker is helped by a colleague, that person puts his or her identifying sticker on the chart, next to the name of the person who performed the AC4P behavior.

The Daniels brothers report dramatic culture change. "Not only does it give recognition for those who help, but it is an antecedent for others to take the initiative in finding ways they can help other team members."[30]

In addition, for more than 20 years I've been promoting the use of a green wristband, embossed with the words "Actively Caring for People," to recognize people for their AC4P behavior. Over the years, I've distributed about 50,000 of these wristbands after my keynote addresses at conferences and organizations. My students have used this recognition approach to reduce bullying by promoting and rewarding AC4P behavior in various educational settings.[31]

For these latter applications, the AC4P wristbands were redesigned to include a different identification number per wristband as well as the website (www.ac4p.org) where people can: a) share their AC4P stories (with the number of the wristband they gave or received), b) track worldwide where a particular AC4P wristband has been, and c) order more AC4P wristbands to reward others for actively caring.

To date, more than 2,000 AC4P stories have been shared on this website, and more than 70,000 AC4P wristbands have been purchased with proceeds going to the Actively Caring for People Foundation, Inc. We believe this particular accountability system for activating and rewarding AC4P behavior has great potential for spreading the AC4P paradigm worldwide and inspiring the development of AC4P cultures.

Genuine appreciation and recognition can have dramatic positive effects on a person's attitude, mindset, and disposition. A recognition system that directly acknowledges AC4P behavior can result in a spiraling cycle of favorable culture change. Positive regard for people's AC4P behaviors increases the frequency of the target behavior directly, while simultaneously feeding the five person-states that set the occasion for more AC4P behavior. These person-states are defined next, as well as ways to enhance them.

The Indirect Approach

Psychological science considers both the observable (outside) and non-observable (inside) aspects of individuals. Indeed, long-term behavior change requires people to change *inside* as well as outside. The promise of a positive consequence or the threat of a negative one can maintain desired behavior while the response-consequence contingencies are in place. But what happens when they are withdrawn? What happens when people are in situations, like at home, when no one is holding them accountable for their behavior?

If people do not *believe* in the AC4P way of doing something and do not *accept* AC4P as a value or a personal mission, they will not choose AC4P behavior when no one's watching. If people are not self-motivated to actively care, the frequency of AC4P behavior will be much less than desired. I explain self-motivation and illustrate ways to enhance this person-state in the next chapter.

Figure 2.5 illustrates how person factors interact with the basic activator-behavior-consequence (ABC) model of behavior-focused psychology, as introduced in Chapter 1.[32] Activators direct behavior and consequences motivate behavior. But as shown in Figure 2.5, these events are first filtered through the person. Numerous internal and situational factors influence how we mentally process activators and consequences. If we see activators and consequences as schemes to control us, our attitude about the

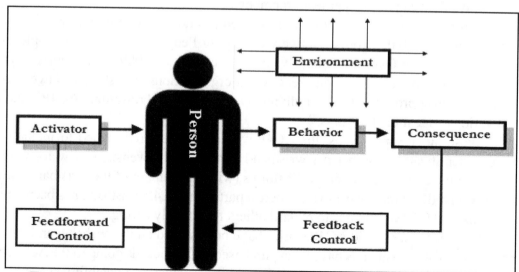

Figure 2.5. Activators and consequences are filtered through the person.

situation will likely be negative.

On the other hand, when we believe the external contingencies are genuine attempts to help us do the right thing, our attitude will be more positive. Personal or internal dynamics determine how we receive activator and consequence information. This can influence whether environmental events enhance or diminish what we do. Let's consider five states that influence one's propensity to perform AC4P behavior.

Self-Esteem (*"I am valuable"*). One's self-concept, or feeling of worth, is a central theme of most humanistic therapies.[33] According to Carl Rogers and his adherents, we possess both a real and an ideal self-concept.

We have notions or aspirations of what we would like to be (our ideal self) and what we think we are (our real self). Our self-esteem decreases as the gap between our real and ideal self-concepts increases. The mission of many humanistic therapies is to help a client reduce this gap.

A healthy level of self-esteem and acting to help others raise their self-esteem has obvious benefits. Research shows people with high self-esteem report fewer negative emotions and less depression than people with low self-esteem.[34] Those with higher self-esteem also handle life's stresses better.[35]

Individuals who score higher on measures of self-esteem are: a) less susceptible to outside influences,[36] b) more confident of achieving personal goals,[37] and c) make more favorable impressions on others in social situations.[38] People with higher self-esteem also help others more frequently than those scoring lower on a self-esteem scale.[39]

Empowerment (*"I can make a difference"*). In management literature, empowerment typically refers to delegating authority or responsibility, or sharing decision-making.[40] In contrast, the AC4P perspective of empowerment focuses on *how a person reacts* after receiving more power or influence.

From a psychological perspective, empowerment is a matter of personal perception. Do you feel empowered or more responsible? Can you handle the additional assignment? This view of empowerment requires the personal belief that "I can make a difference".

Perceptions of personal control,[41] self-efficacy,[42] and optimism[43] strengthen the notion of empowerment. An empowered state is presumed to increase your motivation to "make a difference," perhaps by going beyond your normal routine on behalf of the well-being of another person. Empirical support exists for this intuitive hypothesis.[44] Let's look more closely at these three person states that affect our propensity to actively care.

Self-Efficacy. In other words, *"I can do it"* (or, *"You can do it."*). I'm talking about your self-confidence. This is a key principle in social learning theory, determining whether a therapeutic intervention will succeed over the long term.[45]

People who score relatively high on a measure of self-efficacy perform better at a wide range of tasks, and work harder to achieve a specific goal, according to dozens of studies. These "can do" believers also demonstrate greater ability and motivation to solve complex problems at work, have better health and safety habits, and are more successful at handling stressors.[46]

Self-efficacy contributes to self-esteem, and vice versa; but these constructs are different. Self-esteem refers to a general sense of self-worth; self-efficacy refers to feeling successful or effective at a particular task. Self-efficacy is task focused, and can vary markedly from one task to another. One's level of self-esteem remains relatively constant across situations.

Personal Control. This is the sense that *"I am in control"*. J. B. Rotter[41] used the term *locus of control* to locate the forces controlling a person's life. People with an *internal* locus of control believe they usually have direct personal control over significant life events as a result of their knowledge, skill, and abilities. They believe they are captains of their life's ship.

In contrast, persons with an *external* locus of control believe "outside" and random factors like chance, luck, or fate play important roles in their lives. Externals believe they are victims, or sometimes beneficiaries, of circumstances beyond their direct personal control.[47]

More than 2,000 studies have investigated the relationship between perceptions of personal control and other variables.[48] Internals are more achievement-oriented and health conscious than externals. They are less prone to distress, and more likely to seek medical treatment when they need it.[49]

Having an internal locus of control helps reduce chronic pain, facilitates psychological and physical adjustment to illness and surgery, and hastens recovery from some diseases.[50] Internals perform better at jobs that allow them to set their own pace, whereas externals work better when a machine controls the pace.[51]

Optimism. *"I expect the best"* sets the tone for optimism. It's the learned expectation that life events, including personal actions, will turn out well.[52] Optimism relates directly to achievement. Martin Seligman[53] reported, for example, that world-class swimmers who scored high on a measure of optimism recovered from defeat and swam even faster compared to those swimmers scoring low. Following defeat, the pessimistic swimmers swam slower.

Compared to pessimists, optimists maintain a sense of humor, perceive problems or challenges in a positive light, and plan for success. They focus on what they can *do* rather than on how they *feel*.[54] Optimists handle stressors constructively and experience positive stress more often than negative distress.[55] They essentially expect to succeed at whatever they do, and so they work harder than pessimists to reach their goals.

Optimists are beneficiaries of the self-fulfilling prophecy.[56]

Fulfilling an optimistic prophecy can enhance our perceptions of personal control, self-efficacy, and even self-esteem. Realizing this should motivate us to do whatever we can to make interpersonal conversations positive and constructive. This will not only increase optimism in a certain culture, but also promote a sense of group cohesiveness or belonging – another person state that facilitates AC4P behavior.

Belonging (*"I am a team member"*). M. Scott Peck challenges us to experience a sense of true community with others in his best seller, *The Different Drum: Community making and peace.*[57] We need to develop feelings of belonging with one another regardless of our political preferences, cultural backgrounds, and religious beliefs.

We need to transcend our differences, overcome our defenses and prejudices, and develop a deep respect for diversity. Peck claims we must develop a sense of community or interconnectedness with one another if we are to accomplish our best and ensure our sustainability as human beings.

It's intuitive that building a sense of community or belonging among our friends and colleagues will increase the frequency of our AC4P behaviors. Improvement in behavior requires interpersonal observation, feedback, and recognition. For this to happen, people need to adopt a collective win-win perspective instead of the individualistic win-lose orientation so common in many work and educational settings.

A sense of belonging and interdependency leads to interpersonal trust and caring – essential features of an AC4P culture. In the next chapter, I explain how one's sense of community or relatedness to others affects self-motivation – a person's drive to do something without an external incentive or accountability system.

Someone at my group discussions with employees inevitably raises the point that a sense of belonging or community at their plant has decreased in recent years. Belongingness is a fading concept; "We used to be more like family around here" is a common theme.

For many companies, growth spurts, continuous turnover – particularly among managers – or "lean and mean" cutbacks have left many employees feeling less connected and trusting. People's need level on Maslow's hierarchy has regressed from satisfying social acceptance and belonging to concentrating on maintaining job security, in order to keep food on the table.

Figure 2.6 lists a number of special attributes prevalent in most families, where interpersonal trust and belonging are usually optimal. We are willing to actively care in special ways for the members of our immediate family. The result is optimal trust, belonging, and AC4P behavior for the health, safety, and welfare of our family members.

To the extent we follow the guidelines reflected in Figure 2.6 among members of our everyday peer group, we will achieve an AC4P culture. Following the principles implied in Figure 2.6 will develop trust and belonging among people, and lead to the quantity and quality of AC4P behavior expected among family members – at home, at work, at school, and everywhere in between.

- We use more rewards than penalties with *family* members.

- We don't pick on the mistakes of *family* members.

- We don't rank one *family* member against another.

- We brag about the accomplishments of *family* members.

- We respect the property and personal space of *family* members.

- We pick up after other *family* members.

- We correct the undesirable behavior of *family* members.

- We accept the corrective feedback of *family* members.

- We are interdependent with *family* members.

- We actively care because they're *family*.

Figure 2.6. A family perspective in an organization helps to cultivate an AC4P culture.

A Self-Supporting AC4P Cycle

The five person-states presented here as influencing people's willingness to actively care are shown in Figure 2.7 as an AC4P Model. Each of these person-states has a rich research history in psychology, and some of this research relates directly to the AC4P Model. Research that tested relationships between these person-states and actual behavior has supported this model,[58] although much more research is needed in this domain.

A particularly important question is whether the AC4P person-states are both antecedents and consequences of an AC4P act. It seems intuitive that performing an act of kindness that is effective, accepted, and appreciated could increase the helper's self-esteem, self-efficacy, personal control, optimism, and sense of belonging. This, in turn, should increase the probability of more AC4P behavior. In other words, one act of caring, properly appreciated, should lead to another and another. A self-supporting AC4P cycle is likely to occur.

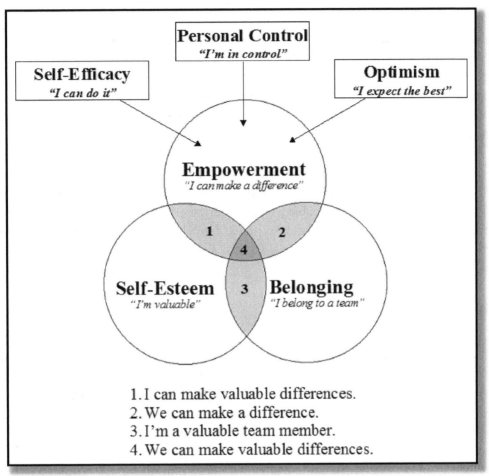

Figure 2.7. Five person-states influence a person's willingness to actively care.

Enhancing the AC4P Person-States

Sometimes participants at my workshops and seminars express concern the AC4P person-state model might not be practical. "The concepts are too soft or subjective," is a typical reaction. Teachers, parents, work supervisors, and individual employees accept the behavior-based approach to performance improvement because it's straight-forward, objective, and clearly applicable to educational, work, and family settings. But person-based concepts like self-esteem, personal control, optimism, and belong-ing appear ambiguous, "touchy-feely," and difficult to deal with. "The concepts sound good and certainly seem important, but how can we wrap our arms around these 'warm fuzzies' and use them to promote an AC4P culture?"

To be sure, person-states are more difficult to define, measure, and manage than behaviors. But we just can't ignore how people *feel* about a behavior-improvement process. For people to accept a behavior-change process and sustain the target behaviors for the long term, we must confront internal person-states when designing and implementing an intervention.

After introducing the AC4P Model (Figure 2.7) at my workshops on cultivating an AC4P culture, I often divide participants into discussion groups. I ask group members to define events, situations, or contingencies that decrease and increase the person-state assigned to their group. Then I ask the groups to derive simple and feasible action plans to increase their assigned dispositional state. This promotes personal and practical understanding of the concept.

The AC4P Model may be soft, but feedback from these workshops shows it's not too hard to grasp. Action plans have been practical and quite consistent with techniques used by researchers. Also, there has been substantial overlap of practical recommendations – workshop groups dealing with different person-states have come up with similar contributory factors and action plans. Let's take a look at what my workshop participants have proposed regarding factors and strategies related to each of these person-states.

Self-Esteem

Participants suggest a number of ways to build self-esteem, including: a) Provide opportunities for personal learning and peer mentoring; b) Increase recognition for desirable behaviors and individual accomplishments; and c) Solicit and follow up on a person's suggestions.

It's essential to give more positive (or supportive) than negative (or corrective) feedback. When offering corrective feedback, it's essential to focus on the act, not the actor. Emphasize an error only reflects behavior that can be corrected, not some deeper character flaw. Don't come off as a judge of character, implying a mistake suggests some subjective personal attribute like "carelessness," "apathy," "bad attitude," or "poor motivation".

Be a patient, active listener. Allow people to offer reasons for their error or poor judgment. Resist the temptation to argue about these. Giving a reason or excuse is just a way to protect one's self-esteem, and it's generally a healthy response. Remember, you already made your point by showing the error and suggesting ways to avoid the mistake in the future. Leave it at that.

If a person doesn't react constructively to corrective feedback, it might help to explore feelings. "How do you feel about this?" you might ask. Then listen empathically to assess whether self-esteem has taken a hit. You'll learn whether some additional communication is needed to place the focus squarely on what is external and objective, rather than subjective and internal.

Self-Efficacy

Self-efficacy is more situation-specific than self-esteem, so it fluctuates more readily.

Job-specific feedback should be directed only at one's perception of what's needed to do a particular task successfully. It should not veer off in the nebulous direction of general self-worth.

Keep in mind that repeated negative feedback can have a cumulative effect, chipping away at an individual's perception of self-worth. Then it takes only one remark, perhaps one you would think is innocuous and insignificant, to "break the camel's back" and activate what seems like an overreaction.

Our communication may not be received as intended. We might do our best to come across positively and constructively, but because of factors beyond our control, the communication might be misperceived. One's inner state can dramatically bias the impact of interpersonal feedback. Note that self-efficacy reflects a perception of competence, and in the next chapter I explain how feeling competent leads to self-motivation.

Achievable Tasks. What makes for a "can do" attitude? Personal perception is the key. A supervisor, parent, or teacher might believe s/he has provided everything needed to complete a task successfully. However, the employee, child, or student might not think so. It's important to ask, "Do you have what you need? We're checking for feelings of self-efficacy." This is easier said than done, because people often hesitate to admit their incompetence. Who wants to concede, "I can't do it?" Instead, we try to maintain the appearance of self-efficacy.

Ask open-ended questions when you give assignments to assess whether those on the receiving end are prepared to get the job done. In large groups, though, this probing for feelings of self-efficacy is impossible. As a result, in the classroom many students get left behind in the learning process (frequently because they skipped classes or an important reading assignment). As they get farther and farther behind in my class, their low self-efficacy is supported by the self-fulfilling prophecy and diminished optimism. Sometimes this leads to "raise-the-white-flag-behavior" and feelings of helplessness.[59]

All too often, these students withdraw from my class or resign themselves to receiving a low grade. In the workplace, employees who cannot keep pace with new procedures might withdraw into themselves or put up defensive resistance.

Personal Strategies. Watson and Tharp[60] suggest the following five steps to increase perceptions of self-efficacy. First, select a task at which you expect to succeed, not one you expect to fail. Then, as your feelings of self-efficacy increase, you can tackle more challenging projects.

A cigarette smoker who wants to stop smoking, for example, might focus on smoking 50 percent fewer cigarettes per week rather than attempting to quit "cold turkey". With early success at reducing the number of cigarettes smoked, the individual could make the criterion more stringent (like smoking no cigarettes on alternate days). Continued success leads to more self-efficacy.

Second, it's important to distinguish between the past and the present. Don't dwell on past failures. Past failures are history – today is the first day of the rest of your life. Focus on a renewed sense of self-confidence and self-efficacy.

Third, it's important to keep good records of your progress toward reaching your goal. Our cigarette smoker should record the number of cigarettes smoked each day, and note when the rate of smoking is 50 percent less for a week. This should be noted as an achievement, and then a new goal should be set. Focusing on your successes (rather than failures) represents the fourth step in building self-efficacy.

The fifth step: Develop a list of tasks or projects you'd like to accomplish, and then rank them from easiest to most difficult to accomplish. Whenever possible, start with the easier tasks. The self-efficacy and self-confidence developed from accomplishing less demanding tasks will help you tackle the more challenging situations on your list.

Focus on the Positive. Many of the strategies I've presented for improving person-states include a basic principle: Focus on the positive. Whether attempting to build your own self-efficacy or that of others, success needs to be emphasized over failure. Thus, whenever you have the opportunity to teach others or give them feedback, you must look for small-win accomplishments and give genuine approval before commenting on ways to improve. Again, this approach is easier said than done.

Failures are easier to spot than successes. They stick out and interrupt the flow. That's why

most teachers are quick to give negative attention to students who disrupt the classroom, while giving only limited positive attention to students who remain on task and go with the flow. Plus, many of us have been conditioned (unknowingly) to believe negative consequences (penalties) work better than positive consequences (rewards) to influence behavior change.[61]

Personal Control

Employees at my seminars on AC4P have listed a number of ways to increase perceptions of personal control, including: a) set short-term goals and tracking progress toward long-term accomplishment; b) offer frequent rewarding and correcting feedback for process activities rather than only for outcomes; c) provide opportunities to set personal goals, teach others, and chart "small wins";[62] d) teach employees basic behavior-change intervention strategies (especially feedback and recognition procedures); e) provide time and resources for people to develop, implement and evaluate intervention programs; f) show employees how to graph daily records of baseline, intervention, and follow-up data; and g) post response-feedback graphs of group performance.

The perception of personal control is analogous to perceptions of personal choice and autonomy. When people believe they are in control of a situation or challenge, they generally feel a sense of personal choice. "I choose to take charge of the mission which is within my domain of influence." Appreciate the similarity between these person-states. In the next chapter I discuss the connection between perceptions of choice and self-motivation.

Optimism

Optimism flows from thinking positively, avoiding negative thoughts, and expecting the best to happen. Anything that increases our self-efficacy should increase optimism. Also, when our personal control is strengthened, we perceive more influence over our consequences. This gives us more reason to expect the best.

Again, we see how the person-states of self-efficacy, personal control and optimism are clearly intertwined. A change in one will likely influence the other two. Note also how these person-states relate to perceptions of choice and competence – determinants of self-motivation, as I explain in the next chapter.

Belonging

Here are common proposals given by my seminar discussion groups to create and sustain an atmosphere of belonging among employees: a) decrease the frequency of top-down directives and "quick-fix" programs, b) increase team-building discussions, group goal-setting and feedback, and group celebrations for both process and outcome achievements, c) use self-managed or self-directed work teams.

Feelings of empowerment and belonging can be enhanced when groups are given control over important matters like developing a behavior-improvement observation and feedback process or a particular AC4P initiative. When resources, opportunities, and talents enable team members to assert, "We can make a difference," feelings of belonging occur naturally. This leads to synergy, with the group achieving more than could be possible from participants working independently.

In Conclusion

Continuous improvement in any endeavor involving human dynamics requires people to actively care for others as well as themselves. The research-based principles reviewed here are relevant to increasing the frequency and improving the quality of AC4P behavior throughout a particular culture. Some practical intervention procedures benefit AC4P behavior indirectly by enhancing the person-states that facilitate one's willingness to actively care. Other strategies target AC4P behaviors directly, but often have an indirect positive effect on the person-states that increase one's propensity to actively care.

Any procedure that increases a person's self-esteem, self-efficacy, personal control, optimism, or sense of belonging or interdependence in a system will indirectly benefit AC4P behavior. A number of communication techniques enhance more than one of these states simultaneously, particularly actively listening to others for feelings and giving genuine praise for other people's accomplishments.

Reflect on your own life to appreciate the power of personal choice, and how the perception of personal control makes you more self-motivated, involved, and committed to a particular mission. The perception of choice can help activate and sustain AC4P behavior.

Perceptions of belonging are important, too. They increase when groups are given control over important decisions and receive genuine recognition for their accomplishments. Synergy is the ultimate outcome of belonging and win-win interpersonal involvement. It occurs when group interdependence produces more than what's possible from going it alone.

AC4P behaviors are the building blocks of an AC4P culture. The more quality AC4P behaviors occurring among people in a given work, school, or family setting, the more likely will an AC4P culture evolve.

It usually takes self-motivation to initiate and sustain the kind of behavior needed for an AC4P culture because people are rarely held accountable for performing AC4P behavior. The next chapter explains how to increase perceptions of self-motivation, thereby setting the stage for effective AC4P behavior. You'll see several direct connections between the person-states that increase one's propensity to actively care and those that enhance one's self-motivation.

Notes

1. Cialdini, R.B. (2001). *Influence: Science and practice* (4th Edition). Needham Heights, MA: Allyn & Bacon; Schroeder, D.A., Penner, L.A., Dovidio, J.F., & Piliavin, J.A. (1995). *The psychology of helping and altruism*. New York, NY: McGraw-Hill, Inc.

2. Geller, E.S. (1998). *Understanding behavior-based safety: Step-by-step methods to improve your workplace* (Revised Edition). Neenah, WI: J.J. Keller & Associates, Inc; Geller, E.S. (2001). *The psychology of safety handbook*. Boca Raton, FL: CRC Press; Geller, E.S. (2002). People-based safety: Seven social influence principles to fuel participation in occupational safety. *Professional Safety, 47*(10), 25-31; Geller, E.S., & Williams, J.H. (2001). *Keys to behavior-based safety*. Rockville, MD: ABS Consulting; McSween, T.E. (1995). *The values-based safety process: Improving your safety culture with a behavioral approach*. New York, NY: Van Nostrand Reinhold.

3. Geller, E.S. (1998). *Beyond safety accountability: How to increase personal responsibility*. Neenah, WI: J.J. Keller & Associates, Inc; Geller, E.S. (2001). Actively caring for occupational safety: Extending the performance management paradigm. In C.M. Johnson, W.K. Redmon, &

T.C. Mawhinney (Eds.). *Organizational performance: Behavior analysis and management.* New York, NY: Springer.

4. Covey, S.R. (1989). *The seven habits of highly effective people.* New York, NY: Simon & Schuster, Inc.; Covey, S.R. (1990). *Principle-centered leadership.* New York, NY: Simon & Schuster, Inc.

5. Peale, N.V. (1952). *The power of positive thinking.* New York, NY: Prentice-Hall.

6. Kohn, A. (1993). *Punished by rewards: The trouble with gold stars, incentive plans, A's, praise, and other bribes.* Boston, MA: Houghton Mifflin.

7. Deming, W.E. (1986). *Out of the crisis.* Cambridge, MA: Massachusetts Institute of Technology, Center for Advanced Engineering Study; Deming, W.E. (1993). *The new economics for industry, government, education.* Cambridge, MA: Massachusetts Institute of Technology, Center for Advanced Engineering Study.

8. Skinner, B.F. (1981). Selection by consequences. *Science, 213,* 502-504.

9. Carnegie, D. (1936). *How to win friends and influence people.* New York, NY: Simon & Schuster, Inc., p. 57.

10. Maslow, A.H. (1943). A theory of human motivation. *Psychological Review, 50,* 370-396; Maslow, A.H. (1954). *Motivation and personality.* New York, NY: Harper.

11. Schultz, D. (1977). *Growth psychology: Models of the healthy personality.* New York, NY: D. Van Nostrand.

12. Maslow, A.H. (1971). *The farther reaches of human nature.* New York. NY: Viking.

13. Frankl, V. (1962). *Man's search for meaning: An introduction to logotherapy.* Boston, MA: Beacon Press.

14. Rosenthal, A.M. (1964). *Thirty-eight witnesses.* New York, NY: McGraw-Hill.

15. Latané, B., & Darley, J.M. (1968). Group inhibition of bystander intervention. *Journal of Personality and Social Psychology, 10,* 215-221; Latané, B., & Darley, J.M. (1970). *The unresponsible bystander: Why doesn't he help?* New York, NY: Appelton-Century-Crofts.

16. Latané, B., & Nida, S. (1981). Ten years of research on group size and helping. *Psychological Bulletin, 89,* 308-324.

17. Beaman, A.I., Barnes, P.J., Klentz, B., & McQuirk, B. (1978). Increasing helping rates through informational dissemination: Teaching pays. *Personality and Social Psychology, 37,* 1835-1846.

18. Hornstein, H.A. (1976). *Cruelty and kindness: A new look at aggression and altruism.* Englewood Cliffs, NJ: Prentice-Hall.

19. Shotland, R.L., & Heinold, W.D. (1985). Bystander response to arterial bleeding: Helping skills, the decision-making process, and differentiating the helping response. *Journal of Personality and Social Psychology, 49,* 347-356.

20. McCarty, S.M., Teie, S., & Furrow, C.B. (2012). *Training students to observe and reward actively-caring behavior.* Technical Research Report, Center for Applied Behavior Systems, Department of Psychology, Virginia Tech, Blacksburg, VA.

21. Rutkowski, G.K., Gruder, C.L., & Romer, D. (1983). Group cohesiveness, social norms, and bystander intervention. *Journal of Personality and Social Psychology, 44,* 545-552.

22. Carlson, M., Charlin, V., & Miller, N. (1988). Positive mood and helping behavior: A test of six hypotheses. *Journal of Personality and Social Psychology, 55,* 211-229.

23. Bierhoff, H.W., Klein, R., & Kramp, P. (1991). Evidence for the altruistic personality from data on accident research. *Journal of Personality, 59,* 263-280.

24. Schwartz, S.H., & Clausen, G.T. (1970). Responsibility, norms, and helping in an emergency. *Journal of Personality and Social Psychology, 16*, 299-310; Staub, E. (1974). Helping a distressed person: Social, personality, and stimulus determinants. In L. Berkowitz (Ed.), *Advances in experimental social psychology*, Vol. 7. New York, NY: Academic Press.

25. Geller, E.S. (1998). *Beyond safety accountability: How to increase personal responsibility.* Neenah, WI: J.J. Keller & Associates, Inc; Geller, E.S. (2001). Actively caring for occupational safety: Extending the performance management paradigm. In C.M. Johnson, W.K. Redmon, & T.C. Mawhinney (Eds.). *Organizational performance: Behavior analysis and management.* New York, NY: Springer.

26. Latané, B., & Darley, J.M. (1970). *The unresponsible bystander: Why doesn't he help?* New York, NY: Appleton-Century-Crofts.

27. Piliavin, J.A., Piliavin, I.M., & Broll, L. (1976). Time of arousal at an emergency and likelihood of helping. *Personality and Social Psychology Bulletin, 2*, 273-276.

28. Clark, R.D., III, & Word, L.E. (1972). Why don't bystanders help? Because of ambiguity? *Journal of Personality and Social Psychology, 24*, 392-400.

29. Schroeder, D.A., Penner, L.A., Dovidio, J.F., & Piliavin, J.A. (1995). *The psychology of helping and altruism.* New York, NY: McGraw-Hill.

30. Daniels, A.C., & Daniels, J.E. (2005). *Measure of a leader.* Atlanta, GA: Performance Management Publications, p. 158.

31. McCarty, S.M., & Geller, E.S. (2011, Summer). Want to get rid of bullying? Then reward behavior that is incompatible with it. *Behavior Analysis Digest International, 23*(2), 1-7.

32. Kreitner, R. (1982). The feedforward and feedback control of job performance through organizational behavior management (OBM). *Journal of Organizational Behavior Management, 4*(2), p. 3.

33. Rogers, C. (1957). The necessary and sufficient conditions of therapeutic personality change. *Journal of Consulting Psychology, 21*, 95-103; Rogers, C. (1977). *Carl Rogers on personal power: Inner strength and its revolutionary impact.* New York, NY: Delacorte.

34. Straumann, T.J., & Higgins, E.G. (1988). Self-discrepancies as predictors of vulnerability to distinct syndromes of chronic emotional distress. *Journal of Personality, 56*, 685-707.

35. Brown, J.D., & McGill, K.L. (1989). The cost of good fortune: When positive life events produce negative health consequences. *Journal of Personality and Social Psychology, 57*, 1103-1110.

36. Wylie, R. (1974). *The self-concept* (Vol. 1). Lincoln, NE: University of Nebraska Press.

37. Wells, L.E., & Marwell, G. (1976). *Self-esteem.* Beverly Hills, CA: Sage.

38. Baron, R.A., & Byrne, D. (1994). *Social psychology: Understanding human interaction* (7th Edition). Boston, MA: Allyn and Bacon.

39. Batson, C.D., Bolen, M.H., Cross, J.A., & Neuringer-Benefiel, H.E. (1986). Where is altruism in the altruistic personality? *Journal of Personality and Social Psychology, 1*, 212-220.

40. Conger, J.A., & Kanungo, R.N. (1988). The empowerment process: Integrating theory and practice. *Academy of Management Review, 13*, 471-482.

41. Rotter, J.B. (1966). Generalized expectancies for internal versus external control of reinforcement. *Psychological Monographs, 80*, No. 1.

42. Bandura, A. (1997). *Self efficacy: The exercise of control.* New York, NY: W.H. Freeman and Company

43. Scheier, M.F., & Carver, C.S. (1985). Optimism, coping and health: Assessment and implications of generalized outcome expectancies. *Health Psychology, 4*, 219-247; Scheier, M.F., & Carver, C.S. (1993). On the power of positive thinking: The benefits of being optimistic. *Current Directions in Psychological Sciences, 2*, 26-30; Seligman, M.E.P. (1991). *Learned optimism.* New York, NY: Alfred A. Knopf.

44. Bandura, A. (1986). *Social foundations of thought and action.* Englewood Cliffs, NJ: Prentice Hall; Barling, J., & Beattie, R. (1983). Self-efficacy beliefs and sales performance. *Journal of Organizational Behavior Management, 5*, 41-51; Ozer, E. M., & Bandura, A. (1990). Mechanisms governing empowerment effects: A self-efficacy analysis. *Journal of Personality and Social Psychology, 58*, 472-486; Phares, E.J. (1976). *Locus of control in personality.* Morristown, NJ: General Learning Press.

45. Bandura, A. (1990). Self-regulation of motivation through goal systems. In R.A. Dienstbier (Ed.). *Nebraska symposium on motivation,* Vol. 38. Lincoln, NE: University of Nebraska Press; Bandura, A. (1994). Self-efficacy. In *Encyclopedia of human behavior,* Vol. 4. Orlando, FL: Academic Press; Bandura, A. (1997). *Self efficacy: The exercise of control.* New York, NY: W.H. Freeman and Company.

46. Bandura, A. (1982). Self-efficacy mechanism in human agency. *American Psychologist, 37*, 122-147; Betz, N.E., & Hackett, G. (1986). Applications of self-efficacy theory to understanding career choice behavior. *Journal of Social and Clinical Psychology, 4*, 279-289; Hackett, G., Betz, N.E., Casas, J.M., & Rocha-Singh, I.A. (1992). Gender, ethnicity, and social cognitive factors predicting the academic achievement of students in engineering. *Journal of Counseling Psychology, 39*, 527-538.

47. Rotter, J.B. (1966). Generalized expectancies for internal versus external control of reinforcement. *Psychological Monographs, 80*, No. 1; Rushton, J.P. (1984). The altruistic personality: Evidence from laboratory, naturalistic and self-report perspectives. In E. Staub, D. Bar-Tal, J. Karylowski, & J. Reykowski (Eds.). *Development and maintenance of prosocial behavior.* New York, NY: Plenum.

48. Hunt, M.M. (1993). *The story of psychology.* New York, NY: Doubleday.

49. Nowicki, S., & Strickland, B.R. (1973). A locus of control scale for children. *Journal of Consulting Psychology, 40*, 148-154; Stickland, B.R. (1989). Internal-external control expectancies: From contingency to creativity. *American Psychologist, 44*, 1-12.

50. Taylor, S.E. (1991). *Health psychology* (2nd Edition). New York, NY: McGraw-Hill.

51. Eskew, R.T., & Riche, C.V. (1982). Pacing and locus of control in quality control inspection. *Human Factors, 24*, 411-415; Phares, E.J. (1991). *Introduction to personality* (3rd Edition). New York, NY: Harper Collins.

52. Peterson, C. (2000). The future of optimism. *American Psychologist, 55*(1), 44-55; Scheier, M.F., & Carver, C.S. (1985). Optimism, coping and health: Assessment and implications of generalized outcome expectancies. *Health Psychology, 4*, 219-247; Seligman, M.E.P. (1991). *Learned optimism.* New York, NY: Alfred A. Knopf.

53. Seligman, M.E.P. (1991). *Learned optimism.* New York, NY: Alfred A. Knopf.

54. Carver, C.S., Scheier, M.F., & Weintraub, J.K. (1989). Assessing coping strategies: A theoretically-based approach. *Journal of Personality and Social Psychology, 56*, 267-283; Seligman, M.E.P. (2011). *Flourish: A visionary new understanding of happiness and well-being.* New York, NY: Simon & Schuster, Inc.; Peterson, C., & Barrett, L.C. (1987). Explanatory style and academic performance among university freshmen. *Journal of Personality and Social Psychology, 53*, 603-607.

55. Scheier, M.F., Weintraub, J.K., & Carver, C.S. (1986). Coping with stress: Divergent strategies of optimists and pessimists. *Journal of Personality and Social Psychology, 51*, 1257-1264.

56. Tavris, C., & Wade, C. (1995). *Psychology in perspective*. New York, NY: Harper Collins College Publishers.

57. Peck, M.S. (1979). *The different drum: Community making and peace*. New York, NY: Simon & Schuster, Inc.

58. Geller, E.S. (2001). Actively caring for occupational safety: Extending the performance management paradigm. In C.M. Johnson, W.K. Redmon, & T.C. Mawhinney (Eds.). *Organizational performance: Behavior analysis and management*. New York, NY: Springer; Geller, E.S. (2001). Sustaining participation in a safety improvement process: Ten relevant principles from behavioral science. *Professional Safety, 46*(9), 24-29.

59. Peterson, C., Maier, S.F., & Seligman, M.E.P. (1993). *Learned helplessness: A theory for the age of personal control*. New York, NY: Oxford University Press; Seligman, M.E.P. (1975). *Helplessness: On depression, development, and death*. San Francisco, CA: Freeman.

60. Watson, D.C., & Tharp, R.G. (1987). *Self-directed behavior: Self-modification for personal adjustment* (7th Edition). Pacific Grove, CA: Brooks/Cole Publishing Company.

61. Notz, W.W., Boschman, I., & Tax, S.S. (1987). Reinforcing punishment and extinguishing reward: On the folly of OBM with SPC. *Journal of Organizational Behavior Management, 9*(1), 33-46.

62. Weick, K.E. (1984). Small wins: Redefining the scale of social problems. *American Psychologist, 39*, 40-44.

CHAPTER 3

The Psychology of Self-Motivation

E. Scott Geller

EXACTLY WHAT IS an external accountability intervention? In the work world, these motivational tools include time sheets, overtime compensation records, peer-to-peer behavioral observations, public posting of performance indicators, group and individual feedback meetings, and performance appraisals.

In schools it's all about grades, and teachers attempt to keep students motivated by emphasizing the relationship between the quality of their school-work and the all-important grade. Psychologists call these "extrinsic motivators," and managers and teachers use them to keep employees and students on track, respectively.

Sometimes it's possible for people to establish conditions that facilitate self-accountability and self-motivation. When people go beyond the call of duty to actively care for the welfare of others they are self-motivated to an extent. Achieving an AC4P culture requires more people to be self-motivated at more times and in more situations.[1] This chapter presents evidence-based ways to make this happen, as gleaned from research in behavioral and psychological science.

Self-Motivation for AC4P

Without safety regulations, policies, and external accountability systems, many more employees would get hurt or killed on the job and on the road, and more students would be victimized in schools. All of us, including employers, police officers, safety professionals, and school teachers need extrinsic controls to hold us accountable to perform safe and AC4P behavior, while avoiding risky and confrontational behavior. Why do we need such extrinsic controls?

The desired, safe, AC4P behaviors are relatively inconvenient, uncomfortable, and inefficient. The soon, certain, positive consequences (or intrinsic "natural" reinforcers) of at-risk and other undesirable behaviors often overpower our self-motivation to be as safe or caring as possible.

Every driver knows it's risky to talk on a cell-phone or type a text message while driving, yet many drivers perform these behaviors regularly. Why?

The immediate and naturally-reinforcing consequences take priority over the low likelihood of a crash. These risky drivers are not self-motivated to actively care for the safety of themselves and others on the road. (See Chapter 15 for the AC4P approach for traffic safety.)

Here's the key question: What can we do to overcome the human nature implied by these profound quotations from B.F. Skinner: "Immediate consequences outweigh delayed consequences" and "Consequences for the individual usually outweigh consequences for others."[2]

In other words, AC4P behavior is seemingly not rewarded by soon, certain, and positive consequences for the individual. Therefore, we need techniques to overcome this natural tendency to avoid AC4P behavior. Some practical solutions are derived from psychological science, especially research conducted by Edward Deci and Richard Ryan.[3]

Human Needs and Self-Motivation

We have three basic psychological needs, and when these needs are satisfied, we are self-motivated, according to Deci and Ryan. Specifically, self-motivation is supported by situational factors (e.g., environmental contexts and other people) that facilitate fulfillment of our needs for autonomy, relatedness, and competence. "Self-motivation, rather than external (or extrinsic) motivation, is at the heart of creativity, responsibility, healthy behavior, and lasting change."[4]

Autonomy

Autonomy is a matter of being self-governing or having personal control. In Chapter 2, I described this condition as a person-state related to one's propensity to actively care for the safety and well-being of others.[5] Autonomous behavior is self-initiated, self-endorsed, and authentic. It reflects one's true values and intentions. Geller and Veazie[1] refer to this attribute as "choice," and plenty of research shows people are more self-motivated when they have opportunities to choose among action alternatives.[5]

Early Laboratory Research. More than 40 years ago when I was conducting research in cognitive science, I conducted a very simple experiment and obtained very simple results. The implications of the findings, however, are relevant to self-motivation in numerous situations.

Half of the 40 participants in this experiment were shown a list of five three-letter words (i.e., cat, hat, mat, rat, and bat) and asked to select one. Then, after a warning tone, the selected word was presented on a screen in front of the participant, and s/he pressed a micro-switch as fast as possible after seeing the word.

The latency in milliseconds between the presentation of the word and the participant's response was a measure of simple reaction time. This sequence of warning signal, word presentation, and participant reaction occurred for 25 trials. If a participant reacted before the stimulus word was presented, the reaction time was not counted, and the trial was repeated. The session took less than 15 minutes per subject.

The word selected by a particular participant was used as the presentation stimulus for the next participant. Thus, this participant did not have the opportunity to choose the stimulus word. As a result, the word choices of 20 participants were assigned to 20 other participants.

This simple experiment had two conditions – a *Choice* condition (in which participants chose a three-letter word for their stimulus) and an *Assigned* condition (in which participants were assigned the stimulus word selected by the previous participant). To my surprise, the mean reactions of participants in the *Choice* group were significantly faster than those of participants in the *Assigned* group.

Although these results were explained by presuming the opportunity to choose their stimulus word increased the motivation of the participants to perform in the reaction time experiment, the large group differences were unexpected. How could the simple choice of a three-letter word influence faster responding in a simple reaction-time experiment? In fact, because I did not feel confident in a basic motivational explanation for these surprising results, I did not pursue publication of these data in a professional research journal. Only years later did I appreciate the real-world ramifications of those findings.[5]

From Laboratory to Classroom. About a year after the simple reaction-time study described above, I tested the theory of choice as a motivator in the college classroom. I was teaching two sections of Social Psychology; one at 8:00 A.M. Monday, Wednesday, and Friday, and the other at 11:00 A.M. on these same days. There were about 75 students in each class.

On the first day of class, I did not hand out a pre-prepared syllabus with weekly assignments, but distributed only a general outline of the course which introduced the textbook, the course objectives, and the basic criteria for assigning grades (i.e., a quiz on each textbook chapter and a comprehensive final exam on classroom lectures, discussions, and demonstrations).

In an open discussion and voting process, the 8:00 class was given the opportunity to choose the order in which the ten textbook chapters would be read for homework and discussed in class. They could also submit multiple-choice questions for me to consider using for the ten chapter quizzes, and they could hand in short-answer and discussion questions for possible application on the final exam.

The 11:00 class received the order of textbook chapters selected previously by the 8:00 class, and this class was not given an opportunity to submit quiz or exam questions.

Thus, I derived *Choice* and *Assigned* classroom conditions analogous to the two reaction-time groups I had studied one year earlier. Two of my undergraduate research assistants attended each of these classes, posing as regular students, and systematically counted the frequency of behaviors reflecting class participation. These observers did not know about my intentional *Choice* vs. *Assigned* manipulations.

From the day the students in my 8:00 class voted on the textbook assignments, this class seemed to be livelier than the later 11:00 class. My perception was verified by the participation records of the two classroom observers.

Furthermore, the ten quiz grades, final-exam scores, and my teaching-evaluation scores from standard forms distributed during the last class period were significantly higher in the *Choice* class than the *Assigned* class. (Although several students from the 8:00 class submitted potential quiz and final-exam questions, none were actually used. Each class received the same quizzes and final exam.)

I'm convinced the *Choice* versus *Assigned* manipulation was a critical factor. The initial opportunity to choose reading assignments increased students' motivation and class participation and this extra motivation and involvement led to more involvement, perceived choice, self-motivation and learning. The students' attitudes toward the class improved as a result of feeling more in control of the situation.

It's likely the "choice" opportunities in the 8:00 class were especially powerful because they were so different than the traditional top-down classroom atmosphere at the time, as typified by the organization of my 11:00 class. In other words, the contrast of the *Choice* class with the students' other courses made the "choice" opportunities in my 8:00 class especially salient, meaningful, and motivational.

A Corporate Safety Example. A decade after my laboratory and classroom research that showed the self-motivating impact of *choice*; I visited a chemical facility of 350 employees that exemplified the power of choice to impact occupational safety. The employees had initiated an AC4P and behavior-focused observation, feedback, and coaching process in 1992, and had reaped amazing safety benefits for their efforts. In 1994, for example, 98% of the workforce had participated in behavioral observation and feedback sessions, documenting a total of 3,350 coaching sessions for the year. A total of 51,408 behaviors were safe and 4,389 were at-risk.

Such comprehensive employee involvement in a behavioral observation and feedback process led to remarkable outcomes. At the start of their process in 1992, the plant safety record was quite good (i.e., 13 OSHA recordables for a TRIR of 4.11). They improved to 5 OSHA recordables in 1993 (TRIR = 1.60), and in 1994 they had the best safety performance among several plants in their company with only one OSHA recordable (TRIR = 0.35).

I've seen numerous companies improve their safety performance substantially with a process based on the principles of people-based safety (PBS),[6] but this plant holds the record for efficiency in getting everyone involved and obtaining exceptional results.

I'm convinced a key factor in this organization's outstanding success was the employees' choice in the development, implementation, and maintenance of the process. The employees owned their AC4P observation and feedback process from the start because they applied people-based techniques *their way*.

There is no best way to implement PBS. Rather, the principles and procedures from behavioral science need to be customized to fit the relevant work culture. The most efficient way to make this happen is to involve the target population in the customization process. At this facility, the entire workforce learned the AC4P principles by participating in ten, one-hour small-group sessions spaced over a six-month period.

These education/training sessions were facilitated by other employees who had received more intensive training in AC4P principles and PBS applications. At these group sessions, employees discussed specific strategies for implementing a plant-wide behavioral monitoring and coaching process, and they entertained ways to overcome barriers to total participation and sustain the process over the long term.

They designed an AC4P process which included employee choice at its very core. Although some specifics of the process have changed since its inception in 1992, the *choice* aspect has remained a constant.

From the start, employees scheduled regular AC4P observation and feedback sessions with two other employees (i.e., observers). That is, they selected the task, day and time for the coaching session. Additionally, they selected two individuals to observe their performance and give them immediate and specific feedback regarding incidences of safe and at-risk behaviors.

Employees chose their observers (and coaches) from *anyone* in the plant. At the start of their process the number of *volunteer* safety coaches was limited (including only 30% of the workforce), but today everyone in the workforce is a potential safety coach. Personal choice facilitated involvement, ownership, and trust in the process.

At first, some employees did not have complete trust in the process and resisted active participation. Some tried to "beat the system" by scheduling their observation and feedback sessions at inactive times when the probability of an at-risk behavior was minimal (i.e., while they watched a monitor or completed paperwork). And most employees were certainly "on their toes" when the observers arrived at the scheduled times.

At the same time, those observed were optimally receptive to constructive feedback and advice from the observers they had selected. Many people (whether observing or being observed) were surprised that numerous at-risk behaviors occurred in situations where employees knew the safe operating procedures and knew they were being observed for the occurrence of at-risk behaviors.

It wasn't long before most employees at this facility began scheduling their coaching sessions during active times when the probability of an at-risk behavior or injury was highest. Frequently, the observed individual pointed out an at-risk behavior necessitated by the particular work environment or procedure (e.g., a difficult-to-reach valve, a hose-checking procedure too cumbersome for one auditor, a walking surface made slippery by an equipment leak, a difficult-to-adjust machine guard).

Many employees chose to use their observation and feedback process to demonstrate that some at-risk behaviors are facilitated or necessitated by equipment design or maintenance, and/or by environmental conditions or operating procedures. This involvement often led to a beneficial change in environmental conditions or operations procedures. More details about various applications of AC4P principles and PBS procedures in industry are given in Part II.

We've All Been There. You need only reflect on your own life circumstances to realize how a perception of choice or personal control increases your self-motivation, involvement, and commitment. We are not always in control of the critical events of ongoing circumstances, and thus we've experienced the frustra-

MAN, DO WE HAVE THIS GUY CONTROLLED. EVERY TIME WE PULL THE LEVER HE GIVES US A FOOD PELLET.

tion, discomfort, and distress of being at the mercy of environmental circumstances or other people's decisions.

And we've certainly experienced the pleasure of having alternatives to choose from and feeling in control of those factors critical for successful performance. How sweet the taste of success when we can attribute the achievement to our own choices.

Bottom Line: The message is clear. Whenever possible, give people opportunities to choose mission-relevant goals and the procedures to reach them. The result: increased self-motivation, engagement, and ownership.

This may require relinquishing some top-down control, abandoning a desire for a "quick fix," changing from focusing on outcomes to recognizing process achievements, and giving people opportunities to choose, evaluate, and refine their means to achieve the ends. The result: more people going beyond the call of duty on behalf of others when no one's watching.

Competence

Several researchers of human motivation have proposed that people naturally enjoy being able to solve problems and successfully complete worthwhile tasks[7]. In their view, people are self-motivated to learn, to explore possibilities, to understand what's going on, and to participate in achieving worthwhile goals. The label for this fundamental human motive is *competence*. "All of us are striving for mastery, for affirmations of our own competence."[8]

Motivation researchers assume the desire for competence is self-initiating and self-rewarding. Behavior that increases feelings of competence is self-directed and does not need extrinsic or extra reinforcement to keep it going. Feeling competent to do worthwhile work motivates continued effort. When people feel more successful or competent, their self-motivation increases. As one behavioral scientist put it, "People are not successful because they are motivated; they are motivated because they have been successful".[9]

The Power of Feedback. How do we know we are competent at something? How do we know this competence makes a valuable difference? You know the answer – feedback.

Feedback about our ongoing behavior tells us how we are doing and enables us to do better. That familiar slogan, "Practice makes perfect" is actually incorrect. Practice makes permanence and without appropriate feedback, well-practiced behavior can be wrong. We hone our skills through practice *and* behavior-focused feedback.

Some feedback comes naturally, like when we recognize our behavior has produced a desired result. But often behavioral feedback requires careful and systematic observation by another individual – a trainer or coach – who later communicates his or her findings to the performer. In each case, feedback enables development of perceived competence and self-motivation.

Feedback is essential to fulfill a basic human need – the need for competence. And helping people satisfy this need increases their self-motivation to perform the relevant behavior. But feedback regarding the *outcome* of a project or process does not reflect individual choices or competence, and thus can be ineffective. Only feedback that is behavior-focused and customized for the recipient can enhance an individual's perception of personal control and competence, and thus bolster self-motivation.

Is Feedback Reinforcing? Technically, a reinforcer is a behavioral consequence that maintains or increases the frequency of the behavior it follows. So, if behavior does not continue or improve after feedback, the feedback was not a reinforcer. Likewise, praise, bonus pay, or frequent flyer points are not reinforcers when they don't increase the frequency of behavior they target; and they often don't. However, interpersonal, behavior-based rewards can increase our perception of competence.

Can well-delivered supportive or corrective feedback increase our perception of competence and self-motivation? Absolutely, but it's not a payoff for doing the right thing. Rather, it's behavior-based information a person uses to feel more competent or to learn how to become more competent.

There is perhaps no other consequence with greater potential to improve competence, self-motivation, and individual performance than behavior-focused feedback. Behavioral feedback, delivered with an AC4P mindset, is usually a reinforcer because it maintains or increases a certain desired behavior.

A Paradigm Shift. This discussion of feedback, competence, and self-motivation calls for a paradigm shift – a change in perspective about AC4P behavior. We should assume people are naturally self-motivated to help others, instead of calling on guilt or sacrifice to get people involved to improve the health, welfare, or safety of other people.

Simply put, we hate feeling incompetent or helpless. We want to learn, to discover, to become more proficient at worthwhile tasks. We seek opportunities to ask questions, to study pertinent material, to work with people who know more than we do, and to receive feedback that can increase our competence and subsequent self-motivation.

AC4P behavior is not a thankless job requiring self-sacrifice, obligation, or a special degree of altruism. Participation in an AC4P process provides opportunities to satisfy a basic human need – the need for personal competence.[7] Effective and frequent delivery of behavior-based feedback provides a mechanism for improving the quality of an AC4P process, as well as cultivating feelings of competence and self-motivation throughout a culture.

Relatedness

The innate need for *relatedness* reflects "the need to love and be loved, to care and be cared for...to feel included, to feel related."[11] This is analogous to the state of belonging – a person-state influencing one's propensity to actively caring for the health, safety, and well-being of others. Geller and Veazie[1] use the term *community* to reflect this person-state because the concept of community is more encompassing than relatedness or belongingness.

A community perspective reflects systems thinking and interdependency beyond the confines of family, social groups, and work teams, as explicated by Peter Block[13] and M. Scott Peck.[14] Community is an AC4P mindset for human kind in general – an interconnectedness with others that transcends political differences and prejudices, and profoundly respects and appreciates diversity.

Systems Thinking and Interdependence. Focus your efforts to optimize the system, W. Edwards Deming tells us in his best sellers on total quality management, *Out of The Crisis* and *The New Economics*.[15] Peter Senge stresses that systems thinking is *The Fifth Discipline*,[16] and key to continuous improvement. And Stephen Covey's discussion of interdependency, win-win contingencies, and synergy in his popular self-help book, *The Seven Habits of Highly Effective People*,[17] is founded on systems thinking and a community perspective.

SON, IT'S NOT WHETHER YOU WIN OR LOSE... UNLESS YOU WANT DADDY'S LOVE.

Geller and Veazie propose and explicate in *The Courage Factor*[18] the amount of courage a person needs to intervene on behalf of another individual decreases as a function of the degree of connectedness between the two people. (See Chapter 4 for more on courage.)

Developing a community or interdependent spirit in an organization, a classroom, or a family unit leads to two primary human-performance payoffs: a) individuals become more self-motivated to do the right thing, and b) people are more likely to actively care for the well-being of others. In their reality-based narrative, Geller and Veazie[1] illustrate the do's and don'ts of building an interdependent community perspective.

More Paradigm Shifts. A systems or community approach to improving people's welfare implicates a number of paradigm shifts from traditional management of an organization, a classroom, and yes, a family. We need to shift from trying to find one root cause of a problem (e.g., interpersonal bullying, sexual abuse, substance abuse, and occupational injuries) to considering a number of potential contributing factors from each of three domains – environment, behavior, and person.

Interdependent systems thinking requires a shift from down-stream outcome-based measures of individual or group performance (grades, injury rates, familial acceptance) to a more proactive and diagnostic evaluation of process variables within the environment, behavior, and person domains.

Systems thinking enables a useful perspective on basic principles of human motivation, attitude formation, and behavior change. The influence of activators and consequences on behavior are thought to be linear, or so we believe. But systems-thinking implicates a circular or spiral perspective.

While an event preceding a behavior might direct it and a particular event following a behavior determines whether it will occur again, it's instructive to realize the consequence for one behavior can serve as the activator for the next behavior. With this perspective, behavior-based feedback can serve as a motivating consequence or a directive activator, depending on when and how it's presented.

Spiral causality and the consistency principle combine to explain how small changes in behavior can result in attitude change, followed by more behavior change and then more desired attitude change, leading eventually to personal commitment and total involvement in the process.[19] Similarly, the notion of spiral causality and the reciprocity principle explain why initial AC4P from a few individuals can result in more and more AC4P behavior from many individuals.

This *ripple effect* can eventually lead to families, work teams, and community groups AC4P regularly for the health, safety, and well-being of each other, with a win-win interdependent attitude and a proactive mindset. In the end we have AC4P synergy. It can all start with systems thinking and one intentional act of kindness from one person to another. (See Chapter 5 for more on this AC4P *ripple effect*.)

How to Increase Self-Motivation

The C-words of *Choice*, *Competence*, and *Community* are used by Geller and Veazie[1] in their narrative as labels for the three evidence-based person-states that determine self-motivation. Dispositional, interpersonal, and environmental conditions that enhance these states, presumed to be innate needs by some psychologists,[20] increase personal perceptions of self-motivation.

Researchers offer the following ten guidelines for increasing self-motivation by affecting one or more of the three person-states (or needs) defined above. Geller and Veazie[1] explain each of these with real-world examples from the workplace, schools, and families.

1. Explain Why.

Rules and regulations should be accompanied with a meaningful explanation (i.e., why?) to provide a rationale for behavior that is not naturally reinforcing. Often, we tell people what to do (with rules and regulations) without including the rationale – the why? At work, managers often quickly delegate without connecting the specific task to the organization's larger mission or vision – the "big picture." In educational institutions, policies regarding student admissions, staff-evaluation, and student grading, as well as changes in textbooks, are often announced without a reasonable rationale.

In the community, some people may choose to ignore residential speed laws (e.g., 20 mph zone) because they don't understand how such a dramatic reduction in vehicle speed improves safety. In this case, it would help to know that pedestrians have an 85% chance of being killed when hit at 40 mph versus a 5% fatality rate when hit by a vehicle traveling 20 mph.[21]

If individuals were able to connect a speed restriction to saving a human life, as opposed to fear of a speeding ticket, there might be less speeding. Or at least those complying with the 20 mph speed limit would more likely perceive personal choice and more self-motivation regarding their decision to obey reduced mph mandates.

2. It's Not Easy.

Acknowledge that "People might not want to do what they are being asked to do."[22] For example, admit certain behaviors (e.g., safety-related behaviors) are relatively inconvenient and uncomfortable, but given the reasonable rationale provided, the personal response cost is worthwhile.

And even though the value of AC4P coaching (i.e., giving a colleague interpersonal feedback to support right behavior and correct wrong behavior) is obvious, acknowledge it's natural to feel awkward in this situation, whether delivering or receiving the feedback. This justifies role-playing exercises to improve people's social skills at delivering and receiving behavior-based feedback. (See Chapter 4 for more on delivering and receiving feedback effectively.)

3. Watch Your Language.

Your language should suggest minimal external pressure. The common phrases "safety is a condition of employment," "all accidents are preventable," "bullying is a rite of passage," or "random acts of kindness" reduce one's sense of autonomy. The slogan, "AC4P is a value of our organization, school, or community" implies personal authenticity, interpersonal relatedness, and human interaction.

In the workplace, injuries are typically referred to as "accidents," implying limited personal choice or control and making it reasonable to think, "when it's your time, it's your time."

In schools, some teachers believe "students are just cruel at this age," or "bullying just happens." As a result they exercise limited personal interaction to prevent bullying behavior. The problem is "beyond their control".

The common phrase "random acts of kindness"[23] has a disadvantage when describing AC4P behavior. Random implies the behavior happened by chance, which suggests it's beyond individual choice or control. A kind act may appear random to the recipient, but it's intentionally performed and is usually self-motivated. Our preferred alternative: *intentional* acts of kindness. Parts IV and V of this book illustrate numerous intentional acts of AC4P.

The language we use to prescribe or describe behavior influences our perceptions of its meaningfulness and its relevance to our lives. Language impacts culture, and vice versa. (See Chapter 6 for more on the role of language in determining effective communication.)

4. Provide Opportunities for Choice.

Participative management means employees have personal choice during the planning, execution, and evaluation of their jobs. People have a need for autonomy, regardless of dispositional and situational factors. In the workplace, managers often tell people what to do as opposed to involving them in the decision-making process.

In schools, students are often viewed as passive learners, because teachers plan, execute, and evaluate most aspects of the teaching/learning process. Students' perceptions of choice are limited. Yet cooperative teaching/learning – where students contribute to the selection and presentation of lesson material – has been shown to be most beneficial over the long term.[9]

5. Involve the Followers.

Rules established by soliciting input from those affected by the regulation support autonomy.[11] Employees are more likely to comply with safety regulations they helped to define. Shouldn't they have significant influence in the development of policy they will be asked to follow? Those on the "front line" know best what actions should be avoided versus performed in order to optimize the safety and quality of their production system.

Similarly, before a rule or regulation is implemented in an educational system, those affected (i.e., faculty and/or students) should certainly be given opportunities to offer suggestions. In a family, as the children mature, certain rules should be open to discussion before being mandated. This takes more time, but the marked increase in effectiveness justifies any loss in efficiency.

6. Set SMARTS Goals.

Customize process and outcome goals with individuals and work teams. The most effective goals are SMARTS: *Specific, Motivational, Achievable, Relevant, Trackable, and Shared.*[19]

Process goals reflect successive behavioral steps to achieve on route to accomplishing a significant outcome goal. A work team might set a process goal to complete a total of ten interpersonal observation-and-feedback sessions per week for one month, aiming to increase the percentage of safe behaviors recorded for their team. Of course, the long-term outcome goal is a reduction in personal injuries, but this can take substantial time to realize, especially if the group's injury rate is already low.

It's important to note and celebrate the periodic accomplishment of measurable process goals related to more remote and nebulous visions such as "culture improvement" and "injury free".

In educational settings, completing certain homework assignments and studying a certain number of hours per week serve as process goals, leading to the outcome of an improved exam grade, and eventually a desirable grade in a particular course. Achieving such process goals and obtaining desirable grades leads to the more remote outcome goal of graduating with honors.

In family settings, goal-setting involving the participation of children may seem unreasonable, but at a certain point of their evolving maturity, full family involvement in defining the required individual and group behaviors (e.g., daily chores, school work, and budget management) to meet desired outcome goals (e.g., house and lawn maintenance, good school grades, and a family vacation) promotes mutual trust, perceived equity, and interdependent participation.

For optimal effectiveness, it's critical to apply the SMARTS acronym to the definition of a process goal. "S" for "specific" means the goal needs to be defined precisely with regard to the specific actions planned within a certain time period (e.g., perform ten coaching sessions per week for one month; complete a certain two-hour exercise routine three times a week for five consecutive months; recognize and reward five AC4P behaviors per week.

Is Your Goal Motivating? "M" for "motivational" refers to the realization of the extrinsic and/or natural consequences acquired following goal attainment. For example, employees might look forward to a group pizza social (an extrinsic reward) after a month of averaging ten coaching sessions per week, and they might also anticipate improved communication skills and more AC4P relationships (an intrinsic reinforcer).

Similarly, an individual could plan for a weekend at the beach after completing the weekly exercise routine for five months (extrinsic reward), and anticipate fitting well in a new bathing suit (intrinsic reinforcer). Moreover, it naturally feels good to reward the AC4P behavior of others with an AC4P wristband, and such action contributes to cultivating an AC4P culture.

The "A" for "attainable" simply means the participants believe they can achieve the process goal, although it will not be easy. Fitting in ten coaching sessions a week for a month, for example, might be considered challenging but feasible. And, sticking to a specified exercise routine for five months will be difficult but doable. Recognizing and rewarding AC4P behavior is easier said than done, but it does get easier with practice.

The "R" for "relevant" refers to a clear, rational connection between achieving the process goal and obtaining an eventual outcome. Participants need to believe working toward accomplishing the process goal is consistent with their mission to obtain an eventual outcome goal. Interpersonal coaching is relevant to preventing injuries; regular exercise will lead to improved fitness, health, and well-being; and recognizing people regularly for their AC4P behavior is consistent with cultivating an AC4P culture of compassion.

The "T" for "trackable" reflects the need to track your progress toward attaining process goals. This implies, of course, goal-relevant behaviors can be counted successively as the participants get closer to realizing their goal. For example, interpersonal coaching sessions are tallied and posted on a chart for team members to observe; every two-hour exercise routine completed is marked on the calendar; and occurrences of

AC4P behavior are indicated on a spread sheet that includes a space to specify the particular AC4P behavior rewarded.

Sharing Your Goal. Finally, the "S" for "share" means it's useful to share your process goal with others. Public announcement of a group or individual goal increases commitment to work toward reaching that goal. And when others know your laudable goal and realize value in accomplishing that goal, they will likely help to support your progress.

For example, you might anticipate friends asking you about your goal-directed behavior, and such expected social accountability could enhance your self-motivation. In fact, just seeing those individuals who know about your goal can serve as a reminder to stay on course. You anticipate the question, "How's your goal progress these days," and you want to answer, "Very well, thank you".

So it's beneficial: a) for a work team to announce their coaching goals to other teams; b) to tell others of a fitness-routine goal, and c) for leaders of an AC4P movement to share their recognition goals with other advocates of an AC4P culture.

Observational learning is a positive side-effect of such goal sharing. When others interested in the mission implied by your goal learn about your goal setting and view your progress, they might consider setting a similar goal for themselves or their team. Your shared goal setting and progress sets an impressive example for others to follow. This was a beneficial result of the following goal-setting story.

Joanne's AC4P Story. Two years ago, my wife Joanne made a New Year's resolution to perform an AC4P behavior every day until her 60th Birthday on March 27th. She announced her goal to family and friends, including leaders of our campus AC4P Movement. She also described each of her AC4P behaviors on the website: ac4p.org. I hope it's obvious this was a SMARTS process goal. As Joanne reports in her personal story (Chapter 19), she did accomplish this goal; but it wasn't easy.

Joanne knew she was setting a "stretch goal," but it was actually more challenging than she had expected. It took significant planning, preparation, and time to achieve daily AC4P behaviors, which varied widely from cooking meals and shoveling snow for neighbors to giving gift certificates to individuals she observed providing noteworthy community service.

Daily sharing of her AC4P actions sustained social support for her commitment, and set an impressive example many AC4P advocates have attempted to emulate on a smaller scale.

For example, each semester we initiate the "AC4P Challenge" among the 50 to 70 research students in our Center for Applied Behavior Systems. We evaluate whether students can attain the goal of performing five intentional AC4P acts in one week. "If Joanne can do 60 in 60," we say, "then surely you can accomplish five AC4P acts in seven days".

Most students willingly sign an "AC4P Commitment Card" for the "AC4P Challenge," but less than 50% report meeting this seemingly easy goal. Actively caring on a daily basis is easier said than done when AC4P behavior is defined as going beyond the norm to benefit the health, safety, or well-being of another person.

7. Use Behavior-Based Feedback.

Supervisors, teachers, and parents are more likely to notice and reprimand undesirable behavior, than discern and acknowledge desirable behavior. This is why the term "feedback" carries negative connotations.

What is one to think if asked, "Can I give you some feedback about your behavior last night"? Likewise, how do you feel after receiving an email from your supervisor that he wants you to come to his office at the end of the day for some feedback? Has your day been ruined? For many of us, the illustration below rings true.

It's unfortunate but true: Most people expect feedback to be more negative than positive. Of course, that perception can be changed if supervisors, teachers, and parents verbalized more *supportive* than corrective feedback.

Suppose that supervisor or teacher who asked to see you at the end of the day for a feedback session gives you only supportive feedback. She defines specific desirable behaviors she has observed you perform, and expresses genuine appreciation for the extra effort you consistently demonstrate to apply your notable skill sets on behalf of the organization's mission.

How would that make you feel? Would "feedback" take on a more positive meaning, at least with this supervisor? Would you share this positive experience with others and likely enhance others' perception of "feedback" and this supervisor's leadership skills? That's the power of interpersonal recognition and approval in cultivating a self-motivated AC4P culture.

***If-Then* Rewards.** Use *if-then incentive/reward contingencies* when individuals are not already self-motivated to perform the desired behavior or intrinsic reinforcers are not available. This does not mean the *if-then incentive/reward contingencies* are bad or undesirable, as some uninformed authors have claimed.[24] Extrinsic rewards influence many behaviors and this is not detrimental to self-motivation; they just might not increase it.

For example, I choose certain airlines and hotels in order to earn "points" that can translate to material rewards or improved service. My awareness of this "manipulation tactic" does not impact my disposition in any negative way. In fact, I'm pleased to be extrinsically rewarded for making certain choices. Indeed, my sense of choice to select the airline or hotel that offers the "if-then" rewards has a beneficial impact on my overall self-motivation.

In the same view, it's not detrimental to reward students for performing certain behaviors relevant to their education, as authors uneducated in psychological science have claimed.[24] The child who doesn't choose to read books, for example, cannot experience the inherent enjoyment (i.e., intrinsic reinforcement) of reading. In this case, an *if-then contingency* can be invaluable. The child is extrinsically rewarded for performing a behavior previously emitted only infrequently. Subsequently, the child may enjoy reading, especially after feeling competent at this worthwhile task. Then self-motivation takes control, and extrinsic incentives are no longer needed.

As I explained earlier, competence fuels self-motivation. People can help others feel competent by offering words of appreciation for behaviors that reflect their personal competence. Hence, genuine approval of a child's reading behavior from a parent increases the child's perception of competence and self-motivation.

Now-That **Rewards.** At times, special rewards of excellence are given to individuals and groups for excelling at performance in a given domain, from accomplishments in teaching and learning to winning an athletic competition. These extrinsic consequences are well received, often to the applause of an approving audience. Such acknowledgment does wonders to an individual's sense of personal competence, leading to more self-motivation to sustain or even enhance the relevant skill set.

It's noteworthy these latter examples of rewarding desirable behavior reflect a *now-that* contingency rather than *if-then*. These rewards do not include an incentive (i.e., the announcement of the availability of a reward if a designated behavior occurs). The behavior might be initiated for a variety of internal, intrinsic, or extrinsic reasons, but the unannounced *now-that* reward is given after the behavior occurs in order to support its occurrence.

In some cases, this rewarding consequence increases the probability the desirable behavior will recur. In most cases, a person's sense of competence increases following sincere *now-that* rewards, fueling self-motivation to continue the rewarded behavior.

Behavior-Based Recognition. In the workplace, managers should intermittently communicate one-on-one with employees to express sincere appreciation for their specific behaviors that contribute to the organization.

In school, teachers' interper-

sonal praise of their students' work are invaluable to boosting self-competence, confidence, and self-motivation to continuously improve. And every parent knows through personal experience the motivational benefits of demonstrating enthusiastic approval of a child's dedication to do well at a particular task.

Words of approval, appreciation, and praise are relatively rare, especially when compared with the use of verbal reprimands, as experience has taught us. Mistakes or disruptive behaviors stick out and invite corrective action; but desirable behavior does not naturally attract attention and seemingly does not require intervention.

By now you certainly see the special advantages of supportive feedback in enhancing self-motivation, right? Still, there are times when it's necessary to correct undesirable behavior. How should this be done?

8. Give Corrective Feedback Well.

Make use of empathy and compassion to correct undesirable behavior. Be non-directive, actively listen to excuses, and emphasize the positive over the negative. It can be uncomfortable to provide others with behavior-based corrective feedback, even when the recipient of your feedback is a family member or friend.

Remind yourself and the feedback recipient that only with specific behavioral feedback can performance be improved. Remember, practice does not make perfect unless the performer receives supportive feedback for right behavior and corrective feedback for wrong behavior.

Incorrect or unsafe behavior is not an indictment of a person's attitude, values, or personality. Our unintentional mistakes do not reflect who we are. So it is critical to emphasize that your corrective feedback is only about behavior you have observed and not a judgment of the person.

Continuous improvement occurs when observers have the courage to give relevant behavior-based feedback, and when those observed have the humility to accept the feedback and make relevant behavioral adjustments. After all, we all want to improve behavior that's important to us, and this often requires behavioral feedback from others

How should you approach someone to give corrective feedback? Your initial words are critical. If you come on too strong when directing a person to improve in a certain way, the "victim" may get defensive and offer excuses for a mistake. Or, if the observer has relevant authority over the victim, which is often the case, the victim might make the behavioral adjustments called for; but the change will not stick if the victim does not agree with and accept the behavioral advice.

How can you get buy-in for the behavioral feedback you have the courage to offer? Your opening words should be inquisitive rather than accusative. If the feedback targets a person's unsafe behavior, my good friend John Drebinger recommends beginning with a question like, "Could I look out for your safety?"[25] Who could say "No" to a request like this?

Then following a "Yes, of course," the observer mentions the behavior that needs adjustment for injury prevention. Often it's best if the observer can mention some desirable behavior first, and then suggest where there's room for improvement.

My partners at Safety Performance Solutions have been teaching behavioral coaching for occupational health and safety for almost two decades, and they've always emphasized the need to be empathic and nondirective when giving co-workers behavior-based feedback.[26] More specifically, an AC4P observer of a certain worker completes a critical behavior checklist (CBC) of safe vs. at-risk behavior, previously designed through interactive group discussions among line workers representative of the relevant workforce.[27] Workers give permission to be observed, and they know what behaviors are being observed. Even with this set up, at-risk behaviors are often observed and observers are challenged to offer corrective feedback to a co-worker.

How do they do this? From the start it's emphasized the observer (unlike a typical athletic coach) is not responsible for directing or motivating corrective action. The observer merely completes the CBC, and then shows the results to the person observed. The two workers might discuss environmental or system factors that discourage safe behavior and encourage at-risk behavior. And they might consider ways to remove barriers to safe behavior. The observer, referred to as an AC4P coach, might offer positive words of approval to recognize certain safe behavior, but gives no disapproving statements or directives related to any observed at-risk behavior.

An AC4P coach is nondirective when communicating corrective feedback. The coach provides specific behavior-based feedback for the person observed to consider. There is no pressure to change. The only accountability is self-accountability. Any adjustment in behavior is self-motivated, activated by the results of a nonintrusive and anticipated application of a CBC.

As I explained in Chapter 2, the perception of personal choice increases the likelihood this kind of corrective feedback will be accepted and lead to a self-motivated behavioral adjustment. Workers choose to be observed by an AC4P coach, and then choose to accept or reject the feedback provided by a CBC.

9. Celebrate to Increase a Sense Community.

Celebrations, when done correctly, can motivate teamwork and build a sense of belongingness and community among groups of individuals, boosting their self-motivation. Of course the key words in the preceding sentence are "when done correctly". Let's consider seven guidelines for celebrating group accomplishments:

Reward the Right Behavior. In the domain of occupational safety, it's common for organizations to give groups of employees a celebration dinner after a particular number of weeks or months pass with no recordable injury. This kind of achievement is certainly worth celebrating, but let's be sure the record was reached fairly. If people cheat to win by not reporting their injuries, the celebration won't mean much.

If a celebration for lower injuries is announced as an incentive, the motivation to cheat is increased. If employees are promised a reward when they work a certain number of days without an injury, it will be tempting to avoid reporting a personal injury if they can get away with it. This is, of course, peer pressure to cheat – a situation that reduces interpersonal trust and promotes a belief that improved levels of organizational safety cannot be reached fairly.

If the accomplishment of process activities is celebrated, then it's okay to establish an *if-then* behavior-consequence contingency, as discussed earlier. In this case, the behaviors needed from the group are specified in order to warrant a celebration. This is group goal setting. If the SMARTS principles discussed above are followed, teamwork for goal accomplishment will be motivated.

A group might decide to celebrate after everyone reports one observation of an AC4P behavior or when every group member performs an AC4P behavior, or after the total number of AC4P behaviors observed and performed by the group members reach a designated total. In these cases, a SMARTS group goal is set and progress is monitored. When the goal is reached, a celebration is warranted. It was earned for a successful journey, destined to eventually achieve an AC4P culture of compassion.

Focus on the Journey. Most of the corporate celebrations I've seen were for excellence in safety, and all of these gave far too little attention to the journey – the processes that contributed to reaching the milestone. Typically, the focus was on the end result, the outcome measure, like achieving zero injuries for a certain period of time.

There was scant discussion about *how* the outcome was achieved. It's natural to toast the bottom line, but there's more to be gained from taking the opportunity to diagnose and recognize process success.

When you pinpoint processes instrumental to reaching a particular milestone, you give valuable direction and motivation. Participants learn what to continue doing for an effective journey. Those responsible for the behaviors leading to the celebrated outcome receive a special boost in competence, personal control, and optimism. Plus, information is added to these individuals' internal recognition scripts which in turn enhances their self-motivation.

Perhaps the most important reason to acknowledge journey activities leading to a noteworthy group outcome is that it gives credit where credit is due. Focusing on the process endorses the people and their actions that made the difference, fueling self-motivation. This leads to the next guideline.

Recipients Should Be Participants. Rarely do participants in a celebratory event discuss the processes they supported in order to reach the outcome. And so a valuable "teaching moment" is missed. Instead, speeches from top management often kick off a corporate celebration. Sometimes charts are displayed to compare the past with the improved present. Often a sincere request for continuous improvement is made, and a manager points out the amount of money saved or profits earned by the group's accomplishment. Sometimes promises for a bigger celebration are made following continued success.

Occasionally a motivational speaker or humorist gives everyone a lift and some laughs. Often special rewards are given to individuals or team captains, along with a handshake from a top-management official. Certificates and trinkets might be handed out, along with a steak dinner.

In the typical corporate celebration, management gives and the employees receive

– certainly an impressive show of top-down support. But the ceremony would be more memorable and beneficial as both learning and motivational if employees were more participant than recipient.

Managers should listen more than speak, and employees should talk more about their experiences than listen to managers' pleasure with the bottom line.

Relive the Journey. Managers should facilitate discussion of the activities that led to the celebrated accomplishment. Relive the procedures that made the journey successful. This "reenactment" strengthens employees' internal scripts that direct and motivate their ongoing support of the effective process. Managers who listen to these discussions with genuine interest and concern are rewarding the participation that enabled the success and empowering employees to continue their journey toward higher-level achievement.

The best safety celebration I ever observed was planned by employees and featured a series of brief presentations by teams of hourly workers. Numerous safety ideas were shared. Some workers showed off new personal protective equipment, some displayed graphs of data obtained from environmental or behavioral audits, some discussed their procedures for encouraging reports of close calls and implementing corrective action, and one group presented its ergonomic analysis and redesign of a work station.

Even the after-dinner entertainment was employee-driven. A skit illustrated safety issues. A talent show had entrants from all levels of the organization, including top managers. There was no need to hire a band for live music – a number of talented musicians were found in the workforce of 600. Luckily, they didn't find a drummer, allowing me to sit in and relive my rock-n-roll gigging from the 1960s.

Discuss Successes and Failures. The work teams in this celebration discussed both successes and failures, displaying the positive results and recalling disappointments, dead ends, and frustrations. Pointing out the highs and lows made their presentations realistic, and underscored the amount of dedication needed to complete their projects and contribute to the celebrated reduction in injuries.

Presentations that point out hardships along the journey to success justify the celebration. The celebrated bottom line was not a matter of luck. It took hard work by many people going beyond the call of duty. The payoff: small-win contributions, pronounced interdependence, win-win collaboration, and synergy.

Make it Memorable. Goal attainment is meaningful and memorable when people discuss the difficulties in reaching a goal. When managers listen to these presentations with sincere interest and appreciation, the event becomes even more significant and credible. And when a tangible reward is distributed appropriately at such an occasion, a mechanism is established to sustain the memory of this occasion and promote its value.

Ideally, the memento should include words, perhaps a theme or slogan, that reflects the particular celebration. The tangible reward should be something readily displayable or usable at work – from coffee mugs, placards, and pencil holders to caps, shirts, and umbrellas, for example.

When delivering these keepsakes, it should be noted they were selected "to help you remember this special occasion and what it has meant to all of us. This small token of our appreciation will remind us how we got here."

One week after the safety celebration I described here, every participant received a framed group photograph of everyone who attended the event. That picture hangs in my office today, and every time I look at it, I'm reminded of the time several years ago when management did more listening than talking in a most memorable and educational group celebration.

Don't Neglect Your Leaders. In every group project, some individuals take charge and champion the effort, while others sit back and "go with the flow". Some people exert less effort when working with a group than when working alone. Psychologists call this phenomenon "social loafing".[28]

Recognize the champions of a group effort one-on-one, and you let them know you realize the importance of their leadership in a team accomplishment. You appreciate their extra-effort contributions. This adds substantially to the self-motivation these individuals had already received from the earlier group celebration. As a result, you've increased the likelihood of their continued leadership for attaining further goals.

Solicit Ideas. When I mentioned to my graduate students I was writing a book chapter on how to celebrate, one of them quickly responded, "That's easy, a $100 bottle of cognac, a $6 cigar, and a special friend". I had to tell him, of course, my focus was on a different kind of celebrating.

But it occurred to me that everyone has his or her own way of celebrating. And when it comes to group celebration, we often inadvertently impose our prejudices on others. We usually don't take the time to ask potential participants what kind of celebration party they would like.

When it comes to organizing a group celebration, many people don't know how to celebrate. Ask people what they want for their celebration, and the discussion likely focuses on tangible rewards. "What material commodity should we receive for our efforts?" This puts the celebration in a payoff-for-behavior mode and is not the real purpose of a group celebration. You want a meaningful and memorable event that increases a sense of belonging and community, and can serve as a stepping stone to even greater achievements.

10. Build Interpersonal Trust.

To cultivate an AC4P culture, interpersonal trust is absolutely fundamental. Trust is the foundation for building a community of people who go beyond the call of duty to give each other behavior-based support and relevant corrective feedback.

Seven C-words capture the essence of building interpersonal trust and interdependence: communication, caring, candor, consistency, commitment, consensus, and character. Let's consider how each of these C-words implicates interpersonal trust and community-building. The phrase associated with the following C-words summarizes the key definitions given in my *American Heritage* and *New-Merriam-Webster* dictionaries.[29]

Communication – *exchange of information or opinion by speech, writing, or signals.* What people say and how they say it influences our trust in both their capability and their intentions.

I'm sure you've heard many times the way something is said, including intonation, pace, facial expressions, hand gestures, and overall posture, has greater impact than what was actually said. And, you've certainly experienced personal feelings of trust toward another person change as the result of how that individual communicated information.

Often we trust certain information because we respect the credentials of the communicator or we like the way the message is displayed. Personal opinion or "common sense" is relied on if the message sounds good to us and if the presentation is given well – with Clarity, Confidence, and Charisma.

Those three C-words suggest how we get others to trust our knowledge, skill, or ability. But what about trusting one's intentions? Do you know people who have impressive credentials and communicate elegantly, but something makes you suspicious about their intentions? You believe they know what to do, but you're not convinced they will do what they say. They have the right talk, but give the impression they don't walk it. This critical issue is reflected in each of the subsequent C-words for trust-building.

However, before moving on to the other C-words, let's consider the most powerful communication strategy for increasing trust in one's intentions – AC4P listening. There is probably no better way to earn someone's trust in your intentions than by listening attentively to that person's communication with an AC4P mindset.

When you listen to others first before communicating your own perspective, you not only increase the chance they will reciprocate and listen to you, you also learn how to present your message for optimal understanding, appreciation, and buy-in.

Caring – *showing concern or interest about what happens.* When people believe you sincerely care about them, they will care about what you tell them. They trust you will look out for them when applying your knowledge, skills, or abilities. They trust your intentions because they believe you care.

You communicate AC4P and build interpersonal trust when you ask questions.

I'm referring to inquiry about a particular task or set of circumstances. Questions targeting a specific aspect of a person's job send the signal you care about him or her. This communication is more credible than the general, "How ya doing?" greeting.

Take the time to learn what others are doing. Listen and observe. Here I'm talking about "listening to the talk, and walking the talk". You want to "talk the walk" so people trust your intentions.

Candor – *straightforwardness and frankness of expression; freedom from prejudice.* We trust people who are frank and open with us. People who don't beat around the bush.

When they don't know an answer to our questions, they tell us outright they don't know and they'll get back to us with an answer.

You have reason to mistrust individuals if their interactions with you reflect prejudice or the tendency to judge blindly. You question their ability to evaluate others and their intentions to treat people fairly.

When people give an opinion about others because of their race, religion, gender, or birthplace, you should doubt these individuals' ability to make people-related decisions. And, you should wonder whether their intentions to perform on behalf of another individual will be biased or tainted by a tendency to pre-judge people on the basis of overly simple and usually inaccurate stereotypes.

Consistency – *agreement among successive acts, ideas, or events.* Consistency is a key determinant of interpersonal trust. Perhaps the *fastest* way to destroy interpersonal trust is to not follow through on an agreement. This is also the *easiest* way to stifle trust.

How often do we make a promise we don't keep? Most promises are *if-then* contingencies. We specify a certain consequence will follow a certain behavior. Whether the consequence is positive or negative, trust decreases when the behavior is not rewarded or punished as promised.

When my daughters were young, I frequently caught myself impulsively making promises (or policy statements) I didn't keep. For example, when they misbehaved while their mom and I were packing the car for a trip, it was not uncommon for one of us to say, "Stop doing that right now or we're not going". Often our daughters stopped the undesirable behavior. The "policy maker" was then reinforced for making the promise.

But what happened when my daughters didn't stop their misbehavior or resumed the undesirable behavior after a brief hiatus? Sure, we still made the trip. The punishment contingency might be shouted a few more times, but regardless, we eventually piled into our car and took off. What did these empty threats teach our daughters?

We would have been far better off promising a less severe negative consequence we could implement consistently, such as delaying the trip until the behavior stops. "We can't go until you stop fighting," would have been much better than a more severe *if-then* threat with inconsistent consequences.

Commitment – *bound emotionally or intellectually to a course of action*. When you follow through on a promise or pledge to do something, you tell others they can count on you. You can be trusted to do what you say you will do.

The consistency principle reflects a spiral of causality and explains how behavior influences attitude, and vice verse. When we choose to do something, we experience internal pressure to maintain a personal belief system or attitude consistent with that behavior. And when we have a certain belief system or attitude toward something, we tend to behave in ways consistent with such beliefs or attitudes. (More about this critical AC4P principle is discussed in Chapter 5.)

Commitment and total involvement result from a causal spiraling of action feeding attitude, then attitude feeding more action, which strengthens the attitude and leads to more behavior.

Researchers have found three ways to make an initial commitment to do something lead to the most causal spiraling and total involvement.[30] First, people live up to what they write down, so ask for a signed statement of a commitment. Second, the more public the commitment, the greater the relevant attitude and behavior change, presumably because social pressures are added to the personal pressure to be consistent in word and deed.

Third, and perhaps most importantly, for a public and written commitment to initiate causal spiraling of behavior supporting attitude (and vice versa), the commitment must be viewed as a personal choice. When people believe their commitment was their idea, the consistency principle is activated. But when people believe their commitment was unduly influenced by outside factors, they do not feel a need to live up to what they were coerced to write down.

Consensus – *agreement in opinion, testimony, or belief*. Whenever the results of a group decision-making process come across as "win-lose," some mistrust is going to develop. A majority of the group might be pleased, but others will be discontented and might actively or passively resist involvement. And even the "winners" could feel lowered interpersonal trust. "We won this decision, but what about next time?" And without solid back-up support of the decision, the outcome will be less than desired. "Without everyone's buy-in, commitment and involvement, we can't trust the process to come off as expected."

How can group consensus be developed? How can the outcome of a heated debate be perceived as a win-win solution everyone supports? Consensus-building takes time and energy, and requires candid, consistent and caring communication among all members of a discussion or decision-making group.

When people demonstrate the C-words discussed above for building trust in interpersonal dialogue, they also develop consensus and more interpersonal trust regarding a particular decision or action plan.

There's no quick fix to doing this. It requires plenty of interpersonal communication, including straightforward opinion sharing, intense discussion, emotional debate, active listening, careful evaluation, methodical organization, and systematic prioritizing. But on important matters, the outcome is well worth the investment. When you develop a solution or process every potential participant can get behind and champion, you have cultivated the degree of interpersonal trust needed for total involvement. Involvement in turn builds personal commitment, more interpersonal trust, and then more involvement.

Character – *the combined moral or ethical structure of a person or group; integrity; fortitude.* Generally, a person with "character" is considered honest, ethical, and principled. People with character are credible or worthy of another person's trust because they display confidence and competence. They know who they are; they know where they want to go; and they know how to get there.

All of the strategies discussed here for cultivating a trusting culture are practiced by a person with character. Individuals with character are willing to admit vulnerability. They are humble and realize they aren't perfect and need behavioral feedback from others. They know their strengths and weaknesses, and find exemplars to model.

By actively listening to others and observing their behaviors, individuals with character learn how to improve their own performance. And if they're building a high-performance team, they can readily find people with knowledge, skills, and abilities to complement their own competencies. They know how to make diversity work for them, their group, and the entire organization.

Having the courage to admit your weaknesses means you're willing to apologize when you've made a mistake, and to ask for forgiveness. There is probably no better way to build trust between individuals than to own up to

an error that might have affected another person.

Of course you should also indicate what you will do better next time or ask for specific advice on how to improve. This kind of vulnerability enables you to heed the powerful enrichment principle I learned from the late Frank Bird, "Good better best, may we never rest until good is better and better is best".[31]

While admitting personal vulnerability is a powerful way to build interpersonal trust, the surest way to reduce interpersonal trust is to tell one person about the weakness of another. In this situation it's natural to think, "If he talks that way about her, I wonder what he says about me behind my back". It's obvious how criticizing or demeaning others in their absence can lead to interpersonal suspiciousness and mistrust.

Back-stabbing leads to more back-stabbing, and eventually you have a work culture of independent people doing their own thing, fearful of making an error, and unreceptive to any kind of behavior-based feedback. Key aspects of continuous performance improvement – team-building, interpersonal observation, and coaching – are extremely difficult or impossible to implement in such a culture. Under these circumstances it's necessary to first break down barriers to interpersonal trust before implementing a behavior-based observation and feedback process.

Start to build interpersonal trust by implementing a policy of no back-stabbing. People with character, as defined here, always talk about other people as if they can hear you. In other words, to replace interpersonal mistrust with trust, never talk about other individuals behind their backs unless you're willing to say the same thing directly to them.

A Summary

The seven C-words offer distinct directives for AC4P trust-building behavior. *Communicating* these guidelines to others in a *candid* and *caring* way opens up the kind of dialogue that starts people on a journey of AC4P trust-building. Then people need to give each other *consistent* and *candid* feedback regarding those behaviors that reflect these trust-building principles.

With *character* and *commitment*, they need to recognize others for doing it right and offer corrective feedback when there's room for improvement. And of course it's critical for the recipient of such *candid* behavior-based feedback to accept it with *caring* appreciation and a *commitment* to improve.

Then, the feedback recipient needs to show the *character* to thank the observer for the feedback, even when the *communication* is not all positive and is not delivered well. S/he might offer feedback on how to make the behavior-based feedback more useful. Dialogue like this is necessary to build *consensus* and sustain a journey of continuous AC4P trust and community-building.

In Conclusion

An AC4P culture requires people to do the right thing on behalf of other people when no other person is holding them accountable. Such self-accountability to perform AC4P behavior usually requires self-motivation. This research-based chapter introduced a number of practical ways to facilitate the self-motivation needed to achieve and sustain an AC4P culture.

This book offers a number of real-world examples of the self-motivation principles and leadership lessons reviewed here, as well as practical ways to apply these principles and lessons for enhancing people's self-motivation to actively care for the health, safety, education, and well-being of others.

Notes

1. Geller, E.S., & Veazie, R.A. (2010). *When no one's watching: Living and leading self motivation.* Newport, VA: Make-A-Difference, LLC.

2. Chance, P. (2007). The ultimate challenge: Prove B.F. Skinner wrong. *The Behavior Analyst, 30, 153-160.*

3. Deci, E.L. (1975). *Intrinsic motivation.* New York, NY: Plenum; Deci, E.L., & Flaste, R. (1995). *Why we do what we do: Understanding self-motivation.* New York, NY: Penguin Book; Deci, E.L., & Ryan, R.M. (1995). *Intrinsic motivation and self-determinism in human behavior.* New York, NY: Plenum; Ryan, R.M., & Deci, E.L. (2000). Self-determinism theory and the foundation of intrinsic motivation, social development, and well-being. *American Psychologist, 55,* 68-75.

4. Deci, E.L., & Flaste, R. (1995). *Why we do what we do: Understanding self-motivation.* New York, NY: Penguin Books, p.9.

5. Geller, E.S. (2001). *The psychology of safety handbook.* Boca Raton, FL: CRC Press; Ludwig, T.D., & Geller, E.S. (2001). *Intervening to improve the safety of occupational driving: A behavior-change model and review of empirical evidence.* New York, NY: The Haworth Press, Inc.; Monty, R.A., & Perlmuter, L.C. (1975). Persistence of the effect of choice on paired-associate learning. *Memory & Cognition, 3,* 183-187; Perlmuter, L.C., Monty, R.A., & Kimble, G.A. (1971). Effect of choice on paired-associate learning. *Journal of Experimental Psychology, 91,* 47-58; Steiner, I.D. (1970). Perceived freedom. In L. Berkowitz. (Ed.). *Advances in experimental social psychology,* (Vol. 5). New York, NY: Academic Press.

6. Geller, E.S. (1994). Ten principles for achieving a Total Safety Culture. *Professional Safety, 39*(9), 18-25; Geller, E.S. (2001). *The psychology of safety handbook.* Boca Raton, FL: CRC Press; Geller, E.S. (2005). *People-based safety: The source.* Virginia Beach, VA: Coastal Training Technologies Corp.; Geller, E.S. (2008). *Leading people-based safety: Enriching your culture.* Virginia Beach, VA: Coastal Training Technologies Corp.

7. White, R.W. (1959). Motivation reconsidered: The concept of competence. *Psychological Review, 66,* 297-321.

8. Deci, E.L., & Flaste, R. (1995). *Why we do what we do: Understanding self-motivation.* New York, NY: Penguin Books, p.66.

9. Chance, P. (2008). *The teacher's craft: The 10 essential skills of effective teaching.* Long Grove, IL: Waveland Press, Inc.

10. Geller, E.S. (1996). *The psychology of safety: How to improve behaviors and attitudes on the job.* Radnor, PA: The Chilton Book Company; Geller, E.S. (1998). *Understanding behavior-based safety: Step-by-step methods to improve your workplace* (2nd Edition). Neenah, WI: J.J. Keller & Associates, Inc; Geller, E.S. (2001). *The psychology of safety handbook.* Boca Raton, FL: CRC Press; Geller, E.S. (2005). *People-based safety: The source.* Virginia Beach, VA: Coastal Training

and Technologies Corporation; Geller, E.S., Perdue, S.R., & French, A. (2004) Behavior-based safety coaching: Ten guidelines for successful application. *Professional Safety, 49*(7), 42-49; Krause, T.R., Hidley, J.H., & Hodson, S.J. (1996). *The behavior-based safety process: Managing improvement for an injury-free culture* (2nd Edition). New York, NY: Van Nostrand Reinhold; McSween, T.E. (2003). *The values-based safety process: Improving your safety culture with a behavioral approach* (2nd Edition). New York, NY: Van Nostrand Reinhold; Weigand, D.M. (2007). Exploring the role of emotional intelligence in behavior-based safety coaching. *Journal of Safety Research, 38,* 391-398.

11. Deci, E.L., & Flaste, R. (1995). *Why we do what we do: Understanding self-motivation.* New York, NY: Penguin Books, p.88.

12. Geller, E.S. (1994). Ten principles for achieving a Total Safety Culture. *Professional Safety, 39*(9), 18-25; Geller, E.S. (2001). *The psychology of safety handbook.* Boca Raton, FL: CRC Press; Geller, E.S. (2005). *People-based safety: The source.* Virginia Beach, VA: Coastal Training Technologies Corp.

13. Block, P. (2008). *Community: The structure of belonging.* San Francisco, CA: Berrett-Koehler Publishers.

14. Peck, M.S. (1979). *The different drum: Community making and peace.* New York, NY: Simon & Schuster, Inc.

15. Deming, W.E. (1986). *Out of the crisis.* Cambridge, MA: Massachusetts Institute of Technology, Center for Advanced Engineering Study; Deming, W.E. (1993). *The new economics for industry, government, education.* Cambridge, MA: Massachusetts Institute of Technology, Center for Advanced Engineering Study.

16. Senge, P.M. (1990). *The fifth discipline: The art and practice of the learning organization.* New York, NY: Doubleday.

17. Covey, S.R. (1989). *The seven habits of highly effective people.* New York, NY: Simon and Schuster, Inc.

18. Geller, E.S., & Veazie, R.A. (2009). *The courage factor: Leading people-based culture change.* Virginia Beach, VA: Coastal Training and Technologies Corporation.

19. Geller, E.S. (2005). *People-based safety: The source.* Virginia Beach, VA: Coastal Training Technologies Corp., pp. 95-98.

20. Deci, E.L. (1975). *Intrinsic motivation.* New York, NY: Plenum; Deci, E.L., & Flaste, R. (1995). *Why we do what we do: Understanding self-motivation.* New York, NY: Penguin Book; Deci, E.L., & Ryan, R.M. (1995). *Intrinsic motivation and self-determinism in human behavior.* New York, NY: Plenum; Ryan, R.M., & Deci, E.L. (2000). Self-determinism theory and the foundation of intrinsic motivation, social development, and well-being. *American Psychologist, 55,* 68-75.

21. United Kingdom Department of Transport (1987). *Killing speed and saving lives.* London, England: Department of Transport.

22. Deci, E.L., & Flaste, R. (1995). *Why we do what we do: Understanding self-motivation.* New York, NY: Penguin Books, p. 104.

23. Conari Press (1993). *Random acts of kindness.* Emeryville, CA.

24. Kohn, A. *Punished by rewards: The trouble with gold stars, incentive plans, A's, praise, and other bribes,* Boston, MA: Houghton Mifflin; Pink, D.H. (2009). *Drive: The surprising truth about what*

motivates us. New York, NY: Penguin Group.

25. Drebinger, J. W. (2011). *Would you watch out for my safety? Helping others avoid personal injury.* Galt, CA: Wulamoc Publishing.

26. Geller, E.S. (2005). *People-based safety: The source.* Virginia Beach, VA: Coastal Training Technologies Corp., pp.95-98; Geller, E. S. (2008). *Leading people-based safety: enriching your culture.* Virginia Beach, VA: Coastal Training Technologies Corp.; Geller, E. S., Perdue, S. R., & French, A. (2004). Behavior-based safety coaching: Ten guidelines for successful application. *Professional Safety, 49* (7), 42-49.

27. Geller, E.S. (1998*). Understanding behavior-based safety: Step-by-step methods to improve your workplace* (Revised Edition). Neenah, WI: J. J. Keller & Associates, Inc.; Geller, E.S. (2001). *The psychology of safety handbook.* Boca Raton, FL: CRC Press; Geller, E.S. (2001). *Working safe: How to help people actively care for health and safety* (2nd Edition). Boca Raton, FL: CRC Press.

28. Latane, B., Williams, K., & Harkins, S. (1979). Many hands make light the work: The causes and consequences of social loafing. *Journal of Personality and Social Psychology, 37,* 822-832.

29. *The American Heritage Dictionary,* (1991). Boston, MA: Houghton Mifflin Company; *New-Merriam-Webster Dictionary* (1989). Springfield, MA: Merriam-Webster Publishers.

30. Cialdini, R.B. (2001). *Influence: Science and practice* (4th Edition). New York, NY: Harper Collins College.

31. Bird, Jr., F.E., & Davies, R. J. (1996). *Safety and the bottom line.* Loganville, GA: Febco.

CHAPTER 4

The Courage to Actively Care

E. Scott Geller

IT'S OFTEN NOT ENOUGH to know what to do in order to actively care effectively (i.e., competence) and to be motivated to perform AC4P behavior (i.e., commitment). The missing ingredient is *courage*. The same five person-states introduced in Chapter 2 as determinants of AC4P behavior are discussed here as precursors to courage.

The simple AC4P intervention strategies presented in this chapter are practical for large-scale application and evidence-based benefits. But, none have been adopted on a broad scale. Why not? Is it lack of compassion, courage, commitment, competence, self-motivation, or something else? Exploring answers to this question will help us determine the next steps in achieving an AC4P culture of compassion.

Interpersonal Intervention and Courage

As with any program designed to improve behavior, people could claim they lack the resources and/or time to implement the intervention. They could doubt the effectiveness of the AC4P technique and wonder whether the time to implement the interpersonal intervention is worth the effort.

However, these excuses are irrelevant for the techniques described here. Why? Because they are straightforward and easy to accomplish with minimal effort. More importantly, empirical research (as cited below) has demonstrated the beneficial impact of these simple interpersonal approaches to promote human welfare and/or prevent harm to people.

Standard excuses for inaction cannot work here. So what is the barrier to large-scale implementation of simple-to-use interpersonal methods that clearly benefit everyone involved?

The key word is "interpersonal". Each effective intervention method requires personal interaction with other people. It is likely many people lack the courage to intervene as an agent of change. This chapter discusses the level of courage needed, and suggests ways to develop that courage in ourselves and others.

Bottom line: What does it take for more people to become interpersonal change agents on behalf of the welfare of others? Effortless evidenced-based techniques to help people prevent harm to themselves and others are available, but at this time it seems too few people have the courage to use them.

What is Courage?

The American Heritage Dictionary[1] defines courage as "the state or quality of mind or spirit that enables one to face danger with self-possession, confidence, and resolution." This denotation is consistent with the two-page description of courage in *Wikipedia* (http://en.wikipedia.org/wiki/courage), except Wikipedia distinguishes between *physical courage* – when confronting physical pain, hardship, or threat of death, and *moral courage* – in the face of possible shame, embarrassment, or discouragement.[2]

Leaders certainly need competence and commitment to be effective change agents.[3] But, interpersonal intervention to prevent possible harm to a person (i.e., proactive AC4P behavior) takes *moral courage*. A person could have both competence and commitment in a particular situation, but not be courageous. Consider the following two authentic incidents related to AC4P, the first was dramatic and reactive while the other was temperate and proactive.

Responding to an Emergency

In the midst of a safety meeting, Joanne Dean, the safety director of a large construction firm in New Jersey is notified of a horrendous "accident." The operator of an industrial equipment truck with an attached auger was pulled into the auger by the weed mesh under the mulch on which he was standing. The worker chose not to stand on the safety platform provided for this task.

Joanne runs to help the bloody victim whose body is severed in half. She assists the on-site nurse with the AED (automated external defibrillator), covers the body parts with a blanket, and stays at the scene until the local EMS (emergency medical service) and coroner arrive.

It took commitment to step up and intervene in this horrible casualty. It's likely Joanne's competence as an emergency-response instructor contributed to her propensity to actively care, but her AC4P behavior took more than commitment and competence.

Indeed, three key safety professionals of the company that hired the construction firm chose not to intervene. They stood at a distance and watched Joanne and the other responders. We can assume these experienced, professional bystanders possessed both the competence and commitment required for their leadership positions. But on this day they appeared to lack moral courage.

Responding to a Risky Situation

While waiting in the lobby of a Fortune-500 company, Bob Veazie, a safety consultant and former culture-change agent for a Fortune-100 company, observes an at-risk behavior. A maintenance worker has climbed to the top of an eight-foot step-ladder to change a light bulb. Because the ladder is not long enough for this job, the individual is standing with one foot on the top step of the ladder. A co-worker is looking up and talking to the man on the ladder, but he's not holding the ladder steady.

Imagining a serious injury from a fall to the hard marble floor of the lobby, Bob walks to the ladder and calls up to the at-risk worker. Holding the bottom of the ladder, he requests the man to come down because, "It doesn't seem safe to stand on the top of that ladder". Then he asks whether a longer ladder is available.

Bob Veazie showed moral courage by intervening with this at-risk stranger. Bob could have faced an unpleasant confrontation, and been publicly embarrassed or humiliated Bob's competence and commitment as a safety trainer and consultant certainly contributed to his inclination to speak up. But competence and commitment were not sufficient for the moral courage he showed. In fact, Bob's training partner who has extensive competence and intense commitment for safety saw the same at-risk behavior, but she chose not say or do anything about it.

How Can Courage Be Encouraged?

Courage is a human characteristic distinct from competence and commitment. But these three qualities of leadership are interdependent to a degree. Individuals with greater competence and commitment in a given situation are more likely to demonstrate courage. One's propensity to demonstrate courage in certain circumstances is increased whenever relevant competence or commitment is augmented.

Developing Competence

As discussed in Chapter 3, behavior-focused training increases one's competence at a particular task. This involves: a) describing and demonstrating a desirable behavior or skill-set, b) giving specific behavior-based feedback during a participant's role-playing of designated target behavior(s), c) practicing the desired behavior(s) with both corrective and supportive feedback, and d) implementing the new competency in real-world situations.[4]

When learners teach this skill-set to others, their perception of competence increases further, along with their personal commitment.[5] And as I commented above, greater feelings of competence and commitment are more likely to support acts of courage.

Developing Commitment

Motivation or commitment to do something is determined by the intrinsic and extrinsic consequences of a task, as well as one's personal interpretation of those consequences.[6] While many tasks are performed for expected soon, certain, and significant consequences, we use self-talk to avoid impulsive reactive behavior and work for long-term goals.[7] Self-talk is also a potential means of overcoming anxiety and reinforcing a commitment to step up and be courageous when called upon.

Cultivating Courage

The moral courage of Joanne and Bob was due to many factors. This suggests cultivating courage is more complex and less straightforward than developing competence and commitment. For example, both Joanne and Bob are extraverts. They gain energy from interacting with people. Both are naturally outgoing and inclined to communicate with others. They would be described as having excellent "people skills."

Another of the Big Five personality traits that facilitated the courage of Joanne and Bob is conscientiousness.[8] I know each of them very well and it's obvious they each carry an AC4P mindset with them at all times – both on and off the job.

Beyond personality *traits*, certain person-*states* increase one's propensity to show AC4P courage. These person-states – self-esteem, self-efficacy, personal control, optimism, and sense of belongingness – were introduced in Chapter 2, along with ways to enhance these dispositions to increase the probability an individual will perform AC4P behavior.

Culture and the Courage to Actively Care

Many of the factors that influence one's propensity to demonstrate AC4P courage can be filed under the general label – culture. Certain cultural factors related to the development and cultivation of courage are exhibited daily by people around us. Another real-life story not only illustrates physical courage, but also demonstrates some practical strategies for promoting the moral courage needed for the kind of interpersonal intervention needed to achieve an AC4P culture.

Physical Courage to Actively Care

On January 16, 2007, Dr. Kevin Brothers, executive director of the Somerset Hills Learning Institute, was wheeled into St. Barnabas' Renal Surgery Center. He was in top physical and mental health, and had never before "gone under the knife" and experienced surgery. He received a three-hour surgical procedure – not for himself but for someone else.

Dr. Brothers donated his kidney to his mentor and professional colleague – Dr. Patricia Krantz, Executive Director of the Princeton Child Development Institute. Seven months earlier Dr. Brothers had learned Dr. Krantz was in severe kidney failure. Without a transplant, she would require dialysis within a few months.

Dr. Krantz was not aware that Dr. Brothers and several other colleagues had agreed to donate one of their kidneys to her. Among all of Dr. Krantz's family, friends, and colleagues who received extensive blood work and tissue sampling, there was only one viable match – Kevin Brothers.

The difference between physical and moral courage is evident in the three real-world incidents I have described here. When we risk social embarrassment or interpersonal confrontation on behalf of another person's welfare, we show *moral* courage. In contrast, when we risk physical harm to ourselves when looking out for another person's well-being, we demonstrate *physical courage*.[2] While Joanne Dean and Bob Veazie demonstrated moral courage, Kevin Brothers' elective surgery exemplifies physical courage.

The AC4P courage of Dr. Brothers was extraordinary. Beyond a number of person factors, including Dr. Brothers' self-esteem, self-efficacy, personal control, optimism and sense of belongingness, a number of cultural factors facilitated this display of courage. Let's consider these cultural factors as potential guidelines for promoting AC4P courage in your culture.

A Group Commitment. Dr. Brothers' first courageous act was to pledge to give one of his kidneys to Dr. Krantz. When Kevin talked with me prior to his surgery, he admitted it was relatively easy to muster the courage to sign the donor pledge. The probability of him being the best antigen match was seemingly low. Surely one of Dr. Krantz's family members would be a better match.

Although surprised he was the best match, Dr. Brothers affirmed strong motivation to honor his commitment to the group of potential donors. He acknowledged the value of this two-part approach to motivate his AC4P behavior – first the promise and then the action. This two-step approach is applicable to many situations.

Suppose each member of a work team signed a group declaration to give each other corrective feedback wherever they saw behavior that could jeopardize the quality or the safety of their job. This commitment could be called a "Declaration of Interdependence." In fact this was the label on a large poster at a leadership seminar for supervisors, safety leaders, and maintenance personnel of Delta Airlines.[9] The commitment poster was signed by more than 100 Delta employees, and is prominently displayed in the maintenance workers' break room at the Hartsfield-Jackson International Airport in Atlanta, GA. (This practical AC4P intervention is explained further in the next chapter, along with photos of the poster signing and the theoretical foundation.)

This group obligation, given voluntarily and publicly within a supportive social context, helps to sustain the moral courage required to give behavior-based feedback. Such courage increases the probability workers deliver AC4P coaching communications to their peers.

Group Support. Both before and after his surgery, Dr. Brothers received substantial social support for his physical courage. This is often crucial in deciding to move forward in a courageous way. His wife Debbie, a registered nurse, and their four daughters totally supported Kevin's decision "to move ahead to give *our* kidney as soon as possible". Dr. Brothers said, "*Our* kidney, because this was a well-informed family decision made with the support of Debbie and our girls." Dr. Brothers' courage was also aided by the dedicated support group of friends and colleagues who pledged to donate a kidney.

Two weeks after a successful surgery, Kevin Brothers returned to work. "What an outpouring of support our family received from our school's parents and staff," reported Debbie Brothers. The parents and staff of the Princeton Child Development Institute were also extremely supportive, sending thank-you cards to Dr. Brothers for helping to prolong Dr. Krantz's life and enable her to continue her important work worldwide.

Substantial research reports verify the beneficial impact of social support on human performance, from enhancing motivation to engage in a challenging task to facilitating recovery from physical illness and injury[10] (e.g., see my cancer story in Chapter 22). This factor relates directly to the person-state of belongingness.

If you feel you belong to a social network or circle of friends or peers, this increases your inclination to actively care for another individual's health, safety, or general well-being. If that AC4P behavior requires an act of courage, strong feelings of belonging create a sense of responsibility or obligation to not disappoint the group. Cultivating social support throughout a particular culture is extremely beneficial to increasing the courage factor and the frequency of AC4P behavior.

Various interpersonal activities can enhance social support and courage, including team goal setting, interpersonal coaching, collaborative work projects, and group celebrations (as described in Chapter 3). Relationship-building conversations are also critical. Methods for cultivating and increasing social support are reflected in the various AC4P applications discussed in Parts II and III of this book.

A Trusting Culture. When Kevin Brothers honored his pledge to give Patricia Krantz one of his kidneys, his courage was bolstered by his feeling that all of the others in his special donor group would follow through on their commitment if they had the best antigen match. He also trusted the expert medical staff at St. Barnabas Medical Center would give Dr. Krantz and him the very best healthcare. He expected a successful kidney transplant.

The topic of interpersonal trust, including the need to distinguish between trusting an individual's ability vs. his/her intentions, is addressed in Chapter 3, as well as in other publications.[11] In Chapter 3, I explained specific ways to increase interpersonal trust. In addition, you might consider asking colleagues or co-workers how specific events, policies, or communications impact their trust levels, and their courage to speak up about safety issues or risks.

Solicit ideas to eliminate barriers to interpersonal trust and nurture courage. Add policies and/or procedures that could enhance people's perception they can trust the intentions and abilities of their supervisors and co-workers. A number of practical action plans will likely result from this process, many similar to those suggested in Chapter 3. Still, just the process of soliciting ways to impact interpersonal trust will have a positive trust-building and courage-building effect.

A Common Worthwhile Purpose. Dr. Brothers and his colleagues in the kidney-donor group admired and greatly appreciated the teaching and research of Dr. Patricia Krantz. Indeed, Dr. Krantz has pioneered the application of behavioral science for the treatment of autism, and she mentored Dr. Brothers while he was a research intern and Ph.D. student. In Dr. Brother's words, "Dr. Krantz gave me the opportunity to learn science, and her teachings continue to be the underpinnings of my career… (and) her guiding me into the field of autism treatment has given more children a chance for a better life".

The group that pledged to donate a kidney for Dr. Krantz had a common and commendable purpose. Likewise, advocates for an AC4P culture have a common and worthwhile mission. In fact, there is perhaps no more esteemed purpose than to actively care for another person's health, safety, and general welfare.

A Family Mindset

It certainly takes more courage to actively care for a stranger than a colleague. In fact, attending to the safety and/or welfare of a family member is usually not even considered courageous but rather an obligation. As I proposed in Chapter 2 (see Figure 2.6), when members of a work team think of their co-workers as "family," actively caring for the well-being of these individuals becomes more an act of commitment than courage.

The probability of AC4P behavior is increased whenever interpersonal behavior supports a family mindset among friends, colleagues, or co-workers. Figure 4.1

illustrates this proposed relationship between the degree of courage needed for interpersonal AC4P behavior and the degree of relatedness or interpersonal connection between the person needing help and the observer.

It's unlikely many readers would undergo elective surgery to give a kidney to a stranger. Fortunately, AC4P does not require the *physical courage* shown by Dr. Brothers.

Indeed, proactive AC4P behavior doesn't require any physical courage – only the *moral courage* to face possible embarrassment, rejection or conflict when giving feedback or advice to improve another person's behavior, or giving personal approval to reward the AC4P behavior of another person. A supportive *family* mindset among people removes the fear of negative consequences from such proactive and behavior-focused actively caring.

Actually, many AC4P actions do not require courage; they only present an inconvenience. If you saw a member of your immediate family get behind the steering wheel of a vehicle and neglect to buckle up, you would not hesitate to intervene. Courage would hardly enter the picture.

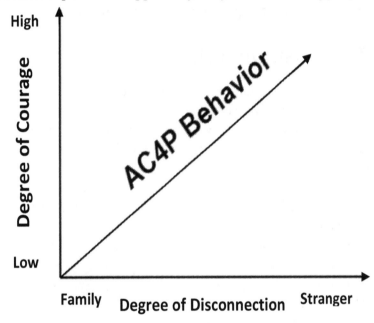

Figure 4.1. The amount of courage needed to actively care increases directly with the degree of disconnection between the observer and the person in need of assistance.

But what would you do if you got in a hotel shuttle van at the airport and noticed the driver and several passengers did not buckle up? Would you offer some proactive AC4P corrective feedback? Would you have the moral courage to intervene on behalf of these at-risk strangers?

You have several excuses for not speaking up, right? It's only a short trip to the hotel and the probability of a crash is miniscule. These folks are adults, and if they want to travel at-risk, that's their choice. Plus, if you say something about this, another occupant might be offended by your meddling and call you a "safety nerd".

So why actively care in this situation? Here's a thought: Consider that your moral courage sets a memorable leadership example. Such behavior could start a constructive AC4P conversation and initiate a ripple effect of AC4P behavior.

Contemplating one's lack of moral courage can activate some disconcerting tension between what an individual thinks s/he *would* do in this and similar situations versus what the person knows s/he *should* do. The more one holds AC4P as a personal value, the greater the tension or cognitive dissonance.[12] Following through with moral courage relieves such tension and exemplifies AC4P leadership.

The following simple and convenient AC4P intervention strategies are straightforward and effortless, and they exemplify the kind of AC4P leadership needed to cultivate an AC4P culture.

Question: Do you have the moral courage to apply any of these, and encourage others to do the same? Implementing these on a large scale would move us one step closer to achieving our vision of an AC4P culture of compassion. And for the most part, they really do not require a great amount of courage.

The Flash-for-Life

Developed initially in 1984 and replicated in several other situations, this rather intrusive but effective intervention merely involves the change agent holding up a card to request a certain safety-related behavior (i.e., vehicle safety-belt use); and if the target individual complies, the "flasher" flips the card over to reveal "Thank You". The top illustration shows my daughter, Karly, at age 3 1/2 holding up the 11 by 14 inch sign to an unbuckled driver at an intersection. When the driver buckled up, she turned over the bright yellow sign with bold black lettering to say "Thank you". Note the ABC

(activator-behavior-consequence) contingency of this intervention.

Here the courage factor is minimized by the physical distance between the actions taking place. In our first study, the "flasher" was positioned in the passenger seat of a vehicle stopped in the left lane at an intersection.[13] Table 4.1 depicts the impact of this simple intervention by specifying the percentage of vehicle drivers who buckled up after viewing the flashcard.

As shown in Table 4.1, seven different vehicle passengers of varying ages, ranging from 3.5 to 23 years of age, "flashed" a total of 787 unbuckled drivers in Blacksburg, Virginia, home of Virginia Tech; whereas only two of these passengers (i.e., Tim and Hollie) showed the Flash-for-Life

card to 300 passengers in the adjacent rural town of Christiansburg, Virginia.

Some drivers did not turn their head to look at the sign, and therefore the compliance percentages are based on only those unbuckled drivers who looked directly at the sign. It's noteworthy this prompting intervention was more successful in the university town than in Christiansburg (i.e., an average of 24.6 vs. 13.7 percent compliance, respectively). The age of the "flasher" did not have a reliable effect on the driver's compliance with the buckle-up prompt.

It's worth noting that this intervention did not result in any verbal or physical harassment. Although the "flasher" did get a few hand signals which didn't mean right or left turn. When my daughter asked, "What do they mean, Daddy," I told her they were signaling, "You're number one, they're just using the wrong finger." Incidentally, none of these one-finger hand signals came from females.

The first applications of the "Flash for Life" occurred before safety-belt use laws, when only about 20% of U.S. drivers buckled up. Twenty years later, with about 80% of U.S. drivers using their vehicle safety belts, my students and I compared the impact of a positive reminder ("Please Buckle Up I Care") with the more common negative-reinforcement prompt (i.e., "Click it or Ticket") on both behavioral compliance and body language.[14]

Table 4.1. Summary of "Flash for Life" Results[13]					
Flasher (Name & Age)	Number of Observations	Number Who looked	Number Who buckled	Percentage Who Looked	Percentage Who Buckled
Blacksburg, VA					
Karly *age 3 ½*	179	154	37	86.0	24.0
David *age 5*	31	21	5	67.7	23.8
Abby *age 7*	68	47	16	69.1	34.0
Carrie *age 7*	64	48	9	75.0	18.8
Dane *age 10*	56	43	6	76.8	14.0
Hollie *age 22*	206	177	43	85.9	24.3
Tim *age 23*	183	148	41	80.3	27.6
Total	**787**	**634**	**157**	**80.9**	**24.6**
Christiansburg, VA					
Tim *age 22*	145	123	19	84.8	15.4
Hollie *age 23*	155	133	16	85.8	12.0
Total	**300**	**256**	**35**	**85.3**	**13.7**

Table 4.2 (on the next page) reveals the percentage of unbuckled drivers who buckled up after viewing one of the two types of cards. This table also shows the percentage of drivers giving positive vs. negative hand signals and facial expressions per type of prompt. It's noteworthy the positive "I Care" prompt was not only more effective at activating buckle-up behavior than the threatening reminder, it also prompted more positive and less negative body language than did the negative-reinforcement prompt (all p's < .05).

Intervention Sign	Percentage who Buckled-Up	Percentage of Positive Hand Gestures	Percentage of Negative Hand Gestures	Percentage of Positive Expressions	Percentage of Negative Expressions
Flash for Life n=895	33.6%	13.2%	.9%	25.0%	3.9%
Click it or Ticket n=927	25.6%	7.8%	2.6%	18.9%	9.2%

Table 4.2. Summary of Results from Positive vs. Negative Buckle-Up Prompting[14]

The AC4P-Behavior Promise Card

This nonintrusive and straightforward strategy is suitable for numerous circumstances and target behaviors.[15] It requires little in the way of courage. It has been used effectively to increase the occurrence of specific safety-related behavior (e.g., the use of safety glasses, gloves, and vehicle safety belts)[16] as well as to promote an interdependent AC4P paradigm or mindset.[17]

Based on the powerful social-influence principle of consistency,[18] this behavior-change tactic merely asks participants to sign an individual "promise card" or a "group pledge" that declares an explicit commitment to regularly perform a particular AC4P behavior for a specified period of time.

For maximum behavioral impact, the pledge-card signing should be public and

AC4P Promise Card

I promise to _____

_____

From _____ until _____

_____
signature   date

voluntary. A generic promise card is depicted below that can be used to increase the occurrence of a number of AC4P behaviors.

The AC4P Polite Light

Taking on the negative emotions of road-rage driving would seem to call for a greater degree of courage. But not so in this case. It involves the use of a vehicle light to signal a simple "Courtesy Code" under relevant conditions. Specifically, one flash means "Please," two flashes reflect "Thank You," and three flashes are used to signal "I am sorry". Vehicle emergency lights can be used to flash this "1-2-3 code," or a small green light as shown here can be affixed to the vehicle's rear window and operated with the convenient push of a button.

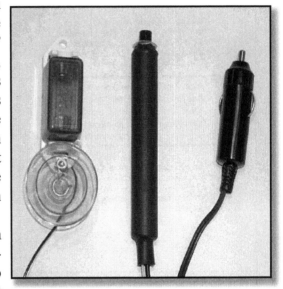

In a community-wide evaluation of this intervention strategy, the polite-driving code was promoted on radio stations and billboards throughout the town of Christiansburg, Virginia, and "polite lights" were distributed at various workshops. Results were encouraging, but the idea was not adopted.

The success of this intervention relied not on courage but on marketing and outreach, and then for people to use the Courtesy Driving Code. Marketing and the minor inconvenience of flashing the Courtesy Code were key barriers that prevented this AC4P behavior from large-scale use. So far, anyway. (More details of our evaluation of this potential "Road-Rage Reducer" are given in Chapter 15.

The Airline Lifesaver

Flying in an airplane requires courage for some people to the degree they need medication to reduce anxiety. Others never think of the risks involved in flying.

For this particular AC4P intervention, courage is needed for one-on-one interaction with a stranger. The 3 X 5 inch card depicted on the next page can be handed to the flight attendant when boarding an airplane. It requests the following announcement be made after landing: "Now that you have worn a seat belt for the safest part of your trip, the flight crew would like to remind you to buckle up during your ground transportation".

To intervene with busy flight attendants by handing them this card and requesting they add on an announcement at the flight's conclusion doesn't require much in the way of courage. Of course there is the fear of possible rejection. "No, I don't have the time."

THE AIRLINE LIFESAVER

Airlines have been the *most effective pro-moters* of seat belt use. Please, would someone in your flight crew consider announcing a statement like the following near the end of the flight.

> *"Now that you have worn a seat belt for the safest part of your trip -- the flight crew would like to remind you to buckle-up during your ground transportation."*

This announcement will show that your airline cares about transportation safety. And who knows -- you might start the buckle-up habit for someone and help save a life! Thank you.

But what this exercise demonstrates is the more committed you are to AC4P, the more passionate you feel about it, the easier it is to risk rejection and go ahead with this simple and convenient intervention. It's also easier if you have extroverted people skills, such as Joanne and Bob in the stories told earlier.

The first Lifesaver Card shown here is the first one I used, beginning in 1985. In 1994, I began using an incentive card that offered the flight attendants a prize if they read the announcement. The back of this card is depicted below, which specifies an *if-then reward contingency.* Later, I alternated the distribution of these two types of reminders to determine the impact of an incentive intervention.

A 17-year study demonstrated substantial compliance with this Airline Lifesaver request,[19] but no current airline has adopted this simple safety-based intervention. And, I know of no individual using this technique consistently when boarding an airplane.

When the request was made without an incentive (i.e., prompt only), 35.5% of 798 recipients read the message. However, when the flight attendant was offered a prize for delivering the buckle-up reminder, 53.3% of 245 recipients complied with the request.

Of course, showing that many flight attendants read the buckle-up reminder when asked to do so does not reveal behavior change directly related to people's welfare. Indeed, it is rare to see such direct benefits of proactive efforts to prevent personal

After you read the "buckle-up reminder," a passenger will give you a coupon redeemable for various prizes.

1 coupon	.... $5.00 *
2 coupons	.... $15.00
3 coupons	.... $30.00

(* Prize equivalent)

For more information call (703) 231-8145
Center for Applied Behavior Systems

injury.

However, two behavior-change benefits of the Airline Lifesaver have been documented.[20] In one case, a passenger who heard the buckle-up reminder asked the driver of the airport commuter van to buckle up, claiming "If a flight attendant can request safety-belt use, so can I."

For a second testimony, I received a letter from a passenger who said he used the back-seat safety belt in a taxi cab because he had just heard the buckle-up reminder at the end of his flight. Traveling over 70 mph, the taxi hydroplaned on a wet road and struck the guardrail. Serious injuries were prevented because this person had buckled up. The actual letter from this individual is printed in my first book on the psychology of safety.[21]

The Driver-Training Score Card

As mentioned earlier, it often requires less moral or physical courage to actively care for family members than for strangers, like in a class of workplace safety trainees. But here is an intervention that has proven successful in both applications.

More than 15 years ago, I documented an effective behavior-change intervention for driver training, which led to numerous adaptations in work settings.[21] Specifically, I worked with my 15-year-old daughter to develop a critical behavior checklist (CBC) for driving. As detailed in Chapter 1, this CBC lists a number of driving-related behaviors, along with columns to record whether each behavior is safe or at-risk, and a column to write comments relevant for a follow-up feedback session.

While much research and even common sense indicates this process works to improve safety-related behaviors, I am unaware of a single adoption of this technique for driver education/training. However, this behavior-change technique is the foundation of behavior-based safety (BBS), and there is much empirical support for the BBS approach to increasing safety-related behaviors and preventing injuries.[22]

As introduced in Chapter 1, BBS has evolved to people-based safety (PBS) and now to AC4P, and more details regarding this approach to cultivating an AC4P workplace are given in Part II of this book.

The Taxi-Cab Feedback Card

At keynote addresses to large audiences, I have proposed that safety leaders record the safety-related driving behaviors of cab, bus, and limo drivers on a simple observation-feedback card; and after the trip, show the results to the driver for valuable behavior-based feedback.[23]

A sample feedback card, applicable in numerous driving situations, is shown on the next page. The top half of the card is given to the driver, while the bottom half has a return address and stamp on the back. This enables tracking of the driver behaviors observed by the passengers of public-transport vehicles.

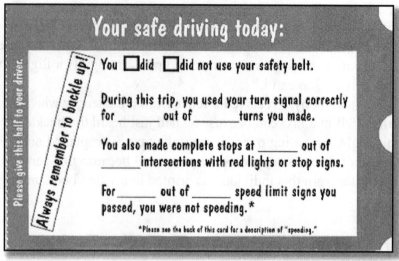

This observation-and-feedback technique reflects another adaption of a basic process of BBS, applied in industries worldwide with remarkable improvements in injury statistics. However, I know of no large-scale application of this evidence-based process for public transportation. It does take substantial moral courage to use this proactive AC4P strategy in taxi cabs, limos, and buses.

The AC4P Thank-You Card

For many years, I have promoted the use of a simple thank-you card for delivery to people following their performance of AC4P behavior.[24] In fact, "thank-you cards" have been customized for particular industrial sites and educational settings. For example, I have distributed the "Virginia Tech Thank-You Card" depicted in Chapter 2 (p. 47) for more than 20 years.

Every semester I make these cards available for my students to use to acknowledge the AC4P behavior of others, but relatively few students take them. Student leaders in our Center for Applied Behavior Systems (CABS) have regularly used this recognition technique for more than two decades, because this recognition process has been institutionalized in our CABS culture. However, beyond applications in CABS, university use of a thank-you card is rare.

Given the power, generic applicability and relative convenience of one-to-one recognition, it's appropriate to end this chapter with evidence-based details about how to give and receive interpersonal recognition. Both prior chapters in Part I on the theoretical and research foundation of AC4P refer to one-to-one recognition.

In Chapter 2, "Actively Caring Thank-You Cards" were introduced as a mechanism to cultivate a sense of connectedness and AC4P throughout an organization. In Chapter 3, I discussed interpersonal recognition within the context of supportive feedback to sustain and potentially increase the occurrence of AC4P behavior. Here I offer specific behavioral strategies for delivering and receiving recognition. First, it's critical to understand and believe in the importance of giving quality AC4P recognition.

In terms of the courage factor, it's worth noting many people are uncomfortable communicating rather intimately on a one-to-one, face-to-face basis. But the value of this sort of interaction makes it important to use whatever means you have at your disposal to overcome fears of interpersonal interaction. Ask for coaching on this critical skill-set. Observe others competent at up-close-and-personal interaction and model techniques that fit your style.

We Learn More from Success

"We can't learn unless we make mistakes." How many times have you heard this? This might make us feel better about the errors of our ways, and provide an excuse for focusing more on people's failures than on their successes, but in reality nothing could be further from the truth.

Behavioral scientists have shown convincingly that success – not failure – produces the most effective learning.[25] Edward Lee Thorndike, for example, studied intelligence at the start of the last century by putting chickens, cats, dogs, fish, monkeys, and humans in situations that called for problem-solving behavior. He then systematically observed how these organisms learned. He coined the "Law of Effect" to refer to the fact that learning depends upon behavioral consequences.

When a behavior is followed by a "satisfying state of affairs" the probability of that behavior occurring again is increased. But, if an "*annoying* state of affairs" follows a behavior, that behavior (considered an error) is less likely to recur.[26]

Which kind of consequence – positive or negative – leads to the most learning? Does an error have to occur in order to solve a problem? We can reflect on our own experiences to answer these questions. A pleasant consequence gives us direction and motivation to continue the behavior. We know what we did to receive the reward, and are thus motivated to earn another.

In contrast, a negative consequence following a mistake only tells us what not to do.

It provides no specific direction for problem solution. An overemphasis on a mistake can be frustrating and discouraging, and de-motivate us to continue the learning process.

Errors are not necessary for learning to occur. In fact, when training results in no errors, made possible with certain presentation techniques, learning occurs most smoothly and is most enjoyable. Errors disrupt the teaching/learning process and can lead to a negative attitude, especially if negative social consequences accentuate the mistake. Even subtle reactions to an error – a disappointed face or verbal tone – can increase feelings of helplessness or despair and turn a person off to the entire learning process.

From the courage perspective, the less focus and talk of errors, the less courage is called for. Offering positive consequences (e.g., supportive feedback) requires substantially less courage, right?

The antidote to depressed learning from the negative consequences of incorrect behavior is to provide positive consequence for correct behavior. And the most powerful positive consequence to support a learning process is interpersonal recognition – the theme of this discussion. Below I offer seven guidelines for giving quality AC4P recognition.

Before leaving this topic of learning from success versus failure, it's noteworthy that Thorndike referred to the type of learning discovered in his problem-solving situations as "trial and accidental success."[26] Many textbook authors have used the term "trial-and-error learning" when describing Thorndike's research, even though Thorndike himself opposed the term because of its inaccurate implications. But let's not focus on this error; rather consider the need to support AC4P behavior with quality recognition.

1. Be Timely.

In order for recognition to provide optimal direction and support, it needs to be associated directly with the desired behavior. This is not necessarily an act of courage, but recognition should be delivered promptly. People need to know what they did to earn the appreciation. Then they might be motivated to continue that behavior.

If it's necessary to delay the recognition, the conversation should relive the activity deserving recognition. Talk specifically about the behavior warranting special acknowledgement. Don't hesitate to ask the recipient to recall aspects of the situation and the commendable behavior. This enables direction and motivation to continue the desired behavior.

2. Make It Personal.

Recognition is most meaningful when it's perceived as personal. Recognition should not be generic, fit for any situation, as in "Nice job". Rather, it needs to be customized to fit a particular individual and circumstance. This happens naturally when the recognition is linked to designated behavior.

When you recognize someone, you are expressing personal thanks. Sometimes it's tempting to say "*we* appreciate" rather than "*I* appreciate," and to refer to company gratitude rather than *personal appreciation.* Speaking for the company can come across as impersonal and insincere.

Of course, it's appropriate to reflect value to the organization when giving recognition, but the focus should be personal. "I saw what you did to support our AC4P process and I really appreciate it. Your example illustrates the kind of leadership we need around here to achieve an AC4P culture." This second statement illustrates the next guideline for quality recognition. Again, being positive and proactive shouldn't require that much courage, but some people are not at ease delivering interpersonal praise.

3. Take It to a Higher Level.

Recognition is most memorable and inspirational when it reflects a higher-order quality. Adding a universal attitude like leadership, integrity, trustworthiness, or AC4P to your recognition statement makes the recognition more meaningful and thus rewarding. It's important to state the specific behavior first, and then make an obvious linkage between the behavior and the positive attribute it reflects.

Our attempts to get college students to recognize others for their AC4P behavior have been less successful than desired. Many claim they didn't observe AC4P behavior worthy of special recognition, whereas others admit lack of courage to present a thank-you card or a Hershey PayDay candy bar (labeled "Pay-It-Forward") as a reward for AC4P behavior.

Some say, "It's unnatural or silly," while others resist because it could come across as manipulative. A sincere verbal "Thank You" is okay, they declare, "But giving someone a material reward could be seen as a ploy to control them."

One of my graduate students claimed he's more comfortable rewarding a stranger with a candy bar or a thank-you card than a friend because, "The embarrassment of using a behavior modification technique would be more personal and aversive among close friends than strangers."

My comeback is, "It's all in the delivery." My students hear this and review the seven steps given here for giving quality AC4P recognition, but the use of thank-you cards and candy bars to recognize AC4P behavior has not markedly increased. However, we have found less resistance to passing on an AC4P wristband when the wristband is viewed as more than a reward for behavior.

More specifically, when the wristband is presented as a symbol of AC4P leadership and worn to show membership in an elite group of individuals dedicated to cultivating an AC4P culture of compassion, my students show more interest and willingness to participate in such a recognition process. The AC4P wristband is given to not only reward AC4P behavior, but to signify membership in a Movement to cultivate AC4P cultures of compassion.

This connection brings the interpersonal recognition to a higher level, enabling positive impact on this recipient's self-esteem, competence, and sense of interdependency and belongingness. As mentioned earlier, courage should not be a significant issue here, but the depth of commitment and passion regarding AC4P can make a difference when "taking it to a higher level."

4. Deliver It Privately.

Because quality recognition is personal and indicative of higher-order attributes, it needs to be delivered in private and one-on-one. This requires a certain degree of courage for those not comfortable in private, one-on-one conversations; especially with people they don't know well. But consider this: The recognition is special and only relevant to one person. So, it will mean more and seem more genuine if it's given from one individual to another.

It seems conventional to recognize individuals in front of a group. This approach is typified in athletic contests and reflected in the pop psychology slogan, "Praise publicly and reprimand privately." Many managers take the lead from this common-sense statement and give individuals recognition in group settings.

Indeed, isn't it maximally rewarding to be held up as an exemplar in front of one's peers? Not necessarily, because many people feel embarrassed when singled out in front of a group.

Part of this embarrassment could be due to fear of subsequent harassment by peers. Some peers might call the recognized individual an "apple-polisher" or "brown-noser," or accuse him or her of "sucking up to management."

When I was in fifth grade, my teacher recognized me in front of the class for doing "an excellent job" on my homework. As depicted in the illustration, I was so embarrassed. Then after school, a gang of boys beat me up on the playground. Unfortunately, that teacher never found out the negative side-effect of her public recognition.

In athletic events the participants' performance is measured fairly and the winners are objectively determined.

However in educational and work settings it's usually impossible to assess everyone's relevant behaviors objectively and obtain a fair ranking for individual recognition.

Therefore, praising one individual in public may lead to perceptions of favoritism from individuals who feel they did equally well, but did not get praised. Plus, such ranking sets up a win-lose atmosphere – perhaps appropriate for sporting events but not in settings where interdependent teamwork is needed to achieve group goals.

It's beneficial, of course, to recognize teams of workers for their accomplishments, and this can be done in a group setting, as I discussed in Chapter 3. Since individual responsibility is diffused or dispersed across the group, there is minimal risk of individual embarrassment or later peer harassment.

However, as I indicated in the prior chapter, it's important to realize that group achievement is rarely the result of equal input from all team members. Some take the lead and work harder, while others "loaf" and count on the group effort to make them look good. Thus, it's important to deliver personal and private recognition to those individuals who went beyond the call of duty for the sake of their team.

5. Let It Sink In.

In this fast-paced age of trying to do more with less, we try to communicate as much as possible when we finally get in touch with a busy person. After recognizing an individual's special AC4P effort, we are tempted to tag on a bunch of unrelated statements, even a request for additional behavior. This comes across as, "I appreciate what you've done, but I need more."

It does take a certain amount of courage or "guts" to tell someone, "I need more out of you". All the more reason to drop the request and let the praise sink in.

Resist the temptation to do more than praise the AC4P behavior you saw. If you have additional points to discuss, it's best to reconnect later, after the rewarding recognition has had a chance to sink in and become a part of the individual's self-talk for self-recognition and self-motivation.

By giving quality AC4P recognition, we give people a script they can use to reward their own behavior. In other words, our quality recognition strengthens the other person's self-reward system. And, positive self-talk (or self-recognition) is critical for long-term maintenance of AC4P behavior. Thus, by allowing our recognition communication to stand alone and soak in, we enable the internalization of rewarding words that can be used later for self-motivation of additional AC4P behavior.

6. Use Tangibles for Symbolic Value.

Tangible rewards can detract from the self-motivation aspect of quality recognition. If the focus of an AC4P recognition process is placed on a material reward, the words of appreciation can seem less significant. In turn, the beneficial impact on one's self-motivation is lessened.

On the other hand, tangible rewards can add to the quality of interpersonal recognition if they are delivered as tokens of appreciation. Rewards that include a relevant AC4P slogan, as on the AC4P wristband, can help to promote the desired behavior. But how you deliver a tangible reward will determine whether it adds to or subtracts from the long-term benefit of your praise.

The benefit of interpersonal recognition is weakened if the tangible is viewed as a payoff for the AC4P behavior. However, if the reward is seen as symbolic of going beyond the call of duty for another person's well-being, it strengthens the praise. Have the courage to tell it like it is: The AC4P wristband or another tangible reward is a token of appreciation or a symbol of going beyond the call.

7. Consider Secondhand Recognition.

Up to this point, I've been discussing one-on-one verbal communication in which one person recognizes another for a particular AC4P behavior. It's also possible to recognize a person's outstanding efforts indirectly, and such an approach can have special advantages. Suppose, for example, you overhear me talk to another person about your outstanding presentation about the AC4P Movement. How will this secondhand recognition affect you? Will you believe my words of praise were genuine?

Sometimes people are suspicious of the genuineness of praise when it's delivered face-to-face. Is there an ulterior motive? Perhaps a favor is expected in return. Or maybe the recognition is seen merely as an extension of a communication exercise and thus devalued as sincere appreciation. Secondhand recognition, however, is not as easily tainted with these potential biases. Therefore, its genuineness is less suspect.

Suppose I tell you someone in your workgroup told me about the superb job you did leading a certain group meeting. What will be the impact of this type of secondhand recognition? Chances are you'll consider the recognition authentic because I was only reporting what someone else said. Because that person reported your success to me rather than you, there was no ulterior motive for the indirect praise.

Such secondhand praise can build a sense of belongingness or group cohesion among individuals. When you learn someone was bragging about your behavior, your sense of friendship with that person will likely increase.

As I emphasized in Chapter 3 when discussing trust-building, gossip can be beneficial – *if it's positive*. When we talk about the achievement of others in behavior-specific terms, we begin a cycle of positive communication that can support desired behavior, as well as activate self-talk for self-recognition and self-motivation.

Have the courage to initiate this cycle of positivism. We also set an example for the kind of interpersonal communication that enhances self-esteem, self-efficacy, personal control, optimism, and group cohesion. As explained in Chapter 2, these are the very person-states that increase the potential for AC4P behavior and the achievement of an interdependent culture of compassion.

A Summary

Referring to classic learning research, I made the case that success is more important than failure in developing and maintaining desired behaviors. This emphasis on success rather than corrective feedback should lessen the need for courage. It's usually more important to recognize people for their correct behaviors than to criticize them for their mistakes. But how we recognize people dramatically influences the impact of our interpersonal interaction. I offered seven basic guidelines to consider when planning to recognize others for their AC4P contributions.

This list of guidelines is not exhaustive, but it does cover the basics. Following these guidelines will increase the positive impact of interpersonal recognition. The most important point is that more recognition for AC4P behavior is needed, whether given firsthand or indirectly through positive gossip. It only takes a few seconds to deliver quality AC4P recognition.

Start giving AC4P recognition today – even for behaviors that occurred yesterday. Delayed recognition is better than no recognition. And, quality recognition does not need to occur face-to-face. Leaving a behavior-based and personal recognition message on phone-mail, e-mail, or in a written memo (formal or informal) can make a person's day. It shows you appreciate what you saw and helps to build that person's self-recognition script for later self-motivation. This behavior takes minimal courage and can reap benefits far greater than the little inconvenience required.

Perhaps realizing the positive impact we can have on people's behaviors and attitudes with relatively little effort will be self-motivating enough for us to muster the courage, if that is what is needed, to do more recognizing. Even more important, however, are the social consequences we receive when attempting to give quality recognition.

The reaction of the people who are recognized can have a dramatic impact on whether AC4P recognition increases or decreases throughout a culture. We need to know how to respond to recognition in order to assure quality AC4P recognition continues. This is our next and final topic of this chapter.

Accept Recognition Well

Most of us get so little recognition from others we are caught completely off guard when acknowledged for our commendable actions. We don't know how to accept recognition when it finally comes. Don't shy away when it does come; have the courage to embrace it.

Remember the basic behavioral-science principle: Consequences influence preceding behaviors. Thus, quality recognition increases the probability the behavior recognized will continue, and one's reaction to the recognition influences whether the behavior of recognizing someone will be attempted again. It's crucial to react appropriately when we receive recognition from others. Let's consider seven basic guidelines for receiving recognition.

1. Don't Deny or Disclaim.

Often when I attempt to give quality AC4P recognition, I get a reaction that implies I'm wasting my time. I get disclaimer statements such as, "It really was nothing special" or, "Just doing my job." The most common reply: "No problem." This implies the commendable behavior is not special and should not have been recognized.

We need to accept recognition without denial and disclaimer statements, and without deflecting the credit to others. It's okay to show pride in our small-win accomplishments, even if others contributed to the successful outcome. After all, the vision of a compassionate AC4P culture includes everyone going beyond the call of duty for the well-being of others. In this context, numerous people deserve recognition daily.

Accept that recognition will be intermittent at best for everyone; and when your turn comes, accept the recognition for your most recent AC4P behavior and for the many prior AC4P behaviors you performed that went unnoticed. Keep in mind your genuine appreciation of the recognition will increase the chance that more recognition will be given by others.

2. Listen Actively.

Listen actively to the person giving you recognition. You want to learn what you did, right? Plus, you can evaluate whether the recognition is given well. If the recognition does not pinpoint a particular behavior, you might ask the person, "What did I do to deserve this?" This will help to improve that person's method of giving recognition.

Of course, it's important not to seem critical but rather to show genuine appreciation for the special attention. Consider how difficult, yes how courageous, it is for many people to go out of their way to recognize others. So, revel in the fact you're receiving some recognition, even if its quality could be improved.

3. Relive It Later for Self-Motivation.

Most of your AC4P behaviors will go unnoticed. You perform many of these when no one else is around to observe you. Even when other people are available, they will likely be so preoccupied with their own routines they won't notice your extra effort. So when you finally do receive recognition for AC4P behavior, take it in as well-deserved.

Don't hesitate to relive this moment later by talking to yourself. Such self-recognition can motivate you to continue going beyond the call of duty on behalf of other people's well-being. As mentioned earlier, self-talk can help you muster the courage to perform more AC4P behavior.

4. Show Sincere Appreciation.

You need to show sincere gratitude with a smile, a "Thank You," and perhaps special words like, "You've made my day." Your reaction to being recognized can determine whether similar recognition is apt to occur again. So be prepared to offer a sincere "Thank You" and words that reflect your pleasure in the memorable interaction. And consider the courage the other person might have needed to give you your recognition.

I find it natural to add, "You've made my day" to the "Thank-You" because it's the truth. When people go out of their way to offer me quality recognition, they *have* made my day. I often relive such situations to improve a later day.

5. Reward the Recognizer.

When you accept recognition well, you reward the person for their appreciation. This can motivate that individual to do more recognizing, especially if the person is more of an introvert and requires courage to step out and speak up to give recognition.

Sometimes, you can do even more to assure the occurrence of more quality recognition. Specifically, you can recognize the person for recognizing you. You might say, for example, "I really appreciate you noticing my AC4P behavior and calling me a leader of the AC4P Movement." Such rewarding feedback provides direction and motivation for those aspects of the AC4P recognition process that are especially worthwhile and need to become routine.

6. Embrace the Reciprocity Norm.

Some people resist receiving recognition because they don't want to feel obligated to give recognition to others. This is the reciprocity norm at work. If we want to achieve an AC4P culture, we need to embrace this norm. When you are nice to others, as when providing them with special praise, you increase the likelihood they will reciprocate by showing similar behavior. You might not receive the returned favor, but someone will.[27] See Chapter 5 for more on the cascading effect of reciprocity.

It's important to realize your genuine acceptance of quality recognition will activate the reciprocity norm; and the more this norm is activated from positive interpersonal communication, the greater the frequency of interpersonal recognition and AC4P behavior.

So accept recognition well, and embrace the reciprocity norm. The result will be more interpersonal involvement consistent with the vision of an AC4P culture of compassion. Again, interpersonal involvement does not come easy to all of us. The quality of AC4P interactions can go a long way to easing one's resistance to involvement.

7. Ask for Recognition.

If you feel you deserve recognition, why not ask for it? In terms of courage, yes, asking for praise is easier if you are an extrovert compared to an introvert.

Your request might result in recognition viewed as less genuine than if it were spontaneous, but the outcome from such a request can be quite beneficial. You might receive some words worth reliving later for self-motivation. Most importantly, you will remind the other individual in a nice way that s/he missed a prime opportunity to offer quality recognition. This could be a valuable learning experience for that person.

Consider the possible beneficial impact from your statement to another person that you are pleased with a certain result of your extra effort, including your performance of particular AC4P behavior. With the right tone and affect, such verbal behavior will not seem like bragging but rather a declaration of personal pride in a small-win accomplishment – something more people should feel and relive for self-motivation. The other person will support your personal praise with supportive testimony, and this will bolster your self-motivation. Plus, you will teach the other person how to support the AC4P behaviors of others.

Many years ago, I instituted a self-recognition process among my research students that increased our awareness of the value of receiving praise, even when it's self-initiated. I told my students during class or group meetings they could request a standing ovation at any time. All they had to do was specify the behavior they felt deserved recognition and then ask for a standing ovation. Obviously, such recognition is not private, personal, and one-to-one, and therefore it's not optimal. Plus, the public aspect of this process inhibited many personal requests for a standing ovation.

However, over the years a number of my students have requested a standing ovation, and the experience has always been positive for everyone. Each request has included a solid rationale. Some students express pride in an exemplary grade on a project; others acknowledge an acceptance letter from a graduate school, internship, or journal editor. The actual ovation is fun and feels good, both on the giving or receiving end. Plus, we all learn the motivating process of behavior-based recognition, even when it doesn't follow all of the quality principles.

The Craving

William James, the first renowned American psychologist, wrote, "The deepest principle in human nature is the craving to be appreciated".[28] A little later John Dewey, the famous American educator who developed the field of school psychology, claimed, "The deepest urge in human nature is the desire to be important".[28] Then in 1936, Dale Carnegie advocated the key to winning friends and influencing people is to "always make the other person feel important".[28] How can we readily fulfill the human need to feel appreciated and important? The answer, of course: Give and receive recognition well.

In Conclusion

Many excuses and barriers can be offered for the lack of large-scale application of effective AC4P interventions analogous to those described in this chapter. I explained three C-words reflecting the leadership qualities needed to achieve an AC4P culture of compassion: Competence, Commitment, and Courage.

Many people are competent and committed regarding the achievement of an AC4P culture. In other words, they know what to do, and are motivated to do whatever it takes to increase the quantity and quality of AC4P behaviors in educational, work, and community settings.

However, I suggest the missing link is often *moral* courage, or the audacity to step up, take an *interpersonal risk* and go beyond one's predictable routine on behalf of the well-being of other people, especially complete strangers.

Beyond competence (or self-efficacy), four person-states that influence courage in this context were discussed in Chapter 2 (i.e., self-esteem, belongingness, personal control, and optimism), and guidelines for cultivating an AC4P culture have been entertained in the first three chapters of this book.

The chapters in Parts II and III, authored by a variety of AC4P leaders, specify cost-effective techniques for increasing the frequency and effectiveness of AC4P behaviors in particular settings and for a designated meaningful purpose. Many of the AC4P applications describe the profound personal and interpersonal advantages of a particular AC4P intervention. These are the special reinforcing consequences that keep all of us in pursuit of an AC4P culture of compassion.

Test your *moral courage* as an AC4P leader by using these various intervention techniques. You can log on to ac4p.org and download airplane lifesaver cards, feedback cards, thank-you cards, and more.

Notes

1.   *The American Heritage Dictionary.* (1991) (2nd College Edition). New York, NY: Houghton Mifflin Company, p.333.

2.   McCain, J., & Salter, M. (2004). *Why courage matters: The way to a braver life.* New York, NY: Random House, Inc.

3.   Blanchard, K.P., Zigarmi, P., & Zigarmi, D. (1985). *Leadership and the one minute manager.* New York, NY: William Morrow and Company, Inc.

4.   Geller, E.S. (1996). *The psychology of safety: How to improve behaviors and attitudes on the job.* Radnor, PA: Chilton Book Company; Geller, E.S. (1998). *Practical behavior-based safety: Step-by-step methods to improve your workplace.* Neenah, WI: J.J. Keller & Associates, Inc.; Geller, E.S. (2001). *The psychology of safety handbook.* Boca Raton, FL: CRC Press.

5.   Kouzes, J.M., & Posner, B.Z. (2006). *A leader's legacy.* San Francisco, CA: John Wiley & Sons, Inc.

6.   Geller, E.S. (1996). *The psychology of safety: How to improve behaviors and attitudes on the job.* Radnor, PA: Chilton Book Company; Geller, E.S. (2001). *The psychology of safety handbook.* Boca Raton, FL: CRC Press; Geller, E.S. (2005). *People-based safety: The source.* Virginia Beach, VA: Coastal Training Technologies Corporation; Geller, E.S. (2006). Reinforcement, reward, & recognition: Critical distinctions and a reality check. *Industrial Safety & Hygiene News, 40(3),* pp. 12,14; Geller, E.S. (2007). Why do people act that way? *Industrial Safety & Hygiene News, 41(10),* 21-22.

7.   Mischel, W. (2004). Toward a integrative model for CBT: Encompassing behavior, cognition, affect, and process. *Behavior Therapy, 35,* 185-203.

8.   Geller, E.S. (2008). *Leading people-based safety: Enriching your culture.* Virginia Beach, VA: Coastal Training Technologies Corporation; Geller, E.S., & Weigand, D.M. (2005). People-based

safety: Exploring the role of personality in injury prevention. *Professional Safety, 50 (12),* 28-36.

9. Geller, E.S. (2001). *The psychology of safety handbook.* Boca Raton, FL: CRC Press., p. 378.

10. Reif, C.D, & Singer, B. (2000). Interpersonal flourishing: A positive health agenda for the new millennium. *Personality & Social Psychology Review, 4,* 30-44; Sarasson, B.R., Sarasson, I.G., & Gurung, R.A.R. (1997). Close personal relationships and health outcome : A key to the role of social support. In S. Duck (Ed.) *Handbook of personal relationships* (2nd Edition) (pp.547-573). New York, NY: Wiley; Sarasson, B.B., Sarasson, I.G., & Pierce, G.R. (1990). *Social support: An interactional view.* New York, NY: Wiley.

11. Geller, E.S. (1999). Interpersonal trust: Key to getting the best from behavior-based safety coaching. *Professional Safety, 44(4),* 16-19; Geller, E.S. (2002). *The participation factor: How to increase involvement in occupational safety.* Des Plaines, IL: American Society of Safety Engineers.

12. Festinger, L. (1957). *A theory of cognitive dissonance.* Stanford, CA: Stanford University Press.

13. Geller, E.S., Bruff, C.D., & Nimmer, J.G. (1985). The "Flash for Life": A community prompting strategy for safety-belt promotion. *Journal of Applied Behavior Analysis, 18,* 145-159.

14. Cox, M.G., & Geller, E.S. (2011). Community prompting of safety-belt use: Impact of positive versus negative reminders. *Journal of Applied Behavior Analysis, 43(2),* 321-325.

15. Geller, E.S., & Lehman, G.R. (1991). The buckle-up promise card: A versatile intervention for large-scale behavior change. *Journal of Applied Behavior Analysis, 24,* 91-94.

16. Streff, F.M., Kalsher, M.S., & Geller, E.S. (1993). Developing efficient workplace safety programs: Observations of response covariation. *Journal of Organizational Behavior Management, 13(2),* 3-15.

17. Geller, E.S. (2001). *The psychology of safety handbook.* Boca Raton, FL: CRC Press.

18. Cialdini, R.B. (2001). *Influence: Science and practice* (4th Edition). New York, NY: Harper Collins College Publishers.

19. Geller, E.S., Hickman, J.S., & Pettinger, C.B. (2004). The Airline Lifesaver: A 17-year analysis of a technique to prompt safety-belt use. *Journal of Safety Research, 35,* 357-366.

20. Geller, E.S. (2005). *People-based safety: The source.* Virginia Beach, VA: Coastal Training Technologies Corporation.

21. Geller, E.S. (1996). *The psychology of safety: How to improve behaviors and attitudes on the job.* Radnor, PA: Chilton Book Company, p. 148.

22. Sulzer-Azaroff, B., & Austin, J. (2000). Does BBS work? Behavior-based safety and injury reduction: A survey of the evidence. *Professional Safety, 45(7),* 19-24.

23. Geller, E.S. (1998). *Practical behavior-based safety: Step-by-step methods to improve your workplace.* Neenah, WI: J.J. Keller & Associates, Inc.

24. Geller, E.S. (1998). *Practical behavior-based safety: Step-by-step methods to improve your workplace.* Neenah, WI: J.J. Keller & Associates, Inc.; Geller, E.S. (2005). *People-based safety: The source.* Virginia Beach, VA: Coastal Training Technologies Corporation.

25. Chance, P. (1999). *Learning and behavior* (4th Edition). Belmont, CA: Wadsworth.

26. Thorndike, E.L. (1911). *Animal intelligence: Experimental studies.* New York, NY; Hafner, p. 174; Thorndike, E.L., (1931). *Human learning.* Cambridge, MA: MIT Press.

27. Cialdini, R.B. (2001). *Influence: Science and practice* (4th Edition). New York, NY: Harper Collins College Publishers; Gouldner, A.W. (1960). The norm of reciprocity: A preliminary statement. *American Sociology Review, 25,* 161-167.

28. Carnegie, D. (1936). *How to win friends and influence people* (1981 Edition). New York, NY: Simon

CHAPTER 5

Social Influence and AC4P Behavior

Cory Furrow and E. Scott Geller

FOR AN AC4P CULTURE to thrive over the long term, self-motivation is essential (see Chapter 3). However, people sometimes need a slight extrinsic nudge to actively care for others, especially strangers. The social influence principles, founded on over 50 years of research by social psychologists, offer practical techniques to help make this happen – strategies to activate and/or support occurrences of AC4P behavior.

Social influence is perceived pressure or support from others that creates notable change in an individual's behavior. Do not confuse this with *persuasion*. We are not seeking to persuade a change in opinion or attitude. Also, persuasion does not necessarily change observable behavior.[1]

In this chapter we define practical behavior-change techniques derived from six basic social-influence principles – consistency, liking, reciprocity, social proof, authority, and scarcity. We illustrate how these principles and related techniques have been (or could be) used to nudge others to perform AC4P behaviors or to increase the probability certain AC4P behavior will continue.[2] Appropriate interventions based on these principles can help cultivate an AC4P culture of compassion, and propel the expansion of AC4P worldwide.

Before defining the social-influence principles and their applications, let's review the concepts relevant for appreciating the applicability of these principles – three types of behavior change and their connection to the Activator-Behavior-Consequence (ABC) Model of Applied Behavior Analysis, as explained in Chapter 1.

Three Types of Behavior Change

Conformity, compliance, and obedience are three types of behavior change that result from social influence. Note that conformity occurs when the social pressure is relatively low, whereas obedience follows the perception of high social pressure.[1]

Conformity

Conformity is an attempt to "fit-in." We conform when we alter our behavior to match the behavior of others.[1] A student will likely drink more beer at a college party if peers consume lots of beer. And one's attire at the party will be formal or informal to match the attire of other party-goers.

Compliance

Compliance comes about when we are directly or indirectly requested to change a behavior.[1] A *direct request* emanates from a interpersonal interaction, usually verbal communication. An *indirect request* uses a message or sign to solicit compliance. Ask a passenger to buckle up in a vehicle and you're taking a direct route to gain compliance. A billboard message, "Click it or Ticket," is an indirect request.

Obedience

When a perceived authority figure requests (or orders or commands) a change in behavior, obedience occurs to appease the authority.[1] Obedience reduces a follower's sense of personal control or choice. This in turn reduces self-motivation, as explained in Chapter 3. The de-motivating effect of obedience occurs whether the authority's request is direct (i.e., interpersonal) or indirect.

The ABC Model

How activators and consequences influence behavior is exemplified by the ABC model of applied behavioral science (ABS). Simply stated, behavior is directed by activators and motivated by consequences.[3]   As illustrated in Chapter 1, activators can be education/training programs, written/verbal prompts, online webinars, and modeling/demonstrations.[4] A stop sign at an intersection is a written prompt, directing a driver to halt at the intersection.

Announcing the availability of a consequence makes for the most influential activators. Incentives activate behavior by announcing a certain reward will follow a designated behavior. In contrast, a disincentive warns people of the negative consequence of a penalty if certain desirable behavior does not occur (e.g., "Click it or Ticket"), or if a designated undesired behavior occurs (e.g., $100 fine for littering).

Consequences vary from rewards to penalties, social approval to disapproval, and to more severe outcomes.[4]   Failing to brake and stop at an intersection stop sign can produce irritating but temporary social disapproval (e.g., other drivers angrily honking their car horn), the more permanent financial cost of a penalty if the behavior is observed by a police officer, or a severe, even fatal incident – colliding with a pedestrian or another vehicle.

Social or interpersonal consequences are desirable to the extent they: a) offer an accurate perception of reality, b) contribute to developing or maintaining meaningful social relationships, or c) contribute to a desirable self-concept, according to Robert Cialdini and Noah Goldstein.[5]

Making an accurate, reality-based decision can have the consequence of helping to attain a goal. Develop meaningful relationships with classmates can make a course more enjoyable and also cultivate support for cooperative learning. A favorable self-concept increases self-esteem and perhaps one's confidence to perform AC4P behavior.[6]

Accuracy, social affiliation, and a favorable self-concept – motivating characteristics of consequences from social interaction – connect to three of the five person-states proposed in Chapter 2 to increase one's propensity to actively care – self-efficacy/

competence (accuracy), belongingness (affiliation), and self-esteem (a positive self-concept).

One behavior can produce these three desirable consequences. You observe your peers make a financial donation to a charity after hearing a persuasive presentation, and you follow up by making a similar donation. This environment-based AC4P behavior (see Chapter 2) is supported by each of three motivating consequences. Your behavior is an "accurate" consequence of a persuasive speech and reflects relevant compliance from peers. You gain social approval and avoid social disapproval from your peers by making a donation. And upon making the AC4P donation, you view yourself more favorably.

Social-influence principles and related techniques can be understood and executed within the framework of the ABC Model of ABS. The six principles and techniques covered in the remainder of this chapter are essentially activators. But each infers desirable or undesirable consequences following relevant behavior. Most of these consequences relate to conformity, compliance and obedience either in combination or alone – the three consequence categories defined by Cialdini and Goldstein.[5]

The Consistency Principle

The first of the six social-influence principles is consistency. Here is how it can work: To pay his way through college, Cory Furrow worked as a cook at a local restaurant in Blacksburg, Virginia. Of the kitchen staff, he was the only one who didn't smoke cigarettes. During one of the "cigarette breaks" a co-worker said he would like to quit smoking for his health. Cory perceived his co-worker feeling guilty about smoking, but this smoker verbalized a convincing rationalization: Cigarettes relieve stress. Before heading back into the kitchen, any guilt about smoking seemed nearly dissipated. Self-talk had this man believing reducing stress overshadowed any future and uncertain costs to his health.

The well-known Theory of Cognitive Dissonance was developed by Leon Festinger.[7] *Cognitive Dissonance* rattles people when they realize their behaviors are inconsistent with their beliefs, attitudes, or values. The smoker experienced dissonance when he said cigarettes are bad while continuing to smoke one. To ease this disturbing dissonance, he identified what he perceived as a soon and certain health benefit from smoking (i.e., stress relief).

Self-Perception Theory, an extension of Cognitive Dissonance Theory, was proposed ten years later by Daryl Bem.[8] According to *Self-Perception Theory* we validate our values, attitudes, or beliefs (internal attributes) by observing our own behaviors. For example, Cory is passionate about outdoor recreation (e.g., mountain biking, hiking, and caving) and environmental conservation. He believes these passions emanate from his dedicated participation in Boy Scouts of America.

As a Boy Scout, he practiced environmental conservation and enjoyed outdoor-recreation activities. Cory includes environmental conservation and protection as a personal value, and he *chooses* to perform behavior consistent with that value.

Note the critical word *chooses*. Self-perception is only influenced by behavior perceived to be personally chosen. Behavior perceived to be influenced completely by external contingencies (e.g., incentives/rewards or disincentives/penalties) does not come to define personal values, attitudes, or beliefs. Likewise, cognitive dissonance is absent when attitude-discrepant behavior is perceived to be controlled by extrinsic consequences (e.g., financial compensation).

The techniques explained below – foot-in-the-door, social labeling and commitment – apply the Consistency principle to influence the behavior of others. Remember the critical role of *choice*. When we believe our inconsistent behavior or attitude was controlled by outside factors, we are not disrupted by cognitive dissonance and do not feel compelled to adjust our behavior, attitude, or perception of self.[9]

Foot in the Door

The *Foot-in-the-Door* (FITD) technique gains compliance with a relatively large request by first obtaining compliance to a smaller, related request.[10] If you want your roommate to help wash the dishes, ask him/her first to take out the trash – a less time-consuming task. Follow with the dishwashing request after your roommate takes out the trash.

Jonathan Freedman and Scott Fraser empirically demonstrated the FITD technique with a seminal field study.[10] The researchers went door-to-door and asked homeowners to post a large sign on their front lawn. For the Large-Request-First condition, homeowners were shown a picture of a large obtrusive sign stating "Drive Carefully,"

and asked if they would allow the researchers to place the same sign in their yard. Of these homeowners (n=24), only 16.7% complied.

In contrast, another group of homeowners were asked if they'd be willing to place a small 3" X 3" sign in their window that stated, "Be a Safe Driver," as a Small-Request-First (or FITD) condition. Two weeks later, those homeowners who complied with the small-sign request were asked if they would place the same large sign used in the Large-Request-First condition in their front yard. Of the 25 homeowners who agreed with the small request first, 76% permitted the large sign in their yard.

Social Labeling

When an individual is assigned a desired attribute, attitude, or belief and is then asked to comply with a behavior related to that label, *social labeling* has occurred.[11] If the social label is desirable, the individual wants to behave consistent with it.

Cory applied the social-labeling technique when managing the data entry/verification process for the Center for Applied Behavior Systems at Virginia Tech. During initial training, Cory gave new researchers supportive and corrective feedback as they practiced the data-processing task. Afterward, he gave especially competent students two positive labels by commenting, "You seem to be detail-oriented and obviously care about doing quality work."

After 15 minutes or so, Cory returned and asked the competent student researchers how things were going as he spot-checked their work. These new researchers were highly focused on their work and asked many thoughtful questions. They appeared to do their best work in order to match the social label Cory had given them.

Supportive Research. To increase charitable donations, Robert Kraut applied a similar social-labeling technique.[12] Homeowners were asked to make a charitable donation for the American Heart Association by a research assistant (RA) acting as a door-to-door volunteer. Participants were split into two conditions, depending on whether they agreed to make a donation (i.e., the Charitable or Uncharitable condition). In both conditions, participants received the same leaflet supporting the charity.

Participants in the Charitable condition were randomly assigned to one of two groups. One group received the leaflet with a card stating, "Charitable people give generously to help a good cause and those less fortunate than themselves. Are you one?"[13] The other received the same leaflet and card, but the RA added the personal statement, "You are a generous person. I wish more of the people I met were as charitable as you."[13]

Similarly, those who didn't make a donation were randomly assigned to one of two groups. One group received the same leaflet given to those in the Charitable condition, but the attached card stated, "Uncharitable people give excuses and refuse to help others. Are you one?"[14]

The second group in the Uncharitable condition, received the same leaflet and card, but a personal label was added: "Let me give you one of our health leaflets anyway. We've been giving them to everyone, even people like you who are uncharitable and don't normally give to these causes."[14]

One to two weeks after the leaflets, cards, and personal labels had been first distributed, the same homeowners were asked by a different RA, posing as a door-to-door volunteer, whether they would like to donate to help raise money for Multiple Sclerosis. Individuals in the Charitable condition (n=37) who had received the personal label donated an average of $.70 (equivalent to approximately $3.67 in 2013), whereas those in the Charitable condition who had not received the personal label (n=62) donated an average of $.41 (equivalent to approximately $2.15 in 2013).[15]

Interestingly, individuals in the Uncharitable condition who received the uncharitable label (n=27) donated significantly less money (p<.05) than did those who had not received the uncharitable label (n=27). Those who got the uncharitable label donated an average of $.23 (equivalent to approximately $1.20 in 2013). Those in the group without the personal statement that implied an uncharitable label donated an average of $.33 (equivalent to approximately $1.73 in 2013).

These results suggest people behave consistently with reasonable labels given to them. Participants who received a charitable label through a personal statement donated more than participants who did not receive the label. Similarly, participants who received a label reflecting uncharitability donated less than uncharitable participants who did not receive a personal statement implying uncharitability.

Consider the disadvantage of giving someone a negative label. A person might behave undesirably to be consistent with a negative label such as being lazy, a poor reader, or an underachiever. A negative label like "underachiever" can be an excuse to put less effort into achieving a personal or group goal. A positive label might activate and/or support desirable behaviors such as being energetic, conscientious, or a diligent worker. However, the type of positive label is critical, according to programmatic research by Carol Dweck.[16]

Ability vs. Effort Labels. Dr. Carol Dweck and her colleagues gave hundreds of early adolescents a set of ten fairly difficult problems from the nonverbal portion of an IQ test. Afterward, all participants were praised individually for their performance on the test, but the nature of the praise was varied systematically. For half of the students, the praise was based on their *ability*. They were each told, "Wow, you got eight right. That's a really good score. You must be smart at this".[17]

The other students were each praised with a positive social label for their *effort* with these words, "Wow, you got eight right. That's a really good score. You must have worked really hard."[18]

Both groups scored equivalently on the IQ test. But researchers noted significant differences in students' behavior following their *ability* vs. *effort* label. All students had the choice to work on a challenging new task they could learn from. Most of those with the *ability* label rejected this opportunity. Apparently "they didn't want to do anything that could expose their flaws and call into question their talent."[18] In contrast, 90 percent of the students praised for their *effort* welcomed the opportunity of a challenging new task from which they could learn.

Later, when all of these students performed less effectively on some additional more difficult problems, their reaction to failure feedback was influenced by the prior label given them (i.e., ability vs. effort). The *ability* kids felt like failures. They believed they did not live up to their ability; and they rated the task as "not fun anymore." The *effort* group saw in their failure a need to try harder. They did not perceive any indictment of their intellect, and they did not indicate a lack of enjoying the problem-solving task. "Many of them said that the hard problems were the most fun."[18]

After experiencing these difficult problems, the researchers gave the adolescents some easier problems to solve. The performance of the *ability*-labeled students plummeted. The *effort*-labeled students performed increasing more effectively. In the profound words of Dr. Dweck: "Since this was a kind of IQ test, you might say that praising ability lowered the students' IQs. And that praising their effort raised them."[19]

A final difference showed up when the adolescents were asked to write out their opinions of the problem-solving tasks they completed for students at other schools. A space was provided on this form for the students to report the personal scores they received on the problems. To the researchers' surprise and disappointment, 40 percent of the *ability*-labeled students reported higher grades than they actually earned. In the author's words, "We took ordinary children and made them into liars by telling them they were smart."[19]

Bottom line: Focus on the process (or effort) rather than the outcome (or results) when praising another person's performance. Cory focused on the process behaviors of the research students rather than giving them an ability label. He did not praise students for being highly competent, but rather for being highly task-focused and for asking thoughtful questions.

Commitment

A few years ago, Cory took out a small loan to purchase his first vehicle. The loan officer reviewed different loan options and payment plans with Cory and his dad. After reviewing the various options, Cory selected the loan that best fit his current financial situation. Then, Cory signed the loan agreement in front of the loan officer and his dad, committing Cory to make monthly payments for a year.

Cory's experience epitomizes the three components that increase the propensity to honor a commitment – choice, active, and public.[20] Cory chose to actively sign the commitment document in the presence of his dad and the loan officer.

Perceived Choice. Imagine helping a young boy dress in nice clothes you have selected for him to wear on his first day of school. This might feel like top-down control to the boy, and he might resist in order to assert his individuality or personal freedom. Consider an alternative: Select two school outfits you would like the boy to wear, and let him choose between the two. More than likely, the young boy will be less resistant because he feels some choice in the clothes he wears to school. Little does he know you're happy with either choice.

When a decision-maker perceives a sense of choice, his or her decision is considered authentic and self-endorsed.[21] People who make a commitment without perceiving some choice are less likely to honor it.[7] Back to the car-loan example: Cory felt personal choice when selecting his car loan. There was really no rational alternative to that particular loan. Cory had to get the loan if he wanted the vehicle. But because Cory was able to choose from various loan options, he perceived his decision as self-directed and self-endorsed.

Active. The second component to increasing the propensity to honor a commitment is to make it active. Signing a document, shaking hands, or succumbing to fraternity hazing are active commitments involving behavior. Cory actively signed the car loan that committed him to make monthly payments. Without such action, a commitment is passive and less binding. It's like verbally making a promise without any active assurance.[22]

Public. Making a commitment in front of others also increases the propensity to honor that commitment. Social consequences are anticipated from behaviors consistent or inconsistent with a public commitment. A public commitment implies possible social approval or disapproval following behavior consistent or inconsistent with the commitment, respectively.[23]

Figures 5.1 and 5.2 depict a public commitment intervention applied at an AC4P safety seminar for safety leaders, supervisors and maintenance personnel at Delta Airlines. After giving a half-day workshop on the AC4P principles and applications for the safety and well-being of others, Scott Geller walked to the back of the auditorium and signed his name to a

Figure 5.1 Scott makes a commitment.

"Declaration of Interdependence" as a public commitment to look out for the safety and well-being of others (Figure 5.1). Then, Scott requested the audience to follow suit.

Social context was probably critical in influencing most of the workshop participants to sign this declaration (Figure 5.2), which is displayed in the break-room for the maintenance employees of Delta Airlines at the Hartsfield-Jackson Atlanta International Airport, Atlanta, Georgia. Scott's request was both public and voluntary in nature. This contributed to the effectiveness of an active exercise to inspire awareness

Figure 5.2. The workshop participants make a commitment.

of the AC4P concepts and the development of relevant action plans.

Consider the discussion of SMARTS goal setting in Chapter 3. The final "S" in the SMARTS acronym represents Shared – making a public commitment. Sharing goals with others creates internal and external accountability. Not only are people motivated to make their behavior consistent with their commitment to achieve a specific goal (i.e., internal accountability), they also want others to see them living up to their commitment (i.e., external accountability).

AC4P Applications

The *Consistency* principle offers a plethora of AC4P applications. The FITD technique can increase the occurrence of AC4P behavior among friends, colleagues, and even strangers. First, start with a small request like "Please wear the AC4P wristband to signify your intention to join the AC4P Movement." Then, follow with a larger request for this person to give another person supportive and/or corrective feedback regarding behavior related to AC4P.

Note these requests can be interpersonal (e.g., from a student to a teacher, a wage worker to another worker, or a parent to a child) or intrapersonal (i.e., self-talk to perform more AC4P behavior). Compliance with the second larger request makes it reasonable to appeal for more effortful behavior (e.g., "Would you watch another person perform that task with a behavioral checklist, and determine the percentage of optimal vs. suboptimal behavior?").

Social labeling is a subtle way to promote AC4P behaviors. Simply give a person a particular desirable and suitable social label (e.g., "You seem to be someone who really cares about the well-being of others") and then follow with a request, "Would you mind providing behavior-based feedback to individuals regarding the safety of their job-related behavior?"

The AC4P label will increase the probability the targeted individual will comply with your AC4P request. Of course, the first request in the FITD example (i.e., to wear an AC4P wristband) reflects social labeling. Those who wear the AC4P wristband display an AC4P label, and this will likely increase their propensity to perform AC4P behavior.

Leaders of the AC4P Movement have used the social labeling tactic to cultivate an AC4P culture in elementary schools.[24] These two students were labeled publically as the "Actively Caring Heroes of the Day," and they proudly wore the AC4P wristband. Systematic evaluations indicated these students performed more AC4P behavior on the days they wore the AC4P wristband, presumably to live up to the positive social label they had received for one day.

A commitment strategy to promote AC4P behavior for environmental conservation was used recently by research students in the Center for Applied Behavior Systems (CABS). Customers leaving a large grocery store were asked by researchers if they'd like to increase their use of reusable grocery bags for purchased groceries. When a customer gave a positive response, the research assistant offered a hangtag to hook on a vehicle's rearview mirror as a reminder. Then, the customer was asked to sign the back of the hangtag as a part of their commitment to use reusable grocery bags.

Notice how this social-influence strategy applied the consistency techniques to enhance people's propensity to honor their commitment. First, customers chose to use reusable grocery bags. Then, they signed the hangtag in front of the research assistant, making the commitment active and public. Subsequently, they were reminded of their pro-environment commitment whenever they looked at the card hanging from the rear-view mirror.

The Liking/Ingratiation Principle

We like to be liked, asserts the *Liking* principle.[25] Naturally, people are more likely to comply with a request from others they like, and to actively care for the well-being of these individuals. *Ingratiation* refers to attempts to get others to like you.[1] Relatively convenient strategies for getting others on board with the AC4P Movement are provided by this social-influence principle of Liking.

Similarity

We tend to like people who are similar to us, and we are more likely to comply with requests from these individuals. Similarities can vary from comparable opinions and attitudes to backgrounds and past experiences, attire, and notable behaviors.[26] It's more likely "birds of a feather flock together" than "opposites attract."

Gaining compliance through similar attire was tested in a field study conducted at Purdue University in 1971. Research assistants (dressed in either collegiate or hippy attire) randomly asked for a dime to make a long-distance phone call from either collegiate or hippy-dressed students (n=384) they encountered in a hallway near a dining facility. Participants were more likely to give a research assistant (RA) a dime when the RA wore similar attire (i.e., collegiate or hippy attire).[27]

In a related study, the experimenter told a RA and the participant they shared a similar fingerprint type. In the Common-Fingerprint condition, the participant and RA were told they shared a common fingerprint type; while in the Rare-Fingerprint condition, the shared fingerprint type was considered rare. In a Control condition, the experimenter did not comment on the relative uniqueness of their shared fingerprint type. After the experimenter dismissed the two individuals, the RA asked the participant to review a document for a class and provide feedback.[28]

Of 29 participants in the Control-Fingerprint condition, 48.3% complied with the RA's request. In the Common-Fingerprint condition, compliance increased to 54.8% of 31 participants. In the Rare-Fingerprint condition, 82.1% of 28 participants complied with the RA's request.

Interestingly, a person can gain favor or compliance by faking or claiming a false similarity. In the fingerprint study, for example, the RA and participant didn't really share the same fingerprint type. But this false similarity was enough to gain compliance.

Now consider this true story: At a calling agency, Stephanie's task was to convince others to make a donation to an organization helping with the clean-up process after Hurricane Katrina. Stephanie was the best at convincing others to make large donations. Her secret: "Appear to be like them." When Stephanie heard a southern accent over the phone, she faked a southern accent. If the person stated a personal opinion or interest, Stephanie faked similarity: "I feel the same" or "I do that too." Stephanie's ability to create a fake similarity enabled her to gain more compliance than her co-workers. Of course, it's critical the apparent similarity is believable, which is not the case in the illustration.

Compliments

Who doesn't like to receive a compliment? Complimenting people is a quick and easy way to gain their favor.[29] You increase the target's self-esteem and perhaps a sense of competence (see Chapter 3). You also set the stage for reciprocity (as discussed later in this chapter). Interestingly, even if the target is aware of an ulterior motive behind the flattery, the target still views the person giving the compliment as favorable.[25]

Professors are suckers for flattery. Many undergraduates seeking a letter of recommendation or acceptance into a graduate program flood professors with compliments and flattery. A student approached Scott and said, "Dr. Geller, your inspirational teaching of the introductory psychology course convinced me to change my major to psychology!" A few weeks later the same student came to Scott with a request: "Dr. Geller, would you write me a letter of recommendation for a summer internship program?"

Even if Scott suspected an ulterior motive behind the prior compliment, the undergraduate still increased the probability of receiving a letter of recommendation. Since students seldom give these kinds of "life-changing" compliments to their professors, the compliment in this case was rare and impacted by the Principle of Scarcity, as explained later in this chapter.

Compliments from a child to parent might be viewed as uncommon and perhaps insincere. Still, parents who receive compliments from their children are extremely pleased and more likely to comply with a child's request.

Bottom line: When people say, "Flattery will get you everywhere," they are probably more right than wrong.

Mere-Exposure Effect

When a new song is first played on the radio, it may not get a positive review from listeners. As the song continues to be played, it may "grow on" the listeners. From mere exposure, listeners can develop a positive attitude toward a song. The impact of repeated exposure was demonstrated in a series of studies conducted by Robert Zajonc.[30]

In one of his experiments, each participant was shown a series of photos. The relative frequency of showing each photo varied among participants. After viewing the photos, participants rated how much they liked each photo. Higher favorability ratings went to those photos viewed more frequently.[30]

Advertisers use the mere-exposure effect constantly to sell their products. We see Coca-Cola products on bill boards, vending machines, in TV commercials, in restaurants, and on the sides of trucks. Does such excessive exposure increase sales of Coke products? Apparently the Coca-Cola Company believes so, given the amount of money spent to promulgate these exposures.

The mere-exposure effect can apply to interpersonal relationships. Initially, one's attitude toward a teacher, co-worker, or neighbor may be neutral. Through frequent interaction, one's impression of another person can become positive. This exposure can then influence one-on-one communication and relationship building. Now we have the possibility of true friendship and increased potential for interpersonal AC4P behavior.

AC4P Applications

The AC4P interventions accomplished by Virginia Tech (VT) students at Chardon High School (CHS) exemplify the influential power of claiming similar backgrounds.[24] Both educational settings were sites of tragic school shootings. After the shootings at CHS in 2012, student leaders contacted AC4P leaders at VT to help recover and move forward.

When the AC4P leaders talked with leaders and students at CHS, they discussed their "common background" to make critical connections. Also, when giving workshops and coaching CHS staff and students, the AC4P leaders wear blue jeans and an AC4P T-shirt customized for CHS, approximating the common attire of most high-school students.

The See-Act-Pass-Share (SAPS) process rewards others for their AC4P behavior, and promotes exposure of AC4P through the social media (ac4p.org).[24] Briefly, this four-step SAPS process includes the following components:

See: Observe an AC4P behavior; ***Act:*** Thank the person for actively caring and reward the individual with an AC4P wristband embossed with a unique ID number; ***Pass:*** Ask the AC4P person to look for AC4P behavior from another individual and then pass on the wristband to reward him/her for the AC4P behavior observed; and ***Share:*** Ask the AC4P person to share their AC4P story at ac4p.org, including the ID number of the wristband received for particular AC4P behavior.

Typically, a compliment is given in the "Act" step of the SAPS process (e.g., "Thank you for actively caring; that was really nice of you"). This initial compliment helps to gain favor from the AC4P individual, and this is supported by the gift of an AC4P wristband. This gained favor increases the AC4P person's propensity to share the AC4P story at the ac4p.org website, and to look for opportunities to reward another individual with the AC4P wristband.

The AC4P Movement gains favorable exposure to expand and grow through the mere-exposure effect, like advertising agencies trying to sell a product. Leaders of the AC4P Movement are already using various techniques to gain favorable exposure, including Facebook.com pages, the ac4p.org website, scholarship (such as this book), t-shirts, media exposure (e.g., radio interviews and local/national television stations), keynote addresses at professional conferences, webinars, as well as the AC4P wristband.

The Reciprocity Principle

Ricky, a father and a husband, suffered a severe stroke that forced him to go on disability. Community members heard about this and came to the rescue. Almost every day for a few months, church members took turns cooking dinner for the family of four. Neighbors and friends transported Ricky to therapy. Financial collections were made to help with the bills. In fact, one relative paid all of the bills for the entire year.

Support wasn't limited to these AC4P behaviors. Community members gathered their resources to construct a new roof on Ricky's home, install heating and air-conditioning systems, and remodel the home to make it handicapped assessable.[31]

These AC4P individuals are certainly caring people and their AC4P behavior is noteworthy, but it's likely the Norm of Reciprocity played a role. While all of these individuals went above and beyond the call of duty, some of their AC4P behavior could have been influenced by a "pay-back" mindset. Ricky, who is Cory Furrow's father, had dedicated much of his time actively caring for others in their community, from leadership at church to Boy Scouts of America. So when Ricky's family needed help, the community stepped to the plate and provided the much-needed support.

Norm of Reciprocity

The Norm of Reciprocity was identified by Alvin Gouldner in 1960 as an obligation to help individuals who have provided you with help, and to retaliate against those who have caused you harm.[32] Many laws and governing societies originate from the Norm of Reciprocity (e.g., Babylon's Code of Hammurabi[33]).

Many human interactions, exchanges, and traditions existing on a smaller scale involve this social norm. In the western culture, gift exchanges occur on special occasions such as birthdays, weddings, baby showers, and holidays. Other reciprocal behaviors develop as families take turns preparing holiday dinners or alternating as host. After being a dinner guest at a friend's home, a couple typically reciprocates with a dinner at their home.

Exchanging holiday cards in December is an enduring tradition in the American culture. Many families go to great lengths to ensure they send holiday cards, including Christmas, Hanukkah, Kwanzaa to important individuals/families in their lives. Plus, when a family receives a holiday card from people to whom they originally failed to send a card, they typically send one in return or at least put the sender on their "holiday-card list" for the following year.

This Norm of Reciprocity was tested by two social psychologists, Philip Kunz and Michael Woolcott. They sent 578 Christmas cards to a random group of Chicago residents they didn't know. To their surprise, 20% of the 578 recipients responded by either calling the researchers to reestablish a lost connection or sending them a Christmas card. Some recipients continued to send these researchers Christmas cards for a number of consecutive years after the first year the experiment was conducted.[34]

The Norm of Reciprocity occurs in two forms: 1) direct reciprocity and 2) indirect reciprocity. Direct reciprocity (DR) is the exchange of helpful or harmful behavior between two individuals.[35] It's helpful when one AC4P act begets another; it's harmful when an individual seeks revenge or "pay back" for an unkind act directed toward him/her.

As shown in the illustration on the next page, a time delay may exist between these behavioral exchanges. Still, the initial exchange can lead to repeated interactions and/or exchanges in the future. Indeed, it's common to experience these repeated interactions between friends, families, and acquaintances.

If exchanges are consistently harmful, the two individuals can easily become long-term enemies, like the Hatfields and the McCoys feuding over old grudges. Even though the negative side of reciprocity is noteworthy, for the remainder of this section we focus

on the positive side of reciprocity and
its connection to AC4P behavior.

Direct Reciprocity

As depicted in Figure 5.3, and
explained previously in the Christmas-
card study, the first AC4P behavior
is initiated by Person A. Person B's
reciprocation is based upon the initial
behavior from Person A. For example,
direct reciprocity (DR) occurred for
Cory when he hosted a spaghetti
dinner at his apartment. After dinner,
one of the dinner guests cleaned all
of the dirty dishes. This mirrors what
many couples do; one cooks, the other
cleans.

Make   the   First   Move.
Reciprocity is a powerful activator
that influences compliance. For this to occur, though, it's important to make the first
move (e.g., be the first to give a gift, provide help, or make a donation); then follow
with a request for AC4P behavior from the recipient.

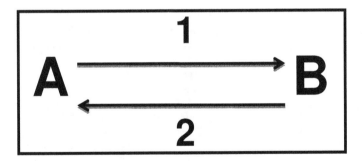

*Figure 5.3. Each letter represents an individual, and "1"
represents the initial AC4P behavior, whereas "2" is the
reciprocal AC4P behavior.*

One study found students who *received* gifts (e.g., t-shirt and travel mug) *before*
a request to reward people's pro-environmental behaviors with thank-you cards were
more likely to pass out the thank-you cards than were students who were *promised* the
same gifts *after* passing out five thank-you cards.[36] Helping or gift-giving prior to a
request is one way to increase probable compliance from others. Making a concession
is another way to obtain agreement with a request. "Door-in-the-face" is the term for
this influence technique, discussed below.

In another study, The Norm of Reciprocity was used to increase the reuse of towels in a hotel to save energy, financial costs, and help protect the environment.[37] Researchers gained 30% participation in the reuse of hotel towels with the following "if-then" contingency: "Partner with us to help save the environment. In exchange for your participation in this program, w*e at the hotel will donate* a percentage of the energy savings to a nonprofit environmental protection organization. The environment deserves our combined efforts. You can join us by reusing your towels during your stay."[38]

Participation grew to 42.5% with the following Reciprocity message: "We're doing our part for the environment. Can we count on you? Because we are committed to preserving the environment, *we have made a financial contribution* to a nonprofit environmental protection organization on behalf of the hotel and its guests. If you would like to help us in recovering the expense, while conserving natural resources, please reuse your towels during your stay."[38]

This study suggests the Norm of Reciprocity is more effective at gaining participation in a hotel towel-reusing program than an "if-then" contingency. Again, being the first to perform an AC4P behavior can activate the Norm of Reciprocity and gain compliance to a follow-up request.

Door-in-the-Face. "Can I have ten dollars?" a person asks you. More than likely you will turn down this plea, unless it comes from a friend who gave you money in the past. After you reject this first request, the person asks, "Could I have one dollar instead?" If you have the dollar, you might honor this request. Here's the critical question: Would you be more inclined to give up one dollar after your refusal to give up ten dollars than if you had never received the first request?

The answer is "yes," according to empirical research. People are more likely to comply after rejecting a request that is more costly, in terms of time, effort, or money. This is called Door-in-the-Face (DITF).[39] The DITF technique increases compliance to a small request by first making a larger related request that is expected to get rejected.

In a seminal study by Cialdini et al., the DITF was used to get college students to volunteer two hours of their time to serve as a chaperon for juveniles.[39] As expected, a low number of college students (16%) agreed to volunteer. But when the same request

followed a larger request to chaperon a group of juveniles for two hours a week for a minimum of two years, significantly more students (i.e., 50%) volunteered.

Now, what if someone asks you for a thousand dollars and then follows up with a request for one dollar. Would you give up the dollar? A small request is likely to be declined if the initial request is too large, research evidence suggests. The request may seem manipulative and illegitimate, and the credibility of the requester is impaired , rationalized Joseph Schwarzwald et al.[40] Additionally, counter-control or psychological reactance may decrease compliance, as discussed later in this chapter.

Indirect Reciprocity

Indirect reciprocity (IR) occurs when the behavior of a third individual is activated following awareness of a previous AC4P interaction between two other individuals.[41] Figure 5.4 illustrates two types of IR: 1) *vicarious reciprocity*, and 2) *pay-it-forward reciprocity*.[42]

Vicarious Reciprocity. Vicarious reciprocity occurs when Person C observes Person A helping Person B, and then Person C chooses to help Person A as a result. For example, in a bullying situation, Person C (the bystander) might defend Person B (the victim) from Person A (the bully) by fighting back or reporting the conflict to an

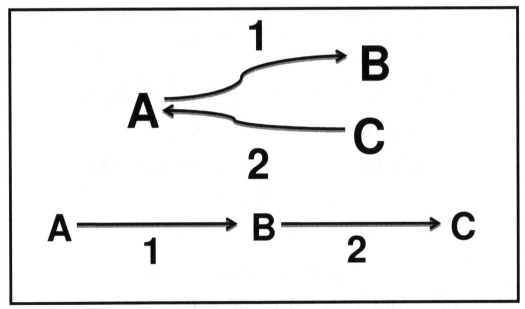

Figure 5.4, Top: Vicarious reciprocity: Person A helps Person B and then Person C helps Person A. Bottom: Pay-it forward reciprocity: Person A helps Person B, then Person B then helps Person C.

authority figure.

Recall the previously mentioned study from Goldstein et al. that increased the reuse of hotel towels. In their reciprocity condition, the researchers induced vicarious reciprocity. That is, the hotel (A) made a financial contribution to an environmental-protection organization (B), and the hotel guest (C) is asked to help the hotel recover financially from its donation by reusing towels.

Pay-it-Forward Reciprocity.   The third individual's behavior (Person C) differentiates *pay-it-forward reciprocity* from vicarious reciprocity. Unlike vicarious reciprocity where Person C rewards Person A, in pay-it-forward reciprocity, Person C is a recipient of the helpful act.[41] Suppose at a coffee shop, Person A purchases the next customer's coffee (Person B); then Person B performs a similar AC4P behavior for Person C by purchasing his/her muffin. Additionally, Person C might continue this linear chain of reciprocity by paying-it-forward to another individual.

Analogously, the Center for Applied Behavior Systems conducted an observational field study of pay-it-forward reciprocity at a university cafeteria.[42] To enter the buffet-style cafeteria, students pay a $6.00 admission fee. Due to the high volume and a rather slow financial transaction process, a long entrance/payment line was common. Periodically, a RA entered this line.

For all conditions, an 8 ½" X 11" sign (illustrated in Figure 5.5) was posted at the cash register, suggesting diners pay for the next person's meal. In the No-Reciprocity condition, the RA entered the line, paid for his/her meal and did not interact with any of the diners standing in line. In the No-Interaction Reciprocity condition, the RA did not interact with the next diner but paid for his/her meal. In the Interaction-Reciprocity condition, the RA turned to the person behind him/her, pointed to the sign and said, "I just read this sign and I want to support the Actively Caring for People Movement, so I am going to buy your meal," and then paid for the meal of

Figure 5.5. The sign at the cash register during all four phases of the study.

this next diner.

In the No-Reciprocity condition, only 6.8% of 148 diners paid for the next person's meal. In the No-Interaction Reciprocity condition, 15.6% of 122 diners paid for the next person's meal; and in the Interaction-Reciprocity condition, 24.6% of 171 diners paid for the next person's meal. In this setting, pay-it-forward reciprocity was most likely to occur when the Norm of Reciprocity was activated with both a prompt (indirect request) suggesting how to reciprocate and a supportive verbal exchange (a direct request).

AC4P Applications

Reciprocity is a fundamental influence tactic in the SAPS process of the AC4P Movement. To clarify: A person rewards another person with an AC4P wristband for performing an AC4P behavior. Once the wristband has been accepted, the recipient may feel a sense of indebtedness. The rewarding individual asks the wristband recipient to use the wristband to reward someone else for his/her AC4P behavior. Such pay-it-forward behavior will alleviate any sense of indebtedness. Compliance with the request to pass on the wristband for AC4P behavior is increased through reciprocity.

The door-in-the-face technique can be used to activate others to actively care. You could challenge people to perform an AC4P act every day for a month. For most people, this would be a difficult task. When this request is rejected, follow with an easier request like: "Perform an AC4P act three times a week for a month." Of course, this same technique can be used to request others to reward observed AC4P behavior or provide behavior-based feedback to benefit another person's health, safety, or welfare.

Let's say you actively cared for an individual and this individual wants to reciprocate. Reciprocation may take place in the form of money, a free meal, or a promise to help you in the future. Regardless, as a result of your AC4P behavior, this individual feels a sense of indebtedness to return the favor. We recommend specifying how this sense of indebtedness can be relieved: "Simply pay it forward by actively caring for another person." Your suggestion may nudge pay-it-forward reciprocity, enabling your one AC4P behavior to have a ripple effect that spreads AC4P behavior.

The Social Proof Principle

Cory joins a group of friends for dinner at a local Blacksburg restaurant. For some time the group exchanges opinions on which entrée seems to be the most appetizing. From their discussions, Cory assumed a wide variety of entrees would be ordered. Brittany is the first to order and selects the grilled chicken salad. Next is Megan, who also orders the grilled chicken salad. Then, Joanne does the same. Each of the girls at the table orders the grilled chicken salad.

We look to others for guidance about which behaviors are appropriate or inappropriate in a particular situation, especially in an unfamiliar setting, according to the *Social*

Proof principle. For instance, the individuals in the opening example discussed which entrée seemed the best to order and then each ordered the same entrée.

People apply the social proof principle through conformity. *Conformity* occurs when people imitate or copy the behavior of one or more persons.[43] Brittany ordering the grilled chicken salad influenced Megan's decision to order the same entrée. Of course, after Brittany and Megan ordered the grilled chicken salad, the remaining girl at the table conformed by ordering the same entrée.

Conforming behaviors are more likely to occur in uncertain or unfamiliar situations.[44] Having never been trained in formal dining etiquette, Cory observes and imitates behaviors of others to learn what behaviors are appropriate. Cory is inclined to observe the behavior of the most senior person at the table because he assumes this person is most likely to be correct. This reflects the role of credibility in determining who is selected to imitate.

Laser-Dot Experiments

Social norms are rules or guidelines for appropriate/inappropriate behaviors.[45] Social approval results from behaviors consistent with a social norm. Behaviors inconsistent with a social norm risk social disapproval. When riding in an elevator, the social norm (in the U.S.) is to face the elevator door for the duration of the ride. Don't believe us? Break this social norm by turning and facing the back wall of the elevator. We guarantee the reactions from the passengers will be priceless.

Muzafer Sherif conducted a series of classic conformity experiments when studying the development of social norms.[46] Many variations exist of Sherif's paradigm, but the basic procedure was as follows. Each participant sat in a dark room. A laser dot was displayed on the wall across from the participant who was instructed to tell the researcher how far the laser dot moved on each trial. Unbeknownst to the participant, the laser dot was stationary.

With a dark room eliminating a visual frame of reference and occasional rapid eye movements, a stationary laser dot appears to move. Perceived movement of the laser dot is an illusion called the *autokinetic effect.*

In the first experiment, each participant evaluated the distance the laser dot appeared to move.[47] The participants' responses ranged from 0.4 inches to 9.6 inches. The wide range of responses allowed Sherif to conduct the next two studies to measure conformity.

The second experiment consisted of four trials per participant.[45] The first trial followed the same procedure as in the first experiment. Then, participants were placed in groups of two or three participants and three additional trials followed. On the second trial, the group members announced their response publically, and their responses varied quite a bit from each other. But on Trials 3 and 4, the variation in the group members' responses decreased significantly. Each group member's response was within one inch of each other's response.

Interestingly, the groups' responses varied across groups. Toward the end of each group's trial, a norm was developed regarding the observed distance the dot moved. For one group, the laser dot moved one inch; for another group, the norm was established at five inches. This showed how group behavior can determine different social norms, and how these norms can affect perception.

When a participant was removed from the group, Sherif found the group's social norm still existed.[48] In this study, a participant and RA reported the distance a laser dot moved for 50 trials and a social norm was established (i.e., the distance the laser dot moved). After the first 50 trials, the RA left and the participant continued to evaluate the distance the laser dot moved for another 50 trials. Sherif found each participant's responses given in the second set of 50 trials were similar to the responses in the first 50 trials. This suggests the social norm established in the first 50 trials remained after the RA left.

Because there wasn't a correct response in Sherif's experiments, participants might question their perception after hearing a conflicting view. As a result, perceptions were apparently altered to conform with those of others. Question: Will people conform to a group's incorrect response when the correct answer is obvious? The answer is "yes," according to research conducted by Solomon Asch.

Matching Line Length Experiments

In a series of studies analogous to those by Sherif, participants in Solomon Asch's studies selected one of three lines to match the length of a specified line – the standard.[49] The correct answer was always obvious. On successive trials, a participant publicly selected the line that matched the standard after several RAs publicly announced their judgments one by one.

The RAs made correct selections for the first few trials. Then, the RAs gave uniformly incorrect judgments for the remaining trials. Even though the correct answer was obvious, for all 12 trials the judgments for only 23% of 123 participants remained completely independent from the group's response. Most participants (i.e., 77%) denied reality in order to conform to the unanimously incorrect judgment of others.

Normative and Informational Influence

Other people's judgments can have dramatic impact on an individual's decisions, as demonstrated by the Sherif and Asch studies. In Sherif's experiments, participants' reports of the movement of a stable dot were influenced by the reported observations of others. In Asch's studies, participants denied their comparative judgments of line lengths to conform with the inaccurate judgments of a group. Why did these participants choose to conform?

People conform in anticipation of two possible consequences (i.e., social approval or social disapproval). People conform to gain approval from others and/or avoid disapproval of others. They also gain information by observing the behavior of others. This is considered normative influence.[44] In Sherif's laser-dot studies, conforming participants modified their perceptions after becoming aware of another participant's reported perception. In Asch's line-judgment studies, incorrect information from others influenced most participants to deny their own perceptions.

Back to the individuals at the dinner table exchanging opinions about which entrée seemed best. As in Sherif's experiments, the judgments of others were used by individuals to be correct in their decisions and/or to gain a sense of social affiliation. These benefits reflect two of the three motivating consequences proposed by Cialdini and Goldstein: accuracy/competence and affiliation/community.[5]

Changing behavior to gain social approval (or peer support) or to avoid social disapproval (typically viewed as peer pressure) results from *normative influence*. In contrast, changing behavior for accuracy or competency is referred to as *informational influence*.

Informational and normative influence can occur simultaneously. At the dinner setting, diners sought information from each other about their opinion on which was the best entrée. When Brittany and Megan selected grilled chicken salads, the other girl might have selected the same entrée because of both normative and informational influence.

Strength in Numbers

The more people performing a certain behavior, the more likely will others will imitate the same behavior. Makes sense, doesn't it? But this is not always the case. To test the impact of group size on conformity, Stanley Milgram, Leonard Bickman, and Lawrence Berkowitz conducted a simple field study.[50] A number of RAs (i.e., 1, 2, 3, 5, 10, or 15 people) simultaneously looked toward the sky at a busy sidewalk in New York City.

Observers noted 42% of 1424 pedestrians looked up when one research assistant looked up. When three RAs looked up, the percentage of pedestrians who looked up averaged about 60%. When five RAs looked skyward nearly 86% of the pedestrians followed suit. But as the number of RAs increased beyond five, the percentage of pedestrians who looked up remained at approximately 80%.

In the line-judgment studies, Solomon Asch found a participant's conformity to a group's decision increased as the group size increased to three people.[49] But the percentage of conforming people remained the same as the group size increased beyond three people. What does this mean?

Results from these studies suggest the increase in people performing the same specific behavior can prompt others to conform. However, as the number of people observed performing the same behavior increases beyond a certain point, one's propensity to conform is only slightly increased, if at all.[51]

Similarity

A person is more likely to conform to someone if the individual is similar to that person with regard to gender, age, career/education, and cultural background.[27] Being of the same age and gender could explain why all of the girls at the restaurant chose the grilled chicken salad.

Injunctive and Descriptive Norms as Activators

Recall a social norm is a rule or guideline for performing or avoiding a certain behavior. Social norms are injunctive or descriptive. An *injunctive norm* defines desirable and/or undesirable behavior. An injunctive norm is what one "ought to do," as Robert Cialdini put it.[52] In the U.S., driving on the right side of the road is an injunctive norm. Strong disapproval is expressed (e.g., via shouting, horn honking, and/or hand gestures) when a driver is observed driving on the left side of the road.

A *descriptive norm* is the behavior of other's. Are people hiking, running, or biking on a trail? In this case, whichever activity is occurring by the most people would be considered a descriptive norm.

Behavior change can be activated by changing one's perception of the injunctive and/or descriptive norm.[52] A credible person performing a certain behavior can alter one's perception of the descriptive norm. One person littering can prompt onlookers to litter. Of course, the same is true if a person picks up litter. In this example, picking up litter is obviously an injunctive norm, while littering is a descriptive norm.

A sign is a low-cost way to inform people of the injunctive norm. Messages stating "no food or drink" are commonly found in office areas and classrooms. The message describes the desirable social norm for that setting. If most people comply, then a descriptive norm is created. As depicted in the illustration on the next page, a descriptive norm can put social pressure on a person to conform even when the norm is not injunctive.

AC4P Applications

Large-scale behavior change is influenced through the *Social Proof* principle. Many people conform to fashion trends or fads because others are doing it. Seeing others wearing the AC4P wristband encourages others to do the same. This demonstrates social approval of the AC4P Movement, and perhaps awareness of how this wristband gets passed on among individuals. Such social proof could activate interpersonal conversation about the AC4P Movement and requests to get involved. For example, a common reaction following our passing of the AC4P wristband is, "Oh thank you, I've seen these around campus and have always wanted one of my own."

The AC4P T-Shirt. The *Social Proof* principle is one of many social-influence techniques used by the leaders of the AC4P Movement. During the early stages of the AC4P Movement, the original AC4P t-shirt included the line "Join the Movement". The phrase, "Join the Movement" implies other people are already a part of the AC4P Movement – a descriptive norm. This message is more influential in getting others to join the AC4P Movement than a message like "Actively Care for People".

After the AC4P Movement gets established in a particular culture, the general "Join the Movement" t-shirt is often customized for the situation. See, for example, the illustration of the t-shirt developed by the AC4P leaders at Chardon High School in Chardon, Ohio.[53]

The AC4P Website. The AC4P website applies the *Social Proof* principle in different ways. It offers a way for others to see the number of wristbands that have been registered and how the wristbands are traveling around the world. During AC4P presentations, AC4P leaders show a map of the world and tell AC4P stories connected to particular AC4P wristbands that have traveled across several countries.[54] See Part IV of this book for representative AC4P stories reported at ac4p.org.

A second way the *Social Proof* principle is used to promote the AC4P Movement is linking the AC4P website to Facebook.com. Through Facebook pages, individuals share their AC4P stories with friends and others. Here we have the influence of both interpersonal liking and a descriptive norm. In this case, the descriptive norm matches the injunctive norm.

Injunctive and Descriptive Norms. Many would agree with an injunctive norm like, "I should actively care for the well-being of others." But behavioral manifestations of this injunctive norm (i.e., performing AC4P behavior) occurs less often than desired, given there can never be too much AC4P behavior.

Negative gossip is promulgated through the news (perceived as a descriptive norm), whereas the AC4P website spreads positive gossip (an injunctive norm). Our vision is to see AC4P behavior become a descriptive norm.

Some schools and communities have organized an AC4P Day to align the injunctive and descriptive norm. Leaders in Newton, Connecticut (site of a tragic school shooting spree) implemented an "Acts of Kindness" day on September 14th, 2013. Community leaders gave speeches and distributed materials to initiate and maintain an AC4P buzz.

Similarly, thousands of students at Virginia Tech (VT) participate annually in "The Big Event" – a day when students volunteer their AC4P service for homeowners throughout the University community. They assist residents with a variety of projects, from planting trees and grooming gardens to cleaning home garages and basements.

Also, VT and many other universities are major financial contributors to cancer research through the annual "Relay-for-Life" event. AC4P behavior is becoming a descriptive norm at VT, partly as a result of the organization of special AC4P days that illustrate the social proof of actively caring.

The Authority Principle

The *Authority* principle reflects compliance to a request coming from an authority figure.[25] The term Authority has negative connotations because many historical examples and studies have illustrated the top-down coercive influence of people abusing their Authority.[56] Still, many people with Authority (e.g., physicians, ministers, teachers, and parents) set the stage for desirable behavior.

Obedience to authority can lead to undesirable behavior. This was shown by Stanley Milgram in a series of seminal experiments in the 1970s.[57] Ordinary people will administer an electrical shock to another person at the request of a perceived authority figure, Milgram discovered. Note the participant's body language in the illustration of Milgram's experiment. She's visibly distressed, as was the case for many participants, while following the anti-AC4P instructions from an authority figure.

In the first study, all 40 participants administered at least 300 volts before refusing to continue administering an electrical shock.[57] Surprisingly, 65% of the 40 participants administered the maximum voltage of 450

volts, even after the shock recipient (a stranger to the shock administrator) pounded on the wall and shouted "Ouch, this hurts!" Fortunately, the shock recipient in these studies was a RA and never actually received a shock.

There's a flip side to Milgram's horrific findings. Ordinary people will help others at the request of a perceived authority figure, according to a 1988 study.[58] A female RA (the requester) dressed as a perceived authority figure and requested a passerby give a nickel to a second RA (the recipient). The recipient posed as if he needed a nickel to pay for a parking meter.

The three conditions in this study were defined by the requester's outfit. In the Common-Clothes condition, the requestor was dressed as a panhandler, wearing an old t-shirt, tattered pants and shoes. Well-tailored business attire was worn by the requestor in the Business-Attire condition. Thirdly, the requester in the Uniform condition wore an official but ambiguous uniform with a patch and badge.

Individuals were much more likely to give the recipient a nickel in the Uniform condition compared to the other two conditions. Of the 150 participants in the Uniform condition, 72% complied with the request. In contrast, compliance in the Business-Attire and Common-Clothes conditions was 48% and 52%, respectively.

In addition to recording the number of participants who gave a nickel per each condition, the participant's verbal behavior accompanying the gift was recorded and classified into four categories: a) altruism, b) unquestioned obedience, c) compliance, and d) ambiguous.

Altruistic responses reflected a desire to help (e.g., "I saw you were in need of a nickel and I wanted to help"). The unquestioned obedience responses lacked the desire to help (e.g., "That person told me to give you a nickel"). A mixture between unquestioned obedience and altruistic responses were categorized as compliance (e.g.,

"I was told to help you, and I figured why not"). Finally, vague responses for helping were categorized in the ambiguous category.

The results demonstrate 27% of 26 participants viewed their gift of a nickel *as more altruistic* when the requester wore common clothes compared to tailored business attire (12.5% of 24 participants) and a uniform (14% of 36 participants).

On the other hand, 62.5% of 24 participants in the Business-Attire condition and 72% of 36 participants in the Uniform condition gave unquestioned obedience responses while giving a nickel to the "beggar." In contrast, only 27% of 26 participants in the Common-Clothes condition gave *unquestioned obedience responses*. Why do people obey an authority figure?

In childhood, obeying a parent's decision is supported through positive and negative consequences, Stanley Milgram proposed.[56] Even in adulthood, consequences are often controlled by an authority figure (e.g., managers or judges). In fact, authority is often defined by the person who controls the most consequences for others in a given situation.

Complying with a request from a manager can increase job security and determine a raise. Disobeying a supervisor can lead to termination.

Bottom line: Human behavior is motivated by consequences and people are likely to comply with requests from those in control of those consequences – the authority figure.

Harsh vs. Soft Factors

Authority figures can gain compliance through situational or person factors. These factors are categorized as harsh versus soft factors.[59] An authority figure who gains obedience from others based on a hierarchical position within a particular social structure represents the *harsh factor* approach. Managers, event staff, and administrators employ harsh factors to gain obedience. A staff member at a football game can instruct a fan to empty a cooler full of alcoholic beverages before entering the stadium.

In contrast, the *soft factor* approach applies person factors (e.g., experience, education, and credibility) to gain obedience. Physicians, professors, and ministers typically can use their person factors to gain obedience within the relevant environmental context. Because of their education and experience, we usually don't question the medicine and dosage amounts prescribed by a physician.

Authority Heuristics

Matt was recently duped by a car salesman. Before purchasing a car, the car salesman agreed to have it inspected at Matt's request. The car salesman took the car to the onsite mechanic. After the car passed inspection, Matt purchased the car.

Within a week, the motor seized up and prevented the car from running. Matt immediately went back to the car salesman to return the car and get a refund. When Matt addressed the issue he discovered the mechanic was a relative of the car salesman who shares the profits for each vehicle sold. Their ploy caused Matt to lose several thousand dollars, and he still was without a functional vehicle.

In this real-life example, Matt became a victim of heuristics. *Heuristics* are mental shortcuts used to make a decision.[60] These shortcuts can save a lot of time and effort in making a decision. For instance, we often don't question a prescription from a medical doctor. After all, the physician is the expert and is looking out for our best interests.

In the car salesman example, Matt made two heuristic mistakes. First he allowed the car salesman to find a mechanic. This saved Matt the trouble of finding a mechanic and an inspection station. The second mistake: assuming the mechanic was a nonbiased third party, as is usually the case.

Bottom line: Individuals can gain obedience from others by creating the perception they are an authority. Bearing titles and wearing certain clothes are two methods people can use to influence the perception they warrant authority influence.[25]

Attire. As a bystander, Cory recently witnessed a person stealing a road sign. Another onlooker approached the thief and strongly suggested he return the sign. The thief ignored the onlooker's request. Shortly after the onlooker's intervention, two police officers approached the thief and requested the sign be returned. Without questioning, the thief immediately obeyed and returned the sign. A uniform can gain more obedience to a request than regular clothes.[61]

To empirically test the impact of attire on onlookers' behavior, a RA dressed differently in two conditions.[62] In the Low-Status condition, the RA wore common clothes. In the High-Status condition, the same RA wore a finely pressed suit. In both conditions, the RA was the first of a number of pedestrians to disobey the pedestrian traffic signal by crossing the street when it displayed "wait." Observers recorded the number of people who illegally crossed the street with the RA and the individuals who waited to cross the street legally.

Significantly more people (14% of 290) illegally crossed the street when the confederate's clothes suggested high status than when the attire of the illegal pedestrian reflected low status (4% of 288).

Titles. Titles define a level of authority because they offer insight into the background of the individual (e.g., education, experience, and leadership). The military uses titles/ranks to signify the chain of command. A doctor's title (e.g., cardiologist, surgeon, and dentist) provides insight to his/her educational background and expertise.

Even when a title is not authentic, bearing one can impact one's decision.[63] Recall Matt getting duped by a car salesman and mechanic. The mechanic may not have been a mechanic at all. Because the individual held the title of mechanic, Matt trusted his decision regarding the condition of the vehicle.

Matt's trusting of the mechanic's credentials through titling relates to an instructive study. Over the phone a researcher claimed he was a medical doctor and instructed different nurses to give a patient a specific drug s/he did not need.[64] The results were terrifying. Almost all (95%) of the 22 nurses studied complied with the researcher's request. Fortunately, a RA stopped each nurse before the medicine was administered and informed them about the study.

That study was conducted in 1966. We wonder whether the same results would be found today, given the current context of frequent internet scamming and phone-call solicitation.

AC4P Applications

Leaders of the AC4P Movement have used various strategies from the Authority Principle to spread the AC4P Movement. Soft-Factor approaches are commonly used by the AC4P leaders. Examples of experience, education, and credibility are often found in resources like the AC4P brochure and on the AC4P website (ac4p.org):

> *"Actively Caring, coined by Dr. E. Scott Geller, refers to any behavior going above and beyond the call of duty for others. For decades, Dr. Geller, alumni-distinguished professor at Virginia Tech, has applied behavioral science to keep people safe at work and on the road."*

To gain credibility via a title, the AC4P leaders are introduced as college students and campus leaders to an assembly of students, from elementary to high-school students. The same leaders wear AC4P t-shirts to display their involvement in the AC4P Movement. To enhance the leaders' credibility, they could add the title: "AC4P Leader" to their shirts.

The Scarcity Principle

On the popular television show *Pawn Stars,* customers bring their rare items to sell or trade at a pawn store in Las Vegas. Occasionally, the rare objects customers bring to the pawn store are far more valuable than realized. Sometimes these customers happily sell their unique items. At other times, customers decide to keep their rare items because they are so unusual and unique. They are presumed to be valuable because they are scarce.

The *Scarcity* principle states we tend to value things that are rare or becoming rare.[25] People pay large sums of money for unique collector items. Our attraction to limited numbers and our attempts to preserve personal control reflect the *Scarcity* principle.

Limited Numbers

Having a limited quantity of a certain product, and increasing one's awareness of the limited availability, increases one's propensity to purchase the product.[24] Advertising companies implement the limited-number technique to sell their products. They claim the item is a "limited release," "limited edition," or "one of a few left in stock." In this latter example, the *Scarcity* principle works in conjunction with the *Social Proof* principle. That is, the message "one of a few left in stock" implies the product is in high demand and becoming scarcer.

Psychological Reactance

We behave to regain our personal control when we perceive a restriction or limitation to our freedom or individuality, according to *psychological reactance* theory.[65] Top-down control tactics can backfire for this reason. A young boy might "fight back" when his parents insist he wear certain clothes to school. The "fighting back" behavior presumes an attempt to regain some personal control. The boy in the illustration is "fighting back" or demonstrating counter-control.[66]

Recall from the section on the Authority Principle that a harsh tactic is one way to gain obedience from others. Due to psychological reactance, though, a top-down approach can be counterproductive.[4] University students getting most intoxicated on Thursday and Friday nights were those whose parents used the most punitive strategies to stop their children from consuming alcohol, according to field research conducted by the VT Center for Applied Behavior Systems (see Chapter 16).

It's called "The Forbidden Fruit Phenomenon." Restricting use of an item makes it scarce, and so the item seems more valuable when one can avoid the restrictions.

AC4P Applications

The *Scarcity* principle can be used to increase the perceived value of the AC4P wristband. For example, at conferences the AC4P leaders inform audience members they brought a limited number of wristbands to the conference. And, the AC4P wristbands can *only* be purchased at the ac4p.org website.

Of course, a social proof message can be added as an explanation for the limited number of AC4P wristbands. For instance, the scarcity of wristbands can be accounted for by explaining a large number of people wanted the wristband prior to the presentation.

Whenever t-shirts are customized for a particular school or community, both scarcity and social proof are activated. Students and teachers want to purchase and wear the special t-shirts because it reflects the common AC4P spirit at their site – a descriptive and injunctive norm. *Scarcity* is implicated because the number of these customized t-shirts is necessarily limited. And this special t-shirt cannot be purchased anywhere except from the local AC4P leaders or on the website: ac4p.org.

In Conclusion

The six social influence principles and strategies described and illustrated here can help initiate and sustain the AC4P Movement at your school, community, and workplace. Throughout this chapter we suggest ways to apply the social-influence principles and techniques to increase another person's propensity to perform AC4P behavior.

The method of delivering an influence technique can be more important than the technique itself. This is worth remembering. A top-down application can actually do more harm than good by activating psychological reactance or counter-control. That's why we call the AC4P approach to cultivate compassion on a large-scale – *humanistic behaviorism*.

We incorporate evidence-based principles of behavioral science to activate and sustain beneficial change. We also use person-centered principles of humanism to assure personal ownership and perceived empowerment. In other words, behavior-change methods are taught, coached, and implemented so both the benefactors and beneficiaries believe in their effectiveness and want to support the AC4P Movement.

Notes

1. Kenrick, D. T., Neuberg, S. L., & Cialdini, R. B. (2002). *Social psychology: Unraveling the mystery* (2nd Edition). Boston, MA: Pearson.

2. Thaler, R. H., & Sunstein, C. R. (2009) *Nudge: Improving decisions about health, wealth, and happiness*. New York, NY: Penguin Group.

3. Geller, E. S. (1996). *The psychology of safety: How to improve behaviors and attitudes on the job*. Radnor, PA: Chilton Book Company; Geller, E. S. (2001). *The psychology of safety handbook*. Boca Raton, FL: CRC Press.

4. Lehman, P. K., & Geller, E. S. (2008). Applications of social psychology to increase the impact of behavior-focused intervention. In L. Steg, A. P. Buunk, & T.Rothengatter (Eds.) (2008). *Applied social psychology: Understanding and managing social problems* (pp. 117-136). Cambridge, MA: Cambridge University Press.

5. Cialdini, R. B., & Goldstein, N. J. (2004). Social influence: Compliance and conformity. *Annual Review of Psychology, 55*, 591-621.

6. Geller, E. S. (2001). *The psychology of safety handbook*. Boca Raton, FL: CRC Press; Geller, E. S., Roberts, D. S., & Gilmore, M. R. (1996). Predicting propensity to actively care for occupational safety. *Journal of Safety Research, 27*, 1-8.

7. Festinger, L. (1957). *A theory of cognitive dissonance*. Stanford, CA: Stanford University Press.

8. Bem, D. J. (1967). Self-perception: An alternative interpretation of cognitive dissonance phenomena. *Psychological Review, 74*, 183-200.

9. Bem, D. J. (1972). Self-perception theory. In L. Berkowitz (Ed.). *Advances in experimental psychology* (Vol. 6) (pp. 1-62). New York, NY: Academic Press.

10. Freedman, J. L., & Fraser, S. C. (1966). Compliance without pressure: The foot-in-the-door technique.*Journal of Personality and Social Psychology. 4*, 195-202.

11. Cialdini, R. B., Eisenberg, N., Green, B. L., Rhoads, K., & Bator, R. (1998). Undermining the

undermining effect of reward in sustained interest: When unnecessary conditions are sufficient. *Journal of Applied Social Psychology, 28,* 249-63; Tybout, A. M., & Yalch, R. F. (1980). The effect of experience: A matter of salience? *Journal of Consumer Research, 6,* 406-413.

12. Kraut, R. E. (1973). Effects of social labeling on giving to charity. *Journal of Experimental Social Psychology. 9,* 551-562.

13. Kraut, R. E. (1973). Effects of social labeling on giving to charity. *Journal of Experimental Social Psychology. 9,* p. 554.

14. Kraut, R. E. (1973). Effects of social labeling on giving to charity. *Journal of Experimental Social Psychology. 9,* p. 555.

15. Retrieved from: www.bls.gov/cgi-bin/cpicalc.pl

16. Dweck, C.S. (2006). *Mindset: The new psychology of success.* New York: Ballotine Books.

17. Dweck, C.S. (2006). *Mindset: The new psychology of success.* New York: Ballotine Books., p. 71.

18. Dweck, C.S. (2006). *Mindset: The new psychology of success.* New York: Ballotine Books., p.72.

19. Dweck, C.S. (2006). *Mindset: The new psychology of success.* New York: Ballotine Books., p. 73.

20. Cialdini, R. B. (2001). *Influence: Science and practice* (6th Edition). Boston, MA: Pearson Education; Lehman, P. K., & Geller, E. S. (2008). Applications of social psychology to increase the impact of behavior-focused intervention. In L. Steg, A. P. Buunk, & Rothengatter, T. (Eds.) (2008). *Applied social psychology: Understanding and managing social problems* (pp. 117-139). Cambridge, MA: Cambridge University Press.

21. Geller, E. S. (2001). *The psychology of safety handbook.* Boca Raton, FL: CRC Press; Geller, E. S, & Veazie, B. (2010). *When no one's watching: Living and leading self-motivation.* Newport, VA: Make-A-Difference, LLC; Ludwig, T. D., & Geller, E. S. (2001). *Intervening to improve the safety of occupational driving: A behavior-change model and review of empirical evidence.* New York, NY: The Haworth Press, Inc.; Monty, R. A., & Perlmuter, L. C. (1975). Persistence of the effect of choice on paired-associate learning, *Memory & Cognition, 3,* 183-187; Perlmuter, L. C., Monty, R. A., & Kimble, G. A. (1971). Effect of choice on paired-associate learning. *Journal of experimental psychology, 91,* 47-58; Steiner, I. D. (1970). Perceived freedom in L. Berkowitz (Ed.). *Advancements in experimental social psychology* (Vol. 5). New York, NY: Academic Press.

22. Fazio, R. H., Sherman, S. J., & Herr, P. M. (1982). The feature-positive effect in the self-perception process. Does not doing matter as much as doing? *Journal of Personality and Social Psychology, 42,* 404-411.

23. Schlenker, B. R., Dlugolecki, D. W., & Doherty, K. (1994). The impact of self-presentations on self-appraisals and behavior. The power of public commitment. *Personality and Social Psychology Bulletin, 20,* 20-33; Tedeshi, J. T., Schlenker, B. R., & Bonoma, T. V. (1971). Cognitive dissonance: Private ratiocination or public spectacle? *American Psychologist, 26,* 685-695.

24. McCarty, S. M., & Geller, E. S. (2014). Actively caring to prevent bullying: Prompting and rewarding prosocial behavior in elementary schools. In E. S. Geller (Ed.) *Actively caring at your school: How to make it happen* (pp. 153-173). Newport, VA: Make-A-Difference, LLC.

25. Cialdini, R. B. (2001). *Influence: Science and practice* (6th Edition). Boston, MA: Pearson Education.

26. Cialdini, R. B. (2001). *Influence: Science and practice* (6th Edition). Boston, MA: Pearson Education, p. 148.

27. Emswiller, T., Deaux, K., & Willits, J. E. (1971). Similarity, sex, and requests for small favors. *Journal of Applied Psychology, 1,* 284-291.

28. Burger, J. M., Messian, N., Patel, S., Prado, A., & Anderson, C. (2004). What a coincidence! The

effects of incidental similarity on compliance. *Personality and Social Psychology Bulletin, 30,* 35-43.

29. Berscheid, E., & Walster, E. (1978). *Interpersonal attraction.* Reading, MA; Addison-Wesley; Howard, D. J., Gengler, C., & Jain, A. (1995). What's in a name? A complimentary means of persuasion. *Journal of Consumer Research, 22,* 200-211; Howard, D. J., Gengler, C., & Jain, A. (1997). The name remembrance effect. *Journal of Social Behavior and Personality, 12,* 801-810.

30. Zajonc, R. B. (1968). Attitudinal effects of mere exposure. *Journal of Personality and Social Psychology, 9,* 1-27.

31. Cory thanks all of the individuals who supported his family during this challenging time. Your AC4P behavior enabled us to heal and move forward.

32. Gouldner, A. (1960). The norm or reciprocity: A preliminary statement. *American Sociological Review, 25*(2), 161-178.

33. Babylon's Code of Hammurabi is one of the earliest known laws. These laws were based upon lextalionis (eye for an eye), which means for every crime committed an equitable punishment should be issued.

34. Kunz, P.R., & Woolcott, M. (1976). Season's greetings: From my status to yours. *Social Science Research, 5*(3), 269-278.

35. Trivers, R.L. (1971). The evolution of reciprocal altruism. *Quarterly Reviews of Biology, 46*(1), 35–57.

36. Boyce, T. E., & Geller, E. S. (2001). Encouraging college students to support pro-environmental behavior: Effects of direct versus indirect rewards. *Environment and Behavior, 33,* 107-125.

37. Goldstein, N. J., Griskevicius, V., & Cialdini, R. B. (2007). Invoking social norms: A social psychology perspective on improving hotel's linen-reuse programs. *Cornell Hotel and Restaurant Administration Quarterly, 48*(2), 145-150.

38. Goldstein, N. J., Griskevicius, V., & Cialdini, R. B. (2007). Invoking social norms: A social psychology perspective on improving hotel's linen-reuse programs. *Cornell Hotel and Restaurant Administration Quarterly, 48*(2), p. 146.

39. Cialdini, R. B., Vincent, J. E., Lewis, S. K., Catalan, J., Wheeler, D., & Darby, B. L. (1975). Reciprocal concessions procedure for inducing compliance: The door-in-the-face technique. *Journal of Personality and Social Psychology, 31,* 206-215.

40. Schwartzwald, D., Raz, M., & Zwibel, M. (1979). The applicability of the door-in-the-face technique when established behavior customs exit. *Journal of Applied Social Psychology, 9,* 576-586.

41. Nowak, M. A., & Sigmund, K. (2005). Evolution of indirect reciprocity. *Nature,* 437(7063), 1291-1298; Stanca, L. (2009). Measuring indirect reciprocity: Whose back do we scratch? *Journal of Economic Psychology, 30*(2), 190-202.

42. Furrow, C. B., Geller, E. S., & McCarty, S. M. (2013). A ripple effect from actively caring. In E. S. Geller (Ed.). *Actively caring for people: Cultivating a culture of compassion* (1st Edition) (pp. 93-101). Newport, VA: Make-A-Difference, LLC.

43. Brecker, S. J., Olson, J. M., & Wiggins, E. C. (2006). *Social psychology alive.* Belmont, CA: Thomson Wadsworth.

44. Deutsch, M., & Gerard, H. B. (1955). A study of normative and informational social influences upon individual judgment. *Journal of Abnormal and Social Psychology, 51,* 629-636.

45. Sherif, M. (1936). *The psychology of social norms.* Oxford, UK: Harper.

46. Sherif, M. (1935). A study of some social factors in perception. *Archives of Psychology, 27*(187), 1-60; Sherif, M. (1936). *The psychology of social norms.* Oxford, UK: Harper; Sherif, M. (1937).

An experimental approach to the study of attitudes. *Sociometry, 1,* 90-89.

47. Sherif, M. (1935). A study of some social factors in perception. *Archives of Psychology, 27*(187), 1-60.

48. Sherif, M. (1937). An experimental approach to the study of attitudes. *Sociometry, 1,* 90-89.

49. Asch, S. E. (1951). Effects of group pressure upon the modification and distortion of judgments. In H. Guetzkow (Ed.). *Groups leadership and men* (pp. 177-190). Pittsburgh, PA: Carnegie Press; Asch, S. E. (1952). *Social psychology.* New York, NY: Prentice-Hall; Asch, S. E. (1956). Studies of independence and conformity: A minority of one against a unanimous majority. *Psychological Monographs: General and Applied, 70* (9), 1-70.

50. Milgram, S., Bickman, L., & Berkowitz, L. (1969). Note on the drawing power of crowds of different size. *Journal of Personality and Social Psychology*, 13, 79-82.

51. Latane, B. (1981). The psychology of social impact. *American Psychologist, 35*(4), 343-356.

52. Cialdini, R. B., Kallgren, C. A., & Reno, R. R. (1991). A focus theory of normative conduct: A theoretical refinement and reevaluation of the role of norms in human behavior. *Advances in Experimental Social Psychology. 24,* 201-234.

53. Generic and customized AC4P t-shirts can be ordered on the website ac4p.org.

54. Case studies are available on ac4p.org.

55. Examples include the Stanford Prison Experiment, Milgram Studies, Rape of Rwanda, and the Holocaust.

56. Milgram, S. (1974). *Obedience to authority: An experimental view.* New York, NY: Harper & Row.

57. Milgram, S. (1963). Behavioral study of obedience. *Journal of Abnormal and Social Psychology, 67,* 371-378.

58. Bushman, B. J. (1988). The effects of apparel on compliance: A field experiment with a female authority figure. *Personal and Social Psychology Bulletin, 14,* 459-467.

59. Koslowsky, M., Schwarzwald, J., & Ashuri, S. (2001). On the relationship between subordinates' compliance to power sources and organizational attitudes. *Applied Psychology: International Review. 50,* 455-476; Raven, B. H., Schwarzwald, J., & Koslowsky, M. (1998). Conceptualizing and measuring a power/interaction model of interpersonal influence. *Journal of Applied Social Psychology. 6,* 161-168.

60. Kahneman, D., Slovic, P., & Tversky, A. (1982) (Eds.). *Judgments under uncertainty: Heuristics and biases.* New York: Cambridge University Press.

61. Bickman, L. (1974). The social power of a uniform. *Journal of Applied Social Psychology, 4,* 47-61.

62. Lefkowitz, M., Blake, R. R., & Mouton, J. S. (1955). Status factors in pedestrian violation of traffic signals. *Journal of Abnormal and Social Psychology, 51,* 704-706.

63. Cialdini, R. B. (2001). *Influence: Science and practice* (6th Edition). Boston, MA: Pearson Education; Hofling, C. K., Brotzman, E., Dalrymple, S., Graves, N., & Pierce, C. M. (1966). An experimental study of nurse-physician relationships. *Journal of Nervous and Mental Disease, 143,* 171-180.

64. Hofling, C. K., Brotzman, E., Dalrymple, S., Graves, N., & Pierce, C. M. (1966). An experimental study of nurse-physician relationships. *Journal of Nervous and Mental Disease, 143,* 171-180.

65. Brehm, J. W. (1966). *A theory of psychological reactance.* New York, NY: Academic Press.

66. Skinner, B. F. (1971). *Beyond freedom and dignity.* New York, NY: Alfred A. Knopf.

CHAPTER 6

Leading with AC4P Communication

E. Scott Geller

Y OU'VE HEARD THE expression, "Talk is cheap." Now consider the remarkable influence of "talking" on our feelings, attitudes, perceptions, knowledge, skills, and behavior. You cannot deny the fact that talking is the most cost-effective intervention we have to improve the human dynamics of any situation.

Simply put, both the quantity and the quality of AC4P behavior can be influenced by interpersonal and intrapersonal conversation. Our interpersonal communication or how we talk to others can influence their AC4P behavior directly or indirectly by affecting their current attitude and person-states, which in turn can increase their propensity to emit AC4P behavior, as covered in Chapter 2.

Our intrapersonal communication or how we talk to ourselves directs our own behavior and influences our attitude and person-states. We can commend ourselves for our AC4P behavior, and thereby increase the probability of performing another kind act. Plus, we use self-talk to direct our ongoing activity, which could include AC4P behavior.

Furthermore our self-talk can increase our sense of self-efficacy and personal control regarding the successful performance of an act of kindness, as well as optimism that our kind act will result in beneficial consequences, including an increased sense of self-esteem and belongingness for ourself and the beneficiary. Thus, the intervention power of conversation to ourselves and others is compelling and prevailing.

Prior chapters in this book have already covered aspects of effective conversation. For example, guidelines for communicating supportive and corrective feedback and for celebrating group achievements were provided in Chapter 3, and techniques for giving and receiving positive words of recognition for AC4P behavior were covered in Chapter 4. Plus, each of the six social-influence principles explained in Chapter 5 involved interpersonal communication to some extent.

This chapter brings us back to some basics in communicating more effectively to others and to ourselves with the overall mission of increasing the quantity and improving the quality of AC4P behavior. Yes, talk is cheap, but it can make or break our efforts to cultivate an AC4P culture of compassion.

The Power of Conversation

Let's start with a common-sense bottom line: Participation in AC4P conversations is key to preventing interpersonal conflict and cultivating cultures of compassion and caring. We're not talking about the high-tech communication referenced in the illustration on the next page, but about one-to-one interpersonal conversation related to AC4P behavior. Such improvement, in turn, benefits our own self-talk or intrapersonal communication and relevant person-states, leading to more AC4P behavior. Yes, we're talking about conversations having the power to activate and maintain an AC4P ripple effect.

This chapter offers guidelines and techniques for getting more beneficial impact from our communications with others, and with ourselves. Then four types of behavior management are presented, each defined by the nature of interpersonal conversation. First, however, let's consider the beneficial consequences of effective conversation. Realizing such consequences can motivate personal time and effort to improve our interpersonal conversations per the guidelines offered here.

Building Interpersonal Barriers

Surely you've seen how lack of communication can escalate a minor incident into major conflict. Here's an example: You see a colleagues and say, "Hello," yet she passes by without reacting. What do you say to yourself? Maybe she didn't see you, or had other thoughts on her mind. Still, it's easy for you to assume the person is unfriendly or doesn't like you.

So the next time you see this person you avoid a friendly, "Hello." You might even talk to others about that person's "unfriendliness". Can you see how an interpersonal barrier might start to develop?

This is only one of many situations that can stifle further interpersonal communication with an individual, and lead to negative feelings and judgments. The result: the possible perception of interpersonal conflict, an unpleasant relationship, lowered cooperation, and reduced willingness for that person to perform AC4P behavior.

Resolving Interpersonal Conflict

If the lack of conversation can initiate or energize conflict, it's not surprising that the occurrence of conversation can prevent or eliminate conflict. "Let's talk it out," as the saying goes. Of course, the quality of that conversation will determine whether any perceived conflict is heightened or lessened.

This issue of conversation quality is covered later in this chapter. Here I only want you to consider the potency of interpersonal talk. It can make or break interpersonal conflict, which in turn enables constructive or destructive relationships. And the nature of relationships determines whether individuals are willing to actively care for another person's safety and health.[1]

Bringing Reality to Intangibles

What is love, friendship, courage, loyalty, happiness, and forgiveness? Of course, you can describe behaviors that reflect these constructs, but where is the true meaning? Don't we derive the meaning of these common words from our conversations? Consider how we "fall in or out of love" depending on how we talk to ourselves and to others. Similarly, we convince ourselves we're happy through our self-talk, and this inner-conversation is obviously influenced by what we hear others say about us.

We define another person's friendship, courage, or loyalty by talking about that individual in certain ways, both to ourselves and to others. Our internal mental scripts and external verbal behaviors rule. They give practical meaning to concepts that define the very essence of human existence. Then when groups, organizations, or communities communicate to explain these concepts, we have a "culture." In fact, our culture is defined by conversations – both spoken and unspoken – and the behaviors influenced by such communication.

Defining Culture

What about "unspoken conversation"? I'm referring to customs or unwritten rules we heed without mention. We might realize, for example, the "teacher's pet" sits in the front row, or the coach doesn't want to hear about a star athlete missing a class, or Mom is more lenient than Dad regarding certain rule-breaking behavior. We might also know characteristics that bias a particular supervisor's performance appraisals, from gender and seniority to one's ability on the golf course.

It might be understood, for example, that a male with high seniority and a low golf handicap is more likely to get the special training assignment, but such prejudice is certainly not expressed. If it were, a productive conversation would be possible – one that could reduce the barriers that prevent optimal interpersonal trust and the achievement of an AC4P culture.

Bottom line: Spoken and unspoken words define a culture, and the culture can change, for better or worse, through interpersonal and intrapersonal conversation.

Influencing Self-Esteem

How we talk to ourselves both influences and reflects our self-esteem. In fact, it's probably fair to say our mental script about ourselves is our self-esteem. We can focus our self-talk on the good things people say about us or on other people's critical statements about us. The result is a certain kind of self-talk we call "interpretation."

Such intrapersonal communication can increase or decrease how we feel about ourselves. In other words, our self-esteem can go up or down according to how we talk to ourselves about the way others talk about us. As the illustration on the next page shows negative self-talk can detract from the consequences of positive experiences that should increase one's self-esteem.

Enabling Breakthroughs

In his provocative book *Leadership & the Art of Conversation*, Kim Krisco[2] defines a breakthrough as going beyond business as usual and getting more than expected. This requires people to realize new possibilities, commit to going for more, and then make a concerted effort to overcome barriers.

In most situations, achieving an AC4P culture requires a breakthrough. So how can we visualize possibilities, show

commitment to go for a breakthrough, and identify barriers to overcome? You guessed it – through conversation.

Krisco warns us to expect barriers and resistance to change. And the greater the change, the greater the resistance. But remember, most barriers to change are perceptions or interpretations derived through people's self-talk about their perceived reality. Conversation, both interpersonal and intrapersonal, enables us to overcome the barriers that hold back the accomplishment of a breakthrough.

The Art of Improving Conversation

Given the power of conversation to resolve interpersonal conflict, define culture, and affect the person-states that influence one's propensity to emit AC4P behavior, we need to apply this powerful tool to support and advance the AC4P Movement. But how do we maximize the impact of our interpersonal and intrapersonal conversations? What kinds of conversations are more likely to provoke and maintain beneficial participation in the AC4P Movement? That's the theme for the remainder of this chapter. Let's start with the most basic aspect of communication – the words we use.

Watch Your Language

Words shape our feelings, expectancies, attitudes and behavior.[3] How you talk about something influences how others feel about it, especially yourself. In other words, our verbal behavior affects our attitudes and beliefs, and these in turn determine more behavior. Question: How might your language increase or decrease involvement in a movement to cultivate an AC4P culture.

Consider for example how some words used in the safety and health fields are counter-productive. They are negative and uninspiring, and probably have a detrimental effect on people's voluntary involvement in organized efforts to actively care for the safety, health, and well-being of others.

Accident Implies Chance. The word accident implies "a chance occurrence" outside one's immediate control. When a young child has an "accident" in his pants, we presume he was not in control. He couldn't help it. Occupational and vehicle "accidents" are usually unintentional, of course, but are they truly chance occurrences? There are usually specific controllable factors, such as changes in the environment, behaviors, and/or attitudes, that can prevent "accidents."

Years ago our President Bill Clinton at the time stumbled on the steps at the home of golf pro Greg Norman in West Palm Beach, Florida. It happened on the morning of March 14th, 1997. When asked about the incident, Clinton was quoted in our local newspaper (*The Roanoke Times*) as giving the statement depicted in the illustration. The logical follow-up comment is, "When it's my time, it's my time." How many times have you heard someone say something like that?

Clinton's remarks reflect the implied meaning of "accident." "Accidents are bound to happen somewhere to someone. It's just a matter of time before it happens here. I just hope my luck doesn't run out and it happens to me." These statements are not far-fetched. They follow logically from the implied meaning of "accident."

Incidentally, do you recall any reports from an "accident investigation" of Clinton's injury? We heard much about the extent of his injury – a tear of his quadriceps tendon, which connects the upper

thigh to the kneecap. And we were told about the surgery to his knee at Bethesda Naval Hospital. We even got a play-by-play of his recovery, progressing from a big brace and crutches to a cane over several weeks. But nothing was mentioned about the factors contributing to the injury.

Were the steps slippery? Did someone distract the President? Did the President fail to use the handrail, or was a handrail unavailable? Did someone "accidentally" push Mr. Clinton? Where were the bodyguards? Could a bodyguard have warned the President about an environmental hazard or offered feedback about his at-risk behavior?

This is just a sample of AC4P questions that could have been asked to enable the kind of injury analysis needed to prevent similar future mishaps to the President and to others in similar circumstances.

Imagine the nationwide impact if a careful AC4P analysis of the potential contributing factors to Clinton's injury had been conducted and reported. Consider the benefits of broad media coverage of the potential environmental, behavioral, and person-based factors that led to the President's injury, and the techniques that could be implemented to prevent future mishaps like this one. Bodyguards might even add observations of safe versus at-risk behaviors of the President and his companions to the regular protective audits they perform. However, none of this AC4P participation for injury prevention is likely to occur with the attitude that, "It was just an accident, and accidents happen to people."

We want to develop the belief and expectation in our culture that injuries can be prevented by controlling certain factors. Therefore, "accident" is the wrong word to use when referring to unintentional injuries. It can reduce the number of people who believe with true conviction that their AC4P involvement in safety efforts can prevent personal injuries. Besides, the word "injury" has more emotional impact than "accident." For the same reason, it's not a vehicle "accident"; it's a vehicle "crash."

Restraints Don't Invite Use. For more than three decades I've been urging

transportation and safety professionals to stop using the terms "occupant restraints" and "child restraints" for vehicle safety belts and child safety seats. These terms imply discomfort and lack of personal control, as shown in the illustration.

Furthermore, these labels fail to convey the true function of these devices. "Seat belt" is better than "occupant restraint," but this popular term is not really adequate because it doesn't describe the function or appearance of today's lap-and-shoulder belts. We need to get into the habit of saying "safety belt" and "child safety device." But actually "life belt" and "life-saving seat" are more appropriate terms.

Priority or Value. Priority implies importance and a sense of urgency. Safety and healthcare professionals are often quick to urge us to make safety and a healthy lifestyle priorities." Similarly, most flight attendants begin their safety announcements with, "Your safety is our priority." This seems appropriate, since my dictionary defines "priority" as "taking precedence logically or in importance."[4]

But everyday experience teaches us that priorities come and go. Depending upon the demands of the moment, one priority often gets shifted for another. Do we really want to put AC4P on such shifting ground? An AC4P culture requires actively caring to be accepted as a value. The relevant definition of "value" in my dictionary is "something (as a principle or ideal) intrinsically valuable or desirable".[5] Shouldn't AC4P be a "value" that people bring with them every day, regardless of the ongoing priorities or task requirements.

Don't Say "Behavior Modification."   Over the years I've seen "behavior modification" used many times for titles of research presentations and keynote addresses at regional and national conferences. I've heard teachers, consultants, coaches, parents, and students use this term to describe behavior-focused approaches to improving individual and group functioning in educational, athletic, and industrial settings, as well as the residence facilities for individuals with developmental, physical, and/or psychological challenges.

Indeed, a flagship research journal of ABS for 37 years is entitled, *Behavior Modification.* And, I've often been introduced at conferences as a specialist in "behavior modification." This is the wrong choice of words to use if we want acceptance and involvement from the folks who are to be "modified." Who wants to be "modified"?

This lesson was learned the hard way more than 30 years ago by the behavioral scientists and therapists who developed the principles and techniques of "behavior modification." Whether applying them to teachers, students, employees, or prisoners, the term "behavior modification" was a real turn-off. It conveyed images of manipulation, top-down control, loss of personal control, and "Big Brother."

Unfortunately, the term "behavior" alone carries negative associations for many – as in, "Let's talk about your behavior last night" – but I can't see any way around using this term. Behavior refers to a process, or the ongoing actions that result in certain output or outcomes. We need to teach and demonstrate the benefits of focusing on behaviors, and on defining behaviors correctly. If we focused more on desirable than undesirable behaviors, as should be the case, the term "behavior" would have more positive than negative connotations.

As detailed elsewhere,[6] the words used to describe behavior should be chosen for: a) clarity to avoid being misinterpreted, b) precision to fit a specific activity, c) brevity to keep it simple, and d) objectivity to refer to actions explicitly observed. Without a clear and precise definition of behavior, most action words can have more than one interpretation, as depicted in the illustration – a reaction to another of President Clinton's "accidents."

If you want to encourage participation in an AC4P process, don't link the term "modification" with behavior. "Behavior analysis" is the

term used by researchers and scholars in this area of applied psychology, as explained in Chapter 1. This implies that behavior is analyzed first, and if change is called for, an intervention process is developed with input from the client(s).

Given that "analysis" can sound cold or bring to mind Sigmund Freud and psychoanalysis, we use "science," as in "applied behavioral science" (ABS) throughout this text. Besides, "science" implies both analysis and intervention based on empirical research.

I hope the basic message is clear. We need to realize how our language can activate feelings and even behaviors we don't want. It can hinder voluntary participation. If we want to communicate in order to "sell" an AC4P process, we must consider how our language will be perceived by those whose participation is needed to make the process work. That's why we refer to the principles and applications of ABS as *humanistic behaviorism*, combining the science of behaviorism with the caring philosophy of humanism.[7]

Ponder the following words and phrases related to the human dynamics of safety, health, or well-being. Do some of the words or phrases on the left suggest negative associations that can stifle involvement in an AC4P Movement? I suggest alternatives on the right, but you might have a better idea.

"Air bag" or "safety cushion"?
"Requirement" or "Opportunity"
"Peer pressure" or "peer support"?
"Program" or "Process"?
"Training" or "Coaching"?
"Loss-control manager" or "Injury-prevention facilitator"?
"Mandate" or "Expectation"
"Compliance" or "Commitment"?
"I got to do this" or "I get to do this"?
"I must meet this deadline" or "I choose to achieve another milestone"?
"I wake up to my alarm clock" or "I awaken to my opportunity clock"?

It's a good personal or group exercise to consider the ramifications of using these terms and phrases. Adding alternatives to this list is even more beneficial. But understanding the critical relationship between words, attitudes, and voluntary participation is only half the battle. We need to change our verbal habits, and this is easier said than done.

Also, the effectiveness of our communication to facilitate involvement in an AC4P process depends on more than the words we use. Let's turn to other aspects of our interpersonal conversations that affect their behavioral and attitudinal impact.

Get Beyond the Past

Has this ever happened to you? You ask for more AC4P involvement from a particular individual and you get a reaction like, "I've tried that AC4P behavior more than once and got no appreciation, so count me out." Or, have you attended a group meeting where people spend more time going over past accomplishments or failures than discussing future possibilities and deriving new action plans.

These are examples of conversations stuck in the past. The dialogue might be enjoyable or a nice diversion, but little or no progress is made. Conversations about past events help us connect with others and recognize similar experiences, opinions, and motives. But, such communication does not permit progress toward problem solving or continuous improvement. For this to happen, the conversation must leave the past and move on.

Kim Krisco[2] maintains leaders need to help people move their conversations from the past to the future and then back to the present. If you want conversation to fuel engagement in an AC4P Movement, possibilities need to be entertained (future talk) after the past is acknowledged, followed by the development of practical action plans (present talk). This is the case for group conversation at a team meeting, as well as for one-on-one advising, counseling, or coaching.

To direct the flow of a conversation from past to future and then to the present, it's first necessary to recognize and appreciate the other person's perspectives. Practice AC4P listening, as discussed later in this chapter. Then shift the focus to the future. "Yes, I understand we've had difficulties with this issue in the past, but what is your vision for an ideal resolution. What specific improvements would you like to see?"

After the ideal AC4P possibilities are explored, shift back to the present. "What can we do today to move us forward toward those ideals."

Seek Commitment

You know your interpersonal conversation is especially constructive when someone makes a commitment to get involved – to join the AC4P Movement. This reflects success in moving conversation from the past to the future and then to a specific action plan for the present.

As discussed in Chapter 5, a verbal commitment also tells you something is happening on an intrapersonal level. The person is becoming self-motivated (Chapter 3), increasing the probability AC4P behavior will continue in the absence of an external accountability system.[8]

Now you can proceed to talk about ways to support the commitment, or methods to hold participants mutually accountable. For example, one person might offer to help a colleague meet an obligation through verbal reminders. Or, an individual might agree to honor a commitment by showing a coach certain behavioral records that verify AC4P involvement. This is the kind of follow-up conversation that facilitates continued participation.

Stop and Listen

Sometimes, in their eagerness to make things happen, managers, coaches, teachers, or parents give corrective feedback in a top-down, seemingly controlling manner. In other words, their passion to make a difference can lead to an overly directive approach to get others to change their behavior.

An indirect or nondirective approach to giving advice is usually more effective, especially over the long term,[9] and this is a basic tenet of humanistic therapy.[10]

Think about it: How do you respond when someone tells you exactly what to do? Now it certainly depends on who is giving the directive, but I bet your reaction is not entirely positive. You might follow the instructions, especially if it comes from someone with the power to control consequences. But how will you feel? Will you be self-motivated to make a lasting change? You might if you asked for the direction. But if you didn't request feedback, you could feel insulted or embarrassed.

Try to be more nondirective when using interpersonal conversation to affect behavior change. This requires empathic listening, or as we say, "AC4P listening."

Dale Carnegie wrote about the value of empathic listening more than 50 years ago in his classic book: *How to Win Friends and Influence People*.[11] His wisdom is reflected in the writing of many authors of popular self-help books, including Stephen Covey's fifth habit of highly effective people, "Seek First to Understand. Then to be Understood."[12]

Carnegie, Covey, and others offer the same basic strategies for AC4P listening; and if you've had any training in effective communication, you've reached the same advice. Let's review these guidelines with four easy-to-remember words, each beginning with the letter "R."

For readers who have received communication training, this review will at least provide a mnemonic for remembering how to listen with an AC4P mindset and teach others to do the same. To be sure, the increasing "lean and mean" and "win/lose" paradigms of contemporary organizations, as well as the focus on impersonal emails and text messages, suggest a dire need to teach and use these humanistic guidelines for AC4P listening.

Repeat. This is the easiest technique to use. Simply mimic (or repeat) what you hear in the same words. This clarifies you heard correctly, and most importantly, prompts the person to say more. Remember the purpose of AC4P listening is to motivate the other person to say more so you can truly understand the problem.

So if a friend tells you he's dropping out of school, you might repeat this statement with, "You're dropping out?" This shows you're attentive and interested, and waiting for more information. Hearing how drastic the statement sounds, the person might reply, "Well, at least I feel like dropping out."

Then, what would you say? Following this "repeat" technique, you would say, "You mean you feel like dropping out?" Or, you might use different words to echo the same meaning. This is the next AC4P listening technique.

Rephrase. Instead of mimicking the content, you might rephrase the statement. In other words, say back the same thing but in different words. In our example, you might say, "You mean you don't like the life of a college student anymore?" By putting the statement in your own words, you're showing genuine interest while also asking for more information. You're also checking for understanding. If you can rephrase the statement correctly, you have received and interpreted the communication accurately.

It's possible your friend miscommunicated or you misperceived something. Your rephrasing gives the other person a chance to explain. And, this is what you want – more disclosure of the problem.

Suppose your friend clarifies, "Well, it's not that I don't like being a student here, it's just that some of my teachers get me so frustrated at times, I feel like quitting." Now, your friend has revealed a more specific aspect of the problem. What do you say?

You could use the repeat strategy and return with, "Your teachers get you frustrated." Alternatively, you could attempt to rephrase with something like, "You mean some of your teachers get you so angry that your motivation to continue attending classes is sapped." Or, perhaps this statement calls for the next "R" of AC4P listening – ratification.

Ratify. With this AC4P listening strategy you demonstrate affirmations or support for the individual's statement by confirming your understanding. In other words, you offer words that show approval for what is being said, and this in turn, encourages more explanation.

In our example, you might ratify your appreciation of the statement by saying, "I know the feeling, I've been frustrated with some of my teachers at times and wonder whether this college life is for me."

At this point, you might be tempted to jump in with probing questions to find out more about the frustration, the teachers, or the situation. What teachers got you so upset? What did they do? Why are you so frustrated that you want to quit? You should resist this temptation to be directive. You probably have not heard enough about the problem to begin a structured (and unbiased) analysis.

More AC4P listening could reveal problems beyond the teachers. Perhaps it's not a teacher per se, but a particular homework assignment or exam grade. Or, the problem might stem from interactions with another student, or a family member, or from feelings of personal inadequacy, including a perceived loss of confidence, self-efficacy, or personal control.

Bottom line: A person's distress signals can come from many sources, and these will probably not come to the surface quickly in one-to-one communication. And, if the relevant causes of a problem were disclosed early, it's unlikely you could give optimal advice at this point – directive action that is both useful and accepted.

Usually, the best we can do is listen actively with repeat, rephrase, and ratify strategies in order to get the problem out in the open. Ultimately, we want the person to express true feelings, as indicated by the fourth "R" word.

Reflect. When people reflect their inner feelings about a situation, they are at the personal root of the problem. Such self-disclosure of person-states can lead to insight into the true cause of the problem (for both the speaker and the listener), and suggest strategies for intervention. However, even at this stage (with outer layers of the onion peeled away), it's usually better to let the speaker entertain a variety of possible intervention approaches.

If you've been an AC4P listener, you might eventually get the ultimate reward for your sensitivity, patience, and emotional intelligence. The speaker will ask you for specific advice. When you hear words like, "What do you think I should do," you have mastered AC4P listening. You have shown you actively care, and now your thoughtful direction will likely be most relevant, understood, and accepted.

"My wife says I never listen to her ...or at least I think that's what she said."

CONCOURSE A

Ask Questions First

Suppose the conversation is not about a serious issue like personal distress, frustration or apathy, but only about a less-than-desired behavior. You see an opportunity for a person to show more or better AC4P behavior in a particular situation. What should you say?

Instead of telling the person what to do, try this. Get the individual to tell you, in his own words, what he should have done to reflect the AC4P principles. You can do this by asking questions with a sincere and AC4P demeanor. Avoid a sarcastic or demeaning tone at all costs.

First, point out certain AC4P behaviors you noticed–it's important to start with positives. Then move on to the undesirable behavior by asking, "Could you have been more actively caring in that situation?" Of course, you hope for more than a "yes" or "no" response to a question like this.

But if that's all you get, you need to be more precise in follow-up questioning. You might, for example, point out a particular situation where AC4P behavior was called for and ask what that behavior should be.

Now we're talking about giving corrective feedback. This was addressed in Chapter 3 with regard to communicating the results of observations with a critical behavior checklist (CBC). But even without a CBC and a systematic feedback process, start corrective feedback with questions.

By asking questions, you're always going to learn something. If nothing else you'll hear the rationale behind not performing in an optimal AC4P manner. You might uncover a barrier to AC4P behavior you can help the person overcome. A conversation that entertains ways to remove obstacles that hinder AC4P behavior is especially valuable if it translates possibilities into feasible and relevant action plans.

Beware of Bias

Every conversation you have with someone is biased by prejudice or prejudgment filters – in yourself and within the other person. You can't get around it. From personal experience, people develop opinions and attitudes, and these in turn influence subsequent experience.

With regard to interpersonal conversation, we have subjective prejudgment filters that influence what words we hear, how we interpret those words, and what we say in response to those words.[13] Every conversation influences how we process and interpret the next conversation.

The illustration makes my point. The female driver is merely trying to inform the other driver of an obstacle in the road. But that's not what the driver of the pick-up truck hears. This driver's prior driving experience leads to a biased interpretation of the warning. You could call such selective listening an "autobiographical bias".[12] Of course, factors besides prior experience can bias interpersonal communication, including personality, mood state, physiological needs, and future expectations.

It's probably impossible to escape completely the impact of this premature bias in our conversations. But we can exert some control. Actually, each of the conversation strategies discussed here are helpful.

For example, the nondirective approach attempts to overcome this bias by listening actively and asking questions before giving instruction. With this approach a person's biasing filters can be identified and considered in the customization of a plan for corrective action.

Certain words or phrases in a conversation can be helpful in diminishing the impact of a prejudice filter. For example, when you say "as you know" before giving advice, you're limiting the perception of a personal insult and the possibility of a "tune-out" filter.

By asking people for their input up front, you reduce the likelihood they will later tune you out. It's the principle of reciprocity (Chapter 5). By listening first, you increase the odds the other person will listen to you without a "tune-out" filter.

If you think a person might tune you out because they heard your message before, you could use opening words to limit the power of tune-out filters. Specifically, you might start the conversation with something like, "Now I realize you might have heard something like this before, but..." In this way you are anticipating the kind of intrapersonal conversation (or mental script) that activates a tune-out reaction, and thereby your opening words can reduce such filtering.

In the same vein, don't let your prejudices about a speaker limit what you hear. Do you ever listen less closely to certain individuals because they seldom had anything useful to say in the past, or because you think you can predict what they will say? If so, you've let your past conversations with these people bias future conversation. Becoming aware of this "stuck-in-the-past" prejudice can enable more AC4P listening.

Don't let a speaker limit what you hear. Tell yourself you're not listening to someone, rather you're listening for something.[2] You're not listening reactively to confirm a prejudice – you're listening proactively for possibilities.

Pay close attention to the body language and tone in conversations. I'm sure you've heard many times that the method of delivery can hold as much or more information as the words themselves. Listen for passion, commitment, or caring. If nothing else, you could learn whether the messenger understands and believes the message.

Perhaps you'll learn a new way to deliver a message yourself. Bottom line: Our intrapersonal conversations can either facilitate or hinder what we learn from interpersonal conversation.

Plant Words to Improve Self-Image

How we talk about others influences interpersonal perceptions. How we hear others talk about us shapes our own self-image. And how we talk to ourselves about these viewpoints can make them a permanent feature of our self-concept or self-esteem. Want to change how others perceive you? Change the conversations people are having about you.

Through proactive AC4P listening, you can become aware of negative interpersonal conversations about you. Then you can interject new statements about yourself into conversations, especially with people who have numerous contacts with others.

If you suspect, for example, colleagues consider you to be forgetful and disorganized, you could mention certain self-management strategies you've been using lately to improve memory and organization. Of course you need to actually practice these techniques so you'll also change your self-talk.

If you focus on new positive qualities rather than past inadequacies in your conversations with others and with yourself, you'll surely improve your self-image and self-esteem. Plant key messages about your commitment to become a more effective AC4P person, and you'll eventually see yourself that way and behave accordingly.

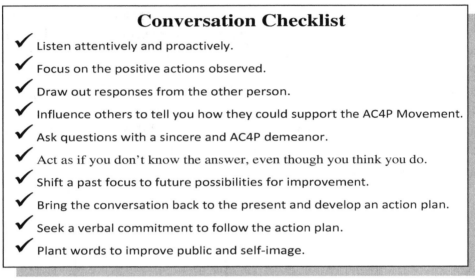

Conversation Checklist

✔ Listen attentively and proactively.

✔ Focus on the positive actions observed.

✔ Draw out responses from the other person.

✔ Influence others to tell you how they could support the AC4P Movement.

✔ Ask questions with a sincere and AC4P demeanor.

✔ Act as if you don't know the answer, even though you think you do.

✔ Shift a past focus to future possibilities for improvement.

✔ Bring the conversation back to the present and develop an action plan.

✔ Seek a verbal commitment to follow the action plan.

✔ Plant words to improve public and self-image.

Figure 6.1. Follow these guidelines for effective interpersonal conversation.

In Summary

The strategies covered here for getting the most from interpersonal conversation are reviewed in Figure 6.1. Each technique is relevant for getting more AC4P involvement from others. Plus, applying these strategies effectively can improve a person's self-talk or intrapersonal conversation. This leads to increased self-esteem, self-efficacy, and personal control – person-states that enhance an individual's willingness to perform AC4P behavior.

First, consider the tendency to focus interpersonal and intrapersonal conversation on the past. This helps us connect with others, but it also feeds our prejudice filters and limits the potential for a conversation to facilitate beneficial change. We enable progress when we move conversations with ourselves and others from past to future possibilities and then to goal setting for present-day behavior.

Expect people to protect their self-esteem with excuses for their past mistakes. Listen proactively for barriers to AC4P behavior reflected in these excuses. Then help the conversation shift to a discussion of possibilities for improvement and personal commitment to apply a practical action plan. This is more likely to occur with a nondirective than directive approach in which more questions are asked than directives given, and when opening words are used to protect self-esteem and limit the impact of reactive bias.

Remember that planting certain words in self-talk and conversations with others can improve your self-image and confidence as a facilitator of beneficial change. Tell others of your increased commitment to facilitate more effective AC4P conversations. Then tell yourself the strategies you will use to improve interpersonal conversation and commend yourself when you do. In this way, intra- and interpersonal conversations work together to help achieve an AC4P culture of compassion.

Conversation for Safety Management

Behavior is managed through conversation, and the success of behavior management is determined in large part by the effectiveness of interpersonal communication. This starts with listening proactively to understand the other person's situation before giving direction, advice, or support.

Then one of four types of interpersonal conversation should occur, depending on what kind of management is called for. As depicted in Figure 6.2 the conversation can reflect coaching, supporting, instructing, or delegating[14] depending on the amount of direction and motivation needed in a particular situation.

Coaching Conversation

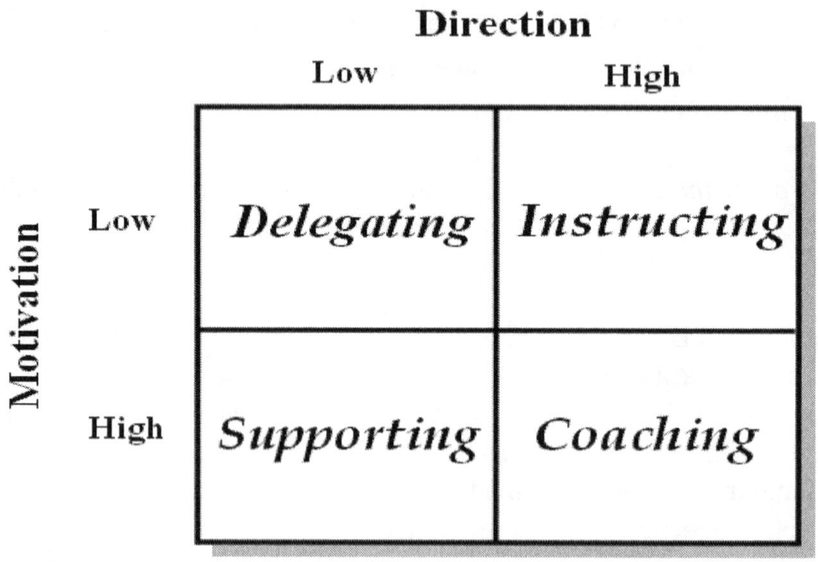

Figure 6.2. Management conversation is determined by the amount of direction and motivation needed.

Coaches give direction and provide feedback. They present a plan, perhaps specific behaviors needed for a certain task, and then follow up with support and AC4P feedback to pinpoint what worked and what did not. Periodic reminders keep people on the right track, while intermittent recognition provide support to keep people going.

Delegating Conversation

Sometime it's best to give an assignment in general terms (without specific direction) and to limit interpersonal behavioral feedback. This is when team members are already motivated to do their best and will give each other direction, support, and feedback when needed. These individuals should be self-accountable or self-motivated, and expected to use self-management techniques (activators and consequences) to keep themselves motivated and on the right track.[15]

Instructive Conversation

Some people are already highly motivated to perform well, but don't know exactly what to do. This is often the case with new hires, beginning students, interns and trainees. They want to make a good first impression, and the newness of the situation is naturally motivating. They are nervous, however, because of response uncertainty. They aren't sure what to do in the relatively novel situation. In this case, managers, teachers, or coaches need to focus on giving behavior-focused instruction.

This type of conversation should also be the coaches' approach at most athletic events. Individuals and teams in a sports contest do not typically need motivation. The situation itself, from fan support to peer pressure, often provides plenty of extrinsic motivation. Such competitors need directional focus for their motivation. They need to know what specific behaviors are needed to win in various situations.

This said, my personal experience with athletic coaches is not consistent with this analysis. For example, are the half-time speeches of team coaches more likely to be directional or motivational?

Supportive Conversation

What about the experienced person who does the same tasks day after day? This individual doesn't need direction, but could benefit from periodic expressions of sincere thanks for a job well done.

There are times when experienced workers know what to do but don't consistently perform up to par. This is not a training problem, but rather one of execution.[16] Through proactive listening a manager can recognize this and provide the kind of support that increases motivation.

This could involve broadening a job assignment, varying the task components, or assigning leadership responsibilities. But at least it includes the delivery of one-to-one recognition in ways that increase a person's sense of importance and self-efficacy. (See Chapter 3 for ways to give quality AC4P recognition.)

A safety celebration with top-down support and bottom-up involvement encourages teamwork and builds a sense of belonging among participants. Therefore, the most effective celebrations are planned by representatives from the group whose efforts warrant the celebration.

At these celebrations, managers do more listening than talking. They show genuine approval and appreciation of the challenges addressed and the difficulties handled in achieving the bottom line.

Discussions of the journey help participants write internal scripts for continued self-talk and self-motivation to achieve more to justify the next celebration. See Chapter 3 for more details about planning the most effective celebration for group support.

Choosing the Best Management Conversation

So how can we know what type of behavior-management conversation to use? This is where empathy is critical. Your assessment of situations and people – through observing, listening, and questioning – will determine which approach to use. And given the dynamic characteristics of most work and educational settings and the changing nature of people, you need to make this assessment periodically per situation and participant.

Consider, for example, the new employee who needs specific direction at first. Then, as this person becomes familiar with the routine, more support than instruction is called for. Later, you decide to expand this individual's work assignment with no increase in financial compensation. This situation will likely benefit most from a coaching conversation whereby both direction and support are given, at least at first.

Eventually, a delegating approach might be most appropriate, whereby varying assignments are given with only a specification of your outcome expectations. These workers are able to manage themselves with self-direction and self-motivation. But as discussed above, these individuals still benefit from genuine words of appreciation and gratitude when expectations are met.

The AC4P leaders of work teams change their interpersonal conversations quite dramatically as groups get more familiar with team members and their mission. In the beginning, during the forming and storming stages of team progress, work groups need structure, including specific direction and support. This implies a coaching or directing format.

Later, when the group members become familiar with each other's interests and talents, and progress to the norming and performing stages of team development, supporting and delegating conversations are needed.[17]

The Role of Competence and Commitment

Figure 6.3 on the next page illustrates how two critical characteristics – competence and commitment – should influence a manager's conversation approach.[14] When competence is high, people know what to do and therefore do not need a directive conversation. However, they need supportive conversations when their motivation or commitment is low. This is particularly evident when employees, students, or athletes perform irregularly or inconsistently. Their good days indicate they know what to do, while the occurrence of bad days suggest a motivation issue.

Causes of low commitment vary dramatically, from interpersonal conflict on the job or athletic field to emotional upheaval at home. Such causes can only be discovered through AC4P listening. At times, the diagnosis and subsequent treatment of a motivational problem requires special assistance. In this case, the best a manager can do is recognize a need for professional help and offer AC4P advice and support.

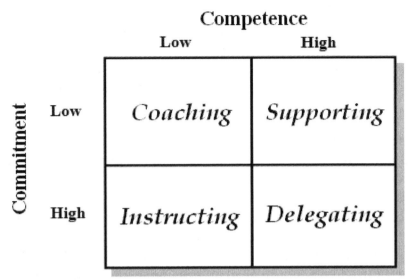

Figure 6.3. Management conversation should be influenced by the recipient's level of competence and commitment.

Five Types of Interpersonal Conversation

We end our discussion of the power of interpersonal and intrapersonal conversation by defining five different types of one-to-one communication. Each plays an essential role in cultivating an AC4P culture of compassion. The strategies illustrated in this chapter for improving the beneficial impact of interpersonal communication connect to each of these types of conversation in unique and important ways.

In other words, each of these types of conversation reflects particular communication techniques aimed at benefitting the human dynamics of a school, work, or home environment. In particular, each type of conversation can play a critical role in increasing the quantity and/or improving the quality of AC4P behavior.[18]

1. Relationship Conversation

Relationship conversations are relatively easy, yet critical to developing a trusting and AC4P culture. Simply put, these conversations occur whenever you show sincere interest in another person, from their home life to their challenges at school or work. This happens, of course, when you talk about particular aspects of a person's family, health, hobbies, work processes, or AC4P-related perceptions.

Indeed, showing genuine interest and appreciation in what a person is doing is probably the best way to give supportive recognition. As Dale Carnegie said years ago, and echoed later by Ken Blanchard and Spencer Johnson, "Help people feel important at doing worthwhile work."[19] This is relationship building – the foundation of an AC4P connection between people.

Specific behaviors you find desirable might surface during a relationship-building conversation. If so, you should certainly acknowledge their occurrence and show appreciation. But your intention is more about developing support and interpersonal trust than influencing behavior.

This approach to interpersonal recognition and support removes the perception of manipulation or "behavior modification," and is therefore more acceptable to both the initiator and receiver of this type of communication. The key is to show genuine interest in the other person's situation, performance, and/or perspective.

2. Possibility Conversation

Relationship conversations often refer to an individual's past. Indeed, we build interpersonal relationships by comparing our prior experiences and looking for commonalities. In contrast, possibility conversations focus on the future. These conversations occur when you share visions with another person.

Leaders of the AC4P Movement are motivated by the vision of an AC4P culture of compassion with interpersonal support predominant over interpersonal conflict and bullying. Possibility conversations target any future situation that reflects desired improvement in environment/engineering conditions, behavioral competence, or person-states.

As discussed earlier, Kim Krisco recommends we begin coaching conversations with a discussion of a person's past, analogous to the relationship conversation discussed above, then progress to a discussion of future possibilities, as defined here.[2]

Subsequently, Krisco proposes the coaching conversation transition back to the present, whereby people define process goals or behavioral strategies relevant to achieving certain possibilities. The next three types of conversation reviewed here help make this happen through improvement-focused interpersonal coaching.

3. Action Conversation

This is behavior-based communication. Given a vision or possibility for improvement, this conversation focuses on what an individual or project team could do to move in a desirable direction. The conversation might be between individuals, as in coaching, or between members of a group.

The action conversation could define a number of different behaviors, some to continue and others to decrease or eliminate. When these conversations occur in group meetings, individual assignments are often needed. Also, action goals are set according to the SMARTS acronym (for Specific, Motivational, Achievable, Relevant, Trackable, and Shared) explained in Chapter 3.

This goal-setting exercise should include an accountability system for tracking progress toward goal attainment. With work groups or teams, it's usually best to monitor both individual achievements with regard to specific assignments, and the group's progress as a team. Next, people look for opportunities to perform their newly-defined and desirable behavior(s).

4. Opportunity Conversation

So you've learned how to do behavior-based coaching, and set a goal for completing a certain number of coaching sessions in one month. Now, it's time to look for opportunities to conduct such a one-on-one session. In some cultures this can be any situation that involves human behavior. However, in other settings the potential participants must agree to be observed before the process can be implemented.

Suppose an individual or a project team chooses to adopt an achievement or success-seeking perspective to actively caring by tracking all AC4P behaviors performed beyond a person's daily routine. This requires an action conversation about the types of behaviors that indicate "going beyond the call of duty," and an opportunity conversation about the various situations that call for various AC4P behaviors.

Bottom line: A practical action plan for achieving particular possibilities includes a definition of behaviors and situations – behaviors needed to fulfill the plan (an action conversation) and the times and places for these behaviors to occur (an opportunity conversation).

After an action plan is completed, it's beneficial to celebrate small-win achievements (see Chapter 3), and set the stage for additional action and opportunity discussions. This is the fifth type of interpersonal conversation.

5. Follow-up Conversation

It's important to acknowledge the achievement of a SMARTS goal. These follow-up conversations are rewarding, and promote a success-seeking mindset – a valuable person-state introduced in Chapter 1.

After noting the acquisition of an action/opportunity outcome, a follow-up conversation turns to discussion of a subsequent challenge. This could include conversations 2, 3, & 4: an identification of new possibilities (2), relevant and acceptable action plans (3), and opportunities calling for certain action (4).

Follow-up conversations target the end result or outcome of an action plan, but they often focus on the process first. In other words, it's useful to have periodic follow-up conversations to check on progress toward a designated outcome.

Suppose, for example, you communicate with a teacher or supervisor regarding a need to have more one-on-one interaction with students or workers. After exploring possibilities, you discuss specific actions and opportunities for meaningful teacher/student or supervisor/employee contacts. You might set a SMARTS goal and even a follow-up reward for goal attainment.

But process-focused monitoring could also be quite helpful. In other words, it would probably be useful to contact this teacher or supervisor periodically for follow-up conversations regarding his or her progress toward goal attainment.

Figure 6.4 on the next page illustrates this five-way classification system, which provides an intuitive sequence for constructive interpersonal talk. For example, action plans will be all the more accepted and accomplishment will be all the more likely, if they are preceded by appropriate relationship conversations.

Please note, however, one type of conversation does not stop with the implementation of the next in the sequence. Relationship conversations, for example, continue throughout action planning, accomplishment, and follow-up. And while it makes sense to define the behaviors in an action plan before considering opportunities, in actual practice people look for opportunities for their action-plan behavior before performing.

   Actually, interpersonal communication varies unsystematically between all five conversation types. Perhaps understanding these different conversations and their different objectives will contribute to increasing the quantity and improving the quality of communications aimed at cultivating an AC4P culture of compassion. When it comes to progressing the AC4P Movement, we can't have too many quality interpersonal conversations.

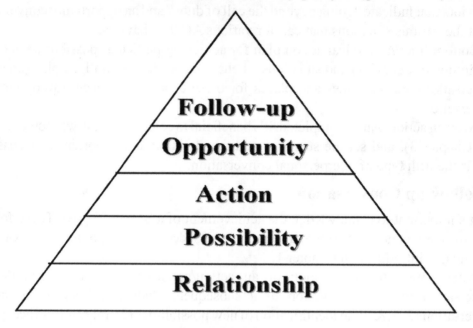

Figure 6.4. Interpersonal conversations occur at one of five levels.

In Summary

   Coaching conversations are needed when a person's competence and commitment regarding a particular task or assignment are relatively low. You can improve competence through behavior-focused direction and feedback, and increase commitment by giving authentic appreciation and AC4P support.

   Anything that increases a person's perception of importance or competence can enhance commitment. What makes that happen? The answer is not always obvious, but if you listen, observe, and ask questions you'll find out.

   Delegating is relevant when people know what to do (competence) and are motivated to do it (commitment). You can often know when an individual or team advances to this level by observing successive progress. But it's often useful to ask people whether they are ready for this level of conversation. If they say "no," then ask them what they need to reach this stage. Do they need more competence through direction or more commitment through some kind of support the institution or organization could make available?

In Conclusion

   I hope you're convinced the level of AC4P in your culture is greatly determined by interpersonal and intrapersonal conversation. We often focus our interpersonal and intrapersonal conversations on the past. This helps us connect with others, but it also feeds our prejudice filters and limits the potential for conversation to facilitate beneficial behavior change. We enable progress when we move conversations with ourselves and others from past to future possibilities and then to the development of an action plan.

Expect people to protect their self-esteem with excuses for their past mistakes. Then help the conversation shift to a discussion of possibilities for improvement and personal commitment to apply a feasible action plan. This is often more likely to happen with a nondirective than directive approach in which more questions are asked than directives given. It's also useful to use opening words to protect the listener's self-esteem and limit the impact of reactive bias.

AC4P listening enables one to determine whether a coaching, instructing, supporting, or delegating conversation is most appropriate. Coaching involves both direction and support, and is needed when a person's competence and commitment in a particular setting are relatively low. In contrast, delegating is relevant when people know what to do and are motivated to do it. In this case, they are both competent and committed, and can direct and motivate themselves. Then, delegating conversations provide clear expectations and show sincere appreciation for worthwhile behavior.

When people are self-motivated to perform well but don't know how to maximize their efforts for optimal performance, an instructive conversation is called for. In other situations, people know what is needed for optimal performance, but don't always work at optimal levels. This reflects an execution problem which can't be solved with directive conversation. Rather supportive conversation is needed. Actually, everyone can benefit from supportive recognition. William James, the first renowned American psychologist wrote, "The deepest principle in human nature is the craving to be appreciated."[18]

Bottom line: Interpersonal conversation defines our culture at home, at school, at work and everywhere in between. It can create conflict and build barriers to performing AC4P behavior. Or, it can cultivate the kind of culture needed to make a major breakthrough in cultivating a culture of compassion. Interpersonal conversation also affects our intrapersonal conversations or self-talk, which in turn influences our willingness to look out for the health, safety, and well-being of ourselves and others.

Notes

1. Geller, E. S. (1994). Ten principles for achieving a Total Safety Culture. *Professional Safety, 39*(9), 18-24; Geller, E. S. (2001). Actively caring for occupational safety: Extending the performance management paradigm. In C. M. Johnson, W. K. Redmon, & T. C. Mawhinney (Eds.), *Handbook of organizational performance: Behavior analysis and management* (pp. 303-326). New York: The Haworth Press.

2. Krisco, K. H. (1997). *Leadership and the art of conversation.* Rocklin, CA: Prima Publishing.

3. Hayakawa, S. I. (1978). *Language in thought and action* (4th Edition). New York: Harcourt Brace Jovanovich, Publishers.

4. New Merriam-Webster Dictionary (1989). Springfield, MA: Merriam-Webster, Inc, Publishing, p.577

5. New Merriam-Webster Dictionary (1989). Springfield, MA: Merriam-Webster, Inc, Publishing, p. 800

6. Geller, E. S. (2001). *Building successful safety teams.* Rockville, MD: Government Institutes.

7. Dinwiddie, F.W. (1975). Humanistic behaviorism: A model for rapprochement in residential treatment milieus. *Child Psychiatry and Human Development, 5*(4), 254-259; Krasner, L. (1978). The future and the past in the behaviorism-humanism dialogue. *American Psychologist,* September, 799-804.

8. Cialdini, R. B. (2001). *Influence: Science and practice* (Fourth Edition). New York: Harper Collins College Publishers; Geller, E. S., & Veazie, R. A. (2010). *When no one's watching: Living and leading self-motivation.* Newport, VA: Make-A-Difference, LLC.

9. Bandura, A. (1997). *Self-efficacy: The exercise of control.* New York: W. H. Freeman and Company; Geller, E. S. (2002). *The participation factor: How to increase involvement in occupational safety.* Des Plaines, IL: American Society of Safety Engineers; Ryan, R. M., & Deci, E. L. (2000). Self-determinism theory and the foundation of intrinsic motivation, social development, and well-being. *American Psychologist, 55,* 68-75.

10. Rogers, C. R. (1957). The necessary and sufficient conditions of therapeutic personality change. *Journal of Consulting Psychology, 21,* 95.

11. Carnegie, D. (1936). *How to win friends and influence people* (1981 Edition). New York: Galahad Books.

12. Covey, S. R. (1989). *The seven habits of highly effective people: Restoring the character ethic.* New York: Simon and Schuster, Inc.

13. Langer, E. J. (1989). *Mindfulness.* Reading, MA: Addison-Wesley.

14. Blanchard, K. (1999, November). *Building gung ho teams: How to turn people power into profits.* Day-long workshop presented at the Hotel Roanoke, Roanoke, VA; Blanchard, K., & Bowles, S. (1998). *Gung ho! Turn on the people in any organization.* New York: William Morrow and Company, Inc; Blanchard, K., Zigarmi, P., & Zigarmi, D. (1985). *Leadership and the one minute manager.* New York: William Morrow and Company, Inc.

15. Geller, E. S. (1998). *Understanding behavior-based safety: Step-by-step methods to improve your workplace* (2nd Edition). Neenah, WI: J. J. Keller & Associates, Inc.; Geller, E. S. (2001). *Beyond safety accountability.* Rockville, MD: Government Institutes.

16. Geller, E. S. (2000). Ten leadership qualities for a Total Safety Culture: Safety management is not enough. *Professional Safety, 45*(5), 38-41;

17. Geller, E. S. (2001). *Building successful safety teams.* Rockville, MD: Government Institutes; Tuckman, B.W. (1965). Developmental sequence in small groups. *Psychological Bulletin, 63,* 384-399.

18. I first heard these five conversation labels during a Progressive Business audio conference in 2003, featuring Bob Aquadro and Bob Allbright.

19. Carnegie, D. (1936). *How to win friends and influence people* (1981 Edition). New York: Galahad Books; Blanchard, K., & Johnson, S. (1981). *The one-minute manager.* New York: William Morrow and Company, Inc.

20. James, W. J. (1890). *Principles of psychology.* New York: Holt.

Part II: Applications of AC4P in the Workplace

E. Scott Geller

IN THE LATE 1970s I began researching applications of behavioral science to increase the use of vehicle safety belts. If the truth be known, I did not get involved in this intervention domain because I was interested in safety. In fact, I didn't even buckle up in those days.

No, my focus was research. I was interested in studying large-scale applications of behavioral science in the community in order to improve quality of life. A few colleagues and I coined the term *behavioral community psychology* to represent this research specialty.[1]

I targeted vehicle safety-belt use because it was possible to observe vehicle occupants in the community and objectively determine their use vs. nonuse of safety belts. My students took to the streets with pens and clipboards, and obtained empirical records of vehicle safety-belt use before, during, and after we implemented a community-based intervention.

Our interventions were designed to activate and/or motivate vehicle occupants to buckle up. We obtained empirical evidence of the relative behavioral impact of various intervention tactics with a Baseline-Intervention-Withdrawal paradigm.[2]

Another reason to target safety-belt use was the low percentage of drivers buckling up in those days (i.e., less than 20% in our university town of Blacksburg, Virginia). Again, it wasn't the life-saving potential of vehicle safety-belt use that attracted my attention. It was the fact we had a behavior with much need for improvement and an objective way to evaluate the impact of various intervention approaches.

The Beginning of Behavior-Based Safety

When colleagues requested a label for our type of research, I called it "behavior-based safety". After all, we were customizing principles and procedures from applied behavioral science (as explained in Chapter 1) to increase the frequency of a safety-related behavior. Behavior-based safety (BBS) was the logical label.

All of our intervention attempts were positive. Our paradigm differed from the ubiquitous punitive approach of "Click it or Ticket". We provided persuasive activators and positive consequences to increase the use of vehicle safety belts. To make a long story short, we set up *if-then* reward contingencies throughout the university town of Blacksburg. Banks and fast-food restaurants gave customers lottery coupons and bingo numbers at their drive-by windows if they were buckled up. Local merchants donated the various prizes for winners of lotteries and "BELTS Bingo".

When directing traffic on campus, police officers spoke into pocket-size tape recorders the license-plate numbers of drivers who were buckled-up and these numbers were translated into lottery coupons for weekly "Get Caught Buckled Up" drawings. Each Week, Virginia Tech President William Lavery drew winners whose names were published in the local newspapers, along with the prizes and the businesses that donated them.

Positive consequences for all. Banks and fast-food restaurants got more patrons using their drive-by windows; local businesses were recognized in local media for their contributions; and most importantly, drivers increased their use of safety belts. These win-win interventions, along with positive media attention, more than doubled the use of safety belts throughout our community.

Word spread beyond Blacksburg. The U.S. Department of Transportation and the National Highway Traffic Safety Administration funded several follow-up studies of our positive approach to improving road safety.

In 1983 the Corporate Safety Director of Ford Motor Company, Dale A. Gray, called to ask if I would teach safety leaders from approximately 110 facilities how to apply BBS principles to increase the use of vehicle safety belts among Ford employees. This marked my entry into the corporate world.

Dale's phone call led my students and me to develop training materials to teach change agents how to *Define* the target behavior (in this case, vehicle safety-belt use), *Observe* and record it's frequency of occurrence, *Intervene* with positive prompts, incentives, and/or rewards to increase the frequency of belt use, and then to *Test* the impact of the intervention by comparing frequencies of the target behavior during Baseline, Intervention, and Withdrawal phases. We called this process "DO IT" for its key steps: *Define*, *Observe*, *Intervene*, and *Test* (see Chapter 1, pp. 15-19).

From the Streets to the Workplace

Safety-belt use among all Ford employees increased from 9% to 54% in 1984.[2] Following the success of this corporate-wide BBS program, the Corporate Safety Director asked me to expand the BBS principles and procedures to address the human side of occupational safety within Ford plants.

This led to me teaching principles and applications of BBS at the facilities of several automobile-manufacturing companies, including Ford, General Motors, and Chrysler. The procedures used in the most successful of these BBS programs are detailed in this section of this book.

The Popularity of BBS

BBS became increasingly popular in industrial settings nationwide in the mid-1980s, and subsequently, throughout the world. Several books detail the principles and procedures of BBS[4] and systematic reviews of the literature provide solid evidence for the success of this approach to injury prevention.[5] But an army of BBS consultants from across the world presented incomplete information and narrow perspectives on BBS.

Here's one example of the unfortunate and ill-informed teaching and misinterpretation of BBS that persists to this day. Many BBS trainers sell BBS on the premise that "95%

of workplace accidents are caused by behavior". To make their point, these safety consultants show videos of workers engaged in extremely risky behaviors and/or workplace "accidents" seemingly resulting from unsafe behavior.

When these BBS sales pitches became popular in the 1980s and early 1990s, leaders of labor unions objected vehemently and justifiably.[6] Why? Because claiming behaviors cause workplace injuries and property damage places blame on the employee and dismisses management responsibility. "Don't blame people for problems caused by the system," warned Dr. Deming.[7]

I never taught BBS from this "blame the worker" perspective. It's wrong to presume behavior is the cause of an injury or property damage. Rather, behavior is one of *several* contributing factors to an injury, along with environmental and engineering factors, management factors, cultural factors, and even person-states, as explained in Chapters 1 and 2 and referred to in each chapter of Part II.

It's ironic the United Auto Workers (UAW) were most vociferous in their objection to BBS, because the BBS I taught Ford Motor Company in 1983 was accepted and appreciated by the UAW. Later, BBS became ill-defined by consultants who marketed and taught their own interpretations of BBS procedures which lacked the profound knowledge of behavioral science as conceptualized and researched by B.F. Skinner.[8]

People-Based Safety

The inaccurate presentations and distortions of BBS led me to introduce a new label for applying psychological science to occupational safety – people-based safety (PBS). Note the term *psychological* science rather than *behavioral* science. This change reflects the fact that PBS draws from areas of psychology beyond behavioral science, including cognitive science, social science, as well as research on perception, emotion, and personality. I describe the principles and applications of PBS for injury prevention in textbooks[9] and journal articles,[10] as well as on CD's and DVD's.[11]

The PBS approach is not an alternative to BBS. It's an evolution. It integrates the best of behavior-based and person-based psychology, as signified by the acronym ACTS: *Acting, Coaching, Thinking*, and *Seeing*. The *Acting* and *Coaching* components are essentially BBS, except self-coaching and self-management techniques are incorporated. These added processes are supported through self-talk, which involve the *Thinking* component of PBS.

The *Seeing* dimension of PBS takes into account the divergent views of safety-related issues held by employers, supervisors and managers, which should be assessed with a perception survey and considered when designing and evaluating interventions to improve safety performance. Personality factors are addressed in this domain of PBS, including the five person-states explained in Chapter 2.

Passion to Make a Difference

After helping to implement BBS for Ford Motor Company in the early 1980s, I was advised to attend national safety conferences sponsored by the National Safety Council (NSC) and the American Association of Safety Engineers (ASSE). Frankly, I was astounded and disappointed by presentations attempting to address the human dynamics of injury prevention. Indeed, it took significant self-control to keep me from leaping from my chair to explain the numerous fallacies.

What I heard time and again was an emphasis on top-down rules and compliance through safety-cop enforcement. Behavioral science informs us this traditional safety approach limits the employee engagement needed to work injury free. The common focus on "safety attitudes" and "think safety" was nebulous and a waste of time without first addressing safe vs. at-risk behaviors.

Furthermore, I knew from research the typical "safety incentive program" that based prizes and financial rewards on avoiding injuries (i.e., the reporting of injuries) encouraged a *failure-avoiding mindset*. Minor injuries would go unreported. And the type of conversations needed to prevent injuries was stifled.

Then, I got my chance to voice my concerns. Dale Gray, a fellow of ASSE, got me on the conference program in 1987, and since then I've offered an ASSE presentation related to the psychology of safety almost every year. Plus, I've given workshops and addresses at The National Safety Conference every year since 1995. You might ask, so what have I accomplished? I have the same question.

I've been told the psychology lessons I've taught at these conferences have significantly changed peoples' perspective of safety management and leadership. Yet I still hear some speakers use the old top-down, command-and-control language when addressing the human side of injury prevention, and misinterpretations and misapplications of BBS are still evident.

My presentations on PBS and the Actively Caring for People (AC4P) principles are well-received by large audiences. But I hear this consistent criticism: "Your research-based principles and lessons about the psychology of safety are certainly reasonable and worth considering. But I don't know what to do with them."

This comes from audience members who want a step-by-step recipe or action plan. I could give the defense I heard Dr. Deming give many times, "That's not my job. I'm here to teach you the theory and principles, and now your job is to develop procedures from these lessons, customized for your culture."[7]

But I want to do better than that. This book was planned and developed to answer this all-to-common criticism. The AC4P principles from which PBS procedures evolved are given in Chapters 1 to 6. Here in Part II, we learn from consultants and safety leaders with regard to their applications of certain AC4P principles and PBS procedures.

In Chapter 7, Dr. Steve Roberts explains the basics of PBS he and our consulting partners at Safety Performance Solutions (SPS) have found successful in numerous implementations. In Chapter 8, Adam Tucker and Dr. Chuck Pettinger, a former senior consultant with SPS, offer their approach to implementing PBS effectively for a global company.

Chapter 9 describes how Dr. Tim Ludwig and his team initiated the development of an AC4P culture among a largely illiterate workforce for a large mining operation in

South Africa. Here we see how the special influence of the AC4P wristband transcended language barriers and a legacy of top-down enforcement-focused management.

In Chapter 10, Joe Bolduc and his team at Shaw Industries describe their pursuit of an AC4P culture, and include empirical findings that link the AC4P person-states (Chapter 2) to Total Recordable Injury Rate.

A special feature of Chapter 10 are the details regarding how the Fibers Division of Shaw Industries progressed beyond BBS to the AC4P approach, and how they plan to continuously improve. Bob Veazie, the author of the next chapter, planted the seeds at Shaw Industries that inspired the leaders to adopt an AC4P mindset.

In Chapter 11, Bob Veazie challenges us to advance beyond the systematic observation-and-feedback procedures of BBS and PBS, and adopt an AC4P lifestyle. While this is easier said than done, Bob's commitment and follow-up behaviors give us direction for turning this ideal into reality, and optimism an AC4P lifestyle is possible.

Chapter 12 reviews a unique AC4P approach to activating, motivating, and maintaining a PBS observation and feedback process that drastically reduced hand injuries among Canadian workers on oil-drilling rigs.

The last two chapters of Part II are personal stories of how involvement in applying AC4P principles for occupational safety led to dramatic beneficial changes in lifestyle, including perceptions, attitudes, and behaviors. You will see how AC4P behavior for safety at work can lead to AC4P beyond safety and beyond the workplace.

These stories reflect a ripple effect from behavior to attitude to more behavior. This cascading spiral of behavior feeding attitude and then attitude feeding more behavior provides optimism for achieving an AC4P culture of compassion.

Notes

1. Geller, E.S., Winett, R.A., & Everett, P.B. (1982). *Preserving the environment: New strategies for behavior change*. New York, NY: Pergamon Press; Glenwick, D., & Jason, L. (Eds.). *Behavioral community psychology: Progress and prospects*. New York, NY: Praeger Press.

2. Geller, E.S. (1982). *Corporate incentives for promoting safety belt use: Rationale, guidelines, and examples*. Washington, D.C.: U.S. Department of Transportation. (Reprinted by General Motors Corporation, 1983); Geller, E.S. (1985). *Corporate safety-belt programs*. Blacksburg, VA: Virginia Polytechnic Institute and State University. (Reprinted by General Motors, Inc. and Motors Insurance Corporation, 1985); Geller, E.S. (1985). *Community safety-belt programs*. Blacksburg, VA: Virginia Polytechnic Institute and State University. (Reprinted by General Motors, Inc. and Motors Insurance Corporation, 1985); Geller, E.S. (1988). A behavioral science approach to transportation safety. *Bulletin of the New York Academy of Medicine, 64*(7), 632-661; Geller, E.S. (1998). *Applications of behavior analysis to prevent injury from vehicle crashes* (2nd Edition). Monograph published by the Cambridge Center for Behavioral Studies, Cambridge, MA.

3. In personal communication, the corporate safety director (Dale A. Gray) estimated this program enabled Ford Motor Company to realize "a savings of over $22 million" and it "saved at least 20 lives and reduced injuries to more than 800 others."

4. Geller, E.S. (1996). *The psychology of safety: How to improve behaviors and attitudes on the job*. Radnor, PA: Chilton Book Company; Geller, E.S. (1998). *Understanding behavior-based safety: Step-by-step methods to improve your workplace* (2nd Edition). Neenah, WI: J.J. Keller & Associates, Inc.; Krause, T.R., Hidley, J.H., & Hodson, S.J. (1996). *The behavior-based safety*

process: Managing improvement for an injury-free culture (2nd Edition). New York, NY: Van Nostrand Reinhold; McSween, T.E. (1995). *The values-based safety process: Improving your safety culture with a behavioral approach.* New York, NY: Van Nostrand Reinhold.

5. Grindle, A.C., Dickinson, A.M., & Boettcher, W. (2000). Behavioral safety research in manufacturing settings: A review of the literature. *Journal of Organizational Behavior Management, 20,*29-68; Sulzer-Azaroff, B., & Austin, J. (2000). Does BBS work? Behavior-based safety and injury reduction: A survey of the evidence. *Professional Safety, 45(7),* 19-24.

6. Hans, M. (1996). Does behavior-based safety work? *Safety and Health,* National Safety Council, June, 44-49; Howe, J. (1998, January). *A union critique of behavioral safety.* Paper presented at the ASSE Behavioral Safety Symposium, Orlando, FL; Hoyle, B. (1998). *Fixing the workplace, not the worker: A workers' guide to accident prevention.* Lakewood, CO: Oil, Chemical and Atomic Workers International Union; Lessin, N. (1997). Workers need real rights. *Industrial Safety & Hygiene News, 31*(10), p. 42; Smith, T. A. (1995). Viewpoint: Rebutting behaviorism. *Industrial Safety & Hygiene News, 40*(3), p. 40; UAW health and Safety Department (1999). Warning: Behavior-based safety can be hazardous to your health & safety program. *UAW Occupational Health & Safety Newsletter, No. 1.*

7. Deming, W.E. (1991). *Quality, productivity, and competitive position.* Four-day workshop presented in Cincinnati, OH by Quality Enhancement Seminars, Inc.

8. Skinner, B.F. (1938). *The behavior of organisms: An experimental analysis.* Acton, MA: Copley Publishing Group; Skinner, B.F. (1950). Are theories of learning necessary? *Psychological Review, 57,* 193-216; Skinner, B.F. (1953). *Science and human behavior.* New York, NY: Macmillan; Skinner, B.F. (1971). *Beyond freedom and dignity.* New York, NY: Alfred A Knopf; Skinner, B.F. (1974). *About behaviorism.* New York, NY: Alfred A. Knopf.

9. Geller, E.S. (2003). People-based safety: The psychology of actively caring. *Professional Safety, 48*(12), 33-43; Geller, E. S. (2006). People-based safety: An evolution of behavior-based safety for greater effectiveness. Proceeding of the 2006 *Professional Development Conference for the American Society of Safety Engineers*; Geller, E.S. (2011). Psychological science and safety: Large-scale success at preventing occupational injuries and fatalities. *Current Directions in Psychological Science, 20*(2), 109-114.

10. Geller, E.S. (2005). *People-based safety: The source.* Virginia Beach, VA: Coastal Training and Technologies Corporation; Geller, E.S. (2008). *Leading people-based safety: Enriching your culture.* Virginia Beach, VA: Coastal Training and Technologies Corporation; Geller, E.S., & Johnson, D. (2008). *People-based patient safety: Enriching your culture to prevent medical error,* Virginia Beach, VA: Coastal Training and Technologies Corporation.

11. *Actively Caring for Safety: The psychology of injury prevention.* (1997). Blacksburg, VA: Safety Performance Solutions [Twelve 30-min. audiotapes with workbook to teach principles and procedures for preventing unintentional injury at work, at home, and on the road]; *The Human Dynamics of Occupational Safety, 2003.* Thibodaux, LA: J.W. Toups, Inc. [24 lessons on audio cassettes and CDs plus memory joggers, action-plan worksheets, and a pocket reference with pen and journal]; *The Safety Performance Coach (2003).* Thibodaux, LA: J.W. Toups, Inc. [An internet education/training service including email, CDs, cassettes, video CDs, and support materials to teach employees principles and strategies for improving the human dynamics of a work culture.]

CHAPTER 7

Actively Caring for Occupational Safety:
Preventing injuries with people-based safety

Steve Roberts

M Y FIRST MEMORY of the term "actively caring" comes from a discussion between Scott Geller, myself, and a group of Exxon Chemical executives in the early 1990s.

One of the company reps complained about the safety culture and said, "No one cares about safety".

Another said, "That's not true, everyone cares about safety".

A third spoke up, "I think you're both right – everyone cares about safety, we just have too few actually doing something about it".

"What you mean is we need more actively caring," said Scott.

At first, the actively-caring person-states seem to have little to do with occupational safety. Perceptions of self-esteem, self-efficacy, personal control, optimism and belonging are likely to be discussed in Human Resource (HR) Management with questions like, "How do we make this a more pleasant place to work as to reduce turnover?"

These factors have much to do with safety, because safety has a lot to do with how people actively care for each other. Are employees willing to observe other workers on behalf of their safety? If workers identify a hazard or at-risk behavior, are they willing to intervene directly and proactively? Will they communicate feedback in a way that builds the person-states and increases the likelihood others will do the same?

Creating an AC4P safety culture requires a broad-based, integrated approach. Unfortunately, many organizations take too narrow a view of injury prevention when attempting to improve safety. Too often, a ramped up or special focus on safety occurs after a recent injury. Sound familiar?

An AC4P safety culture must integrate these six components: 1) Leadership; 2) Systems; 3) Behavior; 4) Employee Engagement; 5) Person-States; and 6) Conditions. The AC4P safety culture is one of empathy and compassion. It's proactive and positive. And it often requires courage.

Leadership

It's the responsibility of leadership to foster an environment of AC4P. How do leaders do this? Let's count the ways:

Compassion

When leaders communicate sincerely that they don't want unnecessary risks to be taken because they care about keeping people safe, they activate and support a deep-rooted, compassionate safety culture as opposed to one focused on only reducing the injury-rate numbers.

Focus on the Process

By focusing on the process, the journey, instead of possibly under-estimating and misleading injury (outcome) numbers, leaders help people see the personal power they possess to make valuable contributions to the organization. The most effective leaders hold workers accountable for accomplishing proactive process behaviors that contribute to group and organizational success in productivity, quality, and safety.

Value Alignment

Leaders must ensure the behaviors discussed, recognized, and rewarded *on the job* are consistent with the stated values of the organization. And safety must be presented as an organizational value rather than a priority. Safety is not just a topic to kick off employee meetings, but an integral part of daily organizational performance.

Actions Speak Louder than Words

Leadership communication is essential, but actions speak louder than words. Managers can contradict support for safety. It's too common for managers to overlook and fail to correct certain at-risk work practices they observe. They might fail to praise or acknowledge safe behavior, and they might herald increased productivity even when the achievement required at-risk shortcuts. Managers might also model at-risk behaviors when they perceive they have less exposure, or when they justify risk-taking from their personal experience and perceived benefits of efficient shortcuts.

Authenticity

From the Leadership perspective, AC4P means managers and supervisors go beyond mouthing the right words about safety to ensuring their actions demonstrate authentic AC4P.

The Leadership Evaluation and Development for Safety (LEADS) process created by Safety Performance Solutions (SPS) provides feedback to leaders regarding their safety-related behaviors, and ensures those behaviors cascade down throughout the organization. Managers evaluate themselves on specific behaviors required of an effective AC4P safety champion. Then personnel above, below, and parallel to this person in the organization provide anonymous evaluations of this targeted individual's safety-related behaviors.

Targeted managers review these feedback evaluations to gain insight into how others perceive their leadership skills in comparison to their self-perceptions, whether their support is being interpreted as intended, and what specific behaviors are expected of them.

Vision for Safety

AC4P leaders should articulate unambiguously the vision for safety within their organization, and maintain focus on safety even when safety is exceeding expectations or when other business areas are doing poorly. Too often senior leaders delegate specification of the safety vision to others (e.g., the Safety Department) or just assume others (e.g., operations directors, plant managers) are properly verbalizing and reinforcing the corporate vision for safety.

Personal Engagement

Leaders should demonstrate personal involvement in safety activities. Important ways senior managers can promote AC4P safety include: a) meeting with safety staff, b) speaking with employees about safety, c) reviewing environmental and behavioral safety audits with site management, d) holding local management accountable for properly managing any safety deficiencies, and e) giving safety topics priority in operational reviews.

Rewards/Recognition

People tend to do what they are rewarded for doing. But organizations often set up systems that fail to consistently reward individuals for their safety-related behaviors and fail to adequately support managers and supervisors who support safety. Rewards relating to AC4P should be delivered in ways to increase self-esteem and perceptions of safety-related competence and personal control.

Interpersonal Trust

Leaders promote safety-related trust through their formal and informal communications. They demonstrate their understanding of the safety challenges facing the organization, and they make decisions that show empathy for employees' safety. Organizational systems, policies, and procedures should motivate safe behavior consistent with the AC4P safety vision. And the safety-related actions of all managers and supervisors should balance key performance indicators – safety, quality, and production (see Chapter 3 for more on developing interpersonal trust.)

Communication

Effective leaders must actively encourage behavior-based feedback to create an open atmosphere. People must feel comfortable expressing their needs and ideas for improving safety. Just as important, leaders must take time to actively or attentively listen to safety-related needs, concerns, and suggestions. Empathic listening is critical to diagnosing a situation and is a key skill of AC4P leaders. AC4P requires patience and an approach that asks questions before giving direction.

Teamwork

Sometimes behavioral observations or acts of AC4P can become competitions or numbers games. This can be motivating, as all competition can be. However, leaders in an AC4P culture must ensure competition does not motivate behavior counter to developing a culture of compassion, teamwork, networking, and the sharing of best practices. Leaders need to ensure competition does not allow one group to excel at the expense of another (e.g., one shift sets production records in a way that leaves conditions in such disarray it's difficult for the next shift to achieve their goals without taking risky short cuts).

Ownership

An AC4P culture relies on leadership expectations rather than mandates. Expectations imply choice and personal control. There's room for individual and group decision-making that builds self-esteem and self-efficacy. When people perceive personal control in how to reach specific goals, they are more likely to own the process and transition from an other-directed to a self-directed mindset (see Chapter 3 for more on self-motivation.)

Systems

Safety-management systems manage risk and decrease the chance of unintentional property damage and injuries. These systems generally include: *safety rules and procedures, safety training, audits, hazard identification and correction, corrective action for at-risk behaviors, injury reporting and analysis, safety communications, safety suggestions, and incentive/reward and recognition programs*. An AC4P safety culture leverages each of these systems for optimal safe production.

An AC4P safety culture not only has well-functioning safety management systems, but these safety systems mesh together with other systems to achieve synergy and enrich the safety culture. A poorly designed, badly implemented, or malfunctioning system can destroy an organization's overall safety culture. Poor features of one system can have negative impact on other systems, making problem areas more difficult to isolate and correct.

For example, effective *hazard identification and correction* requires: a) an atmosphere that fosters *employee participation*, b) sufficient *education and training* on hazard recognition and correction, and c) ample *communication* of the hazard and its sufficient resolution. The lack of closure (e.g., hazard abatement) can reduce employee participation.

Assessment of Safety Management Systems

Cultural weaknesses in a poorly functioning system should be identified and corrected on a regular basis. Use a broad lens when scrutinizing each system. For example, let's take a look at some of the reasons the training system may be ineffective at improving a lockout-tagout process.

Training may be too short, too complicated, poorly conducted, or too general for application on the job. It may be given by employees who lack credibility, or may require overtime either for the trainee or his counterpart covering for him back on the job. This can lead to clock-watching and a lack of focus. Moreover, training should include education about the principles or rationale justifying the particular procedures taught.

Training itself may be top notch but treated by the employee's supervisor as a nuisance or as secondary to "getting the work done". Or the existing environment may not allow the task to be performed on the job as employees were trained. For example, I recently worked with an organization that sent a key group of employees to rigging school. They learned the proper tools and methods for performing heavy lifts and actually felt it was one of the most valuable training courses they had ever received. Thus, they expected the training to greatly improve one of their riskiest tasks.

However, when they returned to the job, they realized they didn't have the proper cables, hooks, and other equipment needed to safely perform their scheduled lifts. They were then quite disheartened when instead of helping secure the proper equipment for the lifts, their supervisor simply told them to use the old methods and they would eventually discuss the need to update the equipment.

All these issues and more can give training a bad reputation, and more importantly, cause it to be ineffective at maintaining or improving employee safety and health.

You might also analyze how *perceptions* of the system are being managed (or not managed). For example, a *safety suggestion process* may be seen as beneficial by only those whose suggestions have been implemented or have received feedback.

Suggestions may be actively solicited, objectively evaluated by a cross-functional team of employees, amply funded, and quickly acted on *but* poorly communicated to the rest of the workforce. Employees then evaluate this system negatively. This situation is easily addressed without revising the entire safety-suggestion system.

Injury Reporting and Analysis

Another system very often telling of an organization's safety culture is the reporting and analysis of *close-calls and injuries*. Sometimes this requires courage to speak up. The level of injury and close-call (or near-hit) reporting is higher in organizations where employees actively care and share trust and a problem-solving perspective. If injury reporting is discouraged, analysis may be impossible, with no communication of findings, and discipline inappropriately practiced. Fear of punishment destroys trust.

System Analysis

Critically analyze each of your systems for alignment with AC4P principles. Be cautious about overhauling existing but ineffective safety management systems too abruptly. For example, employees accustomed to receiving a payoff for working a certain length of time without an injury may be resistant to changing an outcome-based incentive/reward program.

The redesign process is not a "quick fix". You may transition through several intermediate stages before systems reflect employee ownership, achievement orientation, or a systems perspective. AC4P from a systems perspective includes taking a proactive look at the various systems influencing safety, ensuring each system provides its primary function, but doing so in a way that builds an AC4P safety culture primed for proactive injury prevention. Don't wait for injuries to occur on your watch.

Behavior

AC4P from a behavioral perspective includes the systematic identification and analysis of at-risk behaviors. Once critical at-risk behaviors are identified it's essential to explore the underlying systemic reasons. Probing and listening are important parts of AC4P. Figure 6.1 depicts a flow chart for the guidance of questions to be asked and issues to consider after you identify a critical at-risk behavior.

The first issue to consider is whether the employee was aware *at the moment* s/he was performing an at-risk behavior. Of course if an injury results, we can easily determine the behavior was at risk (or there was an uncontrolled hazardous condition – as discussed here as the final component of safety).

But when someone consciously performs an at-risk behavior, we see two possible catalysts: the behavior was supported by the system ("This is the way we always do things around here when the production pressure is strong."); or the individual could have acted outside the system through willful disregard or malicious intent. Malicious intent is very rare (if not, you have a serious problem with your HR Department hiring the wrong people).

Again, it's critical that leaders in AC4P organizations verbalize clear expectations related to at-risk behaviors and work with employees to remove barriers to safe performance. Before labeling an at-risk behavior a willful violation, consider the formal and informal reward/recognition systems that may have encouraged the behavior, the type and quality of the training employees received, the type of corrective feedback given to others for similar behaviors, the availability and condition of the tools and equipment to support safe behavior, and the extent a "just get 'er done" culture is prevalent in the organization. Again, use a wide lens in your AC4P assessments.

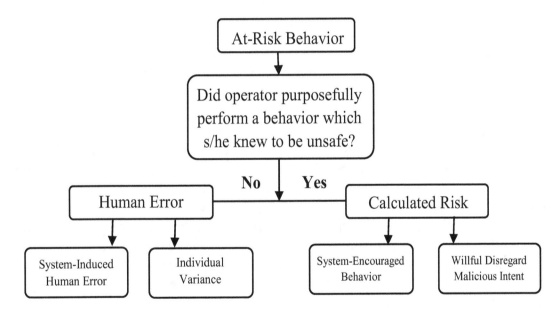

Figure 6.1. Flow chart of issues to consider after identifying a critical at-risk behavior.

Human Error

If the employee didn't realize the behavior was at-risk, we have an example of *human error*. If we identify a systems-level factor for an at-risk behavior, then our corrective action(s) should focus on fixing the system, rather than focusing on the employee.

There's no way to eliminate all human factors contributing to personal injury and property damage. Personal dispositional and situational factors certainly contribute to injuries. Illness, divorce, problems with kids, financial burdens, or drug problems, can make it difficult to focus vigilantly on the job and avoid error. For these reasons, it's important employees and leaders understand the availability and capabilities of Employee Assistance Programs.

We should develop a broad, closely interwoven AC4P "safety net". That is, fault-tolerant systems and recoverability options are needed so when people do experience a 'brain cramp' they won't fall very far. We know people are going to have them; it's not a matter of "if" but "when." There may not be much we can do to prevent cognitive failures. But we must have the courage to step in and actively care when it looks like we might be able to prevent human error.

Behavior Management

Before attempting to change an at-risk behavior to avoid an injury, we should acknowledge that other considerations should typically come first. The following intervention hierarchy should be considered:

1. Eliminate the hazard (substitution of materials, automation)
2. Engineering controls (guarding, interlocks)
3. Warnings (signs, alarms)
4. Behavior change to avoid exposure to the hazard, administrative controls, and training (e.g., following procedures, job rotation, lockout/tagout training, equipment inspections)
5. Using PPE (eye protection, respiratory protection, fall protection)

This hierarchy clearly regards behavior change and PPE as the least effective. However, it is not always feasible to eliminate all hazards or provide engineering controls to create an acceptable risk level. Complex systems in an AC4P culture require a great deal of human contribution to maintain productivity, quality, and safety.

AC4P from a behavioral perspective means not only eliminating or reducing hazards and at-risk behavior, but ensuring the methods used leave people feeling better about themselves, their co-workers, their situation, and the organization. This requires intervention strategies that include elements of choice and personal control, employee involvement and ownership, and focusing on enabling employees to work to achieve valuable outcomes for safety – instead of creating situations where those involved are primarily motivated to avoid negative consequences.

Consideration of people's feelings and other person-states in addition to traditional behavioral factors led Scott Geller to transition to using the term people-based safety (PBS),[1] instead of the now common and often misused and misunderstood behavior-based safety (BBS) which Dr. Geller first coined in 1979.

Behavioral Observation and Feedback

One of the most common applications of the AC4P principles for occupational safety takes the form of a Behavioral Observation and Feedback Process (BOFP). Employees observe co-workers using a critical behavior checklist (CBC) that guides their focus. After the observation, the observer reviews his or her behavioral observations with the person observed.

Supportive feedback is given for safe behaviors and corrective feedback is given for any behaviors thought to be at-risk. The conversation should reveal the organizational or individual influences on the at-risk behavior (e.g., insufficient training or staffing, time pressure, defective equipment, momentary distraction due to personal problems).

If anything can be fixed or improved immediately, the employees (i.e., the observer and the worker observed) attempt to do so. If that is not possible, they contact the appropriate person(s) for support.

Developing the CBC

A cross-organizational Implementation Team (IT) is selected, typically including at least 70% wage workers, to ensure proper employee ownership and buy-in. The IT should also include at least one (but possibly several) members of management to ensure sufficient organizational support and visibility. The IT guides the implementation of the BOFP throughout the organization. After receiving sufficient education and training, the IT develops the initial generic CBC by considering several sources, such as injury and near-hit reports, and job safety analyses.

Critical Behavior Checklist		
Area:_____	Immediate follow-up Needed: YES NO	
Date:_____	Observer:_____	
	Safe	At-Risk	Comments
1. PPE:			
A. Eye/Face			
B. Hearing			
C. Head			
D. Hearing			
E. Breathing			
F. Body			
2. Body Positioning:			
A. Cramped			
B. Ergonomics			
C. Extended			
D. Lifting			
E. Line of fire			
F. PinchPoints			
3. Tools and Equipment			
A. Use			
B. Condition			

The IT selects the top five to ten major or generic categories of behaviors believed to be most critical and includes them on the CBC.

Next, sub-categories are listed within each of the major categories. For example, the major category of *Body Positioning* might include the sub-categories *Lifting, Bending,* and *Twisting*. Moreover, the major category of *Tools and Equipment* may include the sub-categories of *Selection, Condition, and Use*; and the major category of *Housekeeping* may include the sub-categories of *Clean Work Area, Clear Isles/Exits, and Orderly Storage*.

Then the IT determines which demographic information will be included on the CBC. Information such as *Observer Name, Date,* and *Area* are all commonly used.

We strongly discourage the use of the observee's name (i.e., the person being observed). This can damage trust and discourage a frank and open observation and feedback session. Remember, trust and candid yet caring communication are fundamental to an AC4P culture. We encourage the use of a "comments" section on the card to discover and discuss the role of equipment, conditions, and other barriers to safe behavior.

Using the CBC

The IT determines where blank CBCs can be obtained, and where completed CBCs should be deposited. They suggest how many observations should be conducted within an area by each team or employee. And they suggest how long the typical observation should last.

Finally, with appropriate preparation and support, the IT determines how they'll analyze the data, and how they'll share information with the organization.

Before observing a co-worker, the observer asks for permission to conduct the observation. If permission is granted, the observer watches the observee for a short period (10-15 minutes is the average for most organizations). During the observation, the observer records what s/he sees. Comments should include descriptions of the at-risk behaviors, barriers to safe performance, and any ideas for improvement discussed during the feedback conversation.

Giving Feedback

After the observation is complete, AC4P plays a prominent role. The observer: 1) gives empathetic and non-threatening feedback to the observed; 2) provides praise for safe behaviors and corrective feedback for any at-risk behaviors; 3) reviews the entire CBC with the observe; and 4) asks open-ended questions to encourage a meaningful AC4P dialogue.

The approach we typically teach to address target at-risk behaviors is called the DO IT Process, as introduced in Chapter 1.[2] First, *Define* the behavior(s) to target and develop a relevant data-recording sheet (CBC).

Next, employees *Observe* occurrences of the target behavior(s) to derive a Baseline. Decide how you want to *Intervene* to change/influence the behavior in the desired direction. Finally, *Test* to see if your intervention(s) worked by continuing to observe and record occurrences of the target behavior(s).

Participation is Voluntary

This isn't a "gotcha program"; it's all about AC4P. Participation as an observer and observee should be voluntary. Before someone is observed, s/he must grant permission. Although there are some temporary drawbacks from asking permission to observe, the advantages are far more numerous.

First, the process cannot be "employee-owned" if employees don't have the chance to opt out. This also highlights the need to ensure it actually leads to improvements in keeping people safe (intrinsic value). If this intrinsic value is created and well communicated, voluntary participation will be readily obtained.

Second, the voluntary feature promotes the non-punitive nature of the process. Again, the intention is to actively care – to help people recognize risk, perform their tasks more safely, and reveal any system-related facilitators of at-risk behavior. It also increases trust between the observer and the observee.

Customized

The observation and feedback process must be adapted to the unique needs of the organizational culture. This works best when the AC4P principles explicated in Part I are well-understood and fitted to the culture. Customization can occur with outside consultants helping the organization design the process, or with the consultants training organizational personnel to be the "in-house experts" who can design the process with remaining sites, departments, or work teams.

Confidential and Anonymous

Employees find it difficult to participate in the BOFP if they believe the observation data are not confidential. With a guarantee of confidentiality, employees are more likely to agree to be observed, and are more likely to perform their *normal* behaviors. Data are typically tracked by only demographic information such as date, time, and/or work area.

As employees become more comfortable with the process and see no one is being punished as a result of the data, they become far less anxious about having their names on a CBC. In fact, employee groups in some mature observation and feedback processes have decided to include the name of the observee, with no ill effects.

Some of these organizations have also eliminated the "formal permission" aspect of the process. With the trusting, caring mindset of AC4P and continual learning, all employees agree to be observed by their peers (and often by supervisors) whenever the potential for an injury is apparent. (See Chapters 8 and 11 for more on this point.)

Non-Punitive

Negative consequences should never be an outcome of the BOFP. Punitive consequences make a mockery of AC4P. The only outcome of an observation is to give and receive behavioral feedback, and to mitigate any identified hazards. In some situations it may be necessary to stop the job if the observee is in imminent danger.

There may still be occasions when a progressive disciplinary process is warranted, but the BOFP should not be used as input into that system. Care must be taken to ensure the disciplinary process is evaluated and consistent with AC4P principles.

Non-Directive

The intent of the BOFP is not to have the observer tell the observee how to perform his or her job. Instead, feedback is intended to point out with care any behaviors that may place the observee at-risk, and to discuss safer alternatives. This AC4P approach makes it easier for the observee to accept the feedback without becoming defensive.

Of course, there are very rare occasions where clearly unacceptable behaviors occur despite corrective feedback and there is no option but to ensure the behavior is stopped (e.g., lighting up a cigarette in the tank farms of an oil refinery).

Data Entry and Analysis

Data from the observations are entered into a database and analyzed for potential trends. Graphs of the aggregate data are shared with work teams on a regular basis (typically during safety meetings as information for constructive discussion). These trends are then analyzed to determine if systems-level improvements are possible to reduce the probability the identified at-risk behaviors will continue.

Communication

Results from the observation and feedback process, including successes and ongoing challenges, should be communicated regularly within the organization. If the observation process leads to significant behavioral and environmental condition improvements, but people are unaware of these improvements from the PBS process, motivation to continue participation will eventually dissipate.

Employee Engagement

Recently I observed a CEO speaking to the presidents and VPs of each organizational division and subsidiary organizations. When referring to employee involvement he announced:

> *I know you all, I've worked with each of you, and to be honest, you're just not that smart! If we are to become world class with regard to safety, we need help and input from everyone in the organization, especially those with the time and experience doing the hazardous work...*

Although the insult was said in jest, the point was made and accepted by all in the room.

AC4P from the employee-involvement perspective includes genuinely making people feel their input is valued, needed, and seriously considered. However, if you ask for people's input, use it. To ask for input and not use it creates frustration, resentment, and less willingness to provide further input.

Listed below are a number of ideas for promoting more involvement in safety-related activities. As a safety consultant and trainer for more than 20 years, I've seen each of these facilitate employee engagement at a variety of different organizations.

• Regularly communicate with employees about the organization's safety-related processes, both in group sessions and in one-on-one conversations.

- Personally request employee participation.
- Pair experienced with less experienced employees on a safety-related task.
- Use various channels such as safety training, newsletters, and bulletin boards to regularly update all employees on the progress of a particular improvement process.
- Solicit input from employees through one-on-one communication, safety suggestion boxes, and safety meetings.
- Make safety relevant for work and at home and encourage family involvement whenever possible.
- Send memos to supervisors encouraging them to discuss key topics with their employees.
- Post reminders throughout the facility to encourage employees to participate in safety-related projects.
- Involve employees in designing safety signs, posters, newsletters, and emails to promote safety processes.
- Affix highly visible tags or stickers with safety team logos to equipment or areas that have been fixed or improved as a result of a certain safety process.
- Display the names, photographs and contact information of safety-team members who can provide information regarding certain safety issues.
- Provide relevant education and training to all managers, supervisors, employees, new hires, and contractors (when appropriate).
- A couple years after initial training for crucial safety processes, provide relevant refresher education and training to all managers, supervisors and employees that emphasizes any refinements and the beneficial outcomes expected.
- Regularly present the results of safety processes to employees, supervisors and managers.
- Present the latest data that demonstrate both site-wide and area-specific levels of employee involvement and improvements.
- Present the latest process data (quantitative and qualitative) in safety meetings, newsletters, bulletin boards, and other communication outlets.
- Advertise process successes through various channels such as safety meetings, bulletin boards, newsletters, and group emails.
- Provide one-on-one supportive feedback and positive recognition for employees who are actively engaged in safety processes.
- Send personal thank-you cards to employees who frequently provide high-quality participation.
- Provide group celebrations (e.g., steak dinners) for process achievements (see Chapter 3 for procedural guidelines).
- Provide surprise "now-that" rewards (e.g., caps, shirts with a relevant safety message or logo) to employees who are consistently involved in process activities (see Chapter 3 for procedural guidelines).
- Hold supervisors accountable to support safety processes.
- Praise supervisors who effectively encourage and support safety processes.
- Provide adequate time, financial resources, and moral support for the process

committees/teams.

- Hold regular meetings with relevant leadership and process committees/teams to discuss successes, barriers, and overall progress of specific improvement programs.
- Ensure the process committees/teams have adequate representation from various shifts, areas, and organizational levels.
- Encourage the process committees/teams to recruit new members in order to maintain diversity, fresh outlooks, and new ideas.

Person-States

AC4P from the person-state perspective attempts to help others feel better about 1) their job situation; 2) intervening in a crisis; 3) actively listening; 4) recognizing people's contributions; 5) helping someone better perceive previously unrecognized hazards; 6) and other ways of building the relevant person-states (as discussed in Chapter 2).

W. Edwards Deming[3] once said: "It is more important to have an imprecise measure of the right thing than a perfect measure of the wrong thing".

This quote is relevant here because it's difficult (if not impossible) to get a true measure of the AC4P person-states. Still, these factors are part of the "right thing" we need to consider when developing and evaluating personal and organizational improvement activities. And it is possible to estimate AC4P perceptions and person-states with a safety perception survey or a series of structured interviews.

Three types of questions appear on the SPS Safety Culture Survey relevant to assessing different aspects of AC4P: 1) Do participants agree with the concept of AC4P. This is accomplished by asking if people feel they *should* perform a certain safety-related behavior (e.g., "Employees should caution their co-workers when they are observed working at-risk"). 2) Are participants *willing* to perform certain AC4P behaviors? (e.g., "I am willing to caution my co-workers about working at-risk"). 3) Do participants *actually perform* the AC4P behavior? (e.g., "When I see a co-worker working at-risk, I caution him/her").

As shown in Figure 6.3, the results of approximately 200,000 respondents show most people respond favorably to the first two statements. Most have the necessary values and intentions. But far fewer respondents agree with the final statement, indicating there are personal and organizational barriers to actually performing these critical AC4P behaviors.

Analogous to Gilbert's PIP (performance improvement potential) described in his classic text, *Engineering Worthy Performance*,[4] the difference between the "should", "willing", and "do" can be used to estimate the potential for improvement, as well as informing ways to design the most appropriate intervention strategy.

When employees feel they should or are willing to perform these behaviors more than they currently do, a potential for relatively quick improvement can be expected following basic education and training. But if employees say they don't feel they should, they are not willing, and they actually do not perform such behaviors, some one-on-one coaching is called for.

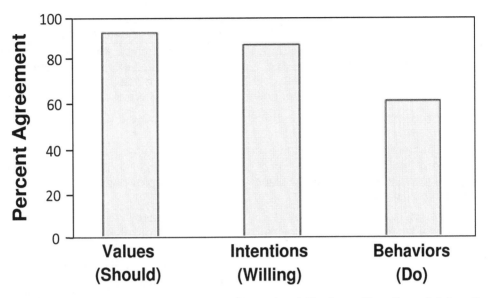

Figure 6.3. Percentage of responses for "should", "is willing", and "does" actively care for others.

Conditions

Although a work environment that minimizes, contains, or controls serious hazards should be a necessary precondition for an ideal AC4P safety culture. We need to consider how safety is supported or inhibited through the interaction of equipment, facilities, procedures, and people.

A number of environmental conditions increase the likelihood of injury. These factors are listed in the table on the next page, as derived from a number of sources, including the Tripod Delta technique described by Reason[5] and the consulting experiences of SPS, Inc.[6]

An AC4P approach proactively addresses these factors before an injury occurs, instead of waiting until someone gets hurt before analyzing what went wrong.

From this perspective, AC4P includes proactively eliminating or improving the physical hazards or hazardous conditions listed in the table on the next page. By taking a proactive AC4P approach to the physical environment, new and improved rules/procedures, equipment fixes, and hazard controls are developed before injuries have a chance to occur.

Participation in this proactive approach is often more difficult to motivate because the consequences of our preventive activities are rarely soon or certain. We will never know how many deaths are prevented by our proactive AC4P behaviors. However, such behavior is required to achieve an AC4P injury-free culture.

Employees at all levels of the organization need to continually search for, discuss, and help to remove these hazards. In order for this to happen, we need to create a culture of AC4P that moves beyond mere hazard recognition skills to a culture of people with the compassion and courage to speak up and identify work environment and situational concerns. (See Chapter 4 on courage.)

Factors Contributing to the Probability of a Workplace Injury
Physical Environment. Are there uncontrolled hazards such as energy sources? Is working at unsecured heights required? Is there uncontrolled exposure to harmful substances? Is there extreme heat, cold, or noise? Is there adequate lighting. Is there sufficient workspace (e.g., not cramped) and proper housekeeping?
Hardware. Are tools, equipment, materials available? Is non-standard use of equipment required to accomplish tasks?
Human-Machine Interface. Are the controls and displays adequate?
Equipment Design. Does the design of equipment provide external cues for proper use. Are the range of safe actions clear, and is feedback provided to the user regarding safe use?
Task Design. Is the workload too high or too low? Is the task performed at inopportune times (end of shift, off shift)? Are operators exposed to distractions? Is the task beyond the operators expected capabilities?
Supervision. Are there adequate pre-job briefings, checks, and scheduling. Is there excessive production pressure? Is progress checked and feedback provided?
Selection of Worker(s). Are workers qualified? Are they fatigued? Do work teams include people with an adequate combination of the needed skills?
New Technology: Does new technology (e.g., automation, new equipment) eliminate some problems while increasing others?
Maintenance Management. Are maintenance activities properly planned? Is maintenance carried out in a timely fashion?
Procedures. Are the procedures accurate, relevant, and practical?
Goal Compatibility. Conflict between an individual's work and personal responsibilities occur when informal norms conflict with the organization's goals, and when different goals of the organization are inconsistent. Does goal incompatibility cause confusion?
Communications. Are sufficient channels of communication available? Is appropriate information transmitted through the communication channels? Is the information timely and understandable? Is there coordination among interdependent groups?
Training. Have task and needs analyses been performed? Has adequate education training been provided on all relevant knowledge/skills? Has sufficient practice with feedback been provided? Was testing for competence performed? Was transfer of training evaluated and periodic refresher training provided?
Feedback. Does the task/job provide intrinsic (i.e., natural) feedback or are systems in place to provide external feedback?
Employee Engagement. Do employees have choice, flexibility, discretion, and feel personal ownership?
Fault-Tolerant Systems. Are errors detectable and recoverable? Are there adequate warnings, protection, containment, escape, and rescue strategies?

Of course, people need to have the education and training to develop hazard recognition skills. But there also needs to be a history of taking concerns seriously. Employees need to see that voicing such concerns leads to serious consideration of the issues and to beneficial AC4P culture change.

In Conclusion

Reducing injuries requires a comprehensive acceptance of safety as an interaction of physical environment/conditions, leadership, organizational systems, the behaviors of all people in the organization, employee engagement, and person-states (e.g., knowledge, skills, abilities, beliefs, expectancies, and personal dispositions). Only by treating safety as multidimensional and integrating AC4P principles into each dimension can the vision of zero injuries be achieved.

Notes

1. Geller, E.S. (2003). People-based safety: The psychology of actively caring. *Professional Safety, 48*(12), 33-43; Geller, E. S. (2005). *People-based safety: The source.* Virginia Beach, VA: Coastal Training and Technologies Corporation; Geller, E.S. (2008). *Leading people-based safety: Enriching your culture.* Virginia Beach, VA: Coastal Training and Technologies Corporation; Williams, J., & Geller, E. S. (2001) (Eds.). *Keys to behavior-based safety from Safety Performance Solutions.* Rockville, MD: Government Institutes.

2. Geller, E.S. (1996). *The psychology of safety: How to improve behaviors and attitudes on the job.* Radnor, PA: Chilton Book Company; Geller, E. S. (1996). *Working safe: How to help people actively care for health and safety.* Radnor, PA: Chilton Book Company.

3. Deming, W.E. (May 1991). Quality, productivity, and competitive position, workshop presented by Quality Enhancement Seminars, Inc. Cincinnati, OH.

4. Gilbert, T.F. (1978) *Human competence: Engineering worthy performance.* New York. NY: McGraw-Hill.

5. Reason, J.T. (1997). *Managing the risks of organizational accidents.* Burlington, VT: Ashgate.

6. Log on to www.safetyperformance.com for information about Safety Performance Solutions (SPS), as well as relevant resources (i.e., books, DVD's, CD's, and articles).

CHAPTER 8

Acting People into Safe Thinking:
Cultivating and sustaining an AC4P culture

Adam Tucker and Chuck Pettinger

SCOTT GELLER'S VISION of cultivating a compassionate culture where people not only actively care but recognize others for their own Actively Caring for People (AC4P) behaviors is ambitious, bold, and seemingly impossible, given the pressures in today's corporate world. Still, a culture of compassion is critical in the face of today's harsh realities: larger workloads, leaner staff, scheduling demands and ever-changing personnel. How can we overcome the inherent barriers to AC4P behavior in today's organizations?

The Safety-Begins-with-Me Culture at Cummins, Inc.

Following is the story of how the Distribution Business Unit in Cummins, Inc. created a safety process based on the fundamental principles of AC4P.

At Cummins, AC4P means everyone in the decision-chain has the compassion to collectively and continuously identify, manage and mitigate risks. Everyone actively cares interdependently for each other. The AC4P culture breaks down interpersonal barriers that prevent co-workers from acting on their sense of caring and provide their workmates with AC4P feedback whenever they see risky behaviors.

In many cases, a safety professional needs a structured change-management process to address the initial barriers to success, track and trend their progress, and act people into thinking differently.

If safety leaders of a global company want to evolve to "world-class," they need to cultivate and sustain an AC4P culture. The lessons and applications revealed in this Chapter reflect our initial attempts to achieve "world-class" through AC4P.

Cummins, Inc. is a global corporation of complementary business units that design, manufacture, distribute and service engines and related technologies, resulting in annual profits of $18 billion and ranking 150th on the Fortune 500 in 2012. It employs approximately 44,000 people with more than 60% located outside of the U.S. The company's customers are in approximately 190 countries that Cummins reaches through a network of more than 600 distributor locations. Clearly, this is a large, complex and diverse company.

The Reality

Imagine a service technician servicing a Cummins engine in an oil field in Wyoming, at night, in the winter, during a snowstorm...alone.

Imagine the dedication of this technician to the customer, to Cummins, to getting the job done.

Imagine the performance pressure on the technician from the customer, from his boss, and from his family whom he had to call and inform he would not make dinner yet again tonight.

These stressors, both positive and negative, represent significant personal challenges for the technician. So will the technician follow safety procedures? Possibly, but motivation to take shortcuts clearly exists.

The technician's various managers are responding to very real pressures to service the customer, get the job done on time, keep the cost down for the customer, and achieve their various performance metrics. Through a series of decisions, these individuals have inadvertently placed this technician in a risky situation.

The Challenge

How does an organization like Cummins move hundreds or thousands of employees from caring to *actively* caring? First, everyone is called on to support a personal commitment to safety. At Cummins it's called, "Safety Begins with Me".

Many organizations have champions to lead such an effort; but in global companies, how do you "bottle" that caring commitment and replicate it across divergent cultures and countries? Organizations need to focus on using change-management strategies that *act* people into AC4P *thinking*. They need to help people think differently, be brave, avoid bystander apathy, and have those caring conversations.

Barriers to Cultivating an AC4P Culture

Flavor-of-the-Month

Employees often see safety programs delivered like a short-term quick fix or a gimmick to motivate safe behavior. Incentive programs are a long-standing, common flavor of the month. Their focus is often on providing a reward in exchange for a reduced injury rate. This inhibits injury reporting and interpersonal conversation or coaching regarding at risk-behavior. Safety bingo, safety jackpot, stop lights and other short-term initiatives sometimes create the expectation among employees that any new safety initiative will be temporary and their participation eventually unnecessary.

Customer Pressure

Cummins technicians face real-time pressure to get an engine generator running, a truck back on the road, or a boat back into a fleet. Pressure not only comes from paying customers; technicians also feel the need to satisfy their internal customers like supervisors or managers.

Technicians are often skeptical about any new process that takes more time away from getting their engines running. They are strongly committed to customer service; take pride in their "efficient" work; and adhere to the schedule provided by managers.

To achieve a viable AC4P culture in this environment, organizations need to manage these pressures and provide technicians the time and resources needed to get the job done safely – while capable to act on any opportunities to offer corrective feedback for risky behavior and supportive feedback for safe behavior.

Limited Resources

The drive to provide on-time, quality customer service can drain resources available for safety. Time, budget, staffing and/or cognitive abilities can all be stretched thin. Employees can feel overworked and understaffed, with safety processes relegated to "just another checklist".

Macro-Scale Culture

Global companies operate in some countries with a very hierarchical society, making a bottom-up intervention on behalf of someone's safety contrary to the social norm. To succeed, AC4P processes need to address any cross-cultural issues/differences and include flexible contingency plans sensitive to cultural contrasts. Leadership must send a strong signal of commitment by making time and resources available for safety.

Person-States

Certain person-states can facilitate or inhibit AC4P behaviors. Employees who have never provided coaching for a risky behavior, received only minimal education/training on feedback skills (see Chapter 3), and rarely work with others, are likely to have limited self-efficacy for interpersonal AC4P behavior and a relatively low sense of group cohesion or belongingness.

Interpersonal coaching performed badly can counter actively caring and undermine the achievement of an AC4P culture. If organizations fail to address the "people-side" of safety appropriately, they "cap" the potential effectiveness of their AC4P process.

Metrics

Metrics are very powerful activators of behavior in organizations because they are personal. No one likes to be "red" on a scorecard.

Countless metrics are used in companies to measure performance such as profit margin, efficiency measures, headcount, injury rate, etc. Unfortunately these metrics are often conflicting and result in confusing directives for the expected behavior.

Cummins technicians are measured on efficiency, but told to take time for a safety process. For safety metrics, injury rate is the lagging-metric used most often to indicate safety-related performance. But this metric is a poor activator for safe behavior.

Injury rate says to an employee, "Don't get hurt", but it does little to direct the behaviors necessary to avoid getting hurt. Organizations that rely on only avoidance-oriented, lagging indicators are uninformed about how to move forward.

How well is your organization cultivating an AC4P culture? Track some key achievement-oriented leading indicators of safety success. Business-process metrics must also be aligned to address those inherent conflicts. Measuring the behaviors expected in an AC4P process drives the desired AC4P behaviors, and enables clear and tangible goal-setting for improvement.

Achieving a Step-Change Toward an AC4P Culture

Cummins invested diligently to create a climate for change. Without this preparation, change efforts are not sustainable. AC4P leaders need to follow a structured change-management process to overcome apathy generated by those superficial quick fixes.

A sense of "urgency" is needed.[1] Without it, people are likely to keep doing "what we've always been doing," expecting to keep getting what they've always been getting. A Design Team is needed to create an AC4P vision to steer the change, and inspire focus for the components of the change process. Change agents on the Design Team must be self-motivated to make proposed changes a reality.

Enabling the Step-Change

Once you gain that urgency, develop your Design Team and set the vision, then roll out the new initiative. Cummins' vision of "Safety Begins with Me" was connected to its job safety assessment (JSA) process rolled-out across all their branches. The JSA process was first piloted by a distributor in Denver to uncover issues and concerns before worldwide implementation.

Once the pilot began, feedback was solicited and potential barriers to success removed. The great success of the pilot provided momentum for the global roll-out of the JSA process with education and training to all Cummins' distributors.

Sustaining the Change

Any organization implementing a new initiative is faced with the same challenge: Sustainability. The key to sustainability is creating a "process" that does not have a beginning and an ending (like a never-ending series of flavor-of-the-month programs).

The process evolves with the culture and is truly a continuous-improvement initiative. "Safety Summits" were held to anchor the change within the Cummins culture. These summits sustained momentum with senior leadership, maintained the urgency, and kept employees engaged in the JSA process.

Cummins' Job Safety Assessment[2]

On the surface, the Cummins JSA process looks like any other behavior-based safety process.[3] But three key aspects of the process are critical for advancing an AC4P culture:

1. Top-to-bottom accountability to drive personal responsibility in the process.
2. Advanced data analysis to demonstrate functional utility.
3. Alignment of expectations and performance metrics with AC4P behaviors.

The Cummins JSA process is a behavioral observation-and-feedback system based on the common continuous-improvement process born in quality systems of Plan-Do-Check-Act.[4] In short, the process goes like this:

Plan

The employee completes a JSA checklist prior to starting each job. The checklist consists of 32 critical behaviors grouped into five categories: Work Practices, Ergonomics, Tools and Equipment, PPE, and Work Procedures. These behaviors were defined within Cummins' Distribution, making them relevant to the jobs being performed.

Because these behaviors were identified internally, they feel "right" to the technician. They have become part of the common Cummins lexicon when discussing safety concerns. With no corporate control of the JSA process, Cummins employees have a "safe harbor" to report problems that may have been long ignored or are contentious.

Do

Cummins employees are expected to execute their tasks while adhering to the safety work plan established through the JSA process. But jobs frequently change mid-stream. Employees are expected to remain vigilant to changing job conditions, ever ready to manage new hazards throughout the job. Hazard recognition training is part of Cummins' JSA process training, providing relevant skill-sets and perceived competence.

Check

At Cummins, a layered observation process involves supervisors observing work being conducted and initiating an AC4P conversation about their observations. Peer-to-peer observations are also conducted. This is where most of the learning occurs. Gaps in critical processes, tools for the job, difficulties with equipment, work conditions, and simple job frustrations that could drive unsafe behavior are captured and discussed.

During these AC4P conversations at Cummins, the employee being observed is in a "safe harbor". S/he cannot be disciplined for any safety "infractions" recorded during the observation period. The purpose is to learn *why* risky behavior is occurring, not to find fault.

Act

This step reflects a learning organization.[5] It completes the continual improvement process. Lessons learned from both the pre-job JSA checklists and the JSA observation events are captured in a robust data-management package. Detailed reports and predictive analytics are used to communicate to all levels of the organization about what issues need to be addressed and where observed patterns of risky behaviors may point to an impending injury.

This is arguably the most important step in the process. This is where the fruits of everyone's labor in the process are realized. Issues are identified, communicated, and ultimately solved.

So how does this JSA process drive an AC4P culture? Let's examine how the three key aspects outlined above can facilitate achieving a robust AC4P culture.

Top-to-Bottom Engagement

Every Cummins employee in the local organization has a role in the JSA process, thus empowering everyone to contribute to the continuous improvement process. Employees have a responsibility to effectively complete the JSA before starting a job (Plan) and execute that job according to their plan, while remaining vigilant to changing hazards (Do).

The key component of their role is not only to work safely, but to identify gaps in the safety systems and working conditions that could lead to at-risk behavior. After all, these employees are closest to the work and likely understand the gaps better than anyone. Identifying and communicating these gaps through the JSA is essential to the continual improvement process.

At Cummins, people perform behavioral observations whether they are employees, front-line supervisors, or VPs, and they are expected to engage in an AC4P conversation if they have any safety-related questions, comments or suggestions.

Leadership at all levels of the organization must learn from the observations and visibly respond to make a difference. Whether this response is changing a procedure, buying a new piece of equipment, purchasing PPE, or providing education/training, leaders must visibly respond with AC4P behavior so the functional utility of the JSA process is demonstrated to all employees.

This follow-up provides an essential positive consequence for participating in the JSA process and eventually increases future AC4P behaviors. When a process helps to facilitate safer operating procedures, momentum is created to move the whole organization toward an AC4P culture.

Applying Your Observation Intelligence

How do companies assess their AC4P-related performance? Ask employees, "How safe is your company?" and they typically answer, "Pretty safe".

How would their safety professionals respond to this question? Most likely they would quote one of many safety-performance lagging indicators like recordable injury rate, total recordable rate, lost workday rate, DART rate, EMR, and fatalities to name a few. In reality, we believe many organizations use only *injury* metrics, not *safety* performance metrics.

It's highly unlikely we will move away totally from reactive lagging indicators. Still, more and more AC4P facilitators look at proactive leading indicators to assess their safety-related performance. Identifying leading indicators can seem overwhelming. However, if these are viewed as activities, behaviors or processes that contribute to an AC4P safety culture, then the only question is, which ones do we choose?

Three key reasons to focus on leading indicators: 1) Leading indicators keep organizations in a proactive, preventive or predictive mindset; 2) Leading indicators are achievement-oriented whereas lagging metrics are avoidance-oriented; and 3) Many organizations have hit a "basement effect" when it comes to injury rates. In other words, injuries occur so infrequently it's difficult to draw statistical conclusions.[6]

Leading indicators are safety-related behaviors including compliance to rules, training activities, safety processes, VPs walking the shop floor, executives attending team meetings and/or monthly safety communications. When measured accurately, these types of actions estimate the effectiveness of your AC4P process.

Use Data to Demonstrate Functional Utility

To become a learning organization, the AC4P process must provide meaningful information that translates into visible results. In the Cummins JSA process, many of the inherent barriers are addressed through the creative use of observation intelligence.

Although participation does not guarantee commitment, it's a leading indicator of initial buy-in to an AC4P process. If a location, business-unit or department is not participating, then some unresolved barrier needs to be addressed. Also, by tracking which safety-related behaviors, conditions or error-prone situations are identified, the AC4P facilitator can proactively address injury potentials and thus prevent harm.

The speed at which data are shared demonstrates the utility of the observation process. In some cases risky behaviors or conditions cannot be resolved on the spot and some form of open-issue or work order needs to be tracked to closure. In this case, the speed at which an open-issue is resolved reflects organizational commitment and responsiveness.

Cummins' JSA Leading Indicators

At-Risk per Audit is a measure of the number of at-risk observations recorded during each JSA audit event. Are we being honest with ourselves during the Plan and Check phases about the safety challenges or are we simply checking the boxes on the form? In other words, are we actively caring for safety?

JSA Audit Target is a measure of how many JSA observations are being conducted during the Check phase. We aim to have an AC4P conversation about safety twice a month per each employee. Are we meeting the two-per-month employee target or do the pressures of the everyday business environment take priority?

Days Past Due is a measure of the responsiveness of leadership to respond and correct action items generated through the observation process. Are we a learning and

AC4P organization, or are we focused on business-as-usual and feeling overwhelmed? Do we lack the resources to actively care for safety?

Employees and leaders have distinct roles in this process. These metrics allow the facilitators to monitor the health of the process, and provide employees and managers with accountability metrics aligned with their respective desired AC4P behaviors.

Specifically, employees are evaluated on whether they are doing their part to sustain the process (i.e., the JSA audit target) and whether they are actively caring with honest observations about the gaps in the safety process (i.e., at-risk behavior per audit). The Days-Past-Due measure assesses the responsiveness of leadership to issues generated from the JSA process.

This is a far more effective approach to learn and improve from objective data than traditional lagging metrics. Individuals can understand how changes in their behavior affect the metrics and then adjust their actions accordingly. Process goals can be set with these metrics to activate designated AC4P behaviors needed to achieve an injury-free workplace.

Alignment of Expectations with AC4P Behaviors

One of the most critical barriers to overcome in the corporate world is misuse or neglect of observation intelligence. Operations often evaluate performance with regard to the desired business results and don't pay heed to the fact metrics can be powerful drivers of behavior.

The Venomous Cycle

If the observation intelligence collected by employees is not used, or used in a way to blame employees, subsequent observations will be of lesser quality. This "venomous cycle" can dramatically distort the information collected, as well as the potential for predicting and preventing injuries.

Here is a common scenario: Employee Bill has just finished conducting his safety observation, and AC4P Facilitator Mike is in the process of reviewing their results. Bill may think, "I'm tired of collecting observations no one does anything with. It just wastes time in my already busy day."

Similarly, Mike could think: "I don't know if I can trust this information. Is it really possible this group has not found a single risky behavior in over six weeks? People are still getting hurt and nobody has seen anything risky; are we doing the observations correctly? What are we doing with all these observations anyway? Is anyone following-up and closing out these issues?"

This spiral of frustration repeats itself thousands of times daily in well-intentioned organizations. Over time, it leads to disillusionment, decreasing participation and deteriorated quality of the observations. Then, the facilitator must go back to beg co-workers to observe and plead with managers to act on the information they don't trust. Frustration, anxiety and fear mount as more people get hurt.

The Virtuous Cycle

To avoid or reverse the venomous cycle, AC4P leaders need to demonstrate functional utility of the process. For those employees already self-motivated to perform AC4P behaviors, this demonstration of usefulness reinforces their participation and deepens their commitment. For other employees who are still "on-the-fence" in terms of truly participating, a demonstration of why participation is valuable to them can help increase their self-motivation to get involved.

Many AC4P processes initially need some external motivation or demonstrated utility to get the behavior started. Once this virtuous cycle begins, participation is motivated by naturally-occurring reinforcers of AC4P behavior, along with using observation intelligence appropriately and visibly.

In Conclusion

During the past two years, Cummins has implemented the JSA process at distributor locations around the world, involving more than 17,000 people. Cummins has accumulated more than 2,000,000 observations, conducted more than 100,000 AC4P conversations arising from observations, and corrected more than 130,000 at-risk conditions and/or behaviors.

The rate of injuries has steadily decreased by 20% each year while lost-work days have been reduced by nearly half. The JSA process has enabled Cummins to actively care for workplace safety.

Most importantly there are signs AC4P is becoming embedded in the culture. The technician working on the Cummins engine in the oil fields of Wyoming faces a very different situation today.

It's still cold. It's still dark at night. He may still be alone. But we now have emergency communication protocols: a "panic button" system for the technician to trigger if he's in trouble, and tracking mechanisms to help keep him safe during his travels.

These improvements all came from people throughout the organization actively caring for this technician and developing solutions for problems like his. The journey is far from over. This technician has many hazards yet to confront on the job. But now he has the tools to recognize and manage these hazards, and the ongoing support of an organization continuously learning how to actively care more effectively for all its employees.

Notes

1. Kotter, J.P., & Cohen, D.S. (2002). *The heart of change.* Boston, MA: Harvard Business Review Press.

2. Special thanks to Cummins Rocky Mountain LLC, a Cummins Distributor, and their Safety Leader, Timothy C. Smith, for their pioneering work in the Cummins Job Safety Assessment (JSA) process.

3. Geller, E.S. (1996). *The psychology of safety: How to improve behaviors and attitudes on the job.* Radnor, PA: Chilton Book Company.

4. Deming, W.E. (1986). *Out of the crisis.* Cambridge, MA: Massachusetts Institute of Technology,

Center for Advanced Engineering Study.

5. Senge, P.M. (1990). *The fifth discipline*. New York, NY: Currency Doubleday; Senge, P.M., Kleiner, A., Roberts, C., Ross, R.B., & Smith, B.J. (1994). *The fifth discipline fieldbook*. New York, NY: Currency Doubleday.

6. Latzko, W.J., & Saunders, D.M. (1995). *Four days with Dr. Deming: A strategy for modern methods of management*. Reading, MA: Addison-Wesley.

CHAPTER 9

Actively Caring for Safety in South Africa:
The power of the AC4P wristband

Timothy Ludwig, Wray Carvelas, Connie Engelbrecht, and Molly McClintock

AC4P WAS BROUGHT to South Africa by a Champion, someone willing to take on the challenges of improving a company's culture while having the vision to impact so much more.

Wray Carvelas, a South African of European descent, was born in 1965, so he really didn't remember too much about the apartheid regime. However, he does remember actively caring about people throughout his childhood. He worked in sprawling black ghettos with his church to empower black children toward a better life. His passion for the safety of his company's black workforce was part of his personal mission.

Wray cut his teeth in the gold and diamond mining industry. He learned very quickly safety management was authoritarian and a dictatorship. He experienced almost every safety management fad that has come and gone. All South African safety programs remained authoritarian and assumed workers are stupid – incapable of looking out for their own safety.

Wray didn't believe workers are stupid. But, because of South Africa's segregated legacy, workers had become incapable of thinking about their own safety and even less about the safety of co-workers.

Wray searched to find a safety program that made sense in modern South Africa. Along his journey, Wray was told he must listen to Scott Geller talk about AC4P and people-based safety (PBS). Indeed, Wray had an epiphany listening to AC4P principles and PBS procedures. For years, he had been searching for an approach like this. An approach that makes the teaching of "love your neighbor as yourself" a part of an everyday practice in the workplace.

After attending a PBS conference sponsored by Safety Performance Solutions (SPS), Wray and Connie Englebrecht combined their considerable energies to start planning a PBS program within their company, DRA, in South Africa. Behind the scenes Wray did an enormous amount of lobbying with executive management and fellow directors. Connie fed off of Wray's vitality, taking complete ownership for PBS and its implementation with her own committed flair.

More than a Routine Kickoff of PBS

The immensity of the challenge to help DRA implement PBS and develop an AC4P culture hit SPS consultants Tim and Molly on their first day while dealing with jet lag. Molly and Tim were to train safety leaders in DRA. Zulus, Afrikaans, British descendants, Zimbabweans, and others gathered in the training room – executive through construction laborers.

During a break Tim was pulled aside and warned, "You must understand… we are not a caring culture". Yes, vigilante violence exploded on all sides during the chaotic times as apartheid fell. That was the history of the culture.

But in this room was the future of the culture. Many volunteers wanted to make a difference. There was an Afrikaan (a man of northern European ancestry) ex-police officer who had enforced apartheid in its waning days. He sat next to a man named Artwell, a Zulu, part of the political resistance during apartheid. Artwell had been hunted, beaten, and left for dead by vigilantes, including members of the police.

A younger generation was present, working for the promise of a middle-class life denied their parents. They sat next to Afrikaans farmers, educated engineers, long-time managers, and safety professionals. They all spoke at least six languages, because they had to in this diverse culture.

With the SPS training complete, the new employee trainers prepared to go to DRA sites, set up implementation teams, develop observation cards, and start the PBS process. But the strategy had to take into account the norm and the legacy of South Africa's top-down, punishment-based management.

The corporate steering team confronted daunting tactical cultural challenges:

- How do you train a largely illiterate workforce and design an observation card they can use? South African law requires 50% of the workforce to be from the local area. In the remote mining regions this usually meant hiring from a local tribe with little education.
- How will this workforce get beyond their fear of punishment and trust the observation process?
- How will employees of multiple tribal backgrounds give feedback to each other in a respectful way when some were hated traditional rivals? Mix in Africans of European origin and their biases and you have a volatile diversity of people learning to live together outside of apartheid, yet within its legacy.
- The more practical complexities of the mining industry also presented obstacles.
- How do you implement PBS when most of the work is done by contractor companies sometimes only on a job for less than six months?
- How do you transfer ownership of the PBS process when the mine was built and production executed by a different company?
- How do you convince an array of Directors, Project Managers, and Construction Managers to implement PBS at their site?

Wray and Connie understood a key strategic point: To gain participation of their site managers and superiors, the success of PBS must be clearly demonstrated. Thus, they decided to set up PBS at three pilot sites, learn from those experiences, and then use their success stories to convince others to get on board.

Small Wins with the AC4P Wristband

Connie had to find a way past the language and cultural divides that could snuff out PBS before it got any traction. She needed a tool the illiterate worker could understand. She needed a tool that gave the white manager a nonthreatening way to communicate with the local black worker.

She needed a tool with a purpose, one that would recognize and reward the AC4P behaviors among the workforce.

One tool she chose was the AC4P wristband. She had thousands produced in a variety of colors. Laminated instructions accompanied the bands,directing users to present the wristband to anyone – anyone – who took a moment to look out for the safety of another person.

In one case, that "anyone" turned out to be a truck driver in Tanzania who stopped to fix Connie's flat tire. Connie was so impressed and thankful that a complete stranger would help out travelers from another country

that she thanked him for his caring act and awarded him an AC4P wristband.

She explained the purpose of the wristband, and promised she would never forget his kind act. He smiled and said his wristband will remind him to always care about other people.

When Connie sits down with skeptical managers at a mining site, she gives them ten wristbands each, and challenges them to recognize AC4P behaviors. She tells her own AC4P stories like that of the Tanzanian trucker. During the following months she advertises the stories of everyday workers and how they earned the wristbands.

The Safety Newsletters are filled with wristband stories, along with relevant photographs. Here are a few examples:

Paul Bantshi received a wristband for stopping a concrete truck driver when the chute of the truck slipped open swinging from side to side narrowly missing a pole close by.

Teichman employee showing he cares! Ngoy Jean Willy saw the DRA team picking up papers on site. He approached one of them and gave her gloves to use. She thanked him for caring and awarded him with a wristband.

Freddy Lwamba moved a rock out of the road near the culvert box cut. He was concerned people may not see the rock and can cause a crash if they hit the rock. Antoine thanked him and told him he showed true caring for people on site by removing the rock.

Aaron Motsi, a Supervisor working for WBHO Civils is proud of his area and maintains it by always keeping it clean, ensuring good housekeeping, maintaining good stacking and storage and excellent barricading standards, setting an example to all the other Supervisors on site. Leon Bessenger (DRA Supervisor) appreciated the efforts of Aaron and thanked him by rewarding him with a wristband as a symbol of caring and lifting the standards at his site.

Gavin Skinner (DRA Mineral Projects Safety Manager) rewarding Piet Moloto from Elan Civils with a wristband for replacing missing rebar caps in their working area.

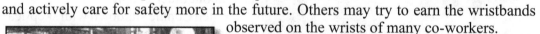

It's a brilliant application of behavioral science. When a wristband is handed to someone, that person is rewarded for AC4P. Ideally, this individual will remember the specific behavior performed and actively care for safety more in the future. Others may try to earn the wristbands observed on the wrists of many co-workers.

Then, people begin or continue coaching others by pointing out risks and hazards, or simply helping to keep a co-worker safe. If this spreads throughout a worksite, it effectively reduces injuries and supports the formal observation and feedback process of PBS.

But this simple process also profoundly impacts the deliverer of the wristbands. Managers handing out the ten wristbands experience inspirational rewards, such as seeing appreciation from recipients and knowing their employees may adopt AC4P into their lifestyle to keep others safe.

Building a Culture of Intervening

The easy part of DRA's conversion to an AC4P culture is rewarding safe behaviors. But, getting workers to intervene when they see at-riskbehavior is a tougher assignment. Connie shares a story:

She was at baggage claim at Oliver Tambo airport eager to get home and relax with her family. A foreign family with two small children was waiting for their baggage. The father allowed his little boy to get on the conveyors while they were not moving. Connie made eye contact with him, but he was not moved. Finally, she asked the father to please remove his child from this dangerous situation.

"As I walked off with my luggage a question popped into my head," said Connie. "Why did I hesitate until after eye contact with the father before I spoke up?"

She realized workers on a site do the exact same thing. They see the danger and realize someone could be killed. They want to prevent an injury. But, they are waiting for someone else, the "responsible party" like the father, to do so before they take action. They may also be afraid of embarrassing the person, or worse, getting them punished.

From that day on, Connie taught people to intervene without waiting. Intervention to prevent an injury is the core of AC4P. It's about that person whose life is being protected. It's not about you, or you offending someone, or you fearing a reprisal, or even you feeling good about what you did. But you will feel good after actively caring effectively for the safety of another person (see Chapter 10), and this should increase the probability you will actively care again.

Changing the Management Culture

Make no mistake; management can kill afledgling AC4P culture. The embedded culture of punishment was difficult to conquer within DRA and among its contractors. It took numerous personal acts of courage to counter the often scary acts of reprisal against workers found working at risk.

Elliot Chataika was a Safety professional working for DRA, truly committed to AC4P every day. Elliot approached people performing at-risk behaviors by treating them with respect. To gain their trust, he actively listened to their reasons for performing risky behaviors. He then coached them about the safest way to perform their task.

Site Supervisors posed a more difficult challenge to Elliott. He had them thanking and awarding wristbands to employees who were performing AC4P behavior. But he was not seeing a fundamental change in the way they managed safety. When an employee was using damaged equipment and accessing unsafe scaffold, Elliott had his chance to confront the culture of punishment.

At a mine in Zambia, Elliot noticed a man named Ethan working on a scaffold that had not been inspected and was tagged as unsafe. Ethan's harness had a broken lanyard and was tied together with a knot on the one side. Elliott asked Ethan to come down from the scaffold, only to discover Ethan was working without supervision. Upon questioning, Ethan said he did not pay attention to the scaffold tag or notice the damaged harness.

After coaching Ethan, Elliot explained he was going to talk to his supervisor to make sure other workers knew the safe way to work at heights. Later in the day,

Elliot received a message from management that they decided to fire Ethan.

Elliot met with the contractors and quickly discovered there was no risk assessment of the area. The dangers had not been discussed with Ethan prior to work, and Ethan had not been provided with appropriate safety equipment.

Blame shifted from Ethan to the Supervisor. Someone had to pay in this punishment-first culture. But, instead of disciplining the Supervisor, Elliot recommended conducting a PBS analysis to determine why Ethan and his Supervisor overlooked the obvious.

The analysis indicated the Supervisor was responsible for three additional areas and could not effectively monitor these areas daily. Additionally, a shortage of PPE supplied by the contractor led to Ethan's use of the damaged harness. After deliberation with the contractor's management, it was understood that blaming Ethan or even the supervisor would not make the workplace safer. Instead management added foremen and updated the PPE.

When Elliot told him he would not lose his job, Ethan broke down in tears, saying:

I am the breadwinner of my family and am supposed to look after them, feed them and most of all pay for my son's medical bills. I left my son in critical condition at the hospital and came to work at the mine. I did not focus on the harness when I took it – my son was on my mind! Elliot, you saved me from losing my job because you listened and cared. You showed me you care about me as a person, a human and not just a worker!

The Road Ahead

AC4P has the power to transform an organization. The greatest reward one can wish for in a successful safety program is to witness the transformation of individuals; people believing their contribution is valued; people beginning to believe in themselves; and people starting to feel they belong.

When people associated with DRA read or listen to some of the AC4P stories, it brings a lump to their throat and a warm glow to their heart. For many associated with DRA, it has been one of the most rewarding journeys in their careers.

Because We Must

During the initial introduction of PBS in South Africa, Tim and Wray took an early morning flight to the Kalahari Desert in the Northern Cape to continue training at one of the bigger construction sites. A large number of San, the local aboriginal people of this area whose rich culture dates back over 20,000 years, had gained employment in the different crafts because of a national law requiring companies and their contractors to hire 50% of their workforce from the local populations. Since mines tended to be in rural areas this meant the local population consisted of farmers, mostly illiterate and poor, with little to no industrial experience. Many supervisors believed their supposed ignorance often led to injuries.

The camp where the miners lived was about 15 kilometers (9.3 miles) from the town and had the normal pre-fabricated units set in rows with service facilities, some recreation, and a mess hall; all surrounded by a tall fence. Next to this camp a shantytown had risen up. It was twice the size of the camp and full of poverty and filth.

"The camp had provided an economy of sorts," Wray explained. "We get these all over Africa because those working in the construction sites get free clothing and food that they distribute to their relatives and friends through the fence."

"The conditions are horrible in those make-shift towns," said Wray while pointing to the cardboard and corrugated metal shacks. "There is hunger, crime, rape... they look to the camps for security."

If DRA is successful in teaching safety and actively caring while building an AC4P culture in this mining industry, the largest in Africa, then a fence should be no barrier to extending the AC4P culture to the wretched shantytowns and their families. Especially when you have champions like Elliott and Connie.

In fact, Connie has already broken thought the fence line. She was approached by one of the local schools in Zambia to coach the children about AC4P and how it works. They wanted their children to apply these principles at school and at home. This happened because some of the parents working in the DRA mines went back home and told their children about this new way: AC4P. They went to school and bragged about their fathers' new way and now the teachers want DRA to share it with them and their children.

As Nelson Mandela once said, "You can never have an impact on society if you have not changed yourself".

CHAPTER 10

Actively Caring to Keep People Safe:
Evolving from BBS to AC4P

Joseph E. Bolduc, Turner Plunkett, Matthew Foy, and
Joseph Dean

UNTIL RECENTLY, THE PSYCHOLOGY that accounts for the human side of workplace injuries eluded us. We were unsure how to respond to this vision statement from a senior executive, "I value a culture where people are comfortable both giving and receiving behavior-based feedback".

The behavior-based safety (BBS) process we implemented did show some promise, but we had yet to develop a culture of people actively caring for each other. The key to truly understanding the executive's statement came with our introduction to Actively Caring for People (AC4P).

Learning About AC4P

In 2009, the Fibers Division of Shaw Industries Group Inc. asked Bob Veazie to deliver the keynote address at the division's annual BBS conference. Bob spoke about transitioning from a culture intermittently conducting behavioral audits to the overwhelming power of an AC4P culture where observation and feedback occurs whenever it's needed. He inspired us to develop a culture where people are encouraged to speak up when something is not right (without fear of retribution).

Six months later Bob introduced us to Scott Geller who, along with the Center for Applied Behavior Systems (CABS) at Virginia Tech (VT), has become our source of research, inspiration, and mentoring in developing an AC4P culture.

Build Relationships using the Platinum Rule[1]

We've all been exposed to the Golden Rule – "Treat others the way you want to be treated". Dr. Geller taught us the Platinum Rule, "Treat others the way *they* want to be treated". We didn't understand this for a long time, but now we do.

For example, all organizations today teach and practice managing diversity. Now, we understand diversity goes far beyond the contemporary model of ethnicity, color, creed and religion to include individuality. It's about developing relationships so we have firsthand knowledge and appreciation for how the individuals and groups in our workplace need to be treated in order for them to perceive a sense of belongingness and interdependency to achieve an injury-free workplace.

Employing the Platinum Rule positions us to better serve and meet the specific needs of each other. We are convinced this is essential to establishing a management climate that enables an AC4P culture. It enables the development of relationships and belongingness needed for behavioral feedback to be given and received constructively in a non-adversarial manner. When such relationships develop, the ability to inspire and influence the achievement of all business objectives is optimized.

Assess Self-Efficacy[2]

At first, we did not understand self-efficacy, but we soon came to realize it's the Achilles Heel of many organizations. Do your employees believe they have the knowledge, skills, and ability to practice AC4P behavior under various circumstances? One training manager put it this way, "The company has spent a lot of money educating people's minds; the work of AC4P brings their hearts and beliefs into the equation".

During the past few years, we've observed that once people have a high personal perception of self-efficacy, they can feel empowered. Dr. Geller taught us that empowerment is being able to provide a "yes" answer to three distinct questions: 1) *Can I do it?*; 2) *Is it worth it?*; and 3) *Will it work?* An operator stopping a process for safety or quality reasons provides a good example of what it means to feel empowered.

Let's say an operator believes a certain process provides an immediate high-loss safety risk. Can he shut the process down? Sure he can. But, will it work? Yes, a serious injury may be averted and the risk is managed by the hazard being removed.

However, the determining factor in the employee's answer to, "*Is it worth it?*" is the expected reaction from management after the process is stopped. Applying these empowerment lessons appropriately puts ordinary people in leadership positions that call for competence and moral courage to do right, even when no one's watching.[3]

An Initial AC4P Survey

After our 2009 Fibers BBS conference, Bob Veazie visited all Fibers Division Manufacturing sites and everyone at his presentation was asked to write numbers 1 to 10 down the left side of a sheet of paper. Then they were asked to rate eight questions on a scale from 1 to 10, with "1" indicating the lowest personal perception of the topic and "10" reflecting the highest personal perception.

The eight questions link to the five person-states outlined by Geller and Veazie in *The Courage Factor.*[4] The eight questions are shown in Table 10.1 on the next page, along with the anchor statements for a "1" vs. a "10" rating.

Out of curiosity, we compared the average site score of all questions to the number of OSHA recordable injuries (or Total Recordable Injury Rate, TRIR) each site had experienced year to date. This was not an exact science; each plant has a different number of associates. Still, it was evident the associates at the three smaller plants (totaling 1,500 associates) had a higher average survey score and 65% fewer injuries than experienced at a large plant of 1,500 associates.

This supported our suspicion that safety is benefited when people have a relatively high personal belief their *competency* can make a positive difference, are *optimistic* about the future, feel high levels of *self-esteem*, know they *belong* in the workplace community, and perceive *choice* in how they work. (See Chapters 2 and 11 for more on these five person-states.)

	Question	Description for "1"	Description for "10"
	Table 10.1.The Initial Eight AC4P Perception Survey Questions		
1	I am heard.	I never get feedback on my ideas.	I always get feedback on my ideas.
2	My ideas contribute to the business.	I can't make a difference.	What I think makes a big difference.
3	I belong here.	I cannot stand coming to work.	I love coming to work.
4	I receive recognition.	I never receive any recognition.	Recognition is excellent.
5	I am competent at my job.	I do not know what I am doing on the job.	I am very capable at my job.
6	I am learning.	I am not learning anything.	I learn something new every day.
7	I have control in how my job is done.	I have no control in how my job is done.	I have control in how my job is done and I follow policies and procedures.
8	I serve others.	I never get involved when I see someone in danger.	I always get involved and help the person I see in danger.

Researching an Improved AC4P Culture Survey

Given this information, coupled with organizational energy to evolve to an AC4P culture, we added a ninth question, "I accept negative feedback and take action to improve based on the feedback." This question reflected our attempt to assess the degree of humility in the culture when employees receive and use safety-related behavioral feedback.

This nine-item perception survey was randomly and anonymously administered via the internet to ten percent of the employees (termed associates) per each of the seven manufacturing sites of the Fibers Division of Shaw Industries Group, Inc.[5] Participants rated each item on a ten-point scale with "1" indicating "strongly disagree" and a score of "10" representing "strongly agree". A rating of "5" was specified as "neutral".

After the data had been compiled, including approximately 40 percent of the associates per site (10% per month x 4 months), the senior author conducted a statistical comparison of each site's survey results with the respective OSHA TRIR in 2010.

Results

A scatter plot of the TRIR vs. the mean total score across all nine questions of the perception survey is depicted in Figure 10.1. The best-fit straight line shows a rather consistent negative relation between TRIR and total score on the nine-item survey. The two sites with zero injuries had the highest total survey scores, while the four sites with relatively high TRIR's had the lowest total mean scores on the perception survey.

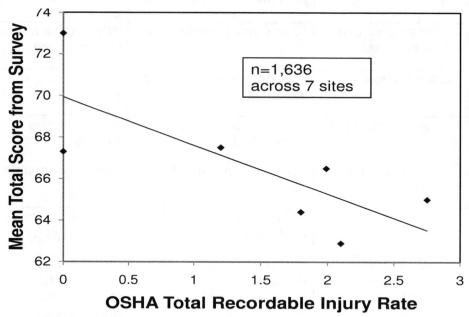

Figure 10.1. Scatter plot of mean AC4P perception survey scores vs. TRIR.

Implications

While these data show strong connections between organizational injury rate and a crude estimation of the safety culture, a cause-and-effect conclusion is obviously inappropriate. Furthermore, these correlations do not support the reliability or validity of the perception survey as a suitable measure of corporate culture.

The Division Survey Committee was convinced the survey activated provocative conversation, but decided certain questions could be improved. Specifically, Question 3, "I belong here" seemed too general for the ethnically-diverse workforce at Shaw Industries. Some associates suggested "here" could mean "this country, this state, or this city". Furthermore, the added ninth item, "I accept negative feedback and take action to improve based on feedback" really asked two questions, "Do I accept feedback?" and "Do I use feedback to improve?"

Thus, the survey was revised to remove confusion and currently contains 12 questions. Question 3 now reads, "I have a sense of belonging among my work team," and Item 9 was expanded to three items, "I receive corrective feedback from my peers," "I willingly accept corrective feedback from my peers," and "When I receive negative or corrective feedback, I react to improve my behavior". This revised AC4P Perception Survey is shown in Table 10.2 on the next page.

Table 10.2. The Twelve AC4P Perception Survey Questions	
1. I feel I am heard because I get feedback on my ideas or concerns.	7. I am self-motivated to do my best work at my place.
2. The ideas I contribute make a difference at my plant.	8. I have personal control over how safely I work each day.
3. I have a sense of belonging among my work team.	9. I actively care about the safety of others at work.
4. I receive recognition for my contributions at work.	10. I receive corrective feedback from my peers.
5. I am competent at my job.	11. I willingly accept corrective feedback from my peers.
6. I learn and develop knowledge and skills at work.	12. When I receive negative or corrective feedback, I react to improve my behavior.

Our Division Vision Statement

Throughout our research with the AC4P perception survey, Division Management understood the importance of empowerment, employee engagement, and inclusion. So, they formed an AC4P Steering Committee. This Committee is made up of Division Management, Plant Managers, Plant Human Resource Managers, Corporate Training and representatives of the corporate management group, including safety professionals and leaders of the BBS process.

> ## *Our AC4P Culture Vision Statement*
>
> *We will work to create a safe environment at Fibers Division Plants in which all employees are actively caring for and committed to each other's safety. We will drive a high level of compassion and encourage employees to raise safety concerns without fear of retribution. Our behaviors will demonstrate that we believe safety is a choice and doesn't happen by chance.*

This team drafted and adopted a vision statement (shown above) everyone in the Division was asked to support. A letter explaining the vision was mailed to all employees' homes, hoping their families would become aware of the vision and "buy in" to its ramifications. Some sites printed the vision on banners and hung them at the entrance to the plant. Employees were asked to assert their commitment to this safety vision by stopping and signing these banners. These signed vision-statement banners still hang in the plants.

Follow-up Focus Groups

The "continuous-improvement" mindset prompted the senior author to contact Scott Geller. We wanted to identify a way to learn more about what associates had to say regarding the safety cultures at the various plant sites. A plan was devised to conduct focus groups at the five plants most geographically proximal. Two VT graduates who had conducted research in CABS were hired as summer interns to lead focus groups tasked with exploring ways to apply lessons learned from the results of the nine-item AC4P Culture Survey.

For 13 consecutive weeks, the two summer interns (termed "facilitators") followed one of two procedures when conducting daily focus groups with plant associates (due to differing capabilities per site) at five different sites. The majority of focus groups included 8 to 12 associates, each sampled from different departments, and each focus-group meeting lasted about 45 minutes in duration. When this method was used, five to seven focus groups were conducted per day.

In some facilities, it was more practical to facilitate focus groups of three to seven associates for a 20-minute time period. This method required facilitation of 12 to 14 focus groups per day.

No standard sampling method was implemented to assign associates to focus groups. Some supervisors selected associates by birthday month, while others merely sent whomever was available and had not already participated. In the end, approximately 40% of the associates at each of the five manufacturing sites had participated in a focus group. Table 10.3 depicts the number of associates per each of the five sites who participated in a focus group.

The Process

Each focus-group session was designed to generate an all-inclusionary, free-flowing conversation around the 12 questions of the AC4P perception survey. (See Table 10.2 on page 221). To ensure participant anonymity, only the first names of the participants were used; and in the facilitators' records, the participants were only identified

Table 10.3. Sample size per plant.		
Plant	Employees	Sample
1	560	140
2	250	100
3	650	260
4	450	180
5	1400	560

by department and work shift.

Facilitators clarified they knew very little about the operations or the culture at Shaw Industries, and were there to learn from the associates. They started by reading an item from the culture survey, which they had learned would generate open discussion (often Items 2, 4, or 8 given in Table 10.2).

The facilitators asked participants their perceptions related to the item (e.g., specifics of their work environment and safety-related behaviors of those around them). Then, they solicited ideas and strategies to raise the perception score for the particular item.

Additional survey items were examined with the same sequence of two questions: 1) What led to the perceptions you feel regarding this survey item?, and 2) What would Shaw need to do for you to be able to rate this question a perfect "10"?

For each focus group, one of the two facilitators led the discussion, while the other recorded (in an electronic database) the associate's comments. To maintain the participants' anonymity, their comments were only identified by the department and shift they represented.

The data from the focus groups consisted of lists of comments that reflected the participants' concerns, opinions, attitudes, and suggestions prompted by a particular question from the AC4P culture survey.

Results[6]

The focus groups at the two plants with no recordable injuries provided the highest number of positive safety-related statements, and the fewest number of negative comments. In contrast, the focus groups at the three plants with relatively

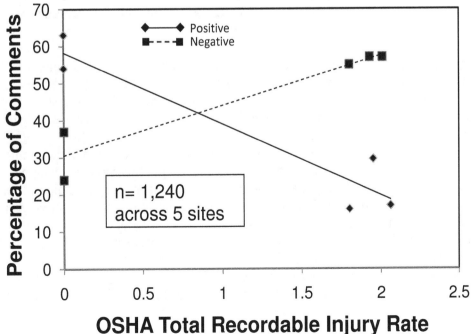

Figure 10.2. Scatter plot of each plant's TRIR vs. focus-group commentary.

high TRIRs gave markedly more negative than positive safety-related comments. The two slope calculations shown on the scatter plot in Figure 10.2 show rather consistent relations between the tone of the commentary and injury rate.

Implications

Given potential bias (e.g., selective perception) regarding the facilitation of the focus groups and the analyses of the qualitative data was minimized, how meaningful or useful are the results summarized in Figures 10.1 and 10.2?

Both the survey and the focus groups assessed participant's attitudes or sentiments regarding their organization's safety-related policies, goals, and procedures, and thus a correlation between these measures and frequency of OSHA recordables was expected. Thus, we were not surprised to find the predicted correlations. These results distinctly support a connection between occupational injuries and safety-related perceptions and attitudes – estimates of a work culture.

Our data suggest, "What is talked about defines culture and culture defines what is talked about." Individuals sharing stories of when they actively care for each other helps sustain the effort. Conversations and activities related to inclusion, self-accountability, self-motivated behavior, and AC4P have direct connections to safety culture and in turn to rate of occupational injury.

In Conclusion

Our efforts to cultivate an AC4P culture informed us of the value of a forum for employees to voice their improvement ideas and receive feedback. Regardless of responsibility or position within an organization, employees who care about their job want to know about the organization's successes and failures, provide input for improvement, be recognized for their useful input, and feel a sense of belonging within the work community.

Management practices that lead to the long heard adage of "I'm just another number" keep many organizations from reaching their potential in all business processes.

This is not to say a "country club" atmosphere is the desired cultural state. Rather, the best organizations maintain passion and dedication to continuously learn with the purpose to continuously improve.

An organization's ability to optimize safety and quality production is determined by its effectiveness at activating and supporting collaborative, constructive, and synergistic relationships at all levels of the organizational structure. Indeed, relationship building is key to developing the interpersonal trust, competence, community, and actively caring needed to cultivate an AC4P culture of interpersonal compassion.

The AC4P Movement has fueled the evolution of numerous positive and productive relationships in the Fibers Division of Shaw Industries, Inc. This is exemplified by the poem given on the next page. It was written by Donald Jones, an electrician at Plant 8S in Columbia, SC. When it comes to actively caring for workplace safety, this poem says it all.

You Are My Friend

I've known you maybe 20 years,
No Matter if one or two,
The very things I want for me,
I desire the same for you.

Life and love, joy and peace,
A job with minimal stress,
So aft your work is safely done,
At home you may find rest.

So think about the things you do,
In haste let none be done,
Consider every circumstance,
Then your battle's almost won.

As you walk along your paths,
Glance now and then at me,
If danger signs come into view,
Please tell me what you see.

We work together, day by day,
I talk, I laugh with you,
It only takes a moment's time,
For joy to turn to gloom.

If I see you in harm's reach,
And resolve to only stare,
Well I've said with loud voice,
My friend, I do not care.

If I fail to right a wrong,
I've shunned to act my part,
Then shall my eyes bow in shame,
When your pain rips my heart.

This prose may not be quoted,
In distant years to come,
As tho was penned by famous men,
With skill to ink a tome,
The important thing at hand,
Is your and my safety,
To know I watch for you,
To know you watch for me.

Notes

1. Allesandra, T., & O'Connor, M.S. (1996). *The platinum rule: Discover the four basic business personalities and how they can lead you to success.* New York, NY: Warren Books, Inc.

2. Bandura, A. (1977). Self-efficacy: Toward a unifying theory of behavioral change. *Psychological Review, 84*(2), 191-215.

3. Geller, E.S., & Veazie, R.A. (2010). *When no one's watching: Living and leading self-motivation.* Newport, VA: Make-A-Difference, LLC.

4. Geller, E.S., & Veazie, R.A. (2009). *The courage factor: Leading people-based culture change.* Virginia Beach, VA: Coastal Training and Technologies Corporation.

5. Asking all employees, salary and hourly, to complete the survey in the month of their birth enabled randomization and ensured all employees had their voice heard annually regarding personal perceptions of their work culture.

6. The research reported here was published in *Professional Safety*, see Geller, E.S., Bolduc, J.E., Foy, M.J., & Dean, J. (2012). In pursuit of an actively-caring safety culture: Practical methods, empirical results, and provocative implications. *Professional Safety, 57*(1), 44-50.

CHAPTER 11

Commitment-Based Safety:
From the workplace to an AC4P lifestyle

Bob Veazie

A T A POWER PLANT in Maryland, 31-year-old Benjamin Heron fell 150 feet to his death in August, 2007 after not hooking his safety harness back on the cable when he moved on the platform to another work area. Two workers on the platform noticed he unhooked and then did not hook back. These workers said nothing and Benjamin fell to his death moments later.

Here is the critical difference between caring and acting: It's not that these workers didn't care, it's that they didn't say anything to remind Benjamin to tie off. His wife and three children likely wonder every day why someone didn't go beyond just caring and say something.

From speaking with thousands of employees in the corporate world, I've learned none of them want to see anyone injured on the job. This is caring. Yet when asked if they go beyond caring to acting – to actually say something to a peer who is working at risk and could get hurt – most admit they do not act on their caring. AC4P is about going beyond just caring to proactive action.

AC4P and Behavior-Focused Safety

Many companies have implemented an evidence-based AC4P program for safety called behavior-based safety (BBS)[1] or people-based safety (PBS).[2] Its purpose is to help people develop the confidence and skills to take care of each other every day (i.e., to be each other's Brother/Sister Keeper) before injuries occur – to be proactive rather than reactive.

As detailed in Chapter 7, employees use a critical behavior checklist (CBC)[3] to remind them of behavioral risks to look for when observing another worker. They check "at-risk" or "safe" on the CBC, based on the behavioral definitions they previously determined in group meetings with their work team.

After completing the CBC, the observer provides the observed worker with supportive feedback for the safe behaviors recorded and corrective feedback for any "at-risk" behavior noted. The CBCs are given to a data processor who tallies the information and distributes a summary to all employees.

At-risk behaviors occurring at the highest frequencies are identified, specifying targets for further improvement. The objective is to cultivate a culture where 100% of the time, every day, any employee who observes another employee taking a risk (including breaking a safety rule) speaks up to remove the possibility of personal injury.

In many workplaces, though, the BBS process is disconnected from the mission of AC4P. Too many employees get caught up in the structure and mechanics of the formal observation process and disregard its core purpose – to actively care for one another, with or without a CBC.

The real value of using a CBC is not the acquisition of tick marks for a computer program and summary output. Rather, it helps all participants become more skilled and comfortable at providing feedback to their co-workers regarding ongoing safe and unsafe behavior.

In fact, the formal observation sessions are actually completed as *practice* to develop competence and courage at providing feedback whenever a person sees someone in potential danger of becoming injured.

Compliance is Not Commitment

At a lunch meeting, the leader of the safety committee at a Fortune-500 company told me he had completed 20 formal BBS observations of other workers that month. How? When he had time he simply went out on the plant floor and walked up to 20 different employees, watched them for six to seven minutes and then completed the employee-designed CBC.

Then he used the CBC to give these workers feedback on how safe they were. If unsafe behavior was observed, he gave the worker specific corrective feedback to improve. After these 20 sessions, the 20 CBCs were entered into a database that included results of the CBCs completed by other employees.

This particular safety leader of a plant with about 1,100 employees had set a record for number of formal CBCs completed, and was the leader that month. His record of 20 CBCs was three times higher than the next highest person, who had completed seven and others who averaged two to three CBCs that month.

Interestingly, most of his CBCs indicated 100% safe. In only two of the 20 observation sessions were there any issues that needed correction. I was impressed with his volume of behavioral observations and interpersonal coaching. This implies exemplary actively caring for safety, right?

That afternoon, we were out walking around and looking at different areas of the manufacturing process. I watched this same individual walk by a worker who was not wearing his safety glasses, and he said nothing but "Hi". Then a short while later, he stopped to talk with another employee who was driving a company vehicle on the property and pulled over to say "Hi". The driver was clearly not buckled up. This safety leader said nothing to remind this individual to comply with a company safety policy.

"Why in the moment of an employee needing your safety advice, didn't you say something," I later asked him. He replied, "They happened so fast that I didn't think to speak up for safety". In both cases, he had noticed unsafe behavior, yet he did not intervene to prevent personal injury.

The formal BBS audit processes is not the bottom line for occupational safety. Keeping people safe requires proactive AC4P observation and feedback whenever an opportunity occurs, whether or not a CBC is available. If we don't personally make a commitment to exemplify AC4P every day on an informal level, we are not authentic "brother's sister's keepers".

An AC4P Lifestyle

AC4P becomes a way of life for those committed to the concept and who act on that commitment. Yet for many reasons, AC4P behavior is often not our nature. The safety leader in the case above cared. He voiced strong commitment to safety. But he did not act consistently on his verbal commitment.

He may have had caring intentions, but he did not actively care beyond a certain BBS process he was held accountable to complete. My friend actively cared enough to complete a formal CBC, yet he lacked the genuine commitment and moral courage (see Chapter 4) to provide critical corrective feedback beyond the formal BBS process.

People sometimes hold back proactive AC4P behavior because they consider the possibility of a negative interpersonal confrontation. You'd think people would be grateful when someone provides them information to prevent personal injury. But many consider it intrusive meddling. "Mind your own business," they think or may actually say aloud. And that's in a workplace where people are told to provide feedback about safety, and the employees know one another. What about offering safety-related feedback to strangers in public places?

The Meaning of Commitment

I recently asked a group of 220 employees if they were committed to ensure no one was injured at their plant. They all yelled out a big "Yes". When I asked them to write down their commitment, most just stared at me. They didn't know what to write. That's because they all had good intentions, but few had a genuine commitment.

The most effective commitments with regard to consistent behavior change meet the following criteria:[4]

1. People freely choose their commitment to act certain ways under designated circumstances.
2. The commitment is defined beyond intention to specific behavior(s).
3. The commitment is measurable and reflects appropriate goal setting. (See SMARTS goals in Chapter 3.) A commitment without a process goal can stagnate and go nowhere.
4. A commitment to achieve a certain goal is shared with others on a daily basis in order to benefit from social support and accountability.

Living Up to My Commitment

I was recently in Anchorage, Alaska in the midst of a snow storm, resulting in 18 inches of snow. The next day it had melted somewhat, and later that night it turned to sheer ice on the surface.

I am entering a Marriott hotel and notice a woman walking to her car with high heels – on ice. I am shocked that anyone would walk on ice in high heels. I just watch for a minute as she gets into her car. Then I realize my mistake, too late. I had failed to provide her timely feedback to keep her safe. I cared, but I did not act promptly on my caring. Upon reflection, I realize it was not too late to actively care.

I enter the hotel and go directly to the front desk. After mentioning what I just saw and asking if anyone knew the guest who was at-risk walking on ice with high heels, the receptionists begin to laugh. When I ask why they are laughing, they reply, "That was Linda; she's our boss". I ask for Linda's email and they give it to me.

That night I wrote Linda a very kind two-page message about the possibility of preventing injuries with certain proactive AC4P behavior. She wrote back the next day, thanking me for caring and letting me know she had just bought a pair of new boots to wear on ice from now on. The high heels were going in the closet until nicer weather.

The Science of AC4P

Proactive AC4P behavior for safety can be difficult. It's usually inconvenient and it's not always well-received. It's both a science and an art. The science of psychology explains a great deal with regard to why we choose to act on behalf of the well-being of another person, or why we might avoid an opportunity to actively care.

I have known and worked with Scott Geller for many years. He has taught me a great deal for which I will be forever grateful. One of the most important domains of learning he taught me is in his book written years ago, entitled *Working Safe*.[5]

This book reviewed findings from psychological science on the five dispositional states that influence whether a person will take the initiative to actively care. These five *states* are called person-*states* rather than *traits* because they change as various situational and interpersonal factors change. They are as follows:

1. *Self-Esteem*: The better I feel about myself, the more likely I will serve others.
2. *Self-Efficacy*: This is perceived competence to intervene effectively.
3. *Personal Control*: The more choice and personal control I perceive in a certain situation, the more likely I will intervene on behalf of another person's welfare.
4. *Optimism*: Optimistic people are success seekers rather than failure avoiders, and expect the best when they intervene to help others.
5. *Belonging*: The greater the personal connection one feels with another person, the less moral courage it takes to intervene proactively for that person's health, safety, or welfare. (See Chapter 4.)

Generative Leadership

These states are important in my organizational work because leaders make a powerful difference in how these person-states show up among employees. The higher these states, the more AC4P behavior.[6] If a leader listens, appreciates or asks about an employee's weekend, the leader may enhance one or more of these person-states, and thereby increase the likelihood this person will perform AC4P behavior. This reflects generative leadership.

Generative leadership[7] is more important than *visible* leadership. The difference is huge. Many leaders know the power of Management By Walking Around (MBWA).[8] Yet, they don't always understand it's not the walking that's important; it's all about their conversations with employees.

If all they do is walk around and tell people what to do or point out their shortcomings, they could be doing more harm than good. A generative leader converses with specific intention to build one or more of the person-states.

Generative leaders understand the importance of building constructive relationships with their employees. They realize how the nature of their conversations with employees can impact the person-states in positive or negative directions, helping or hindering the cultivation of an AC4P culture.

AC4P is not just making noise around people or getting in their space. It is a matter of showing (acting out) genuine concern for people – their person-states and the culture in which they work. That kind of leadership generates self-motivation and optimal performance.

From Acting to Person-States

From my own experience with AC4P, I believe we can have a profound impact on our own person-states. Take self-esteem, for example. When I help another person, as I'm committed to do on a daily basis, I feel better about myself. I feel more valuable after I help another person. And, helping others often boosts my other person-states, from optimism to belongingness.

For example, in the Dulles airport recently I was heading toward security and someone spilled a considerable amount of coffee. I looked all over and finally found towlettes to clean up the spill. Two other people stopped, helped and thanked me.

The woman who helped asked, "You are so nice, why did you stop and do this". I told her we all have an opportunity to make our world better and if we don't people will suffer. She smiled and asserted, "I'm on board".

Here's the kicker. I've also come to experience guilt or a sense of incompleteness when I don't serve another person when I could. My person-states are reduced. By my own choice, I lower my self-esteem, my personal control, my perceived competence, my optimism, and my sense of belonging.

The Win-Win Contingency

When we act to serve others, the victory is not just theirs, it's ours as well – we create a win-win outcome. Their win is obvious, they get our help. Our own win is a boost in one or more of our own person-states which in turn increases the likelihood we will keep serving others.

But, when we choose not to actively care for a person who needs help, we not only lose an opportunity to enhance our own levels of self-esteem, belonging, optimism, self-efficacy and/or personal control, we likely lower one or more of these positive dispositions.

I believe this is why Abraham Maslow[9] concluded near the end of his life that satisfying our need for self-actualization is not the ultimate. Rather, self-transcendence or authentic service to others is the highest need to satisfy in order to be the best one can be. When AC4P behavior becomes part of our lifestyle, we reach the highest level of Maslow's Hierarchy of Needs.

Thinking Fast vs. Slow

In a provocative book by the 2002 winner of the Nobel Peace Prize in Economics, Daniel Kahneman[10] describes the way our minds work, which explains why it's natural to avoid AC4P behavior. Specifically, our minds operate at two different levels – "System 1" and "System 2".

At the System 1 level, our cognitive processing is reflexive, occurring quickly with minimal thinking. We usually get by at the System 1 level, but this level of thinking does lead to mindless mistakes and behavior contrary to our beliefs, values, and/or commitments.

The System 2 level requires more energy and a deeper level of thought. This is our self-motivated AC4P thinking. It occurs when we are mindful of our choice to actively care and help cultivate an interdependent community of people applying their competence to keep each other safe.

Here is where we reflect and determine whether we have honored our commitment to act on behalf of the safety, health, and well-being of our peers. But it's easier and more efficient to operate at System 1, and thus a commitment to actively care can be readily bypassed.

AC4P is not as natural as we would like it to be. Consistent AC4P behavior requires more frequent *reflective thinking* (i.e., System 2). This is far different from our natural *reflexive thinking* (i.e., System 1).

Kahneman's scholarship illustrates our resistance to use System 2 reflective thinking occurs because this level of cognitive processing take more time and energy. However, Kahneman also demonstrates we can choose to live a life of more reflective thinking. In other words, we can operate intentionally at the System 2 level needed for AC4P behavior.

Most of us are running at a fast clip with so much information coming at us it's difficult to just relax and reflect on our AC4P values and ways to bring these to life. To keep up, we multitask and resort to fast and reactive thinking.

A commitment to AC4P requires slow reflective thinking – looking daily for opportunities to actively care and then acting effectively to make a beneficial difference. This takes slow, System 2 thinking which is readily subdued by easy, habitual, and efficient System 1 thinking. Indeed, AC4P is easier said than done.

In Conclusion

It's my hope we all choose to keep our eyes open for opportunities to help others. Then we need to hold ourselves accountable for AC4P action that contributes to making our world a better place – whether our action is an intervention to ensure another person's safety or simply an act of kindness to make a better day for someone else.

This should not be difficult. Yet, I believe it's more difficult than it looks, and takes specific focus, commitment, and slow System 2 thinking to reflect and anticipate feeling good after our AC4P behavior.

Then, when we connect with others for interpersonal accountability and share our AC4P stories, we contribute even more to cultivating an AC4P culture of compassion.

Notes

1. Geller, E.S. (2001). *The psychology of safety handbook*. Boca Raton, FL: CRC Press; McSween, T.E. (1995). *The values-based safety process: Improving your safety culture with a behavioral approach*. New York, NY: Van Nostrand Reinhold; Sulzer-Azaroff, B., & Austin, J. (2000). Does BBS work? Behavior-based safety and injury reduction: A survey of the evidence. *Professional Safety, 45*(7), 19-24.

2. Geller, E.S. (2005). *People-based safety: The source*. Virginia Beach, VA: Coastal Training and Technologies Corporation; Geller, E.S. (2008). *Leading people-based safety: Enriching your culture*. Virginia Beach, VA: Coastal Training and Technologies Corporation.

3. Geller, E.S. (1996). *The psychology of safety: How to improve behaviors and attitudes on the job*. Radnor, PA: Chilton Book Company; Geller, E.S. (1998). *Understanding behavior-based safety: Step-by-step methods to improve your workplace* (Revised Edition). Neenah, WI: J.J. Keller & Associates, Inc.

4. Cialdini, R.B. (2001). *Influence: Science and practice* (4th Edition). Needham Heights, MA: Allyn & Bacon; Geller, E.S. (2002). *The participation factor: How to increase involvement in occupational safety*. Des Plaines, IL: American Society of Safety Engineers.

5. Geller, E.S. (1996). *Working safe: How to help people actively care for health and safety*. Radnor, PA: Chilton Book Company.

6. Geller, E.S. (2001). *The psychology of safety handbook*. Boca Raton, FL: CRC Press; Geller, E.S., Roberts, D.S., & Gilmore, M.R. (1996). Predicting propensity to actively care for occupational safety. *Journal of Safety Research, 27*, 1-8.

7. Klimek, K.J., Ritzenhein, E., & Sullivan, K. D. (2008). *Generative leadership: Shaping new futures for today's schools*. Thousand Oaks, CA: Corwin Press.

8. Packard, D. (2006). *The HP Way: How Bill Hewlett and I built our company*. New York, NY: Harper Collings.

9. Maslow, A.H. (1971). *The farther reaches of human nature*. New York, NY: Viking.

10. Kahneman, D. (2011). *Thinking, fast and slow*. New York, NY: Farrar, Straus and Giroux.

CHAPTER 12

A Hands-On Approach to AC4P

Martin Mudryk and Mike Doyle

IN 2009, THE UPSTREAM In Situ Drilling and Completions Division of Suncor Energy struggled to effectively manage hand injuries. Traditional approaches such as safety stand downs, posters, standard operating procedure revisions and incident reviews met with little success. An innovative solution was required.

An effective job observation process diminishes injuries on a work site by more than 70%, according to research published in 1993.[1] But this methodology involves the uncomfortable component of a worker critiquing a teammate on their own personal work practices,[2] making it challenging to implement observations on a worksite. It was clear a robust job observation process was our solution -- but we needed to integrate it in a manner that resonated with the frontline worker.

Two sets of statistics helped us make this personal connection. In 2009, more than 37,000 hand injuries were reported to the Alberta Workers' Compensation Board. This is the equivalent of approximately 100 injuries per day.[3]

Also in 2009 approximately 100 Albertan women were being diagnosed with breast cancer every month.[4] The upstream drilling and completions industry is male dominated, and all the men have a woman in their life somewhere – mother, sister, auntie, grandmother, wife, girlfriend or daughter – who could be affected by this devastating disease. The safety professionals at Suncor Energy aimed to address these two statistics through a job observation process that could benefit both issues. The *Pink Pinch Point Project,* or *4Pinc* for short, was the newly-created product.

4Pinc Job Observations (The Pink Pinch Point Project)

On the 1st and 15th of each month, the driller (supervisor) of each rig is provided with a pink hard hat and a pair of work gloves with a pink hand skeleton screened on the back of each glove. The skeleton signifies that 27 of the most intricate bones of your body are located in the hand and *'righands keep sticking them in places they shouldn't be'*. The driller is responsible for observing at-risk hand behavior within his team. When he sees a teammate placing his hand in a hazardous location, the driller stops operations and has an empathic conversation with the worker, which includes the following:

1. A sincere, caring discussion occurs on why the worker was at risk.
2. A photo is taken to show where the worker's hands were at risk while wearing the gloves.
3. A second photo with the gloves is taken to show where the worker's hands should have been, according to the standard operating procedure.

4. A job observation form is completed providing additional information on the task, including location, time and overall learning. The observed worker's name is omitted.
5. This job observation is then sent to all the rigs working for Suncor's Oil Sands and the In Situ organization so the proactive observational learning can be visually shared at their next safety meeting.

Once the observed worker understands why he risked a hand injury and commits to changing his behavior – 'tag your it' – he receives the pink hard hat and pink gloves. Now it's his responsibility to observe teammates for at-risk hand behavior. This "observe and tag" gamesmanship continues until the end of the shift. As noted, the submitted job observation form is immediately shared with all Oil Sands and In Situ drilling rigs working for Suncor. To support the process, Suncor En-

ergy makes a donation to the Canadian Breast Cancer Foundation on behalf of the rig crew for every job observation submitted and distributed.

Gaining acceptance for rig hands to wear pink within their industrial setting was the largest perceived risk of implementing *4Pinc*. A key selling feature was that the NHL, NFL, CFL, and MBL all have their 'pink days,' so why can't the oil and gas industry? Our concerns with the job observation process were apparently alleviated by the support of this wonderful charity. And so we achieved our objective of raising frontline awareness on hand-and-health safety.

Pink in fact was a non-issue with frontline employees. Within a group of eight men per rig, at least one knew or cared for someone who was significantly affected by breast cancer. We expected push back on the program but there was none at all during implementation. Instead, some amazing things began to happen. Workers stated, "I do not have any pictures of myself at work. Can I take my observation home to show my wife and kids?" "Yes" is the obvious answer because anytime you integrate work and home safety it's a win for all.

Now children of employees are exposed to safety initiatives taught at work. And, husbands have 'health' discussions with their spouses that would not have occurred otherwise. A roughneck who had taken his *4Pinc* job observation home to show his family offered this humorous story.

"I think I created a monster. Before when I would come home from a two week hitch my boy would run up to me yelling 'DADDY, DADDY I MISSED YOU!'

Now he runs up, stops with both hands on his hips and looks at me with his serious face and asks 'DADDY - DID YOU HAVE TO WEAR A GIRL'S HARD HAT THIS WEEK? So now after every hitch I know my son will be asking if I put my hands in a bad spot… so at the worksite I make the extra effort not to let him down".

Since implementing the *4Pinc* process hand injury rates have been drastically reduced across the organization on a sustained basis. Some rigs achieved recordable-free status for more than a two-year period. And more than $20, 000 has been raised for the Canadian Breast Cancer Foundation to date by the rig crews. The process is now being adopted by companies outside of Suncor.

An email we received on July 18, 2011 is the most gratifying component about *4Pinc*. It was entitled "4Pinc Proof" and contained a job observation completed on July 17th on a SAGD rig. The *4Pinc* process is only scheduled for the 1st & 15th of each month, but this crew felt it was important to complete the process anyway. The email described how a young roughneck put his hands at risk while replacing casing protectors when the crew was pulling liner.

His fellow workers noticed he was placing his hands under the suspended joint as he completed the task. They stopped the work, told him why he was at risk, and had him put on the pink hard hat and gloves so they could take the required photos to complete the *4Pinc* job observation.

Less than an hour later, a near hit occurred. A joint of pipe was prematurely released while over the stump, falling three inches. If the *4Pinc* intervention had not occurred and the roughneck was installing casing protector as he had been doing an hour previously – he would have lost his fingers on both hands. The email closed by thanking us for the program because it works.

Words cannot describe what that email means to us. It will forever be a focal point for making a difference. The *4Pinc* job observation process will be at the top of the list of things we are most proud of when we look back at our safety professional careers.

Notes

1. Guastello, S.J. (1993), Do we really know how well our occupational accident prevention programs work? *Safety Sciences Journal, 16*, 445.
2. Petersen, D. (2003) *Techniques of safety management: A systems approach.* Portland, OR: American Society of Safety Engineers.

3. Work Safe Alberta (2010) "Occupational Injuries and Diseases in Alberta: Lost Time Claims, Disabling Injury Claims and Claim Rates – 2009 Summary", Government of Alberta.
4. Canadian Breast Cancer Foundation (2009). Personal communication from Curtis Charchun, Community Partnerships Coordinator.

CHAPTER 13

Personal Growth from Participating in People-Based Safety

Eric Williams and Deborah Verdugo-Williams

MY EXPERIENCE WITH PEOPLE-BASED SAFETY (PBS), an application of AC4P principles for occupational safety, started when I became a member of the PBS team at Nabors Well Services, in the oil-well-servicing industry.

Before learning about PBS and AC4P, my life story reads like a crime novel – with me as the bad guy. Jail and addiction, along with a few close calls with death, were sprinkled in for excitement throughout 18 years of my life.

The need for personal change became clear to me when I was serving a five-year prison term. After serving my time, I hunted for work opportunities for four months before landing a job with my current employer.

During orientation I was introduced to PBS. I listened actively to how the process works to keep people safe, but I didn't get the profound meaning of this AC4P process until reflecting deeply on two words the orientation instructor had used throughout our education/training –"actively caring".

At first those two words didn't sound right to me. And sitting in a room with others who likely shared some of my history, I'd bet money those words also sounded strange to them. I did not make the connection between my personal safety and AC4P right away, given my personal history in prison was all about *self*-preservation. If you don't look out for yourself every day in that culture, your life is in imminent danger.

But as I listened it dawned on me that AC4P is also preservation, only now the term "preservation" takes on a broader meaning. It's about looking out for the preservation of the men with whom I'd soon be working.

I thought, "Safety here is really not that much different than safety in prison, in that you must be prepared for the unexpected at all times, be alert to your surroundings, and be ever mindful of your actions as they affect you and your co-workers".

The activator-behavior-consequence (ABC) model (see Chapter 1) resonated with me as well, because I understand the critical motivational role of expected consequences. If I stay mindful and actively care for the safety of my co-workers, this job will afford me a good living, and I will never have to repeat my personal history in prison. Thus, I realized PBS is more than a process; it can be a real life saver.

After that orientation in February of 2003, I participated willingly in the PBS coaching process, and by the end of 2003 I was a fully-engaged PBS team member. My personal mantra was, "I'm not going to be injured if I can help it and I'm not going to let a co-worker get hurt if I can help it". Over the next several years, I read *People-Based Safety: The Source* and *Leading People-Based Safety: Enriching Your Culture.*[1]

I became a co-facilitator of the PBS team, all the while working full time in the oil fields as a "rig hand". Since 2007, I have been a full-time area PBS facilitator, teaching the AC4P coaching process to hundreds and sharing what I have learned at annual PBS/AC4P conferences sponsored by Safety Performance Solutions, Inc. (safetyperformance.com).

In 2010, I was promoted to PBS District Facilitator, which allows me the opportunity to work with area facilitators and share their ups and downs but aligned with one common goal – safety for all through AC4P. And this learning/teaching/application experience enriched my life beyond imagination, as exemplified in part by my wife's observations.

First Annoying and Now a Blessing (*A Wife's Perspective*)

At first, it was annoying when my boyfriend pointed out visible safety hazards every time he saw one – even to complete strangers: the car safety belt was not on the child in the passenger seat, or the handle of a hot pot on the stove was hanging over the edge for someone to touch as they walked by.

At first, it was annoying when my purse was missing from my Costco shopping cart when I returned to it after getting milk two aisles away.

At last, it was a blessing when I discovered my boyfriend took my purse to teach me a safety lesson.

At last, our whole family looks for golden opportunities to intervene when we see unsafe situations in our home, at school, at work and even in our community!

As an elementary-school vice principal, it's a blessing to stop students from running in the halls or help them tie their shoelaces so they don't fall down.

At last, it feels good when I radio the custodian and inform him of a wet tile on the floor in the restroom – or about a milk spill in the cafeteria – or about melted ice in front of the ice machine in the dining room, and I ask him to intervene so there are no "slips".

At last, the AC4P mindset has enriched my life.

From the Oil Fields to Our Home and Beyond

Here's how PBS in the oilfields made its way into our home. Ten years ago I met my husband, Eric Williams, who is now known around our house as "Mr. Safety." Mr. Safety (as I will now call him) works in the oil fields and is a member of the PBS Team at Nabors Well Services.

At first, I didn't know what PBS was. At last, PBS is not only something Eric uses at work, but this safety process has become a way of life for our entire family.

At first, these safety issues Eric spoke of were just stories about his work environment. At last, they are integrated into our family environment as well as our daily routines at work, school, and throughout our community.

At first, it was annoying. I can't tell you how many times Mr. Safety started up conversations with strangers out of the blue; and every conversation somehow led to the same subject: *safety*.

One time at "In and Out Burger", Mr. Safety initiated a conversation with the young lady who brought our food to us. After a short two-minute conversation, he said he was from corporate headquarters and proceeded to give her a "heads-up" on what valuable information she just gave to a complete stranger: how much money her company keeps on hand, how much money is made during a shift, how often the money is "dropped" and how the money is taken to the bank.

You could see the fright in her eyes. Mr. Safety then assured her he was not from corporate headquarters; however, he reminded her how unsafe it is to disclose important information to anyone, anywhere, anytime, especially to complete strangers. He could have been a potential robber!

Another example of how AC4P has permeated our daily family life occurred at a local restaurant. When first sitting down, I noticed my chair was a little wobbly. I didn't want to say anything, but Mr. Safety noticed the weak chair right away and motioned for a waitress to come over to our table – how embarrassing!

When Mr. Safety showed her the wobbly chair, the waitress thanked him repeatedly and quickly brought me a safe chair. The owner of the restaurant came to our table to personally thank us for bringing the weak chair to his attention.

Our family loves going to the beach on three-day weekends. We would make the hotel reservations, pack the suitcases, gather the snacks for the road, and load the bikes on the bike rack, and then hit the road as soon as possible.

Mr. Safety would make us so angry when asking, just when we were ready to leave, "Did you check the water, oil and tire pressure on the truck yet?" Of course our answer was "No". Who would ever think to do that? We just wanted to get to the beach.

We got even angrier when Mr. Safety would not let us leave until he had completed "the safety check" on the truck. Now we do the "vehicle safety check" before we do all of those other things. Now we never think of getting on the road without making sure our vehicle is safe to drive – no matter where we are going.

I could share many more examples of how the AC4P approach to safety has spread from the oilfield to our home – and how, Mr. Safety at first frustrated us when he brought hazardous situations to the attention of those who needed to know about them: from wet floors for someone to slip on in restaurants, stores and school functions to exposed electrical cords waiting for someone to trip on at a movie theater, street fair, or coffee house.

Yes, it was annoying. We felt as if we were intruding on the privacy of others. But now, our entire family feels it's our duty to intervene if we see someone doing something we think is unsafe.

From the Home to an AC4P Lifestyle

Mr. Safety has now come up with a new term for this safety intervention process: "Safety Forward". You know how you feel when someone does something nice for you. Doesn't it make you want to do something nice for someone else, as in "Pay it forward"?

This is the point of "Safety Forward". When you see a potential hazard, or people putting themselves in a risky situation, say something, intervene! This in turn influences those people to be more aware of hazards and act on behalf of the safety of others.

I want to thank Nabors Well Services for "planting the PBS/AC4P seed" in Mr. Safety, Eric Williams, my husband. Our personal lives are definitely safer because we have incorporated this process of "Safety Forward" into our daily lives.

I urge everyone to practice "Safety Forward". It might be annoying at first because it will be new to you. Soon enough it will be a blessing, because your behavior will set an AC4P example for others to follow. Get past the annoyance, because soon enough you will contribute to cultivating a more compassionate and safer culture.

Note

1. Geller, E.S. (2005). *People-based safety: The source*. Virginia Beach, VA: Coastal Training Technologies Corporation; Geller, E.S. (2008). *Leading people-based safety: Enriching your culture*. Virginia Beach, VA: Coastal Training Technologies Corporation.

CHAPTER 14

Improving My Quality of Life through AC4P

David McHugh

MANY YEARS AGO, "To each his own" was my motto. Then a moment of clarity: I could have a better quality of life if I had better interpersonal relationships with others. I came to realize I need to help others improve for no personal gain. My reward is their success. In doing so, I develop character.

I began to take on an AC4P mindset. Tolerance and kindness toward others not only benefited them, but affected me in positive ways. I volunteered at work, and sponsored individuals in self-help programs. My quality of life was improving though AC4P.

My Introduction to People-Based Safety

I started work in the oil-drilling industry. With my positive attitude toward safety and my willingness to help others, my supervisor asked me to represent his division in the company's new people-based safety (PBS) program.

This was my first exposure to Scott Geller and PBS. During a three-year period, I volunteered for the PBS safety teams, and contributed as a leader at various safety events, such as motivational seminars and AC4P and PBS study groups.

After three years of volunteering, I was approached by management to apply for a district facilitator position and was selected to lead a PBS program. I was honored – the first individual from the maintenance department to ascend to this level of occupational safety. While I maintained this full-time safety position, I studied a variety of books on PBS.[1] My education in AC4P flourished.

Key Lessons Learned

Two theories stand out to me as invaluable: the ABC model (activator, behavior, consequence) of applied behavioral science (Chapter 1), and the five person-states of humanism (Chapter 2).

If you apply the ABC model to all your affairs, your ability to think a sequence of events through becomes easier. Your awareness of the ABC universality elevates you to become more competent, which in turn builds the three person-states that fuel self-motivation – choice, competence, and community.

With further study I understood that individuals learn in different ways. To teach effectively, I needed to discover what roadblocks or barriers prevented the learning process for certain individuals. The five person-states described in the PBS books[1] helped me identify a person's strengths and weaknesses and laid the foundation for effective interpersonal teaching. I found my quality of life improved at work and at home. The evidence-based AC4P principles are crucial. But practical AC4P applications must be identified for specific problems.

When I took the position of PBS Facilitator, we had a high recordable injury rate of about 30 per year. By applying the AC4P principles and PBS procedures, we reduced our recordable injury rate by 65% after four years. Plus, the severity of injury was greatly reduced.

For me, AC4P is a combination of desire, education, and dedicated effort. With authentic desire, people believe you truly care for them. With education, your interactions have substance and support through research evidence. Dedication shows you are willing to actively care, and individuals believe they have a resource for AC4P assistance. With these three components, I have improved the quality of safety and even the quality of life for numerous employees, as well for myself.

On to Further Accomplishment

As a result of studying Scott Geller's AC4P books and related materials, I have enrolled in college to further my education in this field. My company has used what I have learned and put me in a position to develop new programs in other areas of our organization. This includes leading quality-control audits in the field that help sustain and build on our safety and production successes.

Our company is safety driven from both top and bottom. Because of this and our education in the AC4P principles, the lives of those around me have been enriched. We have a quality of work life that was unimaginable 20 years ago. When I look back and see how far our company has come, along with my own personal growth, I realize the special impact of AC4P. My only regret: I wish I had started sooner so others in my past would not have suffered unnecessarily.

Note

1. Geller, E.S. (2005). *People-based safety: The source.* Virginia Beach, VA: Coastal Training and Technologies Corporation; Geller, E.S. (2008). *Leading people-based safety: Enriching your culture.* Virginia Beach, VA: Coastal Training and Technologies Corporation; Geller, E.S. (2010). Courage, empathy, and the big five for safety. In Williams, J. (2010). *Keeping people safe: The human dynamics of injury prevention.* Lanham, MD: The Scarecrow Press, Inc.; Geller, E.S. (2011). People-based safety and actively caring: Enriching a culture with courage, compassion, and self-motivation. In the *National Safety Council's Supervisors' Motor Fleet Safety Manual.* Itasca, IL: National Safety Council; Williams, J., & Geller, E.S. (2001) (Eds.). *Keys to behavior-based safety from Safety Performance Solutions.* Rockville, MD: Government Institutes.

Part III: Community Applications of AC4P

E. Scott Geller

ISTARTED MY PROFESSIONAL CAREER in 1969 as Assistant Professor of Psychology at Virginia Polytechnic Institute and State University (Virginia Tech). With assistance from undergraduate and graduate students, I developed a productive laboratory and research program in cognitive psychology. My tenure and promotion to Associate Professor was based entirely upon my professional scholarship in this domain.

However, in the mid-1970s I became concerned this laboratory work had limited potential for helping people. This conflicted with my personal mission to make beneficial large-scale differences in people's quality of life. Therefore, I turned to another line of research.

Given my conviction that behavior-based psychology has the greatest potential for solving organizational and community problems, I focused my research on finding ways to make this happen. Inspired by the first Earth Day in April 1970, my students and I developed, evaluated, and refined a number of community-based techniques to increase environment-constructive behaviors and decrease environment-destructive behaviors. This prolific research program culminated with the 1982 book, *Preserving the Environment: New strategies for behavior change*, which I co-authored with Drs. Richard A. Winett and Peter B. Everett.[1]

My students and I applied behavior-based psychology to a number of other societal issues beyond environmental protection. These included prison administration, school discipline, community theft, transportation management, and alcohol-impaired driving.

In the mid-1970s we began researching strategies for increasing the use of vehicle safety belts as explained in the introduction to Part II. This led to a focus on the application of behavior-based psychology to prevent unintentional injuries in organizational and community settings.

From Basic to Applied Research

As suggested above, my early research and scholarship was split between basic (i.e., reaction time) and applied (i.e., behavior analysis) research. After awarded tenure in 1976, I started giving more attention to the domain of behavioral community psychology, which was clearly not mainstream in those days.

My students and I continued to demonstrate the efficacy of applying behavior-focused psychology in community and organizational settings to benefit the environment and people's health, safety and well-being.

By 1979, the year I was promoted to the rank of Professor, my research and scholarship had transitioned completely from basic to applied experimental psychology, particularly the application of behavioral science to improve people's quality of life on a large scale.

Applied Behavioral Science

Every semester since 1979, my graduate students and I have supervised 50 to 70 undergraduate students conducting applied experimental research that reflects our

University motto – *That I May Serve*. They learned the methodology of applying rigorous behavioral science in the field by *doing*, and their *doing* contributed in turn to people's health or safety, or to environmental protection. Thus, in addition to learning the principles and procedures of applied behavioral science through personal involvement, these students have learned the value of Actively Caring for People (AC4P).

A University Research Center

By 1987 our applied experimental research had been awarded enough extramural grant support to justify the establishment of a research center in the Virginia Tech Department of Psychology. That year marked the beginning of the Center for Applied Behavior Systems (CABS). We wanted to be more than a Center for contracts and grant-funded research; we wanted a significant focus on teaching through active involvement.

Following the advice of the wise Confucian principle, "Tell them and they'll forget, demonstrate and they'll remember, involve them and they'll understand," our behavioral research has always involved students in some kind of community service.

By *putting knowledge to work* (our University slogan at the time), these students were experiencing the value of helping others. Now, as an official University Research Center, we were empowered to declare our research, teaching, and service-learning objectives in an official mission statement.

Our Mission Statement

The mission statement below, posted in CABS, defines our purpose and our values as a teaching/learning research center, thereby defining standards to direct our daily process activities and the types of consequences worthy of group celebration.

The Center for Applied Behavior Systems was developed to:

1. Help students, undergraduate and graduate, learn how to conduct research that combines the technology of applied behavior analysis with theories from experimental, social, and applied psychology.

2. Give students real-world, hands-on research experience, from designing methodology and data-analysis strategies to documenting findings in professional publications.

3. Teach, develop, and evaluate community-based interventions.

4. Give students opportunities to participate in leading-edge professional activities.

5. Improve quality of life in the VT and Blacksburg community, and beyond.

6. Teach and demonstrate the value of actively caring for people (AC4P).

Every semester the 50 to 70 VT students who learn and conduct research in CABS receive a comprehensive Handbook that provides an overview of the research planned for the semester, and explains procedures and research projects for the semester. Every semester this Handbook changes to adjust for administrative variations and different research topics and methodology. However, this Mission Statement has remained essentially unchanged since its inception in 1987.

Examples of CABS Research

All of the research discussed in this book illustrate the research conducted by the undergraduate and graduate students in CABS. In fact, all of the data displayed to illustrate the impact of an AC4P intervention were collected by CABS researchers.

Most of the chapter authors received research education/training in CABS, with some currently participating actively in CABS. Those few authors who did not participate directly in CABS report remarkable influence from the findings and implications of our research.

The three research-based chapters in this section are authored by former or current students in CABS, and each reflects remarkable potential for solving serious societal threats to human well-being with AC4P principles and applications.

First, Dr. Chris Dula (a former "cabbie") and Ben Martin discuss the horrendous loss of life from the "war on the highways," and describe AC4P approaches to alleviate this worldwide problem. Some of these AC4P intervention strategies have been applied extensively to improve driving safety; some have evidence-based potential but have not been tried on a large-scale; and others are in the conceptual state, calling for research testing and dissemination.

Chapter 16 addresses the notorious issue of alcohol abuse and alcohol-impaired driving. The senior author of this chapter, Ryan Smith, was a dedicated researcher in CABS since his freshman year at VT until earning a Ph.D. in May 2013. While a M.S. and Ph.D. student, Ryan focused his research and scholarship on preventing excessive alcohol consumption among college students, from their drinking at fraternity parties to downtown bars.

This chapter explores a variety of our attempts to decrease intoxication and its negative side-effects. We provide evidence that many common-sense and popular intervention approaches are not effective, and we discuss some AC4P-principled strategies that show promise but require additional testing. As a research scientist for the Virginia Tech Transportation Institute (VTTI), Ryan continuous to plan and lead this research with university students in CABS.

Chris Downing, author of Chapter 17, has conducted research in CABS for seven years, and will complete his Ph.D. in Industrial/Organizational psychology in May 2014. As he explains in his chapter, Chris has been concerned with the problem of identity theft for many years, and he tested behavioral community interventions to prevent the misuse of credit cards before, during, and after conducting his master's thesis in this domain. After reading this chapter, readers will look at the behavior of credit-card use and ID-checking differently, and perhaps act on this paradigm shift.

The last three chapters in this section are personal stories reflecting AC4P in the community. First, Bobby Kipper shares moments in his personal journey from a paradigm of top-down enforcement as a police officer to promoting AC4P as current Director of the National Center for the Prevention of Community Violence.

Then, Joanne Dean Geller discusses her AC4P challenge to reach out and actively care proactively for one person every day for 60 consecutive days. Imagine the improved communities we would have if significant numbers of individuals and groups attempted Joanne's challenge.

The final story by our Editor, Dave Johnson, exemplifies reactive AC4P. As I indicated in the Preface, the jobs of many people reflect invaluable AC4P behavior on a daily basis, yet even in emergency situations, the quality and/or quantity of actively caring can vary. Dave's story raises the intriguing question: Is it AC4P when helping another person fulfills a job assignment?

Read these chapters to learn the potential of an AC4P approach to improving people's lives beyond industrial work settings. Indeed, these chapters illustrate how AC4P can be applied in a variety of community settings. The need for AC4P community interventions to address so many societal problems is evident. These chapters address only a tip of the iceberg.

We hope these chapters will inspire more people to perform AC4P behaviors for improving road safety, and preventing alcohol abuse and identity theft. But, we also hope these chapters will stimulate more exploration of how AC4P principles can address more community-based problems.

Note

1. Geller, E.S., Winett, R.A., & Everett, P.B. (1982) *Preserving the environment: New strategies for behavior change.* New York, NY: Pergamon Press.

CHAPTER 15

Actively Caring for Traffic Safety:
Decreasing drivers' daring, erring, and swearing

Chris S. Dula and Benjamin A. Martin

TRAFFIC SAFETY IS a serious public health issue in the U.S. and the world. In the U.S. alone, motor vehicle crashes are currently the leading cause of death for people ages five to 34.[1] Specifically, more than 30,000 U.S. residents are killed and over two million injured each year.

Examining 2009 data, annual crash-related costs were estimated at almost $300 billion, where the 'value' of each life was estimated at $6 million, and each injury at $126,000 (based on 13 areas including medical expenses, lost earnings, property damage, etc.).[2] This was double the costs estimated only four years prior, and 2009 estimates were based on only 99 urbanized areas. Actually, the annual costs for vehicle crashes worldwide are much greater than any detailed financial appraisal.

No one can put a 'price' on a death or serious injury, because such losses defy material or monetary evaluations. Nonetheless, the numbers of lives lost and injuries sustained are virtually guaranteed to continually increase as more and more people are driving. Virtually guaranteed, that is, unless we do something. However, we don't seem to value traffic safety in the same way we value other safety issues.

A Matter of Perspective

To powerfully make this point, compare the national attention to dangerous driving with the way the U.S. responded to the terrorist attacks of 9/11/01.[3] We have profound respect for victims and their families, and military personnel and their families, and only make this comparison to highlight a historic shift in national consciousness after such a tragedy.

Following the unfathomable loss of nearly 3,000 innocent people in the 9/11 attacks, our country has undergone a transformation of stunning proportions. This has included debates on striking the optimal balance between preserving freedoms and achieving genuine safety, passing out vast amounts of security-related legislation at all levels of society, creation of the cabinet-level Secretary of Homeland Defense and related Office of Homeland Defense, as well as repeated deployment of hundreds of thousands of troops and support personnel for over a decade.

The 9/11 tragedy has utterly transformed our way of life, especially air travel. Since 9/11, we've prevented a number of terrorist plots in our country, though we've lost over 6,500 members of our military (due to all causes) in Operations Enduring Freedom, Iraqi Freedom, and New Dawn, and many more have been seriously injured.[4] Yet, it's become a national priority to ensure resources are made available to prevent future loss of American lives.

All branches of the military, law enforcement, and many other agencies oversee the reduction of terrorism risk. All are called upon to be watchful and report suspicious activity. And, we frequently have discussions about these serious issues and ways our country could further lower the risk. In other words, fighting terrorism and safeguarding the safety of U.S. citizens from such threats has become a core value for our country –and again, rightly so.

Losses at War vs. on the Road

By way of comparison, considering only an eight-year period from calendar years 2002 to 2010, *over 325,000 Americans lost their lives on U.S. roads*, while many more millions also sustained serious injuries. In other words, in less than 3,000 days, almost a third of a million U.S. citizens were killed on the road. And, as sadly noted by Norman Mineta, past U.S. Secretary of Transportation (2001 to 2006), virtually all these deaths and injuries were preventable. While stark, such comparisons are not new.

Making a similar point, Scott Geller compared the loss of over 58,000 soldiers from 1965 to 1975 in the Vietnam War to the almost half a million lives lost on roadways in the prior decade (1981-1991).[5] Geller noted that in 1991, the U.S. spent $295 billion preparing for war, which was 8,000 times more than funding for research on methods to reduce traffic-related injuries and fatalities.

Using a more current comparison, the U.S. Department of Defense (DOD) requested a budget of $525 billion for 2013,[6] whereas the National Highway Traffic Safety Administration (NHTSA) requested only $981 million.[7] Obviously the DOD has many important responsibilities all over the world; however, this large discrepancy does illustrate a fundamental difference in the way different public dangers are perceived and addressed.

Why don't we take traffic-safety dangers as seriously as terrorist threats or war casualties? Why don't we confront crash-related deaths and injuries with the same type of unbridled devotion we have for reducing terrorism threats and waging war?

Please don't get us wrong. We're not advocating a lessening of the focus on thwarting all forms of terrorism or military risk. No, we're simply advocating that we treat the massive loss of lives and livelihoods from vehicle crashes with the same solemnity. We want an analogous energy to be devoted to making our roadways safer.

Addressing Traffic Safety

To be sure, ever increasing efforts to improve traffic safety are long-standing. Many grassroots programs have arisen to combat the problem. Local and state police are ever on the alert for dangerous drivers. Corporations sponsor advertisements aimed at promoting responsible drinking and reducing texting while driving. And, NHTSA is devoted to the task.

But as noted, NHTSA's annual budget doesn't even reach $1 billion and it operates mostly through state agencies. This is fine, but the reality is that law-enforcement agencies must be continually concerned with all types of public danger. Certainly law-enforcement professionals care deeply about traffic safety, but no agency can devote all its resources to preventing vehicle collisions. And, even if they could, most dangers on the road occur outside the watchful eyes of the law.

Frequently, police are only able to respond after a crash has already occurred, to help the injured, investigate causes, and arrest people who don't comply with traffic laws. At that point, the damage is done.

To reduce the tragic losses from vehicle crashes *traffic safety must become a core value for our country*, not just a priority to be shifted up and down a list of many others. Discussions about traffic safety should be a regular topic of interpersonal communication. So, why aren't these sorts of conversations common?

Well, many feel overwhelmed by the magnitude of the problem and don't see how they can personally make a difference. Also, as crashes and their consequences are rarely experienced by any given individual, it's easy to forget everyone is at risk for involvement in a collision, however small the risk may be at any given time. And, as so much of this book has pointed out, many feel it is not their responsibility to suggest to others, especially strangers, what they should change to make things better or in this case, safer.

Here we discuss ways the AC4P approach could be applied to improve traffic safety, citing research results to support our suggestions.

Dangerous Driving

While some crashes may be caused by factors beyond one's control (e.g., an accelerator sticks due to a manufacturing defect), the vast majority are preventable. That's why we call them crashes instead of accidents.

The term "accident" implies the consequences of a situation were outside our control. Certainly no one *intends* to be in a crash, but we seldom consider how we personally can prevent a crash or lessen the chances for injury or death should one occur anyway.

The critical factor in most crashes is actually driver behavior, which is affected by attitudes, emotions, cognitive processes and the behavior of other drivers. In all driving situations, we must constantly interpret our perceptions, if we're even paying attention, and make choices about how to respond to dangers as they arise. And, some situations are more dangerous than others.

Aggressive vs. Risky Driving

Recent scholarship has identified three independent categories for dangerous driving, namely aggressive driving, negative emotional driving, and risky driving.[8] This stance broke from early researchers' views on "aggressive driving" and "road rage", which had lumped most dangerous driving behaviors under those labels. In the current scheme, a definition of "aggressive driving" must include "intent to harm" which is consistent with decades of research on aggression in other contexts.

While rare, aggression can be directed at others without accompanying negative emotions, such as in the case of someone in the grips of psychopathy. And, almost all drivers experience negative emotions at times without ever intending to harm anyone.

Yet such emotions are dangerous because they can be powerful and distract the driver from important safe-driving tasks. Recent research has demonstrated that people scoring relatively high on the AC4P person-states are less likely to experience negative emotions while driving.[9]

Most drivers who speed, run traffic lights, or weave through traffic, aren't trying to harm anyone; they're just trying to get to their destinations faster. But, because they can't know how drivers around them will respond at any given time, such behaviors are indeed risky, though not aggressive. And, most now consider "road rage" as a mixture of negative thoughts and feelings accompanied by aggressive and risky behaviors.

By defining dangerous driving as any behavior with potential to imperil others, and analyzing its aggressive, emotional, and risky components, we can examine more closely the factors that make these components more likely to occur. Understanding people's emotional, behavioral and cognitive experiences is critical to improving safety.

Safe Driving Practices

It can also be informative to assess dangerous driving by comparing it to safe driving. Danger is often created by a failure to engage in certain proactive behaviors for safety. Some safe-driving practices seem simple enough: stop for red lights and stop signs; follow speed limits and signal lane changing; stay in the rightmost lane except to pass; maintain alertness and attention to driving at all times; slow down in bad weather or on unfamiliar roads; and properly maintain your vehicle (e.g., lights, signals, and brakes). These all serve to prevent situations which put us at risk for a crash.

However, many fail to engage in such safe behaviors consistently. But even if we attend to all of the above and another driver doesn't, his or her failures may result in a collision with our vehicle. Yet even when we can't prevent a crash, we might mitigate potential for harm by using safety equipment. Thus, we should always protect ourselves with proper use of safety belts and child safety seats, and by wearing helmets and other safety gear on a bicycle or motorcycle. Then again, many people don't consistently engage in these safety-related behaviors.

What if everyone always attempted to do the 'right thing' with regard to vehicle safety? In other words, what if we all attended to all driving safety factors virtually all of the time, and assisted others by reminding and encouraging them to engage in specific safe-driving behaviors?

If this happened, crash-related deaths and injuries would most certainly be reduced dramatically. But, could we really achieve such a lofty vision? We contend a nationwide (and eventually worldwide) application of AC4P principles could contribute greatly to achieving this outcome.

Indeed, there is a national movement afoot to change our driving culture. Recently the AAA Foundation for Traffic Safety assembled a compendium of ideas in *Improving Traffic Safety Culture in the United States: The Journey Forward*. Chris Dula and Scott Geller contributed a paper entitled *Creating a Total Safety Traffic Culture,*[3] making the case that large-scale applications of AC4P principles could help increase traffic safety. We revisit those ideas here.

An AC4P Safety Culture

What is an AC4P Safety Culture? As detailed in Part II of this book, an AC4P safety culture involves: honest employee input about safety issues and open ideas for possible solutions; commitment from top- and mid-level management to enable safety-related changes to systems; interpersonal behavior-based observation and coaching by employees; consistent monitoring of leading (proactive) and lagging (reactive) indicators of safety and using data to continually adjust strategies and processes when necessary; and multi-level communication regarding all aspects of a company's safety – past, present and future.

AC4P safety principles and procedures aim to develop an interdependent culture of compassion. The relevant education/training teaches people how to put their caring in motion by giving and receiving behavioral feedback in a respectful, supportive, and constructive manner. Continually thinking about and talking about ways to improve workplace safety becomes the norm.

In such a work culture people daily activate and support safety. This translates back into continuous safety improvement, virtually ensuring mindfulness regarding workplace safety.[3] This is certainly feasible for cohesive groups like factory or office workers, as has been demonstrated time and again across many companies, but you may wonder how it can be translated to a society, much less the entire world. That's the theme of this book. But, you may also ask, how does this apply to traffic safety?

Creating an AC4P Traffic Safety Culture

Traffic safety involves many specific behaviors and persistent attendance to safety issues. And, practicing safe driving is inherently a social activity. We may not see it that way, especially if our daily drive is accomplished alone, but there are people all around us. Most people don't want strangers giving them feedback about driving. But, often people we know are with us in our vehicles and they could provide us with feedback, if we're open to it.

We are all members of various and relatively large cohesive groups, including family members, friends, and co-workers whom we care about and who care about us. Whether with family members, co-workers, our church congregation, fellow students, or others, AC4P processes are relevant at home, school, or church, as well as on the job. What if thinking and talking about traffic safety issues were the norm?

Our current traffic-safety culture can be best described as a 'top-down' system. In other words, a person in a supervisory role (e.g., legislators, administrators, police) decides which driving-related behaviors are safe and at-risk and then typically makes use of threats and penalties to enforce desired behaviors. Legislators are comparable to management within a company. Law enforcement officers can also be thought of as supervisors who issue citations for offenses.

There can be no doubt that traffic safety laws and the people who enforce them have made vast improvements in our collective safety, and they are an important part of the prevention picture. Indeed, they are vital for now, because few citizens feel personally responsible for improving our traffic-safety system. But, that's the direction we need to move.

An AC4P view implies a shift in responsibility toward individuals and subgroups. One mission of this bottom-up system is to get a lot of people feeling empowered and committed to promoting safe-driving practices. People should discuss openly the factors influencing risky versus safe driving. An open dialogue should reveal contributing factors to close calls, as well as reinforcers of at-risk driving.

As with industrial safety (Part II), an analysis of the factors influencing risky driving, near crashes, and vehicle collisions should consider three critical domains: the environment (e.g., road conditions, equipment, and climate), person (e.g., attitudes and person-states), and behavior (e.g., driving routines and interpersonal dialogue).[10]

The bottom-up AC4P approach to driving safety requires drivers and passengers (e.g., families and car-pool participants) to define target behaviors to influence and then to intervene appropriately. We could begin by encouraging individuals who drive safely already to become AC4P leaders in their communities. Safe drivers with training in teaching and/or coaching could provide guidance and support to other potential participants in a community-based program to improve traffic safety.

Let's consider a few areas in which the interpersonal AC4P approach could readily be applied in this domain. Keep in mind these are only a few examples. With dedication, effort, creativity, and persistence, the sky's the limit.

Secure Your Sister and Buckle Your Brother

There is no disputing safety belts save lives and reduce injuries when crashes occur. Instead of *seat* belts, we refer to them as *safety* belts, an important distinction we think. (See Chapter 6.) And, this was the original label given when the buckle-up concept was first patented by Edward Claghorn in 1885.[11]

Safety belts were introduced on a large scale as options by some manufacturers in the '50s, but didn't become standard equipment in most vehicles until the early '60s. And then few chose to use them. Fast forward about 30 years to 1994, and only 58% of all passenger vehicle occupants were using their vehicle safety belts.[12]

Interventions to increase safety-belt use ranged from engineering devices (e.g., dashboard reminders) to top-down legal policies (e.g., safety-belt-use mandates), and community-based efforts (e.g., media campaigns and educational programs). This combination of interventions caused the level of usage to steadily rise in the U.S. until it reached 85% in 2010.[12] This period also saw a mirrored drop in the percentage of fatalities due to unrestrained occupants, falling from 57% to 44%.

While we are collectively better than ever at using safety belts, universal use has yet to be achieved and seems to have peaked at around 85%. In 2011, safety-belt use fell a bit to 84%, with higher rates of use in states where police are allowed to pull over vehicles with unrestrained occupants.[12]

The persistent few who "choose not to use" cite a variety of factors for this choice, like discomfort, forgetting, inconvenience, and even laziness; and of course, many believe they are not really at risk for injury.[13] So, more could certainly be accomplished in this domain, and this should be a priority target for an AC4P traffic-safety culture.

When you see a person unbuckled, whether in your vehicle or another, AC4P requires no more than telling people with genuine kindness you care about their safety and asking if they would please buckle up? You might start with the opening question, "Would you mind if I looked out for your safety?"[14]

How could they say "No" to this AC4P request? Now with a "Yes," a foot-in-the-door, you'll gain courage to ask the person to buckle up, and you can expect compliance. If by chance you did encounter a negative response, you could say something to the effect of, "I understand that it's your choice, but I do care for your safety and hope you'll consider it in the future."

Some large-scale interventions consistent with the AC4P vision have already been used to increase safety-belt use. Scott Geller and others have shown advantages of incentive/reward approaches to increase safety belt use in community, university, and industrial settings.[15] Indeed, use of personal feedback and positive consequences has been shown to effectively promote use of both safety belts[16] and child safety seats.[17]

For some vehicle occupants, simple verbal prompts or reminders have been effective. More specifically, researchers have increased safety-belt use by using promise cards[18], flash cards[19], and safety-belt reminders on airliners.[20] See Chapter 4 for examples of these AC4P techniques to increase the use of vehicle safety belts.

Calming Cognitive-Emotional Commotion

Most drivers occasionally get angry in common situations like traffic jams or if cut off by another driver. One study found drivers felt anger toward another driver on about 10% of their trips and felt frustrated by another driver on about 30% of trips.[21] While a few people may react to anger and frustration with aggression, most don't. But, many drivers simmer in their negative emotions, even if they don't express them openly.

Driving while angry or frustrated is dangerous because it diverts attention from important safe-driving factors. It's probable that experiencing any powerfully negative emotion while driving, such as a potent sadness or jealousy, is likewise dangerous.

One scholar said grieving while driving posed a danger to the driver and others because grieving is "…an intensely demanding process."[22] Theoretically, even a powerful positive emotion could be distracting.

But generally, a positive attitude helps alleviate negative emotions, creates a more charitable interpretation of others' behavior, and promotes forgiveness over anger. And, an AC4P mindset facilitates a positive attitude while driving.

As a driver, how often do you make negative judgments about other drivers? Do these judgments usually lead to negative emotions? Actually, it's common place to think of drivers who are seemingly not concerned for our safety as "careless jerks" or perhaps something worse. This is clearly not an AC4P mindset.

The Fundamental Attribution Error

When attempting to explain the cause of someone's behavior we tend to assume it's the product of some dispositional characteristic of the performer. This is called the fundamental attribution error (FAE) or correspondence bias.[23] It's erroneous because attributing cause of behavior only to a person's character ignores the fact that situations often play a significant role in determining behavior. It's 'fundamental' because humans seem inclined to automatically draw such conclusions about others.

Think about the last time you got cut off by another driver in traffic. You may have automatically said to yourself, or even out loud, "You stupid jerk!" Perhaps your negative self-talk or verbal behavior was more creative and colorful.

Now think of the last time you cut off another driver. Did you say the same type of thing about yourself? Did you say, "I'm such a jerk!" or, "I don't care about anyone's safety!" or, "I'm an awful driver!"? Probably not; this is because you knew when you cut off the other driver, it was unintentional. You may have even wanted to apologize for that behavior.

You likely had a good reason for not condemning yourself, as you interpreted your own behavior in the context of the situation. Maybe you just didn't check your blind spot well enough. Perhaps you were engrossed in thinking about school, home or work. Possibly you were distracted by a conversation with a passenger or child in the back seat. Maybe you were doing something you shouldn't, like texting on a cell phone. At any rate, you probably quickly forgave yourself for your error and wanted the driver you cut off to know you didn't intend any harm.

We tend to forgive ourselves for our errors because we know we don't *intend* to make them. If we didn't intend harm, we shouldn't attribute blame, right? So, why do we think *everyone else* deserves blame? If we usually aren't careless or thoughtless drivers, why do we automatically attribute such negative qualities to others?

What if we drove with an AC4P mindset? What if we gave others the benefit of the doubt and assumed their errors were as unintentional as our own? What if we were willing to forgive errors instead of condemn them?

Such an orientation would promote a much more positive perception and diminish any anger or frustration we might otherwise have felt. Becoming more mindful of the FAE can improve our attitude and our behavior when confronted with the maneuvers of drivers who slow our progress or who put us at momentary risk for a crash.

The Polite Lite

The last time you cut someone off in traffic you may have raised your hand up to waive as a sign of guilt or humility, hoping it would be interpreted as an apology. But, you may avoid such gesturing for fear it could be misinterpreted as insulting or hostile.

Since we can't really understand one another when separated by steel and glass at high speed, it would be helpful if drivers could communicate clearly and quickly on the road. Scott Geller and Jerry Beasley, along with numerous research assistants, designed and tested a concept designed to provide such communication.

Their approach was to use what they called *The Flash* or *Polite Lite*[19] to enable drivers to signal one another with a small but very bright green light which was affixed to the rear windscreen of their vehicle. (See Chapter 4 for a photo of this device.) Vehicles were adorned with a static-cling window decal defining a *Courtesy Code* as: 1 Flash = Please (e.g., allow me to merge into traffic), 2 Flashes = Thank You (e.g., for letting me in), and 3 Flashes = I Am Sorry (e.g., for inadvertently cutting you off).

A major advertising campaign was conducted during the study to make the Code widely known in the study area. Radio and newspaper ads urged drivers to use their hazards lights to flash the code if they didn't have a Polite Lite. Also, the Code was displayed on large billboards along main roads in town (see photo on next page). This campaign was quite effective because after ten weeks, 75% of 599 drivers polled randomly via phone in the region said they were aware of the *Courtesy Code*.

Drivers who participated in a ten-week study of the AC4P intervention were randomly assigned to three groups: 1) Participants in the Polite-Lite Group were told to use the Polite Lite to flash the Code when appropriate, 2) Participants in the Hazard-Light Group were directed to use their hazard lights to signal the Code when they

felt it fitting, and 3) Participants in the No-Code Group were not told anything about the *Courtesy Code*, although they were exposed to the *Courtesy Code* through the billboards and community advertising.

All drivers filled out driving diaries in which they reported behaviors and emotions experienced while driving each week of the study and returned them to the researchers. All took pre- and post-project driving surveys as well. Some interesting between-group differences between groups were detected.

Taken together, drivers instructed to use the Code reported sending an average of 12 positive messages during the eight-week intervention period. Compared to drivers in the No-Code Group (i.e., the Control Group), Code-Group participants reported less speeding, less tailgating, less failure to use a turn signal, less drifting from one's lane, and fewer refusals to let other drivers in traffic. Also, drivers using the *Courtesy Code* reported making fewer negative remarks about other drivers and scored lower on a post-intervention measure of aggressive driving.

These differences are interesting and suggest social validity for an AC4P courtesy-code concept, but it should be noted the number of participants per each group decreased markedly by the end of the study, some differences only approached statistical significance, and differences in verbal report could be partially due to experimenter expectancy.[24] Thus, replication of the study is warranted.

Nonetheless, the trends clearly showed people instructed to engage in positive inter-vehicular communications, and who were reminded to do so by the presence of a static-cling decal on their car (and a switch on the front seat for those with a Polite Lite), reported more AC4P driving behaviors.

Further, of 423 drivers who said they were aware of the *Courtesy Code* during a random phone interview at the study's end, 64% felt such a Code would be 'somewhat' or 'very' helpful if it were widely used. Only 22% thought it would be 'somewhat' or 'very' unhelpful. From these data we might assume most people want to be more courteous and actively care for others while driving.

Among the minority who thought the Code would be *unhelpful*, many presumed some drivers would make some negative use of the Code (e.g., using two flashes to mean something radically different from 'Thank You'). And, some thought drivers being 'flashed' might not be aware of the code and misconstrue the AC4P communication as a threat or insult. Devices used to send positive messages, no matter how advanced, may always carry with them the potential for misuse or misinterpretation.

But even if positive inter-vehicular communication is infeasible for you, you can at least communicate to yourself by using positive self-talk to always remain calm and civil when driving (e.g., deep breathing, avoiding the FAE, choosing to forgive others). And, AC4P-minded passengers can explain relevant AC4P principles to help drivers reduce frustration and anger felt toward other drivers.

By avoiding kneejerk judgments about others, we are far less likely to be distracted by anger or frustration, and to have a more contented commute.

Ditch the Distractions

Driver inattention is a major contributor to highway crashes. An examination of police reports in 2008 indicated at least 25% of reported crashes involved at least one type of driver distraction.[25] Distraction occurs when a driver's attention is diverted from driving-relevant tasks, like monitoring the road and regularly checking mirrors. A wide variety of activities can compete for a driver's attention, but distraction can also result from simply being lost in thought.

The dangers of distractions caused by cell-phone use while driving (i.e., texting, using Apps or the Internet, and talking, with both hand-held and hands-free devices) are well documented and have been known for some time; yet these activities are still ever prevalent.[26]

It seems difficult for many of us to truly appreciate the dangers of driving while distracted (DWD). We'll draw a parallel to another dangerous driving issue once thought not to be that big of a deal, namely, driving while intoxicated (DWI).

Driving While Intoxicated

In the U.S., DWI was not considered a serious problem until the late 20th century. It took a steady stream of research beginning in the mid-1960s,[27] to show the dangers of DWI, namely that crash risk increases precipitously with relatively small increases in blood alcohol concentration (BAC). Although researchers, law enforcement officials, and traffic-safety advocates tried desperately to get DWI on the nation's agenda, many legislators resisted the creation of anti-DWI laws.[27]

It took the grass-roots efforts of Mothers Against Drunk Driving (MADD) to develop an anti-DWI social norm. MADD was started by Candy Lightner and Sue LeBrun-Green, after Candy's 13-year-old daughter (Cori) was killed by a hit-and-run drunk driver. These AC4P-oriented leaders vowed do whatever it took to solve the DWI problem. As reported by former MADD official, Chuck Hurley, "Before the 1980s, drinking and driving was how people got home. It was normal behavior."[28]

Candy also teamed up with Cindy Lamb, whose daughter (Laura), at the age of 5-months, became the nation's youngest paraplegic victim of a DWI-related crash. On October 1, 1980, they held a press conference in Washington D.C. "On that day, public tolerance of drunk driving changed forever".[28] Anti-DWI laws were soon put in place across the country and the public began to change its attitude toward DWI.

DWI vs. DWD

Perhaps a similar grassroots movement will be necessary to change the public's view of DWD. We are in much the same place now with DWD as we once were with DWI. Though DWD is clearly unsafe, it seems the public is much less negative about DWD than DWI. Yet, researchers using a driving simulator found that talking on the phone while driving was *more* dangerous than DWI at a BAC of 0.08%, the upper legal limit in every U.S. state.[29]

While some people agree DWD *can* be dangerous, many more see the risk as low and tolerable.[30] Our DWI parallel also fits well here.

The risk an intoxicated driver will crash on any given DWI trip is actually low, speaking strictly statistically.[31] However, the public has collectively decided that any such risk is unacceptable. Thus, laws with serious penalties were enacted to punish DWI, and alcohol-related crashes have significantly declined, though they do remain a significant problem.[32] But, the laws and public campaigns have helped substantially.

Though some DWD laws have begun to emerge, they do not seem to be helping; at least not yet. For example, one law to curtail cell-phone use while driving seems to have had no discernible effect.[33] If laws against that type of DWD are in place, and people believe the behavior is risky, why does the behavior continue to occur?

The immediately reinforcing aspects of using a cell-phone or text messaging while driving outweigh the seemingly remote risk of negative outcomes. In fact, personal experience tells many people, incorrectly, there is no risk. Every time someone engages in a distracting task and doesn't crash, this view is seemingly supported.

Plus, legal penalties for DWD are not nearly as severe as those with DWI. For example, a recent legislative act doubled the penalties for texting-while-driving in New Jersey.[34] However, that only meant the first offense fine increased to $200, with it being $400 and $600 for the next two. Only upon the fourth offence does it carry a three-point license penalty, which is the case for each offense thereafter.

Compare that to a first-time DWI which results in automatic arrest, some loss of driving privileges, and a stiff fine in all states. In many states a third offense results in automatic and substantial jail time and in some states, permanent license revocation.

Like DWI, unless it's blatant, DWD can be hard for officers to detect,[35] though it occurs with regularity. It will clearly require some new approaches to address this problem if we are to do so effectively.

We know convenience, task accomplishment, social connectedness, curiosity satiation, and fun are powerful reinforcers. We are provided with such reinforcers when we use phones and other devices to talk, text, view videos or listen to audio programs, and to access the Internet.

While the DWD crash risk is likely the same or greater than DWI, people don't yet see DWD as extremely risky. And, there are few, if any, serious legal penalties for DWD behaviors. So, if people don't believe there's a serious risk or potentially substantial cost for these behaviors, why would they refrain from them?

An AC4P Approach

Perhaps people would use cell-phones less while driving if they considered the probability of a crash over a lifetime of this DWD behavior. But, consider this AC4P perspective: While it's likely you will not personally be in a crash while engaging in any given DWD behavior, someone out there will crash and perhaps be killed today as a result of DWD (e.g., search YouTube for "texting-while-driving" to see horrific consequences from this DWD behavior). Do you care?

Of course you care about people being seriously hurt or killed because of DWD, even if you're not an AC4P advocate. Now reflect on the fact that your DWD behavior, viewed by passengers in your vehicle and in adjacent vehicles on the road, sets a risky example for others to follow.

In other words, your DWD behavior supports a risky social norm where such behavior is seen by many as appropriate and acceptable. The ideal norm to prevent vehicle collisions and keep people safe is that no DWD behavior should be considered safe or acceptable.

AC4P leaders should refrain from DWD in order to keep themselves and others safe, as well as set a safe example and support the injunctive norm. In addition, it's critical for the AC4P advocate to use supportive and corrective feedback effectively (see Chapter 3) to promote this safety-based norm with friends, family, colleagues, and even strangers. Do you have the moral courage for this challenge?

When reminding others you care about their safety, and would like to talk about this DWD behavior, be compassionate and not self-righteous. Remind yourself most people who engage in DWD behavior do so because it's convenient to multi-task while driving, and they *believe* they are fully capable of high-quality multi-tasking. They either don't know about the research that refutes this notion, or feel they must be in the 2.5% of population who might be exceptions to the rule.[36] Remember, people don't take risks because they are wild uncaring daredevils; they just don't see the risk as dangerous for them.

Using a cell-phone to stay connected or get work done (talking, texting, browsing) enables drivers to accomplish other goals while driving. Why not get some work done while driving? Why not play a game or use an App to alleviate our boredom? Why not stay in contact with friends and family while in the car? These are the kinds of questions you'll face when trying to convince others of the dangers in DWD.

The AC4P perspective reminds us it's more than changing the behavior of one person on one trip. It's about realizing the large-scale impact of many people applying AC4P feedback techniques to decrease the DWD behavior of many drivers.

Thus, your small-win achievement of convincing one driver to put down his or her cell-phone adds to similar small wins of many other leaders of the AC4P Movement. Your and their AC4P behavior for driver safety can make driving without a cell-phone normative behavior and help cultivate an AC4P culture of compassion.

Initiating a movement for a personal change is relatively easy. But actually changing a culture and sustaining the change is another story. Will you be part of the AC4P Movement for Traffic Safety? Can you give up DWD conveniences, stay calm on the road at all times, eschew DWI, and always buckle up, knowing advocates for AC4P on the road need to set the right example? Will you then champion the AC4P Movement for Traffic Safety and tell others why you changed your driving behavior and why you wish they'd do the same? We hope so!

Intervening for Traffic Safety and Culture Change

There are a host of approaches people can use to transform organizations, including families, churches, and schools. The AC4P principles and procedures can transform individuals, even children, from passive observers to effective changes agents. With the most basic people-based safety (PBS) training, people learn how to design safety interventions, conduct systematic behavioral observations, and give and receive feedback effectively.

Peers can teach the process to one another, and if learned in school, children can teach PBS to their parents. Let's consider the seven principles of Applied Behavioral Science as introduced in Chapter 1, on which PBS[37] and all AC4P applications described in Part II were based.

1. Start with Observable Behavior.

This can be any safe driving behavior, from using a safety belt and a turn signal to keeping one's eye on the road (as opposed to viewing or sending texts, for example).

People-based safety focuses on what people do. *Why* they do what they do becomes a focus to inform the implementation of an evidence-based and behavior-based intervention. Relevant attitudes are not targeted directly, but will change to support the target behavior if the behavior-based intervention facilitates perceptions of empowerment and self-motivation.

2. Look for External and Internal Factors to Improve Behaviors.

Many external factors affect our driving behavior, like someone texting or calling us, or pressure to be at a destination by a certain time. Relevant, internal factors also affect our behavior, like a desire to see who's trying to reach us or holding a value of being on time over driving safely.

Here we look to impact both sides of this equation. On the external side, we want to reduce incentives to engage in unsafe behaviors and increase incentives to engage in safe ones. On the internal side, we want people to engage in self-talk that supports safe over at-risk driving and develops the courage to help others drive more safely as well.

3. Direct with Activators and Motivate with Consequences.

As detailed in Chapter 1, we want to use activators (like signs, posters, stickers and/or verbal reminders) to make drivers more mindful of specific safe vs. risky driving behaviors. The most effective activators remind drivers of positive vs. negative consequences following target behaviors.

Most government-sponsored strategies to motivate safe driving focus on disincentives/penalty-based interventions (e.g., speed enforcement zones, and "Click It or Ticket"). However, as noted above, behavioral community psychologists have developed and evaluated a number of large-scale incentive/reward programs to increase safe driving behavior (e.g., safety-belt use, turn-signal use, complete stopping at intersections, driving the speed limit).

4. Focus on Positive Consequences.

If someone says to you, "I'd like to talk to you about your behavior," what do you expect? By now you realize the AC4P approach puts a positive spin on the term "behavior" by focusing on rewards over penalties. We want people to become success seekers, working to achieve desirable consequences, rather than failure avoiders, working to avoid failure.

Success seekers are more optimistic than failure avoiders and are much more likely to do more than what's required. As discussed in Chapter 3, AC4P behavior requires self-motivation, and positive consequences like supportive feedback and genuine appreciation are critical to developing and sustaining perceptions of self-motivation.

5. Apply the Scientific Method to Design and Improve Interventions.

This is accomplished by using the *DO IT* process (*Define, Observe, Intervene, and Test*). First, we identify (*Define*) the target behaviors to change. In traffic safety these would include such behaviors as using a safety belt and a turn signal, coming to full stops at intersections, turning off a cell-phone before driving, and pulling over to a safe location before making a call or sending a text message.

Risky behaviors to decrease in frequency might also be defined, like turning without signaling or talking/texting on the phone while driving.

Then we measure (*Observe*) the frequency of the target behavior(s) to obtain a baseline. During these baseline observations we look for consequences in the natural environment that could be supporting risky driving or preventing safe driving.

Next, we use the data gathered to create a behavior-change program (*Intervene*) using positive consequences to increase the frequency of safe behaviors. We might also withhold positive consequences and/or provide additional activators (like reminding someone to buckle up) to decrease the frequency of unsafe driving behaviors.

Finally, we objectively determine if our intervention is effective (*Test*). Through continual observation and recording, we can see whether the frequency of a targeted safe behavior is higher than baseline, or whether the occurrence of a targeted at-risk behavior is below the frequency observed during baseline.

6. Use Theory to Integrate Information.

Once you go through the *DO IT* process several times, patterns will emerge. Some approaches will work better than others with some people, in some situations, or within some organizations. As you analyze the consistencies you find you enter the process of developing a data-driven theory to explain your findings and perhaps integrate them with other findings from the rewarding literature. Such theory development is often useful in designing more effective interventions.

7. Consider the Feelings and Attitudes of Others.

People's feelings and attitudes can differ profoundly from person to person, and affect the impact of an intervention. The AC4P approach fosters a concern for the well-being of others, and this includes emotional well-being. Development and maintenance of valued relationships, with a fostering of genuine interpersonal trust, promotes the real teamwork which is needed to achieve an AC4P community.

These factors have been addressed in the six chapters on principles (Part I), as well as in those describing applications. Here we only point out this AC4P perspective targets behavior directly but influences feelings and attitude indirectly. Thus, Scott Geller has appropriately coined this approach "humanistic behaviorism".[37]

End of the Road

We could drive on and on. For example, we haven't addressed details pertaining to many other dangerous driving issues such as drowsy driving and general risk-taking (e.g., red-light and stop-sign running, speeding, weaving, and tailgating). Nor have we touched on matters directly related to age, such as infant/child restraints, teenage driver training, and issues specific to senior drivers.

And, we've not discussed how changes in policy might incorporate an AC4P perspective (e.g., stopping drivers and giving 'tickets' to movies, fairs, concerts, and sporting events for safe-driving behaviors), so improvement of traffic safety is not an entirely punitive enterprise.

Obviously, the AC4P perspective has lots to contribute to so many of society's problems. The bottom line: Traffic safety affects us all, and we all care about safety. Thus, we need to actively care for safe driving practices in a systematic, consistent, and persistent fashion to shift our culture to one that truly values safety, health, and security for everyone, in every situation, including our roads and highways.

Notes

1. Centers for Disease Control and Prevention (2011). Injury prevention & control: Motor vehicle safety. Retrieved from www.cdc.gov/motorvehiclesafety/index.html; National Highway Traffic Safety Administration (2010). Traffic safety facts: 2009 data. Retrieved May 15, 2012: http://www-nrd.nhtsa.dot.gov/Pubs/811392.pdf

2. Cambridge Systematics, Inc. (2011). Crashes vs. congestion: What's the cost to society? Washington, DC: AAA Foundation for Traffic Safety. Retrieved from http://newsroom.aaa.com/wp-content/uploads/2011/11/2011_AAA_CrashvCongUpd.pdf

3. Dula, C.S., & Geller, E.S. (2007). Creating a total safety traffic culture. *Traffic Safety Culture in the United States: The journey forward*. Washington D.C.: American Automobile Association Foundation for Traffic Safety. Retrieved from www.aaafoundation.org/pdf/DulaGeller.pdf

4. U.S. Department of Defense (2012). *Casualty status*. Retrieved from www.defense.gov/news/casualty.pdf

5. Geller, E.S. (1991). War on the highways: An international tragedy. *Journal of Applied Behavior*

Analysis, 24(1), 3-7.

6. U.S. Department of Defense (2012). *Fiscal Year 2013 Budget Request.* Retrieved from http://comptroller.defense.gov/defbudget/fy2013/FY2013_Budget_Request_Overview_Book.pdf

7. National Highway Traffic Safety Administration (2012). *Fiscal Year 2013 Budget Overview.* Retrieved from www.nhtsa.gov/staticfiles/administration/pdf/Budgets/FY-2013_Budget_Highlights.pdf

8. Dula, C.S., & Ballard, M.E. (2003). Development and evaluation of a measure of dangerous, aggressive, negative emotional, and risky driving. *Journal of Applied Psychology, 33*(2), 263-282; Dula, C.S., & Geller, E.S. (2004). Risky, aggressive, or emotional driving: Addressing the need for consistent communication in research. *Journal of Safety Research, 34*(5), 559-566; Dula, C.S., Geller, E.S., & Chumney, F.L. (2011). A social-cognitive model of driver aggression: Taking situations and individual differences into account. *Current Psychology, 30*(4), 324-334.

9. Martin, B.A., Taylor, D.A., Dula, C.S., & Geller, E.S. (2012*). Who cares about dangerous driving: Applying the actively caring model to automobile crash* prevention. Technical Report, East Tennessee State University, Johnson City, TN.

10. Geller, E.S., Bolduc, J.E., Foy, M.J., & Dean, J. (2012). In pursuit of an actively-caring safety culture: Practical methods, empirical results, and provocative implications. *Professional Safety, 57*(1), 44-50.

11. U.S. Patent and Trademark Office (2012). *Safety-Belt. U.S. Patent Number: 312085.* Retrieved from http://patft.uspto.gov/netahtml/PTO/srchnum.htm

12. National Highway Traffic Safety Administration (2011). *Traffic safety facts: Seat-belt use in 2011 – Overall results.* Retrieved from http://www-nrd.nhtsa.dot.gov/Pubs/811544.pdf

13. Begg, D.J., & Langley, J.D. (2000). Seat-belt use and related behaviors among young adults. *Journal of Safety Research, 31*(4), 211-220; Kim, K., & Yamashita, E.Y. (2007). Attitudes of commercial motor vehicle drivers towards safety belts. *Accident Analysis and Prevention, 39*(6), 1097-1106.

14. Drebinger, J.W. (2011). *Would you watch out for my safety? Helping others avoid personal injury.* Galt, CA: Wulamoc Publishing.

15. Geller, E.S. (1983). Rewarding safety belt usage at an industrial setting: Tests of treatment generality and response maintenance. *Journal of Applied Behavior Analysis, 16*(2), 189-202; Geller, E.S., Johnson, R.P., & Pelton, S.L. (1982). Community-based interventions encouraging safety-belt use. *American Journal of Community Psychology, 10*, 183-195; Geller, E.S., Paterson, L., & Talbot, E. (1982). A behavior analysis of incentive prompts for motivating seat belt usage. *Journal of Applied Behavior Analysis, 15*, 403-415.

16. Boyce, T.E., & Geller, E.S. (1999). Attempts to increase vehicle safety-belt use among industry workers: What can we learn from our failures? *Journal of Organizational Behavior Management, 19*, 27-44; Campbell, R.J., Hunter, W.W., & Stutts, J.C. (1984). The use of economic incentives and education to modify safety-belt use behavior of high school students. *Health Education, 15*, 30–33; Geller, E.S., Davis, L., & Spicer, K. (1983). Industry-based incentives for promoting seat-belt use: Differential impact on white-collar versus blue-collar employees. *Journal of Organizational Behavior Management, 5*, 17-29; Geller, E.S., Kalsher, M.J., Rudd, J.R., & Lehman, G. (1989). Promoting safety belt use on a university campus: An integration of commitment and incentive strategies. J*ournal of Applied Social Psychology, 19*, 3-19; Geller, E.S., Rudd, J.R., Kalsher, M.J., Streff, F.M., & Lehman, G.R. (1987). Employer-based programs to motivate safety-belt use: A review of short and long-term effects. *Journal of Safety Research, 18*, 1-17; Grant, B.A. (1990). Effectiveness of feedback and education in an employment-based seat belt program. *Health Education Research, 5*, 2-10; Kello, J.E., Geller, E.S., Rice, J.C., & Bryant, S.L. (1988). Motivating auto safety-belt wearing in industrial settings: From awareness to behavior change. *Journal of Organizational Behavior Management, 9*, 7-21; Pastò, L., & Baker, A.G. (2001). Evaluation of

a brief intervention for increasing seat-belt use on a college campus. *Behavior Modification, 25*, 471-486; Roberts, D.S., & Geller, E.S. (1994). A statewide intervention to increase safety-belt use: Adding to the impact of a belt-use law. *American Journal of Health Promotion, 8*, 172-174; Rudd, J. R., & Geller, E. S. (1985). A university-based incentive program to increase safety-belt use: Toward cost effective institutionalization. *Journal of Applied Behavior Analysis, 18*, 215-226.

17. England, K.J., Olson, T.M., & Geller, E.S. (2000). Behavioral observations find unsafe use of child safety seats. *Behavior Analysis Digest, 12*, 11-12; Greenberg-Seth, J., Hemenway, D., Gallagher, S.S., Ross, J.B., & Lissy, K.S. (2004). Evaluation of a community-based intervention to promote rear seating for children. *American Journal of Public Health, 94*, 1009-1013; Roberts, M.C., Fanurik, D., & Wilson, D. (1988). A community program to reward children's use of seat belts. *American Journal of Community Psychology, 16*, 395-407; Roberts, M.C., & Layfield, D.A. (1987). Promoting child passenger safety: A comparison of two positive methods. *Journal of Pediatric Psychology, 12*, 257-271; Task Force on Community Preventive Services (2001). Recommendations to reduce injuries to motor vehicle occupants: Increasing child safety seat use, increasing safety-belt use, and reducing alcohol-impaired driving. *American Journal of Preventive Medicine, 21*, 16-22; Will, K.E., & Geller, E.S. (2004). Increasing the safety of children's vehicle travel: From effective risk communication to behavior change. *Journal of Safety Research, 35*, 263-274; Zaza, S., Sleet, D.A., Thompson, R.S., Sosin, D.M., Bolen, J.C., & Task Force on Community Preventive Services (2001). Reviews of evidence regarding interventions to increase use of child safety seats. *American Journal of Preventive Medicine, 21*, 31-47.

18. Geller, E.S., & Lehman, G.R. (1991). The buckle-up promise card: A versatile intervention for large-scale behavior change. *Journal of Applied Behavior Analysis, 24*, 91-94.

19. Geller, E.S., Bruff, C.D., & Nimmer, J.G. (1985). The "Flash for Life": A community prompting strategy for safety-belt promotion. *Journal of Applied Behavior Analysis, 18*, 145-159.

20. Geller, E.S. (1989). The Airline Lifesaver: In pursuit of small wins. *Journal of Applied Behavior Analysis, 22*, 333-335; Geller, E.S., Hickman, J.S., & Pettinger, C.B. (2004). The Airline Lifesaver: A 17-year analysis of a technique to prompt the delivery of a safety message. *Journal of Safety Research, 35*, 357-366.

21. Positive Driving Systems, LLC. (2003). *Final report for the National Institutes of Health Project: Innovative Approaches to Anger Management.* Grant #1 R43 MH62263-01A2, Newport, VA: Make-A-Difference, Inc.

22. Rosenblatt, P.C. (2004). Grieving while driving. *Death Studies, 28*(7), 679-686.

23. Ross, L. (1977). The intuitive psychologist and his shortcomings: Distortions in the attribution process. In Berkowitz, L. *Advances in experimental social psychology.* New York, NY: Academic Press. pp. 173-220.

24. Rosenthal, R. (1966). *Experimenter effects in behavioral research.* East Norwalk, CT: Appleton-Century-Crofts.

25. National Highway Traffic Safety Administration (2009). Traffic safety facts: An examination of driver distraction as recorded in NHTSA databases. Retrieved from http://www-nrd.nhtsa.dot.gov/Pubs/811216.pdf

26. Briem, V., & Hedman, L.R. (1995). Behavioural effects of mobile telephone use during simulated driving. *Ergonomics, 38*, 2536-2562; Bener, A., Crundall, D., Özkan, T., & Lajunen, T. (2010). Mobile phone use while driving: A major public health problem in an Arabian society, State of Qatar—Mobile phone use and the risk of motor vehicle crashes. *Journal of Public Health, 18*(2); Cook, J. & Jones, R. (2011). Texting and accessing the web while driving: traffic citations and crashes among young adult drivers. *Traffic Injury Prevention, 12*(6), 545-549; McEvoy, S.P., Stevenson M.R., & Woodward, M. (2006). Phone use and crashes while driving: A representative survey of drivers in two Australian

states. *Medical Journal of Australia, 185*, 630-634; Nemme, H. E., & White, K. M. (2010). Texting while driving: Psychosocial influences on young people's texting intentions and behaviour. *Accident Analysis and Prevention, 42*(4), 1257-1265; Strayer D.L., Drews F.A., Albert R.W., & Johnston, W.A. (2003) Cell phone-induced failures of visual attention during simulated driving. *Journal of Experimental Psychology, 9*(1), 23-32.

27. Borkenstein, R.F., Crowther, R.F., Shumate, R.P., Ziel, W.B., & Zylman, R. (1974). The role of the drinking driver in traffic accidents (The Grand Rapids Study). *Blutalkohol, 11*(1), 1-131.

28. Mothers Against Drunk Driving (2005). 25 years of saving lives: 1980-2005. *Driven*. Retrieved from www.madd.org/about-us/history/madd25thhistory.pdf

29. Strayer, D.L., Drews, F.A., & Crouch, D.J. (2006). A comparison of the cell phone driver and the drunk driver. *Human Factors, 48*(2), 381-391.

30. Hallett, C., Lambert, A., & Regan, M. A. (2011). Cell phone conversing while driving in New Zealand: Prevalence, risk perception and legislation. *Accident Analysis and Prevention, 43*(3), 862-869; Harrison, M. A. (2011). College students' prevalence and perceptions of text messaging while driving. *Accident Analysis and Prevention, 43*(4), 1516-1520.

31. Dula, C.S., Dwyer, W.O., & LeVerne, G. (2007). Policing the drunk driver: Measuring law enforcement involvement in reducing alcohol-impaired driving. *Journal of Safety Research, 38*(3), 267-272.

32. U.S. National Highway Traffic Safety Administration (2012). *Fatality Analysis Reporting System (FARS) Encyclopedia*. Retrieved from www-fars.nhtsa.dot.gov/Main/index.aspx

33. Foss, R.D., Goodwin, A.H., McCartt, A.T., & Hellinga, L.A. (2009). Short-term effects of a teenage driver cell phone restriction. *Accident Analysis and Prevention, 41*(3), 419-424; Goodwin, A.H., O'Brien, N.P., & Foss, R.D. (2012). Effect of North Carolina's restriction on teenage driver cell phone use two years after implementation. *Accident Analysis and Prevention, 48*, 363-367.

34. Friedman, M. (2012). *N.J. Senate passes bill doubling penalty for texting while driving*. Retrieved from www.nj.com/news/index.ssf/2012/06/nj_senate_passes_bill_doubling.html

35. Logana, D. (2012). How do police enforce laws against texting while driving? On *Live 5 WCSC*. Retrieved from www.live5news.com/story/12937810/how-do-police-enforce-laws-against-texting-while-driving; Associated Press (2012). Ore. cops to face problems enforcing cell phone ban. Retrieved from www.policeone.com/communications/articles/1985732-Ore-cops-to-face-problems-enforcing-cell-phone-ban/

36. Watson, J.M., & Strayer, D.L. (2010). Supertaskers: Profiles in extraordinary multitasking ability. *Psychonomic Bulletin & Review, 17*(4), 479-485.

37. Geller, E.S. (2005). Seven basics of people-based safety: Embracing empowerment, ownership, & trust. *Industrial Safety and Hygiene News, 39*(6), pp. 14, 16; Geller, E.S. (2005). *People-based safety: The source*. Virginia Beach, VA: CoastalTraining Technologies Corporation; Geller, E.S. (2008). *Leading people-based safety: Enriching your culture*. Virginia Beach, VA: Coastal Training and Technologies Corporation

CHAPTER 16

Actively Caring to Prevent Alcohol Abuse among College Students:
Research-based lessons from the field

Ryan C. Smith and E. Scott Geller

MAKAYLA GREATHOUSE, a student in Professor Geller's senior seminar on self-motivation in 2012, told us this story:

I met Danny Gilliam my junior year. He lived right above me and my roommates. We spent a lot of time hanging out and saw each other every weekend. One particular Saturday night we were all sitting outside while Danny and his roommates were about to leave for a party. We shared several minutes of conversation and laughs, and then they went on their way.

Around 2:30 A.M. I see a good friend crying outside my apartment and immediately approach her to see what's wrong. The news I hear knocks me off my feet. Danny Gilliam is dead.

Never again will I see him bounding down the flight of stairs or see him laughing with his buddies when I barge into his apartment. It takes me days to process what happened. I watch his family come and move out his belongings with tear-streaked faces. I watch his roommates go through denial, anger and depression, coping with tragedy as best they can, but losing a roommate, a best friend is not easy for anyone.

The mood of our building is solemn, and though people try their best to help by bringing meals to neighbors and offering a listening ear, it takes months for things to return to a new normal.

Her co-worker and good friend Michael had been at the party on Whipple Drive, where the incident happened. Michael reports:

I was at a friend's house off of Whipple Drive and the party above us was huge, probably two hundred people. All at once everyone rushes out so we decide to see what is going on. We don't see cop cars anywhere and when asking the fleeing people what's going on, they would just say "someone fell".

I make my way around the building, and I approach a body on the ground. Only three of his friends are there, all in hysteria. I order someone to call 911 and as a first responder, I begin CPR and check his vitals. The police arrive soon after the call and begin performing CPR, as well. The guy didn't make it; we tried everything but it wasn't enough.

We ask, "Why did everyone flee the scene?" Makayla responds:

Since many students who consume alcohol in college are underage, many are scared to get in trouble. Perhaps, bystander apathy took place. There were so many people; I'm sure many thought someone else would take care of it.

Proactive bystander intervention would have saved Danny's life that night. If someone had stopped him from climbing the balcony, he would have never fallen. There are so many ways Danny could have been convinced to get down. Someone could have told him how dangerous it was or said, "Hey, come get another drink with me" or "Come meet my friend."

A Recurring Tragedy on College Campuses

It's sad how often we turn tragedies into numbers. Take a moment to imagine the full impact of this single loss of life. A father will never again hold his son. A mother will no longer imagine her future grandchildren. Friends will have an irreplaceable void for the remainder of their lives. Classmates will have one less smiling face walking at graduation. Hundreds of people at a party will be left with the haunting and painful feelings they could have intervened proactively and saved a life that ended too soon. Lives are changed forever, and the future will never be quite as bright.

It seems utterly unimaginable this could be a reoccurring story. In 2011, nearly four times as many college students died as a result of alcohol consumption as American soldiers died in both the Iraq and Afghanistan wars combined during the same year. This one tragic story at Virginia Tech (VT) represents only one of approximately 1,800 alcohol-related college student deaths each year.[1]

Alcohol Abuse by College Students

The harm of alcohol abuse is particularly evident on the campuses of our nation's colleges and universities. Not only do college students drink significantly more alcohol than their peers who don't attend a college or university, but they are also more likely to drive under the influence of alcohol.[1] In fact, college alcohol consumption is such a major public health concern that Healthy People 2010 set one of its major ten-year initiatives to reduce the percentage of college students who binge-drink from 39% in 2000 to 20% by 2010.[2]

Binge drinking is typically defined as consuming four standard alcoholic beverages in one sitting for a female and five standard alcoholic beverages for a male. This amount of alcohol leads to the drinker experiencing a host of negative outcomes.

Healthy People is sponsored by the U.S. Department of Health and Human Services as a ten-year blueprint to monitor and improve areas of extreme health risk. Unfortunately, during the decade spanning Healthy People 2010, the percentage of students who report binge drinking actually increased to 44.7%.[1]

Healthy People 2020 once again declared reducing binge drinking among college students as a major initiative, but this time the ten-year goal was set at 36.0% by 2020.[3] This optimistic target would still only reduce the percentage of students binge drinking 3% below the level of 39.0% in 2000.

Clearly, drastic changes are needed in our nation's approach to decreasing alcohol use and abuse among college students. Top-down directives and punitive enforcement tactics are not working. Innovative interventions are drastically needed. New ways of approaching this issue with data-driven solutions must be embraced in order to make headway against alcohol abuse.

The Center for Applied Behavior Systems (CABS) at VT is at the forefront of researching this epidemic, pioneering creative ways to understand and address this large-scale problem from an AC4P perspective.

The Center for Applied Behavior Systems

For over 25 years CABS has been studying alcohol use and abuse among university students. This Center has been working closely with various university organizations, including fraternities and sororities, to provide critical insight into this epidemic.

To date, CABS has received over three million dollars in financial support for research in this domain, published dozens of scientific publications, given hundreds of professional conference presentations, and received multiple community-service awards for researching and preventing excessive alcohol consumption among college students.

These efforts and promising outcomes stem from the unique perspective and approach of CABS. Specifically, the field research is distinguished by data collection at the very locations where people are drinking and its focus on actively caring. Some of this research and solution-relevant results are reviewed in this chapter.

Research in the Field

The research in CABS is distinct because we assess actual levels of intoxication rather than relying on self-report, which is most often used in this research domain. Across all fields of psychological research, self-report is notorious for its inaccuracies.[4] For a variety of reasons, this is particularly true for alcohol research.

In order to ensure the accuracy of self-reported alcohol consumption and survey data, students must not only understand the alcohol concentration of their drinks, but accurately recall each and every drink they consume.

Indeed, it's troubling most alcohol research relies on students' understanding the precise definition of a standard drink in order to report the number of drinks consumed. Both research and common sense show students clearly do not have this level of understanding.[5]

As one example, VT students frequently consume a drink called the "Rail." Despite containing the amount of alcohol contained in over five standard drinks, the "Rail" is often considered by students to be one alcoholic beverage. This impacts more than research accuracy when students think they are safe to drive because they had only one or two "drinks."

In addition to students' lack of awareness and knowledge about the alcohol content of their drinks, self-reported alcohol consumption is also problematic because of the effects of fatigue, blacking out, and social desirability which impedes a drinkers ability and motivation to accurately recall and report the number of drinks they consumed.[6]

The research in CABS is not limited by self-reports. Armed with breathalyzers (the same used by police officers) and clipboards, dozens of undergraduate researchers give up their Thursday, Friday, and Saturday nights to visit fraternity parties, private parties, and downtown bars between the hours of 10:00 P.M. and 2:00 A.M. Yes, these students get academic research credit for collecting data at parties and downtown bars.

Three teams of four undergraduate research assistants set up assessment tables at one of the high-risk drinking locations listed above. Two team members serve as data collectors

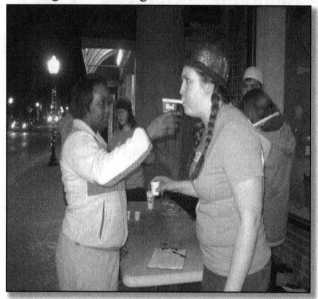

who read survey questions to downtown passersby or partygoers and mark responses. One researcher administers the breathalyzer to the participant after s/he completes the survey. The final researcher serves as a team leader to ensure research protocols are followed.

The results of these field efforts are often startling and revealing. Perhaps the most astonishing result is the average level of intoxication among students across all types of drinking settings.

Specifically, over ten years of data collection, the average blood alcohol concentration (BAC) of drinkers was .082mL/L at private parties, .093mL/L at fraternity parties, and .087mL/L near bar establishments in downtown Blacksburg. This translates into the average drinker at all locations being over the per se legal limit (.08 mL/L) to drive in all 50 states.

The increasing trend in average BACs among college students is also troubling. In 2007, the average downtown BAC was .087mL/L. Yet, the three-year average (Fall 2009 – Spring 2012) was .103mL/L. Out of the more than 10,000 drinkers who were breathalyzed over those three years, nearly 15% were in fact twice the legal limit to drive or higher.

Another surprising, yet consistent finding is the lack of students' awareness regarding their level of intoxication. Results have consistently shown a weak relationship (r's < .15) between a student's intended BAC and actual BAC as measured by the breathalyzer. Furthermore, students are wildly inaccurate in guessing their current level of intoxication.

On average, students are incorrect by .034mL/L in estimating their BAC. Interestingly, students at lower BAC tend to over-estimate their actual BAC, while students at higher BAC generally under-estimate their BAC. These findings shed light on a dangerous-drinking culture where student drinkers are neither in control nor aware of their level of intoxication.

Actively Caring for Alcohol Abuse

The research performed in CABS points to many challenges created by the college-drinking culture. However, the research has also uncovered some promising areas for proactive intervention. It's evident the traditional top-down approach to address college drinking is not working, and certain paradigm shifts are required to reduce the significant harm alcohol abuse is causing our college students.

Here are four research-inspired paradigm shifts we believe are critical in finding practical AC4P solutions to the nationwide epidemic of alcohol abuse on college campuses.

Paradigm Shift #1: From Reactive Responding to Proactive Intervening

Danny's story serves as one demonstration of the negative consequences of only acting after tragedy has struck. While the reactive measures of performing CPR and calling 911 after Danny's fall showed competence and courage, like many AC4P behaviors, they came too late.

If someone had taken the time to help Danny in any number of ways prior to his fall, things would be very different for Danny, his friends, and family. If someone had merely talked to Danny about his excessive alcohol consumption, offered to take him home when he became obviously intoxicated, pulled him down from the balcony he was climbing, or encouraged his friends to look after him, he would be here today. If only someone had actively cared from a proactive stance.

Surprisingly, alcohol problems are almost entirely handled reactively. Our society, friendships, and parenting all revolve around the misconception that alcohol problems only need to be addressed when someone gets caught or when a serious line is crossed.

Problem drinkers are taken to counseling after they become dependent on alcohol or when excessive alcohol consumption negatively impacts interpersonal relationships.

Parents speak to their children about drinking alcoholic beverages after they come crawling home intoxicated or after they get a call from police.

Friends encourage friends to slow down their alcohol consumption only after they have thrown up or are nearly passed out. This delayed AC4P behavior is particularly problematic for drunk driving.

Alcohol-Impaired Driving. The negative consequences of drunk driving are self-evident and tremendous. In 2010, alcohol-impaired driving resulted in 10,228 deaths.[7] In fact, over 30% of all traffic fatalities are the result of alcohol-impaired driving.[8]

While the particular penalties for drunk driving vary by state, a similar reactive approach is used across the entire country. Until a drunk driver gets caught by police or is involved in a vehicle crash, very little happens to a drunk driver. This reactive approach has consistently failed to reduce the number of alcohol-impaired drivers on our nation's roadways.

The utility of these reactive measures are further called into question when they not only fail to produce the needed results, but are also rarely enforced. Specifically, the Centers for Disease Control and Prevention (CDC) estimates the average first offender drives drunk at least 80 times prior to his or her first conviction.[9]

Regardless of the type of reactive punitive consequence originally imposed, drunk-driving recidivism is also extremely high.[10] In fact, it has been estimated between 50 and 75 percent of those whose licenses are suspended because of alcohol-impaired driving continue to drive, sometimes while intoxicated.[11]

Our CABS research in the field sheds a similar light on the problem of drunk driving. Over the past three years, CABS researchers have surveyed and breathalyzed over one thousand designated drivers (DDs) in downtown Blacksburg. Figure 16.1 below shows the BAC distribution of DDs across all nights.

Shockingly, nearly 60% of these DDs had BACs over .08mL/L. Greater than 10% of these DDs had BACs over twice the legal limit. Many of these DDs said they were chosen as the DD because they "were the least intoxicated". Thus, the selection of a DD is too often reactive rather than proactive.

A proactive approach to preventing drunk driving is drastically needed. Society cannot simply rely on reactive legal consequences to sober up drivers on our roadways. We need actively-caring individuals to intervene proactively. This could involve taking

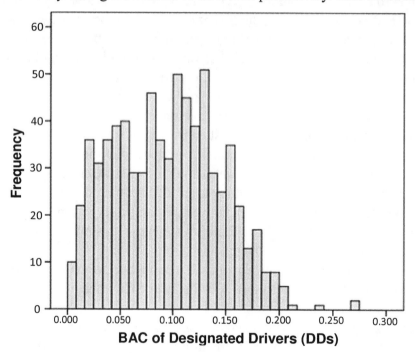

Figure 16.1. Distribution of the BACs of designated drivers.

someone's keys, calling a taxi, or arranging an alternative form of transportation.

We must also shift toward being proactive in selecting our DDs. We simply cannot wait until everyone is intoxicated to make such a critical decision.

While it may be uncomfortable to take keys from a friend or stranger or bring up the topic of a DD before drinking begins, AC4P is all about looking out for the health and safety of others. It's about not letting friends, people we just met, or even total strangers put themselves and/or others in harms way. It's about taking the first proactive step toward preventing a tragedy.

Paradigm Shift #2: From Penalizing to Rewarding

Traditional approaches to dealing with alcohol use and abuse focus almost entirely on penalizing the drinker. This makes sense, after all it's convenient and efficient to resort to punishment. When people get caught driving while intoxicated (DWI), there's a law to penalize them. When people consume too many alcoholic beverages in public, the police can penalize them by throwing them into the "drunk tank". If adolescents come home intoxicated, parents have a variety of penalties they can levy.

Penalities are certainly logical, convenient, and occasionally necessary. It would be foolish to argue for removing all punitive consequences from our system. However, negative consequences often backfire and produce unintended attitudinal and behavioral effects. Critical to this discussion is the distinction between "punishers" and "penalties".

Punishers vs. Penalties. Penalties are negative consequences intended to decrease or discourage a designated behavior. Punishers, on the other hand, are consequences that actually decrease the probability the behavior they follow will recur.

While penalties are usually negative consequences following an undesirable behavior, they do not necessarily decrease the occurrence of that behavior. To the contrary, punishers by definition decrease the frequency of the behavior they follow.

While this terminology distinction may seem picky or unimportant, several implications are noteworthy. It's often assumed the "penalties" used to decrease undesirable alcohol-related behaviors are "punishers". However, a consequence that appears undesirable does not necessarily impact the target behavior. As detailed below, some penalties can actually create resentment which may *reinforce* or increase the very behavior they were intended to stop.

Also, punishers target a specific behavior, whereas penalties target an individual. We say a certain person was penalized for a certain action, but that behavior was punished if the consequences decreased the frequency of the behavior it followed.

Effective punishers typically follow an undesirable behavior immediately and are clearly linked to that behavior. On the other hand, penalties are often delayed and target the individual for misbehaving. The negative outcome is often internalized and can activate reactance, or motivation to perform the undesired behavior more often.[12]

Parenting and Alcohol Consumption. Consider the penalties used by parents to "punish" their children for consuming alcohol. Research in CABS tracked the current alcohol consumption of more than 300 college students and asked these students about their parents' strategies for addressing alcohol consumption while in high school.

A variety of penalties were used by parents in response to their sons' and daughters' consumption of alcoholic beverages including: imposing a curfew, removing access to television/phone, disallowing time with friends, doing chores, and even physical punishment.

Yet, across all types of punitive strategies one consistent finding emerged. Students who were penalized for drinking alcohol in high school consumed significantly more alcohol in college than students who were not penalized.

It could be students who were penalized in high school for drinking were more likely to consume alcohol in college because they consumed more alcoholic beverages in the first place. However, when our statistical tests controlled for the amount of alcohol consumed in high school, this observed relationship between high-school penalties and college drinking still held. The penalties backfired. Parental "punishment" for alcohol consumption was not punishment at all.

As shown in Figure 16.2 this effect was even greater if parents let their children drink, but only with them. College students were asked if they were "punished" for drinking in high school and if they were allowed to only consume alcohol with their parents. Thus, students could fall into the four mutually exclusive categories along the x-axis of Figure 16.2 below. The y-axis shows the average frequency of drinks consumed in the previous two weeks.

As depicted in Figure 16.2, not only did those students penalized for drinking in high school consume more alcohol in college, but this effect was even greater if parents allowed their children to drink with them.

We call this phenomenon a *hypocrisy effect,* distinct from the intrapersonal hypocrisy researched earlier by social psychologists.[13] We're talking about interpersonal hypocrisy

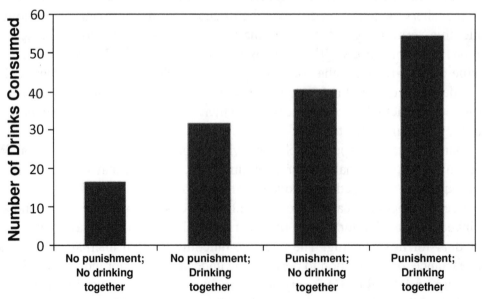

Figure 16.2. Average number of alcoholic beverages consumed per two weeks as a function of parental discipline approach.

whereby the person penalized views an inconsistency in the individual adminsitering the penalty. In this case, the parent is hypocritical by penalizing slectively (i.e., allowing alcohol consumption at home but not elsewhere).

The *behavior* of underage drinking is not punished by those parents who allow alcohol consumption under their own supervision. Thus, when these students are penalized for drinking elsewhere, this penalty is internalized. It's no longer about the behavior, and this can create resentment, confusion, and actually lead to increased drinking in college. Interestingly, this same hypocrisy effect was observed if parents kept alcohol in the house and penalized their children for alcohol consumption.

This research does not inform parents to refrain from all punishment or penalties, especially when it comes to underage drinking. It says, instead, there must be a better way. Mothers and fathers should not wait until after their child starts drinking alcoholic beverages to start parenting on this issue

The AC4P approach advocates rewarding your child for smart, healthy behaviors, rather than just punishing undesirable behaviors. As explained in Chapter 1, sometimes the best way to eliminate undesirable behavior is to reinforce incompatible, desirable behaviors.

Do not just punish your children for drinking, but encourage them to develop positive friendships with those who do not consume alcohol. Motivate your adolescents to attend events and gatherings where alcoholic beverages are not served. AC4P is about developing positive, actively-caring relationships, and finding opportunities to proactively encourage desirable behaviors with positive attention and support.

Alcohol Abuse at Fraternity Parties. Out of all college environments, fraternity parties are among the most infamous for excessive alcohol consumption. In fact, while conducting research in fraternity houses, CABS researchers have observed a wide variety of outlandish behaviors and outrageous themes that set the stage for excessive alcohol consumption.

For example, a few of the observed party themes included *Mardi Gras*, *Cowboys and Indians*, *Bosses and Secretaries*, *Teachers and School Girls*, and *Around the World* where each room contained alcohol specific to a certain country. Several of the other themes were too inappropriate to put in print.

As expected, our field research showed the average BAC to be markedly higher at fraternity parties than at any other typical drinking location. Among 1,525 university students at 19 separate parties, we found BACs were significantly higher at fraternity parties (BAC = .093mL/L) than private non-fraternity parties (BAC = .082mL/L).[14]

It's noteworthy, fraternity brothers at the fraternity parties had a significantly higher BAC than fraternity brothers at private parties. This indicates the environment of a fraternity party may encourage the at-risk drinking behavior more so than just the alcohol-consumption disposition of fraternity brothers themselves. We also found BACs tend to be higher at fraternity parties than downtown Blacksburg, even during "alcoholidays" such as Halloween and St. Patrick's Day.[15]

Each year, our nation's colleges and universities make significant investments in time and money to tackle at-risk drinking at fraternity parties. Similarly, CABS has spent years of intervention research aimed at preventing alcohol abuse at VT fraternity parties. We truly tried every positive approach imaginable, from education to one-on-one demonstrations and feedback.

In one attempt to prevent alcohol abuse, we tried a simple educational approach. In this study, individuals passed out educational cards to drinkers. These cards contained tips for keeping a "buzzed," but safe level of intoxication. The cards also had a BAC chart on the back to help an individual figure out how many drinks it would take to reach his or her desired BAC. Unfortunately, this approach proved wholly ineffective in reducing BACs.

Next, we provided sobriety stations at fraternity parties. These stations included traditional sobriety tests and a few dexterity-based games. In one of these simple tests, participants placed their thumb and index finger an inch apart while a researcher dropped a ruler between their two fingers. Participants could then see how many inches the ruler fell before they were able to catch it with their fingers. Although this clearly showed individuals the severe effect of alcohol on their reaction times, these tests also had no impact on reducing BACs when partygoers exited fraternity parties.

We even went to the lengths of serving pizzas and providing non-alcoholic beverages at fraternity parties. Food slows the absorption of alcohol, and non-alcoholic drinks help individuals pace their level of alcohol consumption. Yet, again, not even this approach was effective in reducing the intoxication of partygoers.

In all the years and methods of attempting to reduce at-risk drinking at fraternity parties, only one tactic was successful at reducing mean party BACs. Instead of focusing on the negative consequences of alcohol consumption, CABS researchers rewarded partygoers for their low-risk alcohol consumption. This created a fun and effective technique for reducing the rates of at-risk drinking.

The success of this intervention was assessed across multiple studies. In each of these studies fraternity parties were divided into *Control* parties and *Incentive* parties. At the *Control* parties, partygoers were informed they could be entered into a raffle for $100 at the end of the night simply by having their BAC taken. At *Incentive* parties, partygoers were informed they could be entered into a raffle for $100 if they maintained a BAC below 0.05mL/L when their BAC was taken at the end of the night.

These two distinct conditions were defined on flyers handed to each partygoer when entering the party location. The flyers distributed defined the experimental condition for the particular party. The two different flyers that defined these two incentive/reward contingencies are depicted on the next page. The flyer for the *Control* condition is on the left, and the flyer for the *Incentive* condition is given on the right.

In the pilot study for this research, fraternity BACs were assessed at the end of the night at four consecutive parties. The first two parties served as Baseline or *Control* parties, and the final two parties served as *Incentive* parties. As shown in Figure 16.3 on page 280, partygoers at the *Incentive* parties had significantly lower BACs. Also, greater numbers of drinkers were below the critical BAC benchmarks of .050mL/L and .080mL/L at the *Intervention* versus *Control* parties.[16]

WIN $100 TONIGHT!

Virginia Tech researchers will be giving free BAC (blood alcohol concentration) assessments tonight.

If you choose to participate, you will be registered in a drawing for $100 to be given away *tonight*.

Flyer for Baseline Condition

WIN $100 TONIGHT!

Virginia Tech researchers will be giving free BAC (blood alcohol concentration) assessments tonight.

If your BAC is *below .05,* you will be registered in a drawing for $100 to be given away tonight.

Here are some tips to help you keep a safe buzz:

* Drink a glass of water between each alcoholic beverage
* Snack on food before and while drinking
* Partake in physical activity, like dancing
* Use the attached chart to estimate a safe number of drinks.

Flyer for Incentive Condition

The results of this pilot study were also replicated in a larger follow-up study of six separate fraternities (n = 207). The results showed significant beneficial impact of the incentive/reward intervention. While individuals at the *Control* party had an average BAC of 0.098mL/L, individuals at the *Incentive* parties had an average BAC of 0.079mL/L. Furthermore, while 40.1% of participants at the *Control* party were over the legal limit to drive, 30.6% of participants in the *Incentive* condition were over the legal limit to drive.[17]

Again, all interventions based on education and negative consequences from alcohol abuse were ineffective at reducing alcohol consumption among college students. Yet, a focus on positive consequences for desirable behavior was shown to reduce at-risk drinking at one of the most challenging and high-risk environments – fraternity parties. Several partygoers (especially women) who did not expect to win the cash prize reported an appreciation for the cash lottery because it gave them an excuse to turn down an alcoholic beverage.

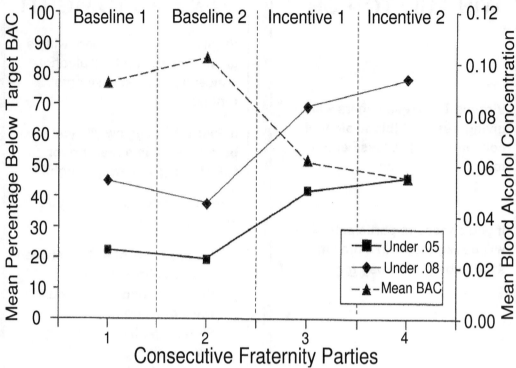

Figure 16.3. Intoxication levels during Baseline and Incentive conditions.

Paradigm Shift #3: From Good Intentions to Data-Driven Solutions

When designing alcohol interventions there's often the misconception good intentions produce good results. Just because an intervention makes sense or sounds good does not mean it works in practice. As we are fond of saying, "Without data you're just a jerk with an opinion." Yet, it seems too many attempts to prevent alcohol abuse are based on someone's common sense rather than empirical evidence.

Thus, AC4P is not about blindly trying to help people. Effective actively caring requires AC4P change agents to be knowledgeable about the problem, the relevant intervention research, and the people they are trying to influence or help. Hope and caring cannot substitute for data-driven solutions.

Multiple empirical studies demonstrate this very point. In fact, the parental punishment study detailed above provides a remarkable example. Well-intentioned parents without proper knowledge often increase alcohol consumption among their teenagers through misguided penalty strategies. In fact, this is quite common for interventions intended to reduce harm from excessive alcohol consumption.

As another example, one of the more intriguing research findings from CABS emerged from a study of students' alcohol consumption on prom night. Well-intentioned high-school faculty and staff designed several interventions to reduce drinking on prom night. These included assemblies, pledge cards, and school-sponsored after-prom parties.

The most noteworthy of these interventions applied Fatal Vision® goggles. These popular and expensive goggles ($150) are designed to simulate alcohol impairment of a designated level when worn. The particular intervention we investigated had students wear these goggles while driving a golf cart around a course marked by traffic cones. A sheriff's deputy sat in the passenger seat of the golf cart to answer students' questions.

This is an innovative and commonly-used intervention at high schools and universities. Students at the particular event we studied had a great time, laughing hysterically while their peers veered around the course.

By all *feel-good* indicators this was a huge success. School administrators felt strongly about repeating this event annually. Unfortunately, our data painted a very different picture than their perceptions.

Students who attended the drunk-goggle event were nearly twice as likely to report consuming alcohol on prom night as their peers not in attendance. This significant difference held even when controlling for students' previous history of alcohol consumption.

Of course, one field study is insufficient and inconclusive. Follow-up studies should be performed before making strong conclusions the "drunk goggles" increase students' consumption of alcoholic beverages. However, our underlying point is that despite well-intentioned efforts, many programs, interventions, treatments, and therapies lack practical effectiveness. Even worse, many of these efforts could actually promote the very behavior they are designed to decrease.

Bottom line: Passion and caring are the foundation of making a difference through AC4P, but these motivating feelings must be supplemented with empirical results from relevant research.

Paradigm Shift #4: From Blame to Empathy

We offer this paradigm shift with a point of caution. It's not intended to remove all responsibility from the drinker, but rather to encourage greater thoughtfulness regarding the effect alcohol has on the body. For example, many alcoholics have a strong desire to remove alcohol from their lives. Most are deeply troubled by the hurt they cause those around them through their drinking. In this case, simply blaming a drinker without considering the addictive properties of alcohol lacks compassion and does not suggest feasible intervention strategies.

Throughout this book, the importance of dispositional variables (e.g., person-states), situational variables (e.g., environmental context and behavioral consequences) and their interaction are revealed. AC4P is about taking the time and effort to understand each of these determinants of human behavior.

It's easy to blame a person for his/her behavior, but this is rarely an effective platform for offering help. AC4P requires the empathy to see the complete picture, and the compassion to act accordingly.

This is certainly true for alcohol-affected behavior. Alcohol consumption provides a context and a physiological change that makes many good people do very bad things. This is not only the case for individuals addicted to alcohol, but for any person with alcohol in their system.

Most people have experienced or observed the negative effects of intoxication.

Physical impairment is a consequence. Drunks may stumble, fall, or slur their words. Mental impairment is a consequence. Those intoxicated may have trouble remembering the occasion; they may say inappropriate things; and their cognitive ability may temporarily decline.

However, few people consider just how significant and fundamental these changes can be for an individual. Few people realize how profoundly someone's perceptions can be altered after only a few drinks. Research in CABS on sexual assault and victimization provides some relevant evidence.

Sexual Assault and Alcohol Consumption. It's estimated a startling one in four females experiences some form of sexual assault or victimization in college.[18] In approximately 85-90% of these sexual assaults the victim knew the attacker.[19] What is not surprising is almost all of these incidents involve alcohol.[20]

It's easy to blame the perpetrator of these horrendous acts, and this is understandable. However, addressing this problem with any hope of reducing the number of sexual assaults and victimizations requires a more comprehensive analysis.

To only examine the people who commit such acts ignores reality and context. Most of these individuals are at least slightly intoxicated at the time of the assault. This is hardly coincidental, but rather in part a result of the effects of alcohol. Research in CABS provides evidence for this very phenomenon from two studies.

In one study, 1,240 drinkers were read a brief vignette by a trained researcher. This story described a fictional, alcohol-related sexual assault between two characters, Steve and Julie. In the most extreme vignette, Steve has sex with Julie while she is completely incapacitated from alcohol. After hearing the vignette, researchers then asked participants several questions about the story.

Even those participants at very low levels of intoxication (BACs ≈ .020mL/L) were significantly more likely than completely sober individuals to say the sexual assault and victimization was not a rape, that Steve was not responsible, and this was a consensual encounter. It was not that individuals with higher BACs were more immoral, but rather that alcohol drastically changed their perceptions of a situation.

Recognizing Facial Emotions. Another CABS study examined the impact of alcohol consumption on the recognition of facial emotions. One's ability to quickly recognize emotions is viewed as a fundamental social skill, but is often taken for granted. In this study, researchers showed 695 participants pictures of several faces from a validated facial-emotion database and asked them to guess the emotion depicted.

On various trials the photo exposure was manipulated between one vs. three seconds and included one face vs. two faces. In the Two-Faces condition, one face served as a distracter and researchers asked for the perceived emotion of the second face. Participants who had consumed alcohol performed significantly worse than those who consumed no alcohol at identifying the negative emotions of *disgust* and *surprise*.

This inability to detect facial emotions was present even at low BACs and offers an explanation for the initiation and continuance of inappropriate sexual advances in a drinking setting. The antagonist may quite literally not be able to detect the negative reaction of the victim. This suggests negative facial expressions are not sufficient to ward off unwanted harassment from an intoxicated individual. The courage to verbalize direct disapproval is necessary.

Again, the purpose of this paradigm shift is not to justify inexcusable behavior, but rather to encourage AC4P intervention agents to consider the entire context of the alcohol consumption. Alcohol can have many pleasing effects, but it can also be the source of addiction and undesirable behavior change.

AC4P means going beyond the simple solution of blaming the drinker. Rather, it's about being empathic and showing compassion for the victims of alcohol. And this includes the drinker.

In Conclusion

Just like most colleges and universities, Virginia Tech has had its share of alcohol-related tragedies. If we as a country are going to seriously begin addressing the extreme rates of alcohol consumption at our nation's colleges and universities, drastic changes are necessary. The paradigm shifts detailed above provide a general blueprint for how AC4P can be a significant part of the solution.

We as a country cannot keep hoping the reactive, punitive, and rarely research-based laws and the legal system will fix our college-drinking epidemic. The optimal solution is not more laws or administrative policies, but actively-caring communities of people. The AC4P paradigm requires all of us to take personal responsibility and ownership of this serious societal problem.

Danny's life was lost because not a single person had the compassion and courage to step to the plate and actively care. We must stop asking why there is a college binge-drinking culture and start asking why more people are not willing to actively care for those around them.

Every alcohol-related death is preventable, and we have the power to drive alcohol-related college deaths to zero. The old way is not working, but the new way requires your competence, commitment, and courage. Are you ready and willing to help?

Notes

1. Hingson, R.W., Zha, W., & Weitzman, E.R. (2009). Magnitude of and trends in alcohol-related mortality and morbidity among U.S. college students ages 18-24: 1998-2005. *Journal of Studies on Alcohol and Drugs, Supplement 16*, 12-20; Slutske, W.S. (2005). Alcohol use disorders among U.S. college students and their non-college-attending peers. *Archives of General Psychiatry*, 62, 321-327; Slutske, W.S., Hunter-Carter, E.E., Nabors-Oberg, R.E., Sher, K.J., Bucholz, K.K., Madden, A.A., & Heath, A.C. (2004). Do college students drink more than their non-college-attending peers? Evidence from a population-based longitudinal female twin study. *Journal of Abnormal Psychology, 113*(4), 530-540.

2. U. S. Department of Health and Human Services. Healthy People 2010. Washington D.C.: USDHHS 2000:26-29

3. U.S. Department of Health and Human Services. Healthy People 2020. Washington D.C. Retrieved

from http://www.healthypeople.gov/2020/topicsobjectives2020/pdfs/HP2020objectives.pdf

4. Schwarz, N. (2007). Retrospective and concurrent self-reports: The rationale for real-time data capture. In Stone, A.A., Shiffman, S.S., Atienza, A., & Nebeling, L. (Eds.). The science of real-time data capture: Self-reports in health research (pp. 11-26). New York, NY: Oxford University Press; Schwarz, N. (1999). Self-reports: How the questions shape the answers. *American Psychologist, 54,* 93-105.

5. Kerr, W.C., & Stockwell, T. (2012). Understanding standard drinks and drinking guidelines. *Drug and Alcohol Review, 2,* 200-205.; Lemmens, P. H. (1994). The alcohol content of self-report and "standard" drinks. *Addiction, 89,* 593-601.

6. Shillington, A.M., Clapp, J.D., Reed, M.B., & Woodruff, S.I. (2011). Adolescent alcohol use self-report stability: A decade of panel study data. *Journal of Child & Adolescent Substance Abuse, 20,* 63-81; Waterton, J.J., & Duffy, J.C. (1984). A comparison of computer interviewing techniques and traditional methods in the collection of self-report alcohol consumption data in a field study. *International Statistical Review, 52(2),* 173-182; Whitford, J.L., Widner, S.C., Mellick, D., & Elkins, R. L. (2009). Self-report of drinking compared to objective markers of alcohol consumption. *The American Journal of Drug and Alcohol Abuse, 35,* 55-58.

7. National Highway Traffic Safety Administration (2012). *Alcohol-impaired driving.* DOT HS 811 606. Department of Transportation. Retrieved from www-nrd.nhtsa.dot.gov/Pubs/811606.pdf

8. National Highway Traffic Safety Administration (2004). *Traffic safety facts: Young drivers.* DOT HS 809 774. Department of Transportation. Retrieved from http://www-nrd.nhtsa.dot.gov/pdf/nrd-30/NCSA/TSF2003/809774.pdf

9. Centers for Disease Control and Prevention (2011). *Vital digns: Alcohol-impaired driving among adults–United States, 2010.* Retrieved from www.cdc.gov/mmwr/preview/mmwrhtml/mm6039a4.htm

10. Rauch, W.J., Zador, P.L., Ahlin, E.M., Howard, J.M., Frissell, K.C., & Duncan, G.D. (2010). Risk of alcohol-impaired driving recidivism among first offenders and multiple offenders. *American Journal of Public Health, 100(5),* 919-924; Rauch, W.J., Zador, P.L., Ahlin, E.M., et al. (2002). Any first alcohol-impaired driving event is a significant and substantial predictor of future recidivism. In D. R., Mayhew, & C. Dussault (Eds). *Proceedings of the 16ᵗʰ International Conference on Alcohol, Drugs and Traffic Safety.* Montreal, Quebec: Council on Alcohol, Drugs and Traffic Safety, 161-167.

11. Nichols, J.L, & Ross, H.L. (1990). The effectiveness of legal sanctions in dealing with drinking drivers. *Alcohol, Drugs and Driving, 6(2),* 33-55.

12. Brehm, S.S., & Brehm, J.W. (1981). *Psychological reactance: A theory of freedom and control.* New York, NY: Academic Press

13. Aronson, E., Wilson, T.D., & Akert, R.M. (2013). *Social psychology* (8th Edition). Pearson Education: Upper Saddle River, NJ.

14. Glindemann, K.E., & Geller, E.S. (2003). A systematic assessment of intoxication at university parties: Effects of the environmental context. *Environment and Behavior, 35*(5), 655-664.

15. Glindemann, K.E., Wiegand, D.M., & Geller, E.S. (2007). Celebratory drinking and intoxication: A contextual influence on alcohol consumption. *Environment and Behavior, 39*(3), 352-366.

16. Fournier, A. K., Ehrhart, I. J., Glindemann,K.E.,& Geller, E. S. (2004). Intervening to decrease alcohol abuse at university parties: Differential reinforcement of intoxication level. *Behavior Modification, 28,* 167-181.

17. Glindeman, K. E., Ehrhart, I. J., Drake, E. A., & Geller, E. S. (2006). Reducing excessive alcohol consumption at university fraternity parties: A cost-effective incentive/reward intervention. *Addictive Behaviors, 32*(1), 39-48.

18. U.S. Department of Justice: Office of Justice Programs (2005). *Sexual assault on campus: What colleges and universities are doing about it.* Retrieved from https://www.ncjrs.gov/pdffiles1/ nij/205521.pdf

19. Koss, M.C., Gidycz, C., & Wisniewski, N. (1987). The scope of Rape: Incidence and prevalence of sexual aggression and victimization in a national sample of higher education students. *Journal of Consulting and Clinical Psychology, 55*(2), 162-170.

20. Abbey, A., McAuslan, P., & Ross, L.T. (1998). Sexual assault perpetration by college men: The role of alcohol, misperception of sexual intent, and sexual beliefs and experiences. *Journal of Social and Clinical Psychology, 17*, 167-195.

CHAPTER 17

Actively Caring to Prevent Identity Theft:
Research in the community

Christopher Downing, Jr.

I REMEMBER IT LIKE it was yesterday. On June 15th, 2005, I receive a phone call from my dad that leaves me stunned. The phone call starts out more awkward than usual. As our phone conversation continues, a deep sigh comes from my dad. I take a deep breath and ask, "Why do you sound down?" "I was a victim of credit-card fraud a couple of days ago," he says in a low-pitched voice that didn't sound like my dad.

A person posing as my dad had used his credit card to purchase more than $3,500 worth of merchandise in stores. Fortunately, this criminal was caught, but not until after the financial and psychological damage was left for my dad to clean up.

Following that phone call, I called my dad every day to see how he was coping with the identity theft, and to find out the steps he was taking to reclaim his identity. I figured it would all be resolved in a couple of weeks. Boy, was I wrong!

The process was an ordeal. The frustration in his voice came across every day when we talked. In the end it took 46 days for my dad to restore his identity and clean up negative information on his credit report. During that time, his bank accounts were frozen. He couldn't pay his bills because all the money from his job was directly deposited into the frozen bank account.

He was forced to borrow from relatives until he could get back on his feet. Compounding his frustration, he had to spend hours on the phone going through various channels to reach the proper authorities about his predicament.

It was hard for me to watch my dad struggle to reclaim his identity. He was the first victim of credit-card fraud I knew, and I understood very little about this crime. I searched the literature to learn about the harm to my dad. The things I uncovered were baffling and disheartening. For one thing, there are so many people in my dad's predicament – unwitting victims of credit-card fraud.

The Credit-Card Fraud Epidemic in the U.S.

Credit-card fraud occurs when a thief illegally charges goods and services in another person's name by using a credit card or any similar payment mechanism in a transaction. Credit-card fraud is one of the most frequently committed types of identity-theft crimes. Of the 250,854 complaints reported to the Federal Trade Commission (FTC) in 2010, credit-card fraud made up 15% of those cases.[1] Credit-card fraud has been the leading identity-theft category reported to the FTC since 2000, with the exception of one year.

This is a crime that usually goes underreported by individuals because many do not know they've been victimized. Victims do not usually find out they've had their identity stolen until they receive a credit-card statement in the mail, are disapproved for a loan, get rejected for a job, or lose their job.

On average it takes 13 months after the theft for the average victim to realize his or her identity has been stolen.[2] By that time, the thief has likely moved on and assumed someone else's identity. And like my dad, victims must straighten up all the damage left by the thief.

Credit-card fraud impacts companies as well as individuals. Every year, the business community loses between $40,000 and $92,000 per individual in fraudulent transactions.[3] The total amount of money stolen is devastating. Credit-card fraud removes millions of dollars from the American economy annually.[2]

Research in the Center for Applied Behavior Systems

As I read through the literature to educate myself on credit-card fraud, I was bewildered. Aside from some common-sense ways to protect yourself, there's no clear-cut solution for how we as a community can prevent this crime. The various sources I read offered tips to individuals on ways to prevent their identity from being stolen. But, unfortunately, the preventive strategies did not work for most victims, partly because the steps were not infallible.

Some of the strategies fail to take into account: a) most information on a victim is obtained through a lost or stolen purse or checkbook; b) most thieves have regular access to victims' houses and/or belongings (since they are usually acquaintances); and c) people cannot keep track of everything mailed to them. My dad followed most preventive strategies, just like many other victims. But identity thieves can still borrow and use peoples' names.

Reading the literature, I was struck by the fact researchers and law-enforcement officers had to beg retailers to check the identification (ID) of their customers when a credit purchase was being made. If retailers would just check customers' ID, credit-card fraud would decrease markedly. As I read this repeatedly, I wondered why retailers did not look out for their customer's safety. Did they not care? Did they simply not know how to actively care?

Disappointed by my literature search and reflecting on my dad's experience and the stories told by many victims, I decided to research ways to prevent credit-card fraud, and therefore reduce its concomitant consequences for hard-working people like my dad.

As a Ph.D. student in industrial/organizational psychology and a research assistant in the Center for Applied Behavior Systems (CABS), I knew I could make a difference with behavioral science. If I could somehow get cashiers actively involved in checking the ID of credit-card users, then I could reduce the number of people ending up like my dad and many other victims.

My mentor Scott Geller and I discussed community-based interventions to activate and motivate cashiers to actively care for identity theft in the check-out process. But, first we assessed the Virginia Tech (VT) community to examine the extent the ID of credit-card users was checked.

Credit-Card Fraud Assessment Study

For this assessment study research assistants in CABS ventured into the VT community and collect data on normal credit purchases.[4] Research assistants went into stores (ranging from local restaurants to Wal-Mart) and made credit-card purchases for items they needed. Once they left the store, the research assistants noted inconspicuously on a data sheet whether the cashier had checked their ID.

Data were collected for eight months. The results of this assessment showed the VT community was in dire need of an intervention. Out of 1,789 credit purchases, only 102 (5.7%) customers were checked for ID.

In a follow-up field study, Dr. Geller and I attempted to address the low ID-checking behavior of the cashiers in the community.[4] We had research assistants make purchases with credit cards again and record ID-checking behavior. This time we studied the impact of a simple prevention intervention with an A-B-A (Baseline-Intervention-Withdrawal) design.

Specifically, after collecting Baseline data, research assistants placed a "PLEASE CHECK PHOTO ID" sticker prompt on their credit cards. This prompting intervention failed. We did not find an increase in cashiers' ID-checking behavior as a result of this prompt. The research assistants reported that cashiers usually did not seem to notice the sticker. Perhaps, we need to make cashiers more aware of their potential to actively care about this issue?

Involving Cashiers to Actively Care

Our next intervention focused on getting cashiers to change the safety culture of their workplace. We aimed to get the cashiers more involved in checking customers' IDs. Using a goal-setting and feedback intervention, we targeted two large grocery stores where ID-checking was particularly low in our earlier observations. One store received an A-B-A reversal design and the other served as a control.[5]

Our CABS research assistants observed the cashiers' ID-checking behavior in these grocery stores for 84 consecutive days. After 39 days of Baseline observation at the Intervention store, I worked with the cashiers to establish a store ID-checking percentage goal. Then, I provided the cashiers with daily feedback on their progress toward achieving their group goal of 15% throughout the Intervention. The Intervention was removed during the Withdrawal phase to examine its durability.

As shown in Figure 17.1 on the following page, we found the cashiers' ID-checking behavior increased from 0.2% at Baseline to 9.7% during the Intervention phase. But when the goal-setting and feedback intervention was removed, the cashiers' ID-checking behavior returned to low Baseline levels (2.3%).

Our intervention made a significant difference but its beneficial effects did not continue after the accountability system was removed. At the Control store, the percentages of identification-checked purchases were 0.3%, 0.4%, and 0.7%, respectively during the A-B-A phases at the Intervention store.

Cashiers' ID-checking behavior can indeed be increased, as the goal-setting intervention showed. By getting cashiers involved in setting goals and holding them accountable, we increased their prosocial behavior on behalf of the identity-theft issue.

Although we only increased cashiers' ID-checking behavior to 9.7%, there is reason for optimism. Consider where the cashiers' ID-checking behavior started. I believe the intervention could have produced greater increases in the target behavior were it not for the cashiers' familiarity with customers. The intervention was conducted in a grocery store where the cashiers frequently interacted with the same loyal shoppers.

Also, promotional events held by the stores interfered with the cashiers' ID-

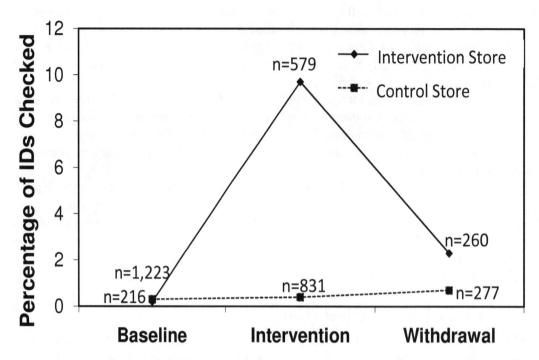

Figure 17.1. The ID-checking of cashiers in the intervention and control stores.[5]

checking behavior. During both the Intervention and the Withdrawal phases, events promoting "Feed the Hungry" and "Environmental Sustainability" were held at both stores. During each event, cashiers were asked to perform additional duties beyond checking out customers. Cashiers might have neglected asking customers for their ID because they were trying to incorporate two donation-soliciting behaviors into their regular check-out routines.

Ongoing Research

The intervention described above focused on creating an AC4P culture within a large grocery-store chain. Then, Dr. Geller and I decided to put the responsibility back on the customer. Specifically, we attempted to increase the impact of the prompt, thereby encouraging customers to actively care for their own safety.

To make the prompt stronger, we used two messages that contained both an antecedent and a consequence instead of only an antecedent. Specifically, the messages read "Check my ID to PROMOTE identity security" and "Check my ID to PREVENT identity theft".

Note that the message in these prompts contained either a positive or negative consequence. We are investigating which consequence is more effective at influencing a cashier's ID-checking behavior – to *promote* security vs. *prevent* theft. We are also comparing a message with no implied consequence, "Please check my ID," with the message about that specify a consequence. Our hypothesis is that messages with a specified consequence will result in more ID-checking than the prompt without a consequence. (See Chapter 1.)

In Conclusion

Credit-card fraud is a major problem, something I did not realize until it hit home after my dad became a victim. I urge others to help me out in this endeavor. I believe a lot more needs to be done to protect the security of individuals.

Future research still needs to be conducted to increase cashiers' AC4P behaviors relevant to protecting customers from credit-card fraud. Indeed, credit-card fraud can be decreased markedly with more actively caring from the community, including both customers and cashiers.

Our survey research showed that a majority of customers do not mind the inconvenience of having their IDs checked.[5] If cashiers knew most customers actually appreciated ID checking, they would likely do it more often.

Perhaps, one solution to this critical societal problem is for cashiers and customers to be more reflective than reflexive when credit cards are used for purchases. Indeed, customers should ask cashiers to check their IDs in order to make ID-checking behavior the norm.

Notes

1. Federal Trade Commission (2011, March 26). *Consumer sentinel network data book for January-December 2010.* Retrieved from http://www.ftc.gov/sentinel/reports/sentinel-annual-reports/sentinel-cy2010.pdf

2. Abagnale, F.W. (2007). *Stealing your life.* New York, NY: Broadway Books.

3. Pastore, M. (2004, November 19). *The identity theft prevention and recovery guide.* Retrieved, from http://www.insideid.com/idtheft/article.php/3438261

4. Downing, C. O., Jr., & Geller, E. S. (2009). Behavior analysts address credit-card fraud. *Behavior Analysis Digest International, 21*(4), 13-14.

5. Downing, C. O., Jr., & Geller, E. S. (2013). A goal-setting and feedback intervention to increase ID-checking behavior: An assessment of both social validity and behavioral impact. *Journal of Organizational Behavior Management, 32,* 297-306.

CHAPTER 18

From Incarcerating Felons to AC4P

Bobby Kipper

GROWING UP IN a southeastern Virginia city, my vision was to become a police officer in my community. My poor, loving family taught me to look out for injustices within our community and do what I could to stop them.

At the age of 20, I became a member of the Police Department of Newport News, Virginia. Early in my career, I believed the number of individuals arrested and punished for their crimes was the best way to measure the impact of successful police work. On a warm day in early June 1983, though, my career path and life-calling changed after a conversation with a little girl at an elementary school.

Per a request from my supervisor, I visited a nearby school to deliver a presentation to a number of young children enrolled in the First Step Educational Program. My talk was on the value of citizenship. Following my presentation, I led the children through a question-and-answer period. To my surprise, the children did not ask questions as prompted, but rather chose to relay stories about their lives.

The last story of the day came from a little girl with cornrows in her hair and wearing a tattered dress. The girl raised her hand, and when I called for her comments she said, "At night, momma forces me to sleep under my bed." Immediately, I was concerned about this child's welfare and possible child abuse or neglect. I reached out further by asking the girl for her name. She stated her name was Keisha.

When I asked Keisha to tell me more, she looked at me with eyes watering and replied boldly, "At night, momma forces me to sleep under the bed so when the bullets from those mean drug dealers come in my window they won't hurt me." Stunned, I concluded the assembly and left the school.

I sat in my patrol car in the school parking lot and reflected on my short, powerful interaction with Keisha. I thought, "How is it possible a six-year-old girl cannot go to sleep at night in her own bed without fear of being killed by gunfire?"

Angered and emotional from that encounter, I searched my own soul and reflected on our impact as police officers. I remember realizing, *we can't arrest our way out of life's social issues.*

Right then and there I renewed my life's mission. I will impact communities nationwide by promoting positive and proactive approaches to reducing crime. I will design intervention programs for those impacted by community violence. Violence is a process, not an event; and to stop that process, we must start with AC4P behavior.

AC4P in Richmond, Virginia

Following my retirement from the Newport News Police Department in 2000, the Attorney General of Virginia, Jerry Kilgore, selected me as Director of Virginia's Gang Reduction Program. I researched gang crime and violence issues, as well as the devastating impact gangs and violence had on individuals and communities.

In 2004, I was invited by the U.S. Department of Justice's Office of Juvenile Justice and Delinquency Prevention to direct a major gang reduction program in Richmond.

My role was to develop and implement a community strategy that would have a lasting impact on gang-related violent crime.

While in Richmond, I developed a concept that would later be known as the P.I.E.R. (Prevention, Intervention, Enforcement and Re-Entry) Program. The program focused primarily on prevention and intervention, and sought to raise the quality of life for ordinary citizens. In turn, this encouraged them to work hard to improve their communities. The success of the P.I.E.R. program, which later became known as G.R.I.P. (Gang Reduction and Intervention Program), is due largely to individuals actively caring for people.

One of the best examples of AC4P in Richmond can be attributed to a local hospital. The hospital provides a van that travels regularly into the community and seeks out citizens needing immediate health care. This project alone led to thousands of people triaged, and a number of them saved from life-threatening illnesses.

In return, these citizens began to take stake in their community and force out those committing evil deeds. By caring for basic human needs and driving out those who would threaten it, high-crime neighborhoods became stable and citizens felt more secure. The beneficial impact of AC4P was obvious.

Another major form of AC4P in Richmond came from the faith-based community. A total of 11 faith-based partners participated in providing services for men and women in Richmond, which included everything from a basic food pantry to job training with placement and continuing education.

Individuals from all walks of faith came together in a united effort to literally wrap their arms around people, including those who had been involved in an ongoing criminal lifestyle. Participants moved beyond the issue of personal judgment and embraced the issue of human rights. By displaying interpersonal, heartfelt support, many lives were transformed.

Just two years after G.R.I.P. was initiated, the crime rate in Richmond fell by 35 percent, and the homicide rate fell by an overwhelming 85 percent.[1] The city went from one of the most dangerous in the nation to a place of thriving businesses and a heightened quality of life for its citizens, thanks to a number of individuals and organizations banding together to unite and become a force for good. The Richmond effort exemplifies the positive impact of AC4P.

On a personal level, the Richmond experience had an enormous impact on me. It reinforced the notion that we, as a society, can no longer deem people *bad* due to their mistakes, nor can we throw away a soul of value simply because of an individual's past behavior.

Our charge must be to care first and address issues as a human process before they turn into negative events. Saving communities must become an issue of saving people. These are issues of the heart and not issues of the government.

Committing crime and violence is a personal decision. In order to impact that decision and save possible victims, we must appeal beyond the social concerns of people and reach deep inside each one of them, actively care, and support positive decisions and lifestyles. By recognizing and rewarding people for AC4P, the end result will be a transitional climate of good over evil, and peace over interpersonal conflict, bullying, and violence.

The National Calling

As a result of my paradigm shift toward proactive intervention and observing the success of the AC4P efforts in Richmond, I formed the National Center for the Prevention of Community Violence (NCPCV). Our Center seeks to teach others that violence is a process that can be interrupted and not an inevitable event. Our Center focuses not on problems, but rather on finding evidence-based solutions to reduce community violence.

Since its inception, NCPCV has accomplished a number of initiatives. Recently, I co-authored a book with Bud Ramey that focuses on solutions to the growing epidemic of gang violence in America. [2] It provides 100 effective strategies to address the issue.

In addition, NCPCV is currently piloting the GreenZone™ Program in York County, Virginia and Phoenix, Arizona. The GreenZone™ concept encourages individuals to treat each other with civility and respect, and to stay in the "green zone" of behavior.

Within the "green zone," citizens use a normal tone and volume of speech, compliment and encourage each other, question others only in an informal manner, and joke only in a non-harmful way. The GreenZone™ is a tool that helps foster civility and aims to stop the process of violence before it becomes an event.

Virginia Tech and AC4P

In the fall of 2011, my daughter became a student at Virginia Tech (VT). One day, early in her VT experience, she called to alert me of a unique approach to violence and injury prevention she felt would interest me greatly. She asked me to reach out to Dr. E. Scott Geller who was one of her professors, and inquire about the AC4P Movement. I quickly learned Dr. Geller directs VT's Center for Applied Behavior Systems (CABS) – the research and outreach domain of the Movement.

Since then, NCPCV and CABS have united, and together work to empower and energize each of the organization's missions to apply evidence-based interventions to cultivate AC4P cultures. I look forward to seeing communities across our nation and worldwide transformed by the power of AC4P.

Notes

1. Charron, T., Floren, R., Jansen, S., & LaBahn, D. (2006) *Prosecutor's comprehensive gang response model.* American Prosecutors Research Institute, Alexandria, VA (p. 33).

2. Kipper, B., & Ramey, B. (2011). *No COLORS: 100 ways to stop gangs from taking away our communities.* New York, NY: Morgan James Publishing.

CHAPTER 19

My 60/60 AC4P Challenge:
When actions speak louder than words

Joanne Dean Geller

LIFE HAS BEEN a delightful ride for me. Sure, there were hard times that could have knocked me down. But the example my parents set with their style of living added appreciation and resilience to how I have lived and handled my life's challenges. I've now lived longer than my mother, who passed away when she was 57. Everyday my heart is warmed when I think of her, wishing I could hold her and tell her how much she has meant to me. She was absolutely an actively-caring person, even when suffering physical disability from a stroke and battling cancer for many years.

My mother had an optimistic aura that was contagious. She never pre-judged anyone negatively, but rather took time to understand the other person's perspective. She was a talented writer with a gift of expressing herself through poetry. She always put her family first and would sacrifice her own needs for ours.

While a mom and career person, she still found time to volunteer at church, and serve as a Councilwoman for our town. She initiated many programs to protect the environment. Indeed, our town planted trees in her memory and placed eight park benches around the fair grounds with her name on them. She made time for everyone and our house was always filled with young people who needed a place to be.

Remembering my mom inspires me to offer special support for the AC4P Movement. I'm proud to be continuing her legacy of AC4P.

I've faced potential life-destroying experiences, but the example of my mom helped me overcome these personal hardships. I had an ovarian tumor removed in high school that led to years of surgeries because of serious adhesions. My intestines had burst a number of times because of this, requiring me to be placed on a stomach pump for three months from these complications.

The doctors were sure I would need a colostomy bag for the rest of my life, but fortunately, I did not. Five years later, the adhesions attached my intestines to my diaphragm and I thought my life was over. But again, competent physicians fixed me up.

Ending a romantic relationship resulted in a person taking his life on my birthday. He left me $100,000 in his only life-insurance policy, but I chose to leave that money to his three sons. I endured the horrible process of terminating my child. Plus, I gave up a meaningful position because I would not compromise my values and tolerate sexual harassment.

I know we all deal with challenges throughout our lives, but for some reason I have been blessed with the ability to be an optimist no matter what. I am so grateful for that.

My 60/60 Commitment

I viewed turning 60 as a gift, and I wanted to share this gift with others. With new knowledge about psychological and behavioral science, as taught to me by Scott Geller,

I now have labels for my disposition to actively care, including courage, commitment, compassion, and self-motivation. Understanding the science behind each of these words provides me with insight to actively care more effectively.

My move to Blacksburg, Virginia four years ago gave me the opportunity to work with faculty and students in the Department of Psychology at Virginia Tech. Graduate and undergraduate students have told me I have been an example for the actions implied by the AC4P concept. This encouraged me to do an AC4P act of kindness for a stranger or friend each of the 60 days prior to turning 60, February 27th, 2010.

This became well-known as "Joanne's 60/60 Challenge". It was actually more of a challenge than I had expected. For me, AC4P behavior is much more than holding a door open for a friend or stranger. It involves reflectively thinking about ways to go out of my daily routine to do something special for another person. I regularly go out of my way to impact other people's lives in beneficial ways; but to give up personal time for AC4P behavior "everyday" was a different story.

My AC4P commitment began on January 1, 2010 and I was enthused. I am an outgoing person, comfortable speaking to almost anyone. But even as an extrovert, I found it challenging to come up with intentional acts of kindness everyday that were beyond the norm. I shared my daily experiences via email and phone calls with a supportive group of close friends who helped keep me accountable to achieve my 60/60 goal.

The Beginning

It's New Year's Day and I'm driving through the quiet town of Blacksburg. There's my first AC4P opportunity right in front of my eyes. Over the past two years, I had observed a young man systematically collecting litter from the sidewalk. I assumed he worked for the town. Now some might judge this "litter-control" job to be insignificant, but I've always appreciated that Blacksburg values keeping the town litter-free and has provided funds for an individual to make this happen.

So there's my "litter control" man picking up papers on New Year's Day. No one's in sight. I pull into the post-office parking lot and run into the local Starbucks to purchase a gift card for this gentleman.

Excited, I run up to him, and actually startle him. I ask for his name and proceed to tell Jason how much I appreciate his efforts to keep our town clean.

With eyes wide open and a friendly smile, Jason says, "No one has ever said anything like that to me". We shake hands and I give him the gift card. I then explain the AC4P Movement and that he's my first choice for the New Year.

What a wonderful feeling that experience gave me, and appeared to give Jason. To this day, two years later, we wave every time we see each other. One simple act of kindness and our brief conversation remind me of the power of putting AC4P words into action.

Meeting My 60/60 Challenge

I continued my daily AC4P behaviors for the next 59 days. On some days AC4P situations just happened, and some days I had to look hard and create opportunities.

My acts of kindness ranged from shoveling mounds of snow for elderly neighbors to cooking meals for families. It was a pleasure to help strangers load groceries into their cars, and to watch a smile come to the face's of cashier's after telling them I appreciate the work they do.

I took a number of days to help friends clean their homes, and I even drove my massage therapist from Blacksburg to Charlotte, North Carolina to give a massage to the wife of a special friend with ALS. (See Chapter 26.)

These are just a few examples of my daily AC4P experiences. Believe me, they were all well received. Some days nearly ended without finding an opportunity for AC4P behavior, and I was challenged to intentionally find someone in need of AC4P behavior.

All in all, I performed a significant AC4P action everyday for the 60 days leading up to my 60th birthday.[1] I reported each of these acts of kindness on the AC4P website for my friends and colleagues to see. Soon after my birthday, leaders of the AC4P Movement gave me a book with 60 AC4P stories, actions reflecting the achievement of my 60/60 challenge.

In Conclusion

An important lesson I learned from this two-month experience: We should appreciate all the people who donate their time on our behalf. We all want an AC4P culture of compassion. Right in front of our eyes people are already donating their personal time to help others. People who come to mind are fireman, first-aid squad members, hospital volunteers, speakers from AA programs, members of the Humane Society and many community leaders.

Growing up in the 1950s, it seemed easier to make time for such groups. In today's fast-pace life it's difficult for many people to dedicate time to others beyond their immediate family. This is why I'm thrilled to help ignite and inspire AC4P behaviors that were seemingly more common in the "good old days".

This story is about putting AC4P words into action, because our actions do speak louder than our words. The AC4P Movement is about bringing to life words of interpersonal caring, and getting on board with volunteering our time on behalf of others, including our own families.

We all have a lifetime to enjoy, and such joy is greatly enhanced when it's shared with others. There are many people out there, young and old, who can benefit greatly from a simple intentional AC4P act of kindness. And when you give some of your precious time to actively care, the enhanced boost in your own self-esteem, optimism, and sense of belonging is priceless.

Note

1. Meeting the 60-day challenge actually required me to continue my daily AC4P behaviors until March 1st, three days after my 60th birthday. But we still celebrated meeting my challenge on February 27th.

CHAPTER 20

The Wayward Safety Expert:
When is help from others AC4P?

Dave Johnson

IN EARLY JUNE, 2012, I made my getaway from the annual meeting of the American Society of Safety Engineers in Denver, Colorado for a five-day road trip through the Dakotas. Very early on the second day, with the sun just starting to climb, I slipped from a craggy clay rock formation in the Badlands National Park in South Dakota and took a seriously bad tumble of which I remember almost nothing.

Next thing I know I'm lying on rocks in a small ravine, my camera ten yards behind me, the camera lens ten yards in front of me. I propped myself up, felt blood dripping into my right eye, and realized my right leg was useless. It was very weak and painful; I thought the femur was broken in my thigh.

No way was I going to stand and walk or hobble out. Seems I had bruises, contusions and abrasions everywhere. I would be at the mercy of others. This kind of vulnerability and humility I always try to avoid. I don't like other folks going out of their way for me; very seldom do I ask for favors. Why? I'm quiet. A much better observer than performer. In a band I'd be the bass player. I like to do my thing without attention.

Well, throw that philosophy down some Badlands crevasse. My tumble triggered more acts of AC4P behavior in one morning, later turning into several days, than I ever experienced in five-plus decades here on the planet. For instance:

The Belgian tourist who discovered me, shielded me from the sun, gave me water, and exhibited a welcomed sense of humor throughout.

Then there was the grandfather with three grandchildren running around, who also provided water and assessed my damages.

His son, whose cell-phone luckily had reception, called in the professional active caretakers.

AC4P Behavior from Professionals

There are of course people who actively care for a living and get paid for it. Teachers, police, fire fighters, social workers, nurses, EMTs, the list of those who serve and get compensated for it goes on. For the most part they don't get paid a lot, which tells me they are drawn to AC4P jobs, not for the paycheck, but because of the natural rewards they get from helping others.

A photo from a newspaper story about my rescue shows ten of these AC4P pros loading me into a chopper for a 75-mile ride to the Rapid City, South Dakota regional hospital. You can barely see me on the stretcher for all the folks lifting the stretcher, holding my head firm, giving me water, opening doors, judging best how to fit me in the chopper, and asking again and again if I'm doing okay.

Let's see, we had ambulance crews from nearby Kadoka and Philip, the Jackson County Sheriff's Office, the South Dakota Highway Patrol, a Black Hills Life Flight helicopter crew, and the National Guard. "Isn't that a little bit of overkill for a guy who

just had a bruised leg?" a reader posted in his newspaper after reading my story. Easy for you to say, fella, four weeks later I'm still feeling that bruise.

But in fact all those folks were not on the scene to actively care for me. Some did try to make me feel better, saying, "This happens all the time. You're just the first this season. Five, six times a year we fetch people who are trapped, can't get up or down." Others seemed to be simply hanging out.

I didn't tell anyone I was the Editor of a safety magazine. I feared actively caring would turn into actively ribbing. Who could blame them?

The Life Flight chopper ride to Rapid City was smooth and fast. A fellow in a helmet and visor sat right next to me the whole flight, checking and checking again if I was comfortable and needed anything.

Is Helping Others Always AC4P Behavior?

I must say my admiration for this AC4P behavior diminished a few weeks later when Life Flight sent me a bill for $30,000 for their service. This brings up an interesting point about AC4P and serving others. When one gets paid for providing that service, or charges for the service, helpful as it may be, I don't see it as an act of AC4P.

Scott Geller defines AC4P behavior as going *above and beyond* the call of duty. Well, the Life Flight crew was simply doing its duty. It's a business that provides a service for a fee. It didn't go above and beyond anything. Good, competent, compassionate and if need be courageous guys, but I would not attach them to the AC4P Movement. If that were the case, the Movement would include every fire department, rescue squad and nurse in the country.

The same kind of professional AC4P occurred throughout my stay in the Rapid City Regional Hospital. From the moment three nurses whisked me off the chopper and took me straight to X-Ray, I received commendable care. The nurses were certainly active, they moved fast, and they obviously cared about my well-being, but we expect this kind of caring in hospitals.

This hospital did offer a service I did not expect: Two so-called Patient Liaison Officers helped put me at ease by giving me a list of travel agents I could pick from to arrange to get me from Rapid City to Denver on Sunday to make my original flight back home to Philadelphia.

And they gave me a list of 20 nearby hotels and motels where I could stay after the hospital released me. I'd need a room for Friday and Saturday nights. And a place with room service because I wasn't getting around very well.

These two Patient Liaison Officers were definitely *active* in their care for me, hustling up these lists of travel agents and hotels. Their demeanor was very kind, warm and encouraging, as in, "Don't worry, we'll get you out of here". Which was exactly what I needed to hear.

Their final act of caring was a bit unusual. All my clothes were in my rental car, and the whereabouts of that rental was a mystery as I prepared to leave the hospital. "Don't worry, we'll scrounge up some clothes for you," they told me. So I left the hospital wearing a XXL pink t-shirt, gray sweatpants I could swim in, and a pair of socks, without shoes. My feet were swollen and I couldn't fit into my sneakers, the only clothes I had.

Did these Patient Liaison Officers go above and beyond their call of duty? For the most part *no*, but I don't think their job description called for outfitting patients in pink tees, sweats and socks.

The hospital shuttle bus driver did go above and beyond the call of his duty. When we rolled up to the Best Western where I'd be staying, he said, "Wait here (like where was I going to go?) and let me see if I can get a wheelchair for you." Minutes later there he was, wheelchair in hand. He loaded me into the chair and wheeled me up to the front desk.

The two girls behind the counter were smiling and out-of-their-way kind, probably prompted by my bizarre appearance: the huge pink tee and the sweats and socks, and my blood splattered face, bulging black eye, matted hair and bloody palms, wrists and forearms. I must have looked like a homeless refugee from some slasher flick.

The hotel shuttle bus driver also went above and beyond. He drove me to the Rapid City airport Sunday morning, carrying my backpack, laptop and duffel bag that had arrived the day before courtesy of Enterprise Car Rental.

Enterprise ended up towing my rental from the parking lot where I left it in the Badlands, across South Dakota to the Enterprise branch in Rapid City, where one fellow cleared out all my gear and dropped it off at my hospital room. He did an excellent job; I didn't lose a thing.

The Enterprise employees certainly did something out of the ordinary for me, but I wouldn't say they had *caring* in mind. What about the fellow who gathered up all my stuff, packed it nicely, and brought it to my hospital room? I'd say his personal touch and concern for getting me everything qualified as actively caring. He didn't have to be so organized and thorough.

There's no way I could have made my way across the country that Sunday without the help of the airlines, which put me in the most comfortable seats they could find. And the wheelchair pathfinders – those folks wheeled me from the gate to my seat, from my seat across the vast Denver airport to my next flight, and then deposited me at my seat.

Then in Philadelphia, the woman who wheeled me to baggage claim, waited with me outside until my wife drove up. She was so patient and helpful. I tipped her $20. Does that gratuity disqualify her as an actively-caring person? We don't tip actively-caring people, do we? Isn't that outside the volunteer ethos of the Movement?

A Wife's Duty to Actively Care

For the past four weeks my wife, Suze, has been a spinning top of AC4P behaviors. She's my coach, my cheerleader, my driver, my cook, my errand-runner, and my line of defense against well-meaning neighbors who I'm often too tired to tell the same story over again. She keeps my family and friends updated on my progress, and when I get depressed, she gets me out of the house and neighborhood.

Now I ask for a ruling from the AC4P Movement leaders: Is my wife actively caring? Or is she simply doing a very fine job at what she signed up for those many years ago when we married: taking care of me in good times and bad, for better or worse? Her so-called "duty".

We family members can be pretty demanding and set the bar pretty high in terms of the caring we expect from others in the family in our times of need. In these cases I see AC4P being taken for granted. By nature I take little for granted and say Suze is doing one hell of an AC4P job.

Part IV: Personal Stories of AC4P Behavior

Joanne Dean Geller

ACTIVELY CARING IS A get-well card sent to a friend or even a stranger, a cup of tea and a listening ear, returning found merchandise to its rightful owner, or shoveling a pile of snow out from an elderly person's driveway. AC4P means we appreciate people for who they are, rather than what they've achieved. When stressors and life's conflicts take the heart out of us, we need to know someone cares about our difficulties and believes in us. And we need to reciprocate, and do the same for others.

This basic level of AC4P can make a lasting difference in our lives. It's not about being judgmental, slashing people's self-esteem, and picking over faults. No, AC4P values the uniqueness of people. It recognizes human potential, and plays positively to people's strengths.

Empathy is a prerequisite. We need to perceive and care about the concerns or predicaments of others. When called to act on our caring for others, we must draw on our inner compassion and courage to act.

The following chapters include personal stories that demonstrate principles and applications of AC4P. They range from challenges of family, dealing with cancer, to the value of making time for others.

These stories will inspire you to carve out more time to actively care for family, friends, colleagues, and even strangers. Each story illustrates how AC4P helps bring out the best in both the giver and the receiver.

The testimonies cited in these chapters make an important point: AC4P behavior strengthens the compassion and caring of the person giving. Imagine the AC4P ripple effect if increasing numbers of individuals experience the rewarding, good-feeling consequences of actively caring for others.

Leaping to the self-transcendence state that sits atop Maslow's Hierarchy of Needs fulfills lower-level needs, especially our need for self-esteem and belongingness.

Self-efficacy, personal control, and optimism are also enhanced through AC4P behavior. Empowerment and self-motivation are fueled by all of these person-states, and vice versa.

Our greatest challenge is to help others feel the rewarding power of AC4P behavior. To do this, we must develop the context and implement contingencies to motivate initial occurrences of AC4P behavior. The stories in Part IV provide practical suggestions for stoking the fires of self-motivation. The positive-reinforcing consequences of AC4P behavior, witnessed and experienced time and again in the personal stories that make up these chapters, support the premise that AC4P behavior is naturally rewarding and self-sustaining when nurtured within a supportive culture.

These personal stories were not due to the competence, commitment and courage of *one* heroic person. Friends, family members, teachers, co-workers, and even strangers provided direction, mentorship or supportive consequences. Performing AC4P behavior affected many authors' way of life, inspiring them to adopt an AC4P lifestyle.

Each personal story illustrates how the AC4P principles enable the development of an AC4P culture – a culture of compassion at home, at work, at school, and throughout our communities.

CHAPTER 21

Memorable AC4P Experiences:
Special impact of a green wristband

Justin Graves

MY DISCOVERY OF THE AC4P Movement came through an interaction in a Virginia Tech (VT) classroom. My experience as a college student and as an individual would never be the same again.

I was a freshman when I first heard about the Movement, with a purpose reflected by my University motto, *Ut Prosim* (That I May Serve).

I learned about the Movement by asking a fellow classmate – one stranger at the time – what his green wristband represented. At the time, in late 2008, there were several different silicone wristbands in circulation with a range of colors, messages, and purposes. I wanted to learn more about the AC4P wristband, and about the founder of the AC4P concept.

My quest found its destination inside Williams Hall, to Dr. Geller's office. But the timing was not right. Heavily-involved in extracurricular and leadership activities, I was unable to commit the time and energy to help the AC4P Movement. That only held true until my senior year.

My First AC4P Wristband

While I was commuting into Washington D.C. from my parent's home in Northern Virginia for a summer internship with the federal government, I was gifted a green AC4P wristband. I remember the day as if it were yesterday.

It's raining when we trek to the above-ground metro stop at L'Enfant Plaza. I ask a gentleman, "How are you doing?" He shares the story of his miserable day at work, and the prospects of an hour-long wait at the metro stop for his wife to pick him up after tending to their sick child. I listen attentively to his difficulties, and then he hands me the AC4P wristband. He had received it from a VT student while he was visiting Blacksburg.

When I got home, I turned to Google for more information about AC4P. I promptly ordered a t-shirt to support the AC4P Movement – one I still wear proudly to this day. I decided to seek out Dr. Geller again when I returned to Blacksburg. Receiving the AC4P wristband had made my day, and I wanted to join the AC4P team.

My AC4P Transformation

I sent an e-mail to Dr. Geller and Shane McCarty, asking for more information about the Center for Applied Behavior Systems, and about acquiring additional wristbands. Dr. Geller promptly e-mailed me back, and invited me to visit with him when I returned to Blacksburg. I then organized a meeting with Joanne Geller, who delivered me a box filled with 100 AC4P wristbands.

I now had my own AC4P challenge, similar to Joanne's 60/60 Challenge. (See Chapter 19.) My goal: Recognize at least one person with a wristband daily until the wristbands are gone. After giving someone a wristband following his or her AC4P behavior, I filled out a brief survey to document how I felt after rewarding a person's act of caring.

Before embarking on the AC4P challenge, I had set an easier goal: Meet one new person every day. Although it was sometimes awkward, and sometimes unnatural, the number of people I had met through my own AC4P challenge was remarkable. I made several new friends, many Hokies and some formerly complete strangers. I enjoyed the positive reactions I received whenever I explained the AC4P Movement.

After meeting this goal, I took a step up to the next AC4P goal. If I could meet one new person every day, then I could try and help one new person every day. I was optimistic and kept trekking through the academic year, trying to meet my commitment.

What Goes Around Comes Around

In my fourth year of volunteering at a local elementary school (Spring 2012), I met a unique first-grader – let's call him Riley. This young student had a profound impact on me throughout my weekly visits to the school. If I had gotten a haircut – Riley noticed. If I wore a different ring on my finger – Riley noticed. When I wore a new pair of shoes – Riley noticed. When I debuted my new wheelchair – Riley noticed.

One morning, just after I had received a new AC4P wristband on campus, Riley notices. "Justin," Riley asks, "What's that green wristband for?" I explain the AC4P Movement to him – the meaning of the wristband, and the pay-it-forward nature of the process. "One day, I hope to receive a green wristband of my own," Riley replies. I make note of this.

Months later, Michelle Obama, the First Lady of the U.S., was the commencement speaker for my college graduation ceremony. One week prior to the commencement, I had received a call from the White House.

The First Lady wanted to mention me in her speech. She was struck by my goal of trying to help one new person every day, having learned of this goal from a story published by the University. I was invited to meet the First Lady for a conversation prior to her speech. I saw this as a grand opportunity – an opportunity to share the AC4P message with Mrs. Obama.

The night before meeting the First Lady, I scoured my home, looking for an AC4P wristband. I rehearsed the purpose of the wristband numerous times in my head before I gave her one. Later, I saw her wearing it during interactions with University officials throughout the day. This was remarkable. Even more remarkable were her comments during her speech:

> *And one of today's graduates, a young man named Justin Graves, has committed himself to helping at least one person every single day. Way to go. As he put it, and these are his words – Justin said, 'Life is all about what you have done for other people.*

Then, Mrs. Obama indicated that Virginia Tech could teach the rest of the world about the spirit of serving others... Wow!

Two weeks later, I'm back at the elementary school, helping out students, including Riley. The students present me with an illustrated book, each page containing students' heartfelt words of appreciation for my AC4P behavior. Then, the teacher sets

Michelle Obama discusses her 2012 commencement address with Justin Graves.

up a projector and shows a video. Low and behold, it's the video of Mrs. Obama's commencement address.

Afterwards, Riley approaches me as we walk to the lunchroom, and says, "Justin, I have something for you". I wonder what he's going to pull from his pocket. He presents me with an AC4P wristband and announces:

> *I got this bracelet at Virginia Tech some time ago. And I want you to know I really like the way you helped us in the classroom this year. Plus, you helped a lot of people too, so here's another green wristband for you to add to your collection, 'cause I bet you have a lot.*

What Goes Around *Really* Comes Around

In the summer of 2012, a close friend and I share a meal in a local Blacksburg restaurant. We start talking about the "Hokie Bucket List" – a set of items a VT student organization claims you should do before you graduate if you are a "true Hokie." Weeks earlier, the university ran a publication with an interview of me that dubbed me as "the Ultimate Hokie" and it documented reflections of my time of leadership and service at the university. I was definitely honored, but once I discover the Bucket List I realize there are some things there I would never be able to accomplish.

In November 2012, when my friend Scinju recommends we go on a local hike, I am floored. I wasn't floored because it was almost December and it had just finished snowing. I was floored because of my disability. I am a paraplegic. I ambulate with a wheelchair but always hesitate to say I am "confined" to a wheelchair because it's not a confinement. Instead, I use my disability to touch as many people as possible when they may not expect it.

After weeks of planning said hike, Scinju and I make our way to the Cascades in Giles County, Virginia with more than ten others - some are close friends, some are strangers. But by the end of the day we will have accomplished something fascinating. Scinju and friends build a make-shift cot that allows me to complete Item Number 10 on the Hokie Bucket List: Hike the Cascades Falls.

This rugged, four-mile roundtrip hike was not only something I never imagined I'd do, but something I had admired. All of my closest friends, at some point, took the trip and took photos of the beautiful natural waterfall you meet at the two-mile point. "The Cascades" hike was an activity I had to participate in to feel I really earned that title of "the Ultimate Hokie."

Not long after I completed the hike, a video of it became viral. It wasn't all the attention it received that moved me. It was the power of AC4P that moved me. I never ever expected to be able to make this hike. I never expected to see the waterfall in person. However, thanks to some of the greatest friends on this Earth caring for me, in as active a way as possible, I was able to conquer something I thought I never could. My disability was put on the shelf when these friends stepped in to help me. And of course I had to recognize each of them with an AC4P wristband. I look forward to hearing how they use those wristbands to recognize others' AC4P behavior.

Unexpected AC4P Behavior

Here's how my motivation to help is enhanced. Everyone wants social approval and appreciation. This is the basic human need of belongingness (see Chapter 2). Indeed, lives can be enriched when you help someone – when you actively care for them – especially when the AC4P behavior is *unexpected*.

As a paraplegic, people often hold a door open for me. I love opportunities to make other people's day by holding a door open for them.

When a Radford student helped me put my groceries in my car at the local Wal-Mart, he didn't think I'd gift him anything, much less an AC4P wristband for him to pass on.

When I met Antwon, a homeless man on a street in Downtown Atlanta, he was just looking for money to get into the shelter on a hot summer night – not a green wristband.

When Ted Faulkner greeted me to help me meet my goal of meeting one new person every day – he didn't expect the wristband, even though he made my day.

When a prospective VT student found a Hokie ID card on the ground during his campus tour and gave it to me, he didn't expect anything in return. It's always such a pleasure to reward a person's AC4P behavior with the AC4P wristband and then share the meaning of this "small token of my appreciation".

My parents taught me to make sure people see me as an individual, before they see my wheelchair. As a disabled student at VT, I faced this challenge daily. After I became immersed in the AC4P Movement, my physical challenge became easier to handle. I looked for ways to actively care for others and for opportunities to show explicit appreciation for their AC4P behavior.

With more and more people actively caring for others, recognizing the AC4P actions of others, and sharing their stories at ac4p.org, AC4P behavior will become the norm. The result: a world we all desire to live in – a world filled with compassion.

CHAPTER 22

Living with Cancer:
The survival power of AC4P

E. Scott Geller

IREMEMBER AS IF it were yesterday. On Friday, May 3, 2002 I received unexpected, grim, and shocking news from an urologist: "You have cancer". I tell you this – not for pity or sympathy – but because of the insight I've gained from dealing with this life-threatening disease.

My life changed dramatically from that unforgettable news forward, from daily debilitating distress to a new appreciation of life and interpersonal relationships. I've intentionally avoided a disposition of despair and a focus on avoiding failure. With a mindset of hope, I've focused on achieving success through personal control. And, I've become more mindful of the many treasures of everyday living.

It Won't Happen to Me

I'm overwhelmed with optimism waiting for my urologist to reveal the results of the biopsy. Leading indicators gave me a 1 in 5, or 20% chance of having prostate cancer. But those statistics are based on the average 60-year old.

I consider myself much less at-risk for cancer than the average person – I don't smoke or consume much alcohol, and eat very little red meat. I exercise regularly and take antioxidant vitamins daily. I eat lots of tomatoes (which contain lycopene – a presumed protector against prostate cancer), and I spend a lot of time in the sun, providing me plenty of vitamin D (another presumed protector against this type of cancer).

I had done everything I knew to do to prevent this relatively common type of cancer. I consider my cancer an "accident," not only because it was unintentional but because it was unexpected and unpreventable with my current knowledge, tools, and methods.

Cancer of course is scary. So many of its contributing factors are unknown and/ or uncontrollable (as in the genetics that likely contributed to my current plight). But through research these unknowns can be revealed, and some of the ordeals I describe in this narrative can be prevented.

The Power of Personal Control

The immediate result of my biopsy is debilitating. I feel distressed and helpless. At the dinner table, I announce, "Well I guess it's just my time. I've lived an active 60 years, and have seen enough of this life." My 23-year-old daughter retorts, with tears streaming down her face, "But Dad, you haven't seen enough of me".

My daughter's words bring me to my senses. Why am I giving up? I can fight this thing. Famous people like Lance Armstrong, Mayor Rudy Giuliani, and General Norman Schwarzkopf have come back strong after a cancer diagnosis – I can too!

I began reading books and scouring internet information about prostate cancer, eventually deciding removal of the prostate was the best therapeutic approach for me.

I scheduled surgery with an urologist who had performed over 350 radical retro pubic nerve-sparing prostatectomies.

I conducted substantial research to gain a perception of control over my adversity. And after this, I felt much better. Hopefulness took the place of helplessness; motivating stress overcame debilitating distress.

The Power of AC4P Support

The sense of personal control over my disease would not have occurred without AC4P behavior from family, students, friends, and colleagues. My family reassured me with words like, "We'll help you get through this". My graduate students brought me relevant books and internet material. My department chairman gave me contact information for reputable urologists.

My partners at Safety Performance Solutions, Inc. offered me optimism, including encouraging stories of their family members who have survived prostate cancer. Students in my university classes sent me e-mails to express appreciation for my teaching and to wish me success in overcoming my setback.

At the end of several classes, students approached me with words of sincere concern and comfort. Some gave me a hug, and after everyone left my introductory psychology class of 600 students, a few asked if they could pray for me. Here I am, standing in front of a mostly empty auditorium and teary-eyed, while three students take turns asking God to keep me healthy so I can keep teaching.

Research has shown over and over that interpersonal support is critical for overcoming physical illness and emotional conflict. Now I had experienced this firsthand. Through AC4P support I received the information and the inspiration to gain personal control. Indeed, without substantial actively caring I could not have maintained sufficient self-motivation and courage to endure the intense and prolonged treatment ordeal required to fight my disease – nor frankly would I want to.

I learned there's a great amount of AC4P support available when we need it, if we are willing to ask for help. As Ramakrishna said, "The winds of grace are always blowing, but you have to raise the sail".

I raised my sail in May 2002 with my announcement of being diagnosed with prostate cancer. I received a remarkable amount of genuine caring, concern, and support. All of a sudden, friends, colleagues and students expressed appreciation for my daily contributions as a teacher and researcher, along with strong sentiment and hope I will be able to continue my worthwhile work.

I soon found I would need this level of interpersonal AC4P for extended periods of time. My Senior Partners at Safety Performance Solutions, Inc. commissioned a local artist, George Wills, to draw the cartoon depicted on the next page. The message hit home for me and made me laugh out loud.

More Difficult Than Expected

I heard convalescence from prostate surgery was painful and arduous, but it was worse than I anticipated. The three-day hospital stay was a breeze compared to the following weeks of post-surgery recuperation. The only memorable problem in the hospital was lack

of sleep, largely due to intermittent interruptions by nurses who were seemingly more disruptive than necessary. It was obvious the hospital staff could have benefited greatly from some basic lessons about AC4P and applications of interpersonal observation and feedback.

I should have stayed in the hospital longer. My rush to go home and get some welcomed sleep led to extra pain and discomfort. I won't bore you with details, but the lesson is important for all kinds of recovery. Be patient and appreciate the need for incremental healing. This is a critical lesson for the doctors and hospital staff, also. They should not let unrealistic wishes and optimism of their patients overcome their empirical observations and more informed judgment.

Set Reasonable Goals

My impatience to leave the hospital was fueled by a goal to attend and participate at the 2002 Professional Development Conference of the American Society of Safety Engineers (ASSE). I was scheduled to give a day-long, pre-conference ASSE workshop just 16 days after surgery, and I had no time to lose. Yes, I gave that workshop and a keynote address two days later, and I was very glad to be able to make that trip.

Upon reflection I realize (as many had advised me) the goal I set and reached was not realistic, nor in my best interest. I'm convinced I slowed the recovery process because I tried to do too much, too fast. Bottom line: Goals are critical motivators for recovery from illness or injury, but be realistic. Trying to do more than you're physically ready for can be detrimental.

More Power from AC4P Support

My attendance at the ASSE conference was a "psychological high". While the experience may have hindered my physical recovery, it did wonders for my psychological state, including my self-esteem, self-efficacy, perception of personal control, optimism, and sense of belonging and interdependence.

I do not point out this inconsistency between mind and body healing to pit medicine against psychological science. I still believe the trip slowed my overall physical recovery and helped make the month following surgery the longest in my life. Rather, I want to demonstrate the power of AC4P support from others.

I presumed a large number of people expected and wanted me to make it to the ASSE conference, and I believed I would make some worthwhile contributions if I participated. Indeed, I signed several hundred copies of my book, *The Participation Factor: How to increase involvement in occupational safety* which was debuted at that conference.

It's noteworthy however; I could not have participated at that level without the continual assistance of my daughter, Krista. Indeed, I needed her to help me walk from one event to another. This is just more evidence for the special power of AC4P, especially from family members.

Fortunately, my interpersonal support extended far beyond my immediate family. Friends, colleagues, and total strangers called and e-mailed me with advice, well-wishes, and statements of appreciation for my prior contributions to occupational safety. Many expressed hope I would be able to get back to my research, teaching, and scholarship quickly and continue in a healthy state of mind and body.

Especially supportive were communications from others who have experienced the same illness and recovery challenges. It's so easy to feel isolated and depressed during the inactive phase of convalescence. Hearing from people who had experienced the same distress and discomfort, and who have recovered, can be extremely encouraging. These individuals can have genuine empathy, and thus can offer the most convincing advice and reassurance.

No Longer Cancer-Free

A post-surgery PSA above 0.001 indicates the presence of cancer. The patient is not cancer-free. After surgery, and for five consecutive PSA tests (i.e., 2.5 years), my score was 0.001. I was cancer-free. After three of these ideal test results, my urologist's office only scheduled me annually for a PSA test. In fact, this PSA test was self-initiated. I had not yet received a postcard to prompt a PSA check. But, I realized it had been a year since my last assessment and wanted verification of "cancer-free".

Waiting for my test results on Friday, August 17th, 2005, I'm as optimistic as I had been on that much earlier Friday, May 3rd, 2002 before learning I had prostate cancer. The doctor is friendly and cheerful as he grabs the computer printout from the holder on the door. Suddenly, his demeanor changes notably. I know something is wrong. He puts his chewing gum in a paper towel, and with a look of surprise, he delicately tells me my PSA was 0.18.

While 0.18 is close to zero, I know this is not good news. It means cancer is in my body, and can certainly grow to be debilitating and life-threatening. The urologist reviews my records and notes how unusual it is to see cancer after surgery and post-operative assessments as successful as mine. Such rhetoric does not make me feel any better.

Then he surprises me with the following: "At this time, I see no need for radiation, chemotherapy, or Lupron". (Lupron is a last-resort drug that acts like a female hormone and can have a number of undesirable side-effects, including hot flashes and complete loss of libido.) Then the doc asks me to schedule a re-assessment of my PSA in four months.

Fighting Complacency

My doc says, "Come back in four months for a reassessment. Then we'll see how fast the cancer is growing." I think: Are you kidding? The PSA test says I've gone from cancer-free to cancer-present in less than a year, and now I'm expected to wait around for another four months. Can I afford to accept this failure, and do nothing until another assessment?

Accepting my current cancer state until future PSA results indicate the need for radical treatment is the most convenient option, and is perhaps accompanied by the least amount of distress. Keep on doing what I'm doing, and I might not be worse off. In essence, this is the advice of my urologist. Keep doing what I'm doing and hope to avoid failure.

The urologist gave me no new strategy for returning me to cancer-free. He never asked me what I had done to remain cancer-free in the past, nor what I had done differently to elevate my PSA. But if he had, I couldn't have offered any meaningful answers. From my perspective, my behavior had not changed. Was the return of my cancer only a matter of bad luck? Must I accept the perspective, "Wait and watch and hope for the best?"

Must I accept the viewpoint my cancer is uncontrollable at this point? Should I keep on doing what I had been doing and merely hope my PSA does not increase dramatically? Such perceived loss of personal control does not feel right, but without evidence-based advice, that's really the only alternative. Without a credible AC4P action plan for gaining control of a personal problem, it's easy to become complacent and accept the failure you're attempting to avoid.

Raise Your Sail

Drafting this story reminds me of my most inspirational keynote address. On Wednesday, August 24th, 2005 I'm giving the closing general-session keynote at the 21st Annual Voluntary Protection Programs Participants' Association (VPPPA) Conference in Dallas, TX. A crowded room of about 2,000 listen intently as I introduce the audience to the enviable qualities of an AC4P culture and the barriers to achieving this ideal state. They display passionate and energetic reactions to my concepts, stories, and illustrations.

Then, without pre-planning or forethought, I tell my cancer story – emphasizing how AC4P support got me through pre and post-surgery as well as the disheartening news I had heard just five days earlier.

Receiving Inspiration

This was "my most inspirational" keynote not because of anything I said, but because of how intensely the audience inspired me. I was touched by the many caring emotions displayed on the faces of the attentive listeners. And after a standing ovation, I am swamped by an onslaught of participants expressing approval, wishing me good health, and telling me I'll be in their prayers.

Many ask for my email address so they can send me information relevant for my fight with cancer, including the names of cancer specialists I could contact. Two participants wait more than 30 minutes to independently pray for me.

I left the ballroom 45 minutes after my 1.5 hour keynote feeling inspired and more ready than ever to fight again to be cancer-free. That special audience lifted my self-esteem and optimism higher than I thought possible in my current state.

In a world that seems to be experiencing more interpersonal mistrust, selfish entitlement, and debilitating fear, it was so uplifting to see so much genuine caring from so many people. Their actively caring inspired me to fight the good fight – against my cancer and for more AC4P behavior.

Living with Cancer

After 35 radiation sessions, January - February, 2006, my PSA returned to 0.004, an indication I was once again cancer free. However, the lab report I received on July 13th, 2009 burst my "health bubble" once again. My PSA had risen to 0.15; I was again no longer cancer-free. Subsequent to this distressing news, I began seeing a prostate-cancer specialist in Charlottesville, VA, who prescribed monthly PSA tests to track the growth of my prostate cancer.

My last blood test (taken April 1st, 2014) showed a PSA of 0.730, reflecting a slow but consistent germination of my prostate cancer. This doc reacted to my concern with "Wait until your PSA reaches 2.0, and then you can have a test to determine the location of the cancer. If your cancer is not systemic and found in one place, you will be a candidate for a new type of radiation therapy."

Frankly, this diagnosis and prescription is not consoling, to say the least. Again, I feel a severe loss of personal control over my disease, leading to feelings of complacency or *learned helplessness*.

I am encouraged by the informative book, *Cancer: 50 Essential Things to Do.*[1] Greg Anderson was diagnosed with metastasized lung cancer in 1984, and was told he had only 30 days to live. Refusing to accept this hopeless state, he searched for individuals who had survived cancer which doctors had labeled "terminal".

He looked for common patterns among more than 500 interviews, and from these derived his own action plan. In 1985, Mr. Anderson started the Cancer Conquerors Foundation, which later became the Cancer Recovery Foundation of America (greganderson.org).

To date, Mr. Anderson has surveyed 16,000 people who survived cancer, and he travels extensively to conduct workshops on his findings. His book on cancer survival is practical and hope-filled, and includes lessons for cancer survival, as well as overall wellness. Three of his most important strategies for surviving cancer relate directly to the AC4P principles and applications discussed in this book.

1. Take Personal Control and Expect the Best

Those who triumph over cancer do not stop with conventional treatment. They believe wellness is not a matter of luck, but requires daily commitment and effort. Active involvement is essential. They maintain a healthy outlook on life.

However, Anderson reports cancer survivors "have a refreshing sense of skepticism about 'just-think-positive' solutions". They are tough-minded realists. They don't deny the negative consequences associated with a lack of personal involvement in wellness. They maintain focus and self-motivation by imagining the most negative consequences that could occur if they don't stay actively involved. But, as we all know, many victims of cancer have done everything they know to fight this disease but still lose the battle.

2. Maintain a Sense of Purpose

Anderson reports that cancer triumphants believe they are needed – their lives have special and unique purposes. "Many are energized by an inner, even transcendent, life mission."[1] But, the author adds, "survivors balance this profound idea of life purpose with a lighter, more playful attitude of fun for fun's sake".[2]

Furthermore, Anderson writes, "Survivors feel they are privileged to be able to help others in meaningful ways. "In helping others, they help themselves."[1] Although the author is referring to cancer survivors, this is true for the survival of most any life difficulty.

People in professions that improve the quality of life in others can take solace in the fact their daily job helps others in meaningful ways. Their professional mission statement epitomizes *self-transcendence* – the highest level of Maslow's Hierarchy of Needs[2] – which means going beyond one's self-interests to benefit others. That's AC4P behavior.

3. Nurture Supportive Relationships

From my cancer diagnosis to recovery, AC4P support from family, friends, colleagues, and students made success possible. People gave me purpose to get beyond traditional treatment and return to my pre-cancer lifestyle. While my recovery was inspired by others, I also became more aware of the value of developing profound relationships with others.

Anderson found, "Cancer survivors invest more time and emotional energy in relationships that nurture them and invest less in those that are toxic".[2] In other words, survivors become "relationship sensitive," evaluating the benefits and costs of maintaining the variety of interpersonal relationships in their entire social-support system. This often leads to change that reduces negative or debilitating emotions.

Less emotional turmoil means less distress, greater reality awareness, and more opportunity for positive emotions. And positive emotions in a work, educational, or family setting lead to interdependency and AC4P behavior. Positive emotions lead to increases in self-esteem, optimism, and a sense of belonging, and these person-states increase the likelihood a person will actively care for the well-being of others.

In Conclusion

Every year since the start of my challenges with prostate cancer, I've attended the annual "Relay-for-Life" event at Virginia Tech (VT). Often I've been asked to offer a few words at the opening ceremony about the human dynamics of cancer and the value of this special fund-raising event for cancer research.

My keynote address has been different each time, except for two points. First, I point out the bold "Cancer Survivor" words displayed on my shirt and the shirt worn by over 300 other participants are wrong.

We are not cancer survivors but are *surviving* cancer. Only through continual research can treatment strategies be developed to make "Cancer Survivor" a reality. Indeed, several of the participants who wore the "Cancer Survivor" shirt at one or more of these events are no longer with us. An effective remedy had not yet been developed to save them.

The second theme I emphasize is the special value of an interdependent community of actively-caring people. This is exemplified by the impressive turnout at each of our annual "Relay-for-Life" events. In fact, for the past six years VT has led all universities nationwide in the amount of funds received at this event for cancer research. This reflects an extraordinary level of AC4P which brings to life the VT motto: *Ut Prosim* (That I May Serve).

Students, faculty, staff, family and friends walk or run around the quarter-mile track all night, each lap representing a certain amount of money donated to the American Cancer Society. Those wearing "Cancer Survivor" shirts walk the first lap. People line both sides of our entire course, cheering loudly and continuously, reaching out to shake hands or to slap high-fives with us smiling walkers.

The power of AC4P support from an interdependent community of like-minded people is exhilarating and healing. It reminds us of life's most meaningful purpose – to reach Maslow's state of self-transcendence.[3] Here we overcome our own selfish interests and issues to experience the exceptional intrinsic reinforcement that comes when we actively care for the health, safety, and general well-being of others.

Notes

1. Anderson, G. (1993). *Cancer: 50 essential things to do*. Harmondsworth, Middlesex, England: Penguin Group.

2. Anderson, G. (1993). *Cancer: 50 essential things to do*. Harmondsworth, Middlesex, England: Penguin Group, pp. 14-15.

3. Frankl, V. E. (2000). *Man's search for ultimate meaning*. New York. NY: Basic Books; Maslow, A.H. (1971). *The farther reaches of human nature*. New York, NY: Viking Publishers.

CHAPTER 23

My Starting Block and AC4P:
Developing and applying moral courage

Shane M. McCarty

AS A RESIDENT ADVISOR during my sophomore year at Virginia Tech (VT), I lived in Pritchard Hall, which at the time was one of the largest, all-male residence halls on the East Coast with 1,016 males. After hearing the words "gay" and "faggot" an average of ten times a day, I decided to act. Those unkind words made me feel uncomfortable and motivated me to actively care for beneficial change, at least among the 42 residents on my floor.

I placed a logo of the *Collegiate Times*, our school newspaper, at the top of the following words, as if they were contained in an anonymous letter to the Editor. Then, I attached this apparent letter in five bathroom stalls on my floor.

Letter to the Editor: *"Gay" is Not a Word to Use Loosely*

I am a homosexual male growing up in a heterosexual world. I feel uncomfortable almost everywhere I go. Have you ever looked down in class and seen the word faggot carved into a desk? I see it, but I also feel it. I feel that same knife cut me out – away from the group of those other Hokies around me.

The distance, the difference, between you and me, increases exponentially each time I read the word on a desk in McBryde Hall. I have seen it so many times at this point; the distance between us can no longer be measured in inches but rather in miles. I no longer feel a part of this community.

Why do you fear me? Do you fear me because I am different? I don't call you names or go out of my way to hurt you. I don't yell redneck, hick, or white trash to those of you who so proudly display your Confederate heritage. I don't judge you, the entitled upper class, for the endless privileges your parents provide – your tuition paid in full, your new car, and your designer clothes in hand with no questions asked.

If you don't want to be me, then don't discriminate against me. You throw the words faggot and gay around as if it's okay, as if nobody cares. Why do you use these words to degrade me? Is your vocabulary so limited you must attack me with the words "gay" and "faggot"? The dictionary definition of "gay" is keenly alive and exuberant.[1] Since when did that word mean *annoying* and *stupid*?

Please stop and think. Ponder your words and their impact on others. Please ask yourself the question: Who does this hurt? Because it hurts me more than you will ever know.

The Truth About That Letter

I am the last person you'd expect to author that letter, because I am a heterosexual, Caucasian, upper-middle class, Roman Catholic, male college student. Because of these identity markers, opportunities are extended to me daily. I am among the privileged class and I *realize* it. I wrote that letter to invoke reflection and potentially start a conversation among my 42 residents that could help them realize their own privileges.

If life were a race, the referee would flag me down for cheating, because my starting block was much farther along than many others. A person's starting block is mostly a product of a number of critical and sometimes invisible environmental factors (e.g., socio-economic status, ethnicity, and education level).[2]

It seems from my interactions that most people rarely consider the position of their starting block, and fewer use their privileged starting-block positions to help others. But I can't help others effectively without understanding their life experiences. Many of us consider ourselves empathic, but do we truly attempt to understand others by stepping into their shoes?

I remember my first attempt to understand the experiences of male homosexuals. Two male friends shared stories of victimization, fear of violence, and the pain caused from being different. Their college experience was markedly more stressful than mine simply due to differing sexual orientations. To reduce my own prejudices, I listened empathically to my new college friends and then attempted to capture their emotions and experiences into a letter as if I were walking in their shoes.

I wasn't born with an elevated capacity for empathy, nor did I inherit an AC4P gene. I learned how to actively care and what to care about from other people. After all, our behaviors, attitudes, and beliefs are largely determined by the various social interactions and behavioral consequences we experience throughout our lives. My family, friends, peers, and VT professors taught me the value of empathic listening, servant leadership, and the moral courage to act on my values.[3]

A Transformational Night

On a cold winter night in Blacksburg, Virginia, my understanding of passive caring versus actively caring, right versus wrong, majority versus minority, were transformed.

I'm chatting with two friends, Brandon and Joey, when I notice a group of students standing by a bus-stop shelter. The cold night causes the glass of the shelter to fog up. I see one of the group members writing a message on the glass, finishing the "t" of "faggot," I ask myself: "Why?" I've seen this scene play out too many times. The 'in' crowd ridiculing minority or less popular students.

I stride briskly over to the group. "Why did you write "faggot" on the window for everyone to see?" I ask the perpetrator. Silence. Nobody responds. But there is tension now where there hadn't been before.

The group looks at their friend in a way that tells me they disagree with his action. I look hard into their eyes as I erase the word "faggot" from the window. "That really offends me and I am not even gay," I say. I sense discomfort from the perpetrator's friends, but nobody says a word.

In the past, I would have reacted in a much different way. I expected those most affected (e.g., homosexuals) to say something – to intervene and stand up for themselves. I would have blamed the victims, thinking they must deserve it, especially if they let the ridicule occur so frequently.

But now I think: It's not exclusively the victims' responsibility to defend themselves. It's my responsibility too, and the responsibility of all bystanders, especially those with privilege and influence to exhibit moral courage[4] and speak up on behalf of others who are mistreated.

As explained in Chapter 2, intervening to help a stranger is not easy. After all, what do you say? And how do you say it? It can even be difficult to provide corrective feedback for a close friend who uses degrading or inappropriate remarks. If you have used similar language, you might assume it's not your responsibility to correct someone's verbal behavior, or you may lack the necessary skills to intervene. As discussed in Chapter 4, it takes moral courage to act contrary to the relevant social norm.[4]

From Caring to Acting

I never wrote "faggot" on a bus-shelter window, but as a high-school student only six years ago I might as well have been that person I confronted at the bus stop. Numerous people heard "he's so gay" spew from my mouth. Fortunately, a telephone conversation with my Aunt Betsy shifted my paradigm.

When referring to a high-school teacher, I said "He's so gay" in place of "He's so stupid". She knew *punishment* was ineffective, so she provided invaluable *corrective feedback*: "You might want to think about your word choice a bit more, because using that word in such a way can really hurt people".

Sometimes people come into our lives who affect us in profound ways. It's not their beliefs that affect us; it's their AC4P behavior. My aunt displayed *moral courage* when she provided honest *corrective feedback* about my inappropriate behavior. It wasn't easy for her, but it was worth it. That single feedback conversation changed my life, and potentially the lives of many others.

Our seemingly small actions can have a far-reaching ripple effect. As I came back to my two best friends at the bus stop, I wondered how my actions affected them and the perpetrator's friends, but I never knew the direct impact of that AC4P behavior. I never mentioned that cold night at a Blacksburg bus stop again.

Two years later, I was seated at the dining room table with my family and my friend Brandon. Brandon shared that bus-shelter story when discussing courage and the challenges associated with doing the right thing. Clearly, Brandon was impacted by my act of moral courage, as were my parents after hearing that story, but what about those at the bus stop?

Did the perpetrator's verbal behavior change as a result of my corrective feedback? I believe it did. Like me, he probably never realized the negative impact caused by such hurtful words.

To this day, I wonder who I would be – my values, attitudes, and behaviors – if family, friends, colleagues, and strangers never provided me with *corrective AC4P feedback*. Numerous courageous bystanders showed genuine caring and *moral courage* when they offered me critical feedback, planting seeds for my development.

The Silent Majority

Martin Luther King, Jr. said: "In this era of social transition, the greatest tragedy is not the blaring noisiness of the so-called bad people, it's the appalling silence of the so-called good people."[5]

Those in the majority have a moral obligation to stand up for the minority. This isn't a religious obligation or a federal law, but our moral responsibility as human beings to actively care for one another.

Most human beings care about social injustice, racism, poverty, world hunger, and the many other social issues of our time, but caring alone is not enough. When we hear homophobic remarks spewing from friends' mouths, do we tell them to stop? Each day, we face choices like this one that define our character and have the potential to create a positive ripple effect we may never see.

Every time we act to benefit a stranger, we remind ourselves of a fundamental belief: Despite the differences between people, our common humanity matters most. When I graduated from high school, I had the whole world in my hands with countless opportunities, because of my advantageous starting block.

Five years later, the same world remains in my hands, but now, I feel its weight. The world feels much heavier today, and it will only get lighter if I use my privilege and moral courage to improve it for others.

Notes

1. Gay. In *Merriam-Webster.com*. Retrieved from http://www.merriam-webster.com/dictionary/hacker

2. Foroohar, R. (2011, November 14). What ever happened to upward mobility. *Time*.

3. I am grateful for the countless people who have actively cared for me throughout my life. Upon reflection, I am indebted forever to those people who helped me during the most challenging and influential academic year of my life (2008-2009). Thank you Bo Hart, Brandon Carroll, Joey Zakutney, Ryan King, and Taris Mullins for inspiring me to become the person I've always wanted to be. A special thanks to each person who changed my paradigm that year, especially mentors who became close friends: Betsy Shane, Edward Spencer, John Driessnack, Leon McClinton, Lis Ellis, Ray Williams, and Steve Skripak. Finally, I am so thankful for the intentional AC4P behavior of one Hokie, because it allowed me to meet my mentor Scott "Doc" Geller, his wife Joanne Dean Geller, graduate students Ryan Smith and Chris Downing of CABS, and find my life's work using behavioral and psychological science to actively care for people.

4. Geller, E.S., & Veazie, B. (2009). *The courage factor: Leading people-based culture change*. Newport, VA: Make-A-Difference, LLC.

5. King, Jr., M.L. *Martin Luther King quotes*. Retrieved from http://www.inspirationpeak.com/cgi-bin/search.cgi?search=Dr.%20Martin%20Luther%20King&method=all

CHAPTER 24

AC4P in My Military Career:
Mentors who had my back

Douglas R. Hole

MANY ASPECTS OF A military career truly fit the AC4P Model, especially the "I have your back" norm embedded in the military culture. My personal story transcends both my college and military experiences, and highlights several people who not only understood the AC4P philosophy but practiced it on a regular basis.

I begin with my head football coach at the College of Wooster – Phil Shipe. Phil was a good coach, but a better mentor and actively-caring person. He actively cared about all of his players as individuals. He wanted us to be the best athletes we could be. More importantly, he wanted us to grow and become outstanding contributors to society.

Promotions in the Military

As an Air Force officer, making regular promotions in an "up-or-out world" is part of the military culture. You are promoted to the next higher rank or you are deemed no longer useful. In some cases your career is cut short.

In my career, promotions came on time, up to Major. Four years after this promotion and in my 15th year, I was considered for promotion to Lt. Colonel. But I was not promoted. I feared my time in the Air Force would be cut short, and I would be separated with no retirement benefits.

Here comes my mentor, Colonel Whitey Barrows. He was the Deputy Chief of Intelligence for Tactical Air Command. He called me in and gave me a profound and thoughtful talk about continuing to do the right thing and to not be discouraged by my setback.

He advised, "Don't wear this disappointment on your sleeve. Continue to be the outstanding contributor you have been."

I followed his advice and was selected for promotion to Lt. Colonel the following year. This enabled at least a 20-year retirement.

Four years later, I faced a similar hurdle for promotion to Colonel. Again, I did not get promoted on time. But with nearly 21 years of service, I was not too concerned. As a non-flying officer, my chance of a promotion was slim at best. Brigadier General (U.S. Army) Mike Pfister, my boss at the time, put me in positions to excel with the senior leadership at U.S. Central Command. He had confidence I had "The Right Stuff" to be a Colonel in the Air Force.

The next year, 1986, I was promoted to full Colonel – a rank I could not have envisioned when I entered the Air Force in 1964. After all, only five of 100 2nd Lieutenants in the Air Force are ultimately promoted to Full Colonel.

I was immediately sent to Bahrain for a three-month stint on the USS Lasalle, the Command Ship Navy Forces in the Persian Gulf. My title was U.S. Central Command Liaison to *Commideast for* a 2-Star Admiral. It was a long title with limited responsibility. Still, I was the 3rd or 4th ranking U.S. Military Officer in the region.

A Cultural Lesson

On the day after Thanksgiving in 1986, the Intelligence Officer for the Lasalle, Marine Lt. Col. Forest Lucy and I decided to explore the Island of Bahrain, where the ship was based. One of our stops was Sheik's Beach, a private beach for westerners run by the Royalty of Bahrain.

Upon arrival, we were invited by the Emir of Bahrain, Sheik Isa bin Sulman al Khalifa, to have coffee with him and his entourage. It happened to be the day the Iran-Contra Scandal broke open, and as representatives of the U.S., we had to tread diplomatically on what was a troubling revelation for many in the Arab world.

Sheik Isa spoke of his wonderful trip to the U.S. and his wonderful host, then Vice President George Bush. He wanted to know why all the people who had been so nice to him wouldn't accept the Rolex watches he offered. Diplomatically we reiterated government employees are not authorized to accept gifts of this nature.

He talked about his family and said he had nine children, five girls and four boys, and he had only made five mistakes (not joking). He asked me how many children I had and I said, "None". He immediately turned his back on me; I became invisible.

I vowed to have a different answer if I received this offspring question from Arab leadership. I wrote to my sister's son, told him the story, and asked if he would mind being my son for this purpose. From then on I carried a picture of Mike Roark for conversations with Arab leadership about children.

An AC4P Mentor

Back in Wooster in the Fall of 1987, I go to see Coach Shipe. I tell him of that most enlightening and embarrassing experience, since he and his wife Pem had no children either.

He sits for a moment and looks at me and asks, "Do you have a picture of you in uniform as a Colonel?" I give him one and ask, "Why?" He replies, "The next time I'm asked if I have any kids I'm going to show him your picture and say you are my son".

This was one of the most monumental and moving experiences of my life. Coach Shipe actively cared once again. He made me feel like his most important player, though I know he felt the same about all of us. From this memorable experience, I learned the power of a few AC4P words. The AC4P phrase, "I've got your back" comes to life in many forms.

CHAPTER 25

AC4P in Australia

Martin Ralph

S INCE 2001 I'VE been privileged to serve as the CEO of the Industrial Foundation for Accident Prevention (IFAP), based in Western Australia. IFAP was founded in 1962 and is a Registered Training Organization providing national and international public and corporate safety courses. It has six training centers in Western Australia and in Queensland (the second-largest and third most populous state in Australia) located in the northeast of the country. We annually train more than 23,000 people and currently employ more than 1,800 personnel.

I regularly attend safety conferences in the U.S., and 17 years ago I met Scott Geller in New Orleans at a conference sponsored by the American Society of Safety Engineers (ASSE). I had been invited to a special book-signing event for the release of his watershed publication, *Working Safe: How to help people actively care for health and safety.* Four trips to Australia and many air miles together have seen us forge a bond that tests the many miles that separate our respective countries.

More than 600 West Australians attended Scott and Joanne's most recent trip "Down Under" as the duo presented forums to share the message of the AC4P Movement. A bit of context: Western Australia has a hard-won reputation of being an outpost community, dominated by the mining industry, with entrenched machismo attitudes, a can-do spirit and an aversion to "touchy-feely" approaches to life.

The majority of the attendees at Scott and Joanne's forums were long-term stakeholders in IFAP. I was impressed when I actively sought the opinions of many of those stakeholders, and received similar reactions: "How do we achieve an AC4P culture in our organization?" I couldn't help but wonder whether the perception of the hardened Western Australian was akin to the legend of Crocodile Dundee – nothing more than a popular myth.

So what about this AC4P Movement, and how to make it work? The prescription is so simple it's actually complex. It all comes down to the individual's willingness to go out of his or her way to help a fellow traveller in life. But this requires compassion, courage and a capacity to demonstrate personal leadership. Of these three characteristics, leadership is the most difficult to define. The academic world is only now starting to properly define what it takes to be a leader, which includes the context of both leadership and followership behavior.

Scott and Joanne have this unique ability to invigorate your soul, and to inspire you to want to go beyond the call of duty to help and/or recognize the positive actions of others. It was at a meeting in Chicago in 2011, and subsequently reinforced by Scott and Joanne in mid-2012, that my personal inspiration for the AC4P Movement began. This is the story I share here.

Contrasting Cultures

First an observation: When I was in Chicago I was privileged to witness the pride and honor on display at the Past-Presidents' reception when the then president of the ASSE,

Ms. Terrie Norris, introduced her son– a serving member of the U.S. military on leave from assignment in the Iraq conflict. The audience of esteemed contributors to the advancement of occupational safety and health in the U.S.stood to attention spontaneously and applauded the achievements of this fine young man. It was a heartwarming moment that brought a lump to the throat of this "hardened" West Aussie.

Throughout my tour of the U.S. in 2011, I saw many examples of how the serving military were given homage, from special mentions at public events to being offered first-to-board opportunities at airports. (Although I've never seen a single uniformed member of the military accept this offer.) Even for a died-in-the-wool pacifist, it's difficult to mount a case against this code of honoring those who serve to protect the rights and welfare of the civilian populace.

Yet in Australia, the land of the great down-to-earth understatement, we do not venture to bring attention to those who deserve such honors. About five percent of the IFAP workforce includes ex-armed services personnel. Prior to my 2011 trip to the U.S. we did nothing particularly special to honor their contribution to our great country. We do now. And so my AC4P story begins. But first a cultural insight.

The Australian armed services have a long and proud history which semi-officially commenced in 1899 when the Boer War broke out in South Africa. Australia was made up of six colonies on the verge of becoming a federation. The war was seen as an opportunity for the emerging federation to show its commitment to Britain and to define its identity.

After the Australian Federation commenced in 1901, the new Commonwealth Government continued to support the war until its eventual conclusion in 1902. The Australian troops' reputation for bravery, toughness and cool-headedness during the Boer War became the foundation for the Australian warrior image.

Remembrance Day (also known as Poppy Day or Armistice Day) is observed on the 11th of November to recall the end of the hostilities of World War I on that date in 1918. This also serves as a memorial day to remember the members of the armed forces of the Commonwealth who had died in the line of duty. Hostilities formally ended "at the 11th hour of the 11th day of the 11th month," in accordance with the Armistice signed between the warring parties.

Australian armed services also commemorate ANZAC day on the 25th of April. This is in remembrance of the landing of the Australian and New Zealand Army Corps (ANZACs) on the shores of the Gallipoli Peninsula (Turkey)in 1915.Aiming to secure a sea route to Russia, the British and French launched a naval campaign to force a passage through the Dardanelles. After the naval operation, an amphibious landing was undertaken on the Gallipoli peninsula to capture the Ottoman capital of Constantinople (Istanbul).

The small cove on the Gallipoli Peninsula in and around which Australian and New Zealand troops landed became known as "Anzac Cove." This sector became known as "Anzac." After eight months the land campaign failed, and the invasion force was withdrawn to Egypt. The cost: 8,709 Australians killed and 19,441 wounded. New Zealand lost 2,721 soldiers, with 4,752 wounded.

The campaign is often considered to mark the birth of national consciousness in Australia and New Zealand and the date of the landing, the 25th of April, is known as

"ANZAC Day." To this day, April 25th is the date on which the sacrifice of those who had died in the Great War, and subsequent arenas of armed conflict, is remembered.

We "tough" Aussies care, but only when the country has an outpouring of nationalistic pride, which manifests itself at ANZAC day, do we *actively* demonstrate caring for our troops. I question whether this is an appropriate level of recognition. And so begins my story of AC4P.

An AC4P Paradigm Shift

In September 2011, I was fortunate to visit Istanbul, Turkey, with my wife, Michelle. I convinced Michelle to take the gruelling 20-hour round trip by road to visit Gallipoli, particularly to visit Anzac Cove, the ill-fated landing place of our armed services in 1915. Anzac Cove holds a special place in the hearts of all Australians, especially our military personnel. But as I learned, many contemporary servicemen and women never get to visit the site during their years of service.

Anzac Cove is a truly inspiring spot. It's difficult to avoid getting swept up into the mystique and unfortunate history of the place. The thought of so many young lives being cruelly cut down in a land so far from home fills one with a sense of loss that is difficult to define. It's perfectly understandable why this place is so important to our serving personnel.

While standing on the rocky beach of the Cove a thought struck me, "If IFAP's ex-servicemen and women on staff had been unable to get to this place, why not take some of this place to them?" Without much forethought I swept up a handful of the pebbles on the beach, handpicked some of the more shaped and colored ones, and stuck 13 of them in my pocket. After a thorough cleaning at the hotel, I transported them with me back to Australia.

A Special Remembrance

The closest memorial date to my return was Remembrance Day – 11th of November, 2011. Without their knowledge, I traced where each of the ex-servicemen and women on the IFAP staff would be on that day. As luck would have it, four were on duty, two at our head office, one at IFAP's southern-most site approximately 20 kilometres from our head office, and the last staff member at a remote site, 40 kilometres north of our head office.

I advised the managers of the two IFAP sites I wished them to host a formal Remembrance Day ceremony to be overseen by the ex-servicemen and women – a one-minute moment of silence at the rising of the 11th hour and flags at half-mast. The three staff at the IFAP sites were overjoyed to be honored this way. My managers willingly collaborated with my request, stopping classes and joining the ex-servicemen and women at the flag-lowering ceremony. About 70 people, staff and course participants alike, joined in at each site.

However, no flagpole was available at the remote site. Without prior knowledge of my staff member, I arranged for a television broadcast of the official flag-lowering ceremony to be broadcast from our nation's capital in Canberra to the remote site. I then opted to drive to the remote site to pay a "surprise visit" for my ex-serviceman colleague.

I arrived at the site around 10:30a.m., and checked out the facility, ensuring arrangements were as expected. At about 10:50a.m., I let myself into the room and advised my colleague of the broadcast.I asked him to officiate the "ceremony" to be held adjacent to his training room. He was astonished I would do something like that for him.

The broadcast went smoothly. We were joined by his class of about 20 course participants; and after a short coffee break, we reassembled in the training room. At this juncture I told the class of my colleague's (Rod's) service, in arenas of conflict from the Middle East, Southeast Asia and Papua New Guinea.

In typical knockabout Aussie fashion, Rod tried to dismiss his contribution as "just doing my job," but his justifiable sense of pride at being recognized was self-evident. I then presented Rod with a green AC4P wristband I had received previously from Scott when we were in Chicago. I told him it was a fitting tribute for his service. (He still wears that wristband today, despite my cajoling to "pass it forward".)

At this juncture, Rod became noticeably emotional. I then presented him with one of the pebbles I had collected from Anzac Cove, and told him of my story of how I had thought about him and my other colleagues who were ex-servicemen and women while I was taking in the Anzac Cove panorama. Rod was visibly moved.

To see this man, who had fought in some of the toughest campaigns in modern warfare, hug me and tear up was one of the most moving experiences in my life. That moving experience served to form a lasting bond between the two of us. To this day, Rod jokes with me that he will "get even," but I know he has mounted that little pebble with his war medals, and that it holds a special place of pride for him.

The same scenario (minus the flag ceremony) was repeated at the other two sites I visited during the day. My colleagues at the head office, Fiona (an ex-submariner) and Jacqui (Navy), both burst into tears upon receipt of their AC4P wristbands and pebbles. Days later they were still talking about the ceremony.

My other colleague, Dave, ex-SAS (Special Air Service), did not display such open emotion. However, he later showed me his pebble which he had mounted into a pendant he wears attached to a neck chain.

Sustaining AC4P Remembrance

This AC4P story is more than a single-yet-significant event. At IFAP we now celebrate both Anzac Day and Remembrance Day with flag-lowering ceremonies at our campuses, presided over by our ex-servicemen and women who are encouraged to wear full uniform to the functions. I have encouraged the permanent adornment of our office doorways with memorabilia of the regiments in which they served so as to mark that a proud regiment member resides within. And of course, I am in the throes of planning a major event for 2015 to mark the centenary of the fateful Anzac Day landing at Gallipoli.

Thank you Scott, Joanne and the others for inspiring me to demonstrate AC4P behavior by recognizing my ex-servicemen and women colleagues in 2011, and beyond.

CHAPTER 26

Making Time for People:
Don't delay to actively care

Joanne Dean Geller

WE HAVE ALL SAID to others or to ourselves, "I will get to that later or maybe I will have time next week." Let's be real about this and consider that waiting to do the important things we talk about can set us up for disappointment and missed opportunities. Reflect on those times you said to yourself, "Why didn't I call or visit that person when my instincts told me to do so?"

We think we have all the time in the world, but of course we don't. When it comes to AC4P we must grab opportunities to actively care as soon as we see them. This book is about inspiring you to embrace those AC4P opportunities sooner rather than later. The following experiences illustrate the meaningfulness that can come from acting on caring as soon as an opportunity presents itself.

Meeting a Distinguished Professor

For eight years now, my husband has spoken to me about an eminent professor he once worked with at the University. I've heard him say many times, "I need to visit John Cairns." Although Scott spoke so highly of this former colleague, he never acted on his words of caring. These are just those situations that call for action. If it's important, don't delay to actively care.

Formerly the Director of the University Center for Environmental and Hazardous Materials Studies at Virginia Tech (VT), Dr. John Cairns is now retired. An esteemed University Distinguished Professor Emeritus who committed his life to his family and academia is now alone. He's just the person who needs a visitor.

"So, this is it," I tell myself as I go off to find this gentleman. I had discovered Dr. Cairns lives in a Care Center in Blacksburg, Virginia. This Sunday afternoon I enter the Center and ask for his whereabouts. I find his building and am told to go to Room 207 on the second floor and knock on his door. A deep voice responds, "Just come in, I am laying in bed".

With a smile on my face, I pop my head around the corner and notice a very handsome, grey-haired gentleman. I smile and say, "I am married to Scott Geller and I just had to find you because he has spoken so highly of you." He replies, "Come sit down," and he immediately reminisces about his work with Scott, claiming, "We were both such mavericks at the University".

My next move is to call Scott, and when he answers I say, "Here's someone who wants to talk

Dr. John Cairns, Jr.

with you." I hand my cell-phone to John and John's face just lights up. I then listen and learn about the fascinating career of Dr. Cairns. Before I leave I promise to bring Scott on the next visit.

That next visit happened the following week, and listening to these two creative scholars was an opportunity I wouldn't have missed for the world.

After a few days I delivered a few of Scott's books to John. I promised to bring Scott back with three of his best students who are interested in ecological sustainability, the research domain in which John and Scott had collaborated. The research these men have accomplished will enlighten and inspire these young people.

This story exemplifies the ripple effect – how the positive impact of one kind act for one person can spread to many others.

From One Kind Act to Another

As the clock ticks, it's time to share my AC4P experience with Billy. One sunny Sunday in October of 2011 after participating in an AC4P meeting at our Make-A-DiffRanch, I drive to Christiansburg, Virginia and pass a young man walking with difficulty. I had seen this individual before on the same road and now I think to myself, "I wonder what his story is and how had he been injured".

When I arrive at the shopping mall, I sit in my car and reflect, "If I am really an actively-caring person I should go back and offer him a ride." I do not ask strangers if they need a ride, but my instincts tell me to alter my paradigm this time.

I turn around and pull up next to this man and ask, "May I give you a ride?" He smiles and I tell him not to be afraid and that it would mean a lot to me if I could help. He replies, "Yes" and enters my vehicle with a smile. I ask him what had happened to him and he shares his story.

As a young man he was shot in the head because he was in the wrong place at the wrong time. He has endured years of rehabilitation and continues treatment to this day. He is lame and unable to use his right arm. He lives with his mom and walks everyday to get exercise. I ask him if he is a VT fan and he says, "Absolutely". "Do you have a VT sweatshirt?" I ask. "No I don't", Billy replies. Well since you are going to the mall to pay some bills how about I treat you to a VT sweatshirt? He displays the biggest smile, and we drive to the store.

I then tell Billy about the AC4P Movement and that he's providing me the pleasure of doing something nice for someone else and I'm so grateful. I ask him if he had ever been to Panera Bread and he responds, "Never". So we have lunch at Panera.

Scott, Billy, and Joanne before a CABS research meeting.

Subsequently, I have taken Billy to some of Scott's large introductory psychology classes and to several of our weekly research meetings. Scott and I have also provided him with some work he can do with his one useful arm.

My instincts were so right on this one. If I hadn't stopped that day to offer a kind deed, I would not have met Billy and developed a special friendship to share with others. Billy is truly an inspiration to all of us, and his involvement with our group enables him to feel useful and appreciated, and to experience a sense of community.

Many of my visits to see Billy have included conversations with his mom. It's humbling to spend time with them and see the love and loyalty they have for each other. They are a very modest family, and every time I pick up Billy to attend one of our classes at VT I smile inside for this special opportunity to actively care. AC4P behavior is rewarding and self-motivating.

The Dick Sanderson Story

My next anecdote has timeless and heartfelt meaning for me and it has touched the lives of many in special ways. This is the story of my special high-school friend, Dick Sanderson, who was stricken with ALS (Amyotrophic Lateral Sclerosis), commonly known as Lou Gehrig's disease.

Eight years ago, Dick called and asked me to reach out to our high-school friends and tell them he has ALS and soon would not be able to talk. That simple phone call provided me with opportunities that have given new meaning to my life. The photo on the next page includes my classmates from the Class of 1969 who have met each year to raise money for the Sanderson family. This challenging experience has provided us all the opportunity to actively care for Dick and his family.

As I write this story, Dick Sanderson is totally paralyzed, requires a machine to breath, and is fed through a tube. He can hear, see and think, but is incapable of any output. He is trapped in his body with no means of communicating to others. His psychological courage to hang on under these most difficult circumstances inspires all of us to complain less about our misfortunes and to reach out to help others less fortunate.

Dick's wife Dawn and their three children work together to care for him 24/7 with daily support of in-home nurses and friends. It's both humbling and heartening to experience the interpersonal support this man has captivated. Dawn, his leading caretaker, will tell you she is blessed with opportunities to actively care for her husband with never-ending love and devotion.[2]

All of us share this story of Dick Sanderson, which in turn motivates others to take more time to appreciate their friends and family. Each year, more than 5,000 U.S. residents are diagnosed with ALS; and following diagnosis the average ALS patient lives two to five years.[1] We have profound sympathy for those stricken with ALS, count our blessings, and embrace opportunities to actively care for individuals less fortunate than we.

My experience with John, Billy and Dick remind me each day of the power of AC4P through simple one-to-one personal communication. Make time for people and your time on earth will be enriched.

Center: Dick Sanderson. Second row: Lorna Schmitt Danckwerth, Karen Steffan Gannon, Dawn Sanderson, Dan Fagan, Wayne Meyer, Betsy Hanna Sollenberger, Sue Schwab Windt, Lynda Martenis Burns. Back row: Suzy Coutts Selby, Arnie Scalio, Michele Corona Grajewski, Ernie Blane, Steve Thomas, Rod Dorman, Brian Peters, Eddie Thomas, Joanne Dean Geller, Dan Windt, and Annie Paterson.

Note

1. Kibbs, L. (2006). ALS and Driving 4 Life. In J. Dean, & E.S. Geller (Eds.). *The power of friendship: Dick Sanderson's positive fight with ALS* (pp. 3-25). Newport, VA: Make-A-Difference, LLC.

2. On November 6th, 2013, Dick Sanderson passed away peacefully at home, surrounded by his family. Three days later, I attended his emotional funeral and an overflowing and moving memorial service.

CHAPTER 27

Cultivating an AC4P Family:
Bringing AC4P home

Corrine Picht

GROWING UP I LIVED on a farm with all the standard farming responsibilities. I often took risks and some might have classified me as your typical tomboy. Growing up on the farm I can honestly say thinking about my safety or anyone else's was the farthest thing from my mind. I was just lucky I was never hurt, nor any of my other family members.

After graduating from high school, I was hired at a local manufacturing facility. Ten years went by in the blink of an eye and soon I found myself just punching the time clock. One day my supervisor came to me and asked if I'd be interested in learning about people-based safety (PBS) and the AC4P Movement.

The opportunity to be a member of our PBS Team sounded interesting, so I took him up on it, although I didn't know what I was signing up for. I could never have imagined how much AC4P was going to impact my life, both in and outside the workplace.

Building an AC4P Culture among Co-Workers

As a member of the PBS Team, my challenge was to get co-workers to talk to each other about their safe and unsafe behaviors. So, we developed a formal safety coaching process where one co-worker observed another co-worker and gave AC4P behavioral feedback. Our mission was to learn from one another and share new ideas, but to also point out things that looked risky. In the beginning, this was quite a challenge because interpersonal observation and feedback is not common among co-workers.

One of my more memorable experiences involved trying to convince a co-worker to participate in AC4P coaching. He and I were chatting while walking by one of our assembly lines. During our conversation he began giving me a hard time about being so actively involved with PBS and AC4P. Our conversation went back and forth about this subject for several minutes.

Then to my surprise, he stopped talking to me and instantly stopped another man working on the assembly line. The co-worker was doing something extremely risky. Not only did he explain why the behavior was at-risk, but he also showed his co-worker the safe way to perform the task.

I just stood there in amazement, while waiting for him to finish his conversation with the co-worker. When he returned I smiled and looked him right in the eye and said, "If that wasn't actively caring then I don't know what is."

His reaction was just a simple smile. He felt good about speaking up to his co-worker and so did I. Sometimes workers just need a little encouragement to see how important AC4P is to the culture of our workplace culture.

Taking AC4P Home

Since I was discovering this deep passion for AC4P at work, I found myself incorporating the same concepts in my personal life. AC4P became a part of the way I interacted and communicated with people at home and in my community, as well as at work. I started to connect with people on different levels, whether they were co-workers, family, or friends. I always felt I was giving something back when I actively cared for others.

My children soon picked up on my AC4P behaviors, and very often played a large role in promoting these principles in their lives. I didn't realize the impact of AC4P on their lives until one day I was out shopping in a grocery store with my six-year old. He pointed out the way a shelf was loaded and how unstable it was. We reported it to one of the store employees. After that experience, both my boys have continued to look for different ways to actively care for the safety and welfare of others.

Several weeks later, I was out shopping again and my youngest son, who was only four years old at the time, saw an older lady drop an item on the floor. My son went right over to pick it up for her. She thanked him and commented, "What a nice little boy you are".

When he returned to me, I also thanked him for his actively caring. His response, "I'm closer to the ground than she is and I didn't want to see her get hurt".

The kids began to ask themselves and others the question, "Is what I'm about to do safe or not?" As a mother, that was and still is a priceless moment for me.

From stories like these and the impact AC4P was having on my two boys, I then made up a fun game for us all to play in the car. We started with road signs and traffic lights. The boys had to explain what they meant and how they influenced the driving of other vehicles on the road.

Next, we progressed to making lane changes safely and then safety-related items we should always have in the vehicle (e.g., flashlight, first-aid kits, jumper cables). They also had no problem letting me know when I wasn't following the proper driving procedures.

The Journey Continues

As you can only imagine, we are still working on how to give effective AC4P feedback to our co-workers. The AC4P principles have changed my life in so many different ways. They have helped me develop self-confidence and enhance my capabilities to influence others. I'm sure the potential was always there, but getting involved in AC4P helped me turn good intentions to action.

Indeed, my interaction with others and my outlook on life has totally changed. I look forward to going to work where we are being more proactive rather than reactive in safety. I'm proud to say AC4P is a value I have now instilled in my children.

CHAPTER 28

Barriers to AC4P in Families:
What's the quality of AC4P on the home front?

Dave Johnson

I WAS 12 YEARS OLD when my father died suddenly, completely unexpectedly. I remember a neighbor down the street, a teacher, telling me, "Oh, you're really at a tough age for your dad to die. You were just starting to know him."

My dad came from a large family, and I recall my aunts and uncles, especially my uncles, trying to show their own form of actively caring, telling me, "Dave, we'll go to games. I'll take you to games." Maybe they included movies and watching me play sports, I don't remember.

But I know for a fact my uncles, well meaning as I think they were, never came through and took me to any games – or movies or whatever they intended as substitute dads. No AC4P behavior from them to me. I think AC4P applications in the complicated dynamics of family is damn difficult.

I didn't harbor any resentment about my uncles not coming through, at least not consciously. Instead, I was preoccupied at the time with sticking out, being different than my friends because I was the only one in seventh grade who didn't have a dad. I dreaded that first day of the school year when the teacher went around the class asking everyone what their fathers did for a living.

I don't think I even really wanted to go out with my uncles. It would be weird, not normal. During early adolescence, you want to fit in and not stick out. So the actively caring that dissipated didn't really bother me. At least I don't think it did. My uncles were raising their own kids, my cousins, and their AC4P intentions for me couldn't keep up with reality.

How Do Families Actively Care?

That did leave a mark on me, however, and it relates to AC4P, though of course I never called it that. You would think the most intimate and sustained AC4P occurs within immediate families.

You might also think love and caring between parents and children, or within more extended families, is something so biologically and culturally embedded is does not qualify as AC4P. After all, if AC4P should occur naturally in any situation, it's within the family, right?

Not so. For many parents AC4P nurturing for their kids is neither instinctual nor easy. Working mothers often feel deep guilt over not doing enough, not being there, especially for their young kids.

Fathers, not as biologically connected to their offspring, nowadays join clubs and workshops on how to be better dads. Plus, fathers can feel guilt over too much business travel or long hours immersed in their work which means less "quality time" with their kids. I equate AC4P with quality time. It's a quality act.

The Quality of AC4P in Families

My future son-in-law recently told my wife and me he believes only the kids who have had easy and continual access to both parents, and years of parental support and encouragement, end up physically and mentally healthy, without resentment or outright anger directed at their parents.

So what's so difficult about giving your kid quality AC4P behavior? All they need is access, listening, questioning, observing, staying close, behavioral praise and corrective feedback, and supportive discipline? Simply put, parents need to be there for their children.

Woody Allen said life is 90% just showing up. Is it that difficult for parents to "show up" for their children? Too often the answer is "Yes".

AC4P time is problematic for many parents, especially for two-income families. Many moms and dads love their jobs, not more than their kids of course, but to the degree they will work nights and weekends. In these cases, there is simply not enough time left over to give quality AC4P to the kids.

Many moms and dads trudge through more than one job they hate in order to cover basic living expenses. The fatigue and stress, anxiety and depression, and eventual burnout, robs many parents of the ability to give quality AC4P time to their kids.

Then there are the fathers who walk out on the family. The kids are raised by their grandparents. What about parents addicted to gambling, sex, alcohol, meth, coke, and so on? So we have broken-down families and alienated children. No AC4P behavior there.

The AC4P Challenge at Home

I believe it's easier to apply AC4P principles in workplaces, schools, the military, even penal colonies than in families. Rules govern these other institutions. Behavior is easier to regulate. Peer pressure exerts itself. Families are more fluid, less structured. Unless dad is an ex-military guy running a very tight ship, which certainly happens.

Most families live in tight quarters, year after year, with so many good and bad interpersonal experiences, that all types of feelings arise among all the family members that can squeeze out opportunities for pure, unadulterated quality AC4P behavior. Call it pain, blame, scars, tension, or as the kids get older and drive and head to college, parents are just running around doing their own thing, with little occasion for sharing and caring behavior.

Finally, I think AC4P faces challenges on the home front because many moms and dads do not have the self-esteem, competence or feeling in control enough to engage in quality AC4P behavior for their kids. Maybe they had kids too young. Or they had too many kids. Or maybe they didn't get the support they needed from their own parents.

Perhaps they thought proper parenting is instinctual, and they never learned how to be an effective mom or dad. There was no sense of belonging. And so ineffective parenthood is passed down – a very undesirable example of *pay it forward*.

By the way, everything I've touched on here is relevant for spouses caring for each other. And the AC4P applications can be broadened to include extended families: grandparents, aunts and uncles, cousins.

In some cultures outside the U.S., such as Japan and other Eastern countries, and some European countries, AC4P is an unspoken multi-generational cultural bond.

The Quantity of AC4P in Families

One more thing: Missing out on my father's actively-caring love, counsel, coaching, general feedback, guidance and, yes, even corrective discipline when I could have used it during my middle-school, high-school, college years and beyond, did deeply commit me to making sure I was present and accounted for to actively care for my daughter and son. Now they are both young adults, and looking back, I may have gone overboard with AC4P behavior. Is that possible? I think so.

A number of us Baby Boomers, raised by remote fathers, the norm for those "Mad Men" times, have vowed to be closer to our kids. You know, the "helicopter parents" who hover over their kids, text them daily in college, do their homework if necessary, and pace the sidelines at every youth soccer, baseball, basketball, football, ice hockey, you name the sport, since the kids were, oh, maybe five.

I believe many of us Boomers felt our parents did not actively care enough. So we more than made up for that by spoiling and codling and pumping up our kids' self-esteem to the point they demand A's from their teachers, more playing time from coaches, lucrative jobs right out of college, and often expect immediate gratification, and oh, with no adversity please.

In Conclusion

AC4P behavior is a tricky balancing act when performed in the highly emotional environment of a family and within the complexities of parenthood. This is different, and I think more challenging than AC4P applied to random strangers, or in schools and workplaces, where emotions don't run so high and organizational structure can include rules, education/training, and incentive/reward programs to prompt and motivate AC4P behavior.

I'd love to see the AC4P Movement include AC4P workshops for families. Cohesive, actively-caring families sustain society. What's more important than that? The workplace? Middle schools? Prisons? No disrespect, but healthy, caring, well-balanced families come first in my book.

Part V: Wristband Stories from ac4p.org

AUTOPILOT: functioning in an unthinking or reflexive manner. Most of you are familiar with this term. Most people do it, function on autopilot that is. It's easier to think at System 1 and perform our daily routines, focused only on ourselves and the tasks at hand. Too often we don't think beyond ourselves and use System 2 thinking[1] to recognize those around us who might need our help.

Aly Neel was adapting to a busy schedule in a new city while interning with the Cook Political Report in Washington, D.C., but it didn't stop her from reflecting and taking time for others.

Dozens of people jam into a D.C. Metro train during rush hour – a diverse crowd of students, business people, and politicians perspiring from the heat, noses stuck in others' armpits. Conversations with riders one doesn't know is rare. On this day sly glances are made at a man catching a snooze in the corner. He's snoring obnoxiously, but no one says anything to him, no hands poke him in the arm. Strangers are not to be bothered – right?[2]

Aly Neel's Metro Story

After living in D.C. for some time and riding the Metro during many rush-hour mornings and nights, I have become well aware of the unwritten rule, "You just ride".

On my way home from work one day, I catch the red-line train toward Union Station per usual. A young man, wearing a suit, is sitting inches away from me. He's so close I can almost reach him. I look up and notice he seems very upset – wringing his hands, shaking his head. Unintentionally, I stare at him. I try but can't look away because he looks as if he is on the verge of tears.

I immediately think, "What can I do?" I know I have to say something, but I'm uncertain how to reach out. We finally make eye contact, and I give him a smile – the empathetic kind I would give a friend whose family member just died. I want him to know I'm sorry for whatever he is going through. Immediately after our exchange I look down, sort of embarrassed. I remember people aren't *supposed* to smile at each other on the Metro!

The Metro slows down and comes to a stop. The guy, still shaken up, stands to get off the train, but then pauses to touch me on my shoulder. He says: "You probably already forgot what you did. It didn't seem like a big deal, but this year has been the worst year of my life. What you just did a second ago, though really small, is probably the most anyone has reached out to me in this past year."

Rolling up his shirtsleeve, he tells me, "It represents a pay-it-forward notion." He hands me a green wristband, embossed with the words "Actively Caring for People".

My mouth is agape. I had heard of this AC4P Movement, but I had never received a wristband until now.

Aly N.
Washington, D.C.

ac4p.org Launch[3]

That wristband was one of the 2,000 AC4P wristbands distributed on the Virginia Tech (VT) campus eight months prior. After hearing this story, our AC4P team knew the AC4P wristbands could create a widespread movement far beyond VT. So, we took the green wristbands, embossed with "Actively Caring for People" that Scott Geller had been distributing at safety conferences for two decades, and added a numbering system that enabled computer tracking of the AC4P *See*, *Act*, *Pass*, and *Share* (SAPS) process.

Specifically, we asked individuals and groups to look for AC4P behavior (i.e., See) and reward such behavior with an AC4P wristband (i.e., Act). Wristband recipients are requested to look for AC4P behaviors from others and pass on the wristband (i.e., Pass). These interpersonal exchanges are documented on the AC4P website (see www.ac4p.org) with the wristband number (i.e., Share). Tracking these positive interactions worldwide rewards and thus motivates people to follow suit and do more.

ac4p.org Stories

Stories posted on ac4p.org tell of interpersonal exchanges between people receiving and giving AC4P wristbands after specific AC4P behaviors. Wristband recognition occurs for simple gestures – such as holding the door for a stranger – and more complex acts requiring skills, financial stability, and time. These acts occur in various locations, including schools, restaurants, highways, community streets, and stores.

Many stories reflect competence, commitment, and courage. They involve people acting on behalf of family, friends, co-workers, and strangers in both reactive circumstances and in proactive situations.

Some individuals receive a wristband for actively caring in reactive situations, such as standing up for a friend after hearing a racist remark (wristband #407), rebuilding a home after tornadoes devastated Joplin, Missouri (#4766), helping after a sibling's car broke down (#2974), and saving the life of a motorcyclist after a crash (#240).

Others are recognized for proactive AC4P behavior, such as helping a friend, holding the door for extended periods of time, walking an intoxicated stranger to her home safely, taking care of a sick roommate, and giving a wallet filled with money back to the stranger who lost it.

From Random to Intentional Kindness

Every story is unique, with different people, places, and behaviors. However, one thread runs through each act of kindness: Intention. I bet you've heard of "Random Acts of Kindness".[3] This popular slogan implies that acts of kindness "just happen" without planning or forethought. Most compassionate acts of helping others are not random.

Every AC4P good-doer reminds us to be mindful and intentional (i.e., System 2 thinking[1]) regarding opportunities to actively care. Additionally, these AC4P stories suggest the helpers receive much in return: Smiles from strangers and genuine appreciation from friends. They think to themselves, "That could've been worse if I hadn't actively cared" or "I really made my friend's day".

We hope these stories inspire you to recognize others with AC4P wristbands wherever you see intentional acts of caring. Such AC4P behavior will range from small acts of kindness to heroic demonstrations of courage. Your AC4P servant leadership will help cultivate a culture of compassion worldwide.

The following AC4P stories were selected from more than 2,000 posted on the ac4p. org website since January, 2011. The stories depict instances of individuals going "above and beyond the call of duty," intervening as a concerned and compassionate bystander on behalf of the health, safety, and/or well-being of someone else.

"Above and Beyond" Stories

From an AC4P Wristband to an AC4P Lifestyle

My freshman year I was lucky to have some crazy roommates who truly tested everything about me. At this point, I was a rough and temperamental personality trying to fit my way into the world, but struggling to adapt. However, I was given something from Benjamin Caleb George. It was a green wristband with the following words inscribed: "Actively Caring for People". At first, I wore the wristband to make Ben happy (sorry Ben but hey it's true), but the words started to etch their way into my life. I found myself trying to become better for everyone, including my friends.

It was tough and I can be a dramatic handful at times, but my life became better and I found myself smiling every day. Today, I lost that green wristband – the one that has been with me for two years, showing up in every good and bad photo. I didn't notice until I looked down and it was gone.

Its weight and words have truly sunk into my skin and I guess it has done its job. So I want to thank Ben for giving me something he might not even know would have a huge effect on my life. And for everyone who has been by my side this whole time, I know it isn't easy and you didn't have to be there, but you did. For that, I thank you. I still have more work to do to better myself, but at least I have a great start.

Nathaniel C.
Richmond, VA

A Compassionate Truck Driver

I am currently on my way back home to Virginia from New York. Long story short, my car broke down. Stuck on the side of the road we called AAA. A tow truck came, with a driver by the name of Taka (Take-a). This man is trying everything in his power to get us all the way from Middletown, Delaware to Virginia Beach, Virginia (some 215 miles) without charging us $500 dollars. He is sticking his neck out to do something for two stranded women that wouldn't benefit him at all. True human compassion! *Wristband #2974*

Jenee E.
Middletown, DE

Offering a Seat

Today, I was in Au Bon Pain and saw two girls offer a seat at their table to a blind student during the busy lunch hour. Then, they proceeded to put down their homework, and have a conversation with her as well as refill her drink when she ran out.

Without acts of kindness like these, I don't know if the student would have ever found a table during the rush hour at Au Bon Pain! I was so ecstatic to be able to give out my first wristband, especially to somebody who truly went out of her way to make somebody else's day! *Wristband #168*

Elise C.
Blacksburg, VA

Students First

I gave a wristband to Shawn Wells, Principal at Bollinger Canyon Elementary School. This is a public school that hosts five intensive special-education classrooms for students with autism and other developmental disabilities.

During the past several years, the special-education population at Bollinger Canyon has grown quite a bit, and Shawn has continued to build and support a culture that accepts, understands, and invites special education.

Just a few weeks ago, Shawn designated one of the "staff only" bathrooms to be used for an intensive toilet training program for a seven-year-old student who was not yet potty trained. This student now successfully uses the toilet on a daily basis for the first time in his life. Additionally, his parents no longer need to spend countless dollars purchasing diapers. Shawn attends and actively participates in nearly all of her student's IEP's and makes frequent visits to the special education classrooms to check in on students and ensure she is familiar with their programs.

With such a large population of special education students, this adds quite a bit of work to Shawn's already busy schedule...but she makes it happen...and she always does it smiling. In my work with Shawn, she has always put the needs of her students first. Thank you Shawn...for Actively Caring about all of your students and their families!! *Wristband #1294*

Joel V.
San Ramon, CA

Coming to the Rescue

My car has had a lot go wrong with it in the past year or so. I never take care of it. The "Check Engine" and "Maint Required" lights have been on for as long as I can remember, and it's been a joke that any day now the thing might explode (not really, I hope).

I let my boyfriend borrow my car one day, and when he returned it my brake light was fixed, the "Check Engine" and "Maint Required" lights were off, there was a brand new cap on my gas tank (I had lost it before), my oil had been checked, and fluid had been put in my windshield wiper thing.

Turns out my boyfriend had taken my car in to get a full list of what was wrong with it (a long list) and wanted to fix everything. But he doesn't know a lot about cars. Turns out Dave came to the rescue! Dave is my boyfriend's roommate. He happens to know a lot about cars and took the extra time to look over and fix the long list of things wrong with it, just because! *Wristband #22549*

Michelle L.
Blacksburg, VA

Helping a Missing Child

I was at Great Wolf lodge when the front desk called to ask if I was missing a child. I said, "No". When I woke up the next morning, I saw a lady with the missing boy.

The missing child had been in the lobby all night with the lady. She got him blankets and held him. I learned she'd been there for seven hours taking care of that boy. The boy's dad didn't even know when he woke up that his son was gone. I gave my wristband to "the lady of the night," someone actively cared! *Wristband #1425*

Logan O.
Charlotte, NC

A Compassionate Student Patrol

A student safety patrol, Eli, showed compassion to another student who boarded my bus in tears. The student proceeded to fight with her older siblings; one of them being Eli's peer.

Eli handled the situation beyond what is required of a safety patrol. She was able to immediately calm the child and find a resolution to what would have surely escalated into something very distracting for me as the bus driver. It allowed me to carry on instead of waiting for a safe place to pullover to address it myself. I gave him *wristband #8215*

Jennifer S.
Great Falls, VA

Recognition in the Worst of Times

This past February there was a shooting at my school: Chardon High School. It's been rough for everyone – some more than others. Like many teenagers, I feel as if I'm fighting the world alone, not sure if what I'm fighting for is even right. I just finished track. I'm not a star runner; I'm actually quite slow, but I do it because I enjoy it. The other faster kids are still in season and still being coached.

Anyway, after the shooting my high school received thousands of cards. They mean more to me than any of the other gifts my high school has received. Sadly we must take them down "to move on" as I keep being told. It seems as if half the kids in the school already forgot why the cards are there, anyway.

Nevertheless, I feel as if I need to read the cards just so a person's actively caring is not thrown into some box without the slightest thought. I volunteered two times to help take down the cards. Both times I read each one before sorting them into their boxes. I try not to cry but there is no shame in getting teary-eyed.

Of course some of the cards hit home, others made me smile, but in general I feel that after the clean-up I have renewed strength to deal with the confusing mess of feelings.

I can tell myself I did this clean-up for those who wrote the letters, or for the victims of the shooting, or to help the janitor who would have to deal with the thousands of cards, but I did this for me. I wanted to and that's why I did it.

The day I was taking down the cards I was extremely sad. I was thinking how I truly haven't accomplished anything since February. My grades dropped, track was not a particularly successful season. The worst part is that my relationships with friends and family are strained. I keep reading the cards, taking the strengths those individuals sent, trying to feel it.

Amazingly my track coach, Bartley comes up behind me one day and says, "You're a good kid, you know that?" I needed to hear those words more than anything. He pulls off his AC4P wristband and gives it to me. I was speechless. This told me I was doing something right. I had always liked and admired him, but this was something more than I ever expected. That was my coach actively caring for me, and I look forward to paying it forward and passing on this wristband *#47735*

Megan W.
Chardon, OH

A Very Grateful Student and Fellow Hokie

I don't usually post stories but I thought this one was an awesome testament to the kind of people we have in Blacksburg. I am driving down Southgate toward Airport Drive and hit something in the middle of the road. My tire immediately bursts and I have to pull over. Of course I have no idea what to do. I get out and call my parents, as if they can help from four hours away.

With no answer I'm scared and unsure what to do. The first few cars fly by me and then finally an older gentleman offers to help. He immediately starts changing the tire and asks me to simply direct traffic. As I'm standing in the middle of the four-way intersection a student walks by. He drops his book bag and rushes over to help me.

After a few minutes of feeling like I'm going to be hit in the middle of the intersection, I call the Blacksburg Police Department to take over. In a matter of minutes two officers respond and thank me for doing the best I could. I have the spare tire in place, the student begins describing the "actively caring" campaign and he gives the older gentleman one of the green wristbands we have all seen around campus.

Until now I didn't know what "paying it forward" really meant. My crazy day turned out to be a story I'll never forget and one I will tell a million times to show people what it really means to be a Hokie. I wouldn't trade this school and town for anything in the world. UT PROSIM, and GO HOKIES. *Wristband #52517*

Kelley C.
Blacksburg, VA

Bystander Intervention Stories

AC4P Behavior Saves a Life

I witnessed a man wreck a dirt bike through a glass window. Once I heard the breaking glass, I ran to the scene and saw lacerations on his arm and several on his leg. I knew this was serious when I saw the amount of blood he lost in the 20 or so seconds it took for me to get there.

I, along with another Appalachian State University student, used t-shirts to stop the bleeding and make him comfortable until the paramedics arrived. He received more than 200 stitches for all of his wounds. We were told he would have bled out if the bleeding would not have been stopped right away. *Wristband #240*

Riley S.
Boone, NC

Corrective Feedback for a Racist Remark

I invited my friend to hang out over at our fraternity house. You might not know right away by looking at him, but he has a white mother and a black father. For most members of the fraternity, this is not an issue.

However, when we were on the porch one of the brothers, unknowing of my friend's ethnicity, begins yelling racist remarks. I immediately confronted my bro in front of guests and other brothers and told him to stop, that his bigotry was unacceptable.

After the fact, I felt guilty to belong to an organization where this kind of racism was present, and I felt incredibly troubled that my guest experienced this at my house. I didn't know the impact of me standing up for my friend until he presented me with this green wristband. The next chapter meeting we established a rule and judiciary system to handle out of line hostile or harrassing behavior. *Wristband #10805*

Scott M.
Statesboro, GA

Stopping to Help on I-95

It was the day after Christmas on a Sunday morning at 6 A.M. I'm a nurse and was driving into Baltimore for work.

I was cruising on I-95 just like every morning and saw a car that appeared stalled in the middle of the interstate about 100 feet ahead. I pulled into the right lane and slowed down. As I approached, I realized this car in the middle of the road was totaled and none of its lights were on. I immediately pulled onto the side of the road and reached into my pocket to pull out my phone to dial 911.

Before I was able to call, a woman squeezed out of the wrecked car and came running to the side of the road where I was, holding her chest. I got out of my car and asked what had happened. She told me her car was hit by another car, causing her to spin, and then a tractor trailer hit her vehicle. Both the other car and tractor trailer drove off, leaving her car smashed in the middle of the road.

I got on the phone with the police while helping to keep her calm and assessing her to make sure she was alright. As this was going on, cars were weaving around her car, which was still in the middle of the road. All of a sudden an SUV slams into her car, causing it to go flying to the side of the road about 30 feet from where we were standing. That's when I really realized: This situation is extremely dangerous.

The SUV driver got out and came running to where we were. I helped keep both of them calm, got their medical history, and assessed them for injuries – all before the police and an ambulance finally arrived. As the woman was being loaded into the ambulance, I noticed she too was wearing scrubs and was a nurse on her way to work, just like me.

I just told my brother this story today and when I did, he pulled off his wristband and gave it to me, telling me to tell my story and pass on the wristband. So that's what I will do. *Wristband #17630*

Alicia C.
Baltimore, MD

Helping a Stranger on the Side of the Road

The other day my car battery died and left me stranded. When I finally got a hold of my mom, she came and tried to jump my battery, which unfortunately fried her car's battery too, leaving us both in a rut.

While my mom started her trek to her nearest friend's house, I waited by our cars. After about 20 minutes of watching cars whiz by, a student from a neighboring district pulled over and asked if I needed any help. Not only did he stay with me as it started to get dark, but he also called his dad who happened to be an auto mechanic. His dad selflessly came and fixed both my mother's and my own car.

I gave my wristband for actively caring to the boy for being the one out of the majority who pulled over to help me – a complete stranger. *Wristband #38955*

Abi C.
Chagrin Falls, OH

Caring for Victims of a Car Crash

I showed up on the scene of a head-on car crash that happened in front of us. Myself and several friends got out to help. I went to one of the cars that had some serious damage and found a young girl inside. Both drivers' side doors were stuck shut.

When I went around to the passenger side I discovered her legs were pinned between the seat and steering wheel/dashboard. While another passerby dialed 911, I got her to give me her parents' phone number. I called them to let them know what was going on.

I stayed with her and tried to keep her calm until the paramedics arrived.

Later, after some time went by, she got my number from her parents and called me. She said she had a wristband to give me and wanted my address. A little while later I got the wristband in the mail. *Wristband #12548*

Joey B.
Chesterfield, VA

Compassionate Helping

Compassion During Times of Hardship

My sister's husband recently passed away after an extended illness. As she completed the difficult task of going through his closet, she wondered what do to with his nearly new (and even some brand new) business and casual clothes. She saw the bus driver for the faith-based school where she teaches and noticed he always wears t-shirts and jeans. She was aware this was because of financial hardship and not a fashion statement. She asked his size and he was the same size as her husband's new clothes.

She gave him all of the clothes that fit him – outfitting him with an entirely new wardrobe. He and his family are so grateful. I've sent the wristband to my sister and I know she'll not only pass it on – but continue (as she has) to actively care for people. She is an inspiration to me and all of our family. *Wristband #15260*

Theresa S.
Taylor, TX

Strengthening Friendship

I recently passed a wristband on to one of my friends at Summer Residential Governor's School. A girl I know was giving me a hard time while a bunch of our friends were spending time together. I left the room, clearly upset, to spend the rest of the night in my dorm rather than provoking the girl even more. My friend, agreeing the girl's comments were out of line, came up to spend the rest of the night in my dorm room with me. We talked mostly about other things.

I thought it was incredibly sweet of my friend to go out of her way to cheer me up. By giving her the wristband I let her know she means a lot to me as a friend and I really appreciate her. She got a little teary-eyed (in happiness of course).

My first experience giving someone an AC4P wristband was one I will truly never forget because I grew much closer with that friend as a result. :] *Wristband #12576*

Melissa D.
Radford, VA

What Goes Around Comes Around

I have always been a proponent of *pay it forward* and when I initially heard of AC4P, I felt like a younger generation now had to chance to pay it forward and understand the benefits.

My story began last winter at a restaurant. I saw a family who was told by the hostess to stand outside in the cold. I quickly finished my dinner and asked that they be seated at our table. The family was from out of town, visiting their daughter, and was truly appreciative.

Fast forward to this summer. My youngest daughter and I were at a local supermarket. I had forgotten my wallet, but had checks. However, since I did not have my license, the clerk told me to put my groceries back. Out from behind in the line, a young female said "I will pay for her". I thanked her and tried to write her a check, but she would not take it.

Then, a different young female came from the door and ran up to the girl who paid for me. She said, "You are actively caring, here's a wristband for you, pass it on." I screamed with joy and my seven-year-old child smiled.

After leaving, I realized the girl who paid for me in the grocery store was Catherine – the same young girl to whom I gave my seat at the restaurant six months earlier. Pay it forward! Actively Caring for People can become a global Movement with your help!

Donna Wertalik
Blacksburg, VA

From One AC4P Act to Another

A few weeks ago, Dr Geller came through the door, buzzing with excitement. He had just been to his bank and Dalton, one of the bank tellers, told him she had a story she needed to share.

She had been at Panera Bread, venting on her cell-phone about an unpleasant event. Frustrated, Dalton hung up after saying, "I'm in Panera now, I'll call you later."

After she ordered, the man behind the counter smiled and told her he'd pay for her meal because she was having a bad day. Grateful and her day brightened, Dalton prepared to pass on the wristband she'd received weeks before only to realize she forgot it at home.

She explained this to him, saying she wanted to pass him the AC4P wristband. Matt proudly displayed his wrist, revealing a green AC4P wristband, "It's alright, I already have one." He had received *Wristband #57071* two weeks earlier from Joanne Dean Geller.

Eric Cunningham & Ilana Elias
NSF & MAOP Students
Blacksburg, VA

Notes

1. Kahneman, D. (2011). *Thinking, fast and slow*. New York, NY: Farrar, Straus and Giroux.

2. We are grateful to Lindsey Brookbank (Writer), Kelly Wolff (General Manager), and the entire Educational Media Company at Virginia Tech for allowing us to reprint an excerpt from: Brookbank, L. (2011, January 27). Chain reaction: Actively caring seeks widespread impact. *Collegiate Times*.

3. We are grateful to the following AC4P leaders who volunteered as undergraduate students to make Part V of this book a reality: Aly Neel (wristband recipient), John Kurlak (AC4P website developer), Harry Rosenbaum (wristband and graphic designer), Matt Wolk (AC4P website designer), and Ryan King (AC4P website manager).

4. Conari Press (1993). *Random acts of kindness*. Emeryville, CA.

Epilogue: Where Do We Go From Here?

E. Scott Geller

I BELIEVE MOST PEOPLE want to do the right thing, and they care profoundly about the hardships of others. Unfortunately, this majority remains silent until after tragic consequences.

Consider this profound quotation from Martin Luther King, Jr., "In this era of social transition, the greatest tragedy is not the blaring noisiness of the so-called bad people; it's the appalling silence of the so-called good people."[1]

Our challenge is to speak up sooner rather than later. This call for proactive AC4P behavior is easier said than done. We don't instinctively know how to offer advice, feedback, or support to promote well-being or prevent a possible mishap. And, it's certainly easier to avoid proactive AC4P behavior and reflexively continue working for soon, certain, positive, and self-serving consequences.

But this book introduced and explained effective techniques for intervening on behalf of the welfare of others. Lack of knowledge is not an excuse. This book also shared stories of the soon, certain, and positive consequences resulting from AC4P behavior. Indeed, it *is* better (i.e., more rewarding) to give (i.e., to actively care) than to receive. So a lack of motivation should not be an excuse.

To the silent majority, let's remain silent and inconspicuous no longer. Reflect on these issues and resolve to join our AC4P Movement to make the people of our world safer, healthier, better educated, and more positive. Just reading and understanding the contents of this book are not enough. You need to teach others the AC4P principles and applications shared in this book. But, teaching is not enough.

Practice AC4P Principles

If we are to make the vision of an AC4P culture of compassion real, we need you to put AC4P principles into practice. And, please make note of the worthwhile outcomes of your AC4P efforts.

When you document the methods and results of your AC4P behavior on behalf of one or more persons' well-being, your competence to teach the AC4P approach to others and convince them to get on board will be enhanced considerably.

The best teachers relate the information they're teaching to personal experiences. Interspersed throughout this book are personal stories from individuals who observed direct or indirect benefits of a particular AC4P intervention. In some cases, these authors experienced a spread of the positive intervention effects to other circumstances and settings.

Documenting your involvement with AC4P principles and practice can do more than increase your effectiveness at teaching others techniques for cultivating an AC4P culture. Your reporting of AC4P experiences can contribute to making a culture of compassion happen.

Post your AC4P stories on the ac4p.org website; email your friends and business colleagues about your positive exposures to the AC4P philosophy; write a brief newspaper report or magazine article about one or more AC4P stories; and contact your local T.V. news stations about your notable AC4P experiences.

Bottom line: An AC4P culture of compassion can only become a reality if the AC4P principles and applications are disseminated and practiced by large numbers of people. To meet this monumental challenge, we need your help to spread the word.

Our challenge is to convince ourselves and others that effective AC4P behavior is followed by soon, certain, and positive consequences. How do we do that? Through practice and feedback, of course. We need the humility to accept behavior-based feedback from others about ways to improve; and we need the courage to offer behavior-based feedback whenever it can support or improve AC4P-related behavior.

Humanistic Behaviorism

Please consider the humanistic principles of empathy, empowerment, and compassion when giving and receiving behavior-based supportive and corrective feedback. Yes, actively caring integrates the best of humanism and behaviorism – *humanistic behaviorism*. After all, *actively* means action (behavior) and *caring* is feeling (humanism).

It's noteworthy the American Humanists Association, founded in 1941 to be a clear, democratic voice for Humanism in the U.S. and to develop and advance humanist thought and action, awarded B.F. Skinner "Humanist of the Year" in 1972.[2]

B.F. Skinner has been one of my life-long inspirations. Indeed, the behavior-based safety I developed in 1979 was founded on the principles of Applied Behavioral Science (ABS) which evolved from the Behaviorism defined and researched by Professor Skinner.[3] Skinner's legacy: We act to gain positive consequences or avoid negative consequences; and the more immediate the consequence, the greater it's behavioral impact. Furthermore, consequences for the individual usually outweigh consequences for others.

Psychologist and scholar Paul Chance purports we must prove Skinner wrong in order to solve the major problems facing humanity.[4] I agree it's a challenge to move people beyond their self-serving desires to achieve soon, certain, and positive consequences. And I can't disagree entirely with his point that these primary principles of behaviorism give us "impulses that undermine our health; impel us toward violence; turn us into cheats, liars, and brigands, and threaten to make our world uninhabitable."[5]

However, I disagree with the implication that self-serving contingencies compel us *all* to perform undesirable behaviors, from cheating and lying to engaging in interpersonal conflict and violence. These are the individuals we hear about all too often in the news and over the internet, perhaps convincing some of us these undesirable actions reflect normative behavior.

I must also disagree with Dr. Chance's premise the ultimate challenge is to prove B.F. Skinner wrong.[4] Skinner was not wrong. We *are* motivated most by soon, certain, and positive consequences, and effective AC4P behavior *is* followed by soon, certain, and positive consequences – for others and for ourselves.

Integrating Research with Practical Applications

This book offered leading-edge strategies you can readily use to improve the health, safety, and well-being of people in various situations – from the workplace to schools and beyond.

Throughout my lengthy career as teacher, researcher, and author, I've had the good fortune to play the role of both an academic professor and an organizational consultant. While the academic researcher in applied psychology develops and evaluates interventions to improve the behavior of individuals and groups, the consultant selects and implements interventions to address problems defined by a particular client.

Consider the advantage of learning from professionals in both the academic and consulting worlds. This can assure the most effective intervention technologies are applied to current problems in ways that are acceptable, cost-effective, and employable by indigenous personnel.

Such was the mission of this book. All of the intervention tactics in the application chapters were developed from the results of both empirical research and practical implementation.

Only the Beginning

In his Foreword, Dave Johnson calls this book "Exhibit A" regarding the exposition of an AC4P Movement that "aspires to increase the competence, commitment, and courage needed to sustain AC4P behavior in all the nooks and crannies of daily life."

Actually, this edition is actually "Exhibit B," with five new chapters and numerous improvements since the first publication of this book in 2012. Plus, we have published Exhibit C – a revision of this text for application in schools, entitled *Actively caring at your school: How to make it happen*. In addition, my students, colleagues, and I are currently expanding and developing sections of this book into a college/university textbook to be published by the Cambridge University Press. Thus, Exhibit D will teach college students ways to enrich their lives with AC4P principles and applications.

Yet, we've only started to address large-scale, people-related problems that can be mitigated with AC4P interventions. Indeed, many of the AC4P methods in this book are incomplete, inconclusive, or inefficient. The potential is obvious, but much more research, development, and dissemination are needed to realize the long-term beneficial impact of the proactive interventions illustrated in this book.

Please contact us with ideas and application possibilities for researching the implementation of AC4P principles. The Actively Caring for People Foundation, Inc. was recently established to explore and evaluate applications of AC4P principles to improve the health, safety, and well-being of people worldwide.

Continuous Learning

Tim, a participant at a recent leadership retreat at my home – Make-A-DiffRanch in Newport, Virginia – made my day with the following comment. He shook my hand and said:

What a pleasure it was to hear your latest thoughts about person-to-person actively caring to benefit individuals, organizations, and communities. I first became aware of your research and scholarship when attending your day-long workshop at the ASSE (American Society of Safety Engineers) Convention in 2002. Since then I've read four of your books, and taught many of your principles to my colleagues at Cummins Rocky Mountain, LLC.

I'm not sharing this comment to show off, but rather to provide context for the rest of Tim's commentary, which was most rewarding to me.

Obviously, I was genuinely pleased to hear those kind remarks, but I had to interject, "It's so nice to learn that my teachings are reaching others through other teachers. But since you've already read several of my recent books, much of my workshop material today was redundant, right?" He replied:

For sure, I understood where you were coming from and I predicted where you were going throughout that session, and it was reassuring to hear it again. But what I really liked best was learning how your perspectives, principles, and application suggestions have evolved over the ten years I've been following your work.

That last comment was the big reinforcer for me. My teaching of practical ways to apply psychology for solving real-world problems has progressed significantly over the years, as I continuously learn from ongoing research and from my own and others' consulting experiences.

Contrary to the illustration on the next page, we're never too old to learn. For me, it's so meaningful to have an organizational leader recognize, understand, and appreciate the evolution of recommendations for managing the human dynamics of organizational and societal problems.

Why? Because it justifies continuous collaboration and mutual learning from researchers and consultants. Tim's commentary also validates the mission of this book – to connect research and practice for optimal intervention design and application relevant to cultivating cultures of compassion.

We've merely scratched the surface of societal problems that can be solved in part by applications of AC4P principles and procedures. The particular issues addressed in this book were limited largely to workplace and traffic safety, and alcohol abuse among college students. Our companion AC4P book focuses on AC4P applications in educational settings, from elementary school to universities.[6] The AC4P interventions within each of these problem domains are far from being comprehensive and optimal. We have so much more to learn from the synergistic integration of behavioral and humanistic psychology – *humanistic behaviorism.*

Please share your AC4P ideas and document your AC4P stories. They could incite relevant research, suggest real-world practice, or inspire participation by others. The outcome could very well end up in a subsequent edition of this book – Exhibit E, F, or G. More importantly, your AC4P leadership is necessary to encourage others to live an AC4P lifestyle and help lead the AC4P Movement.

Notes

1. King, Jr., M.L. *Martin Luther King Quotes.* Retrieved from http://www.inspirationpeak.com/cgi-bin/search.cgi?search=Dr.%20Martin %20Luther%20King&method=all

2. *American Humanist Association.* (2008). Retrieved September 9, 2012 from http://www.americanhumanist.org/

3. Skinner, B.F. (1976). *About behaviorism.* New York, NY: Knopf.

4. Chance, P. (2007). The ultimate challenge: Prove B.F. Skinner wrong. *The Behavior Analyst, 30*(2), 153-160.

5. Chance, P. (2007). The ultimate challenge: Prove B.F. Skinner wrong. *The Behavior Analyst, 30*(2), p. 158.

6. Geller, E. S. (Ed.). (2014). *Actively caring at your school: How to make it happen.* Newport, VA: Make-A-Difference, LLC.

Acknowledgements

For more than 30 years I've taught AC4P principles and applications in workshops and keynotes at regional and national conferences, as well as at various Fortune 500 Companies. The evidence-based AC4P lessons have always been well-received. But, periodically my evaluations have included a negative comment such as, "I appreciate the theory and principles presented by Dr. Geller, but I don't know how to apply his teachings. In other words, I like the ideas, but he didn't tell me what to do with them."

This book addressed this legitimate concern in the best way possible. How? By combining the principles with tried-and-true applications designed to address timely and costly societal issues. The application chapters were written by authors who developed and/or implemented research-based AC4P interventions and observed their beneficial effects. Plus, interspersed throughout the application chapters are personal stories from individuals who experienced benefits of a particular AC4P intervention.

Thus, it's fitting to first acknowledge the 30 authors of the application chapters and/or personal stories exemplifying the impact of practicing one or more AC4P principles. These authors are listed in the following pages, along with their education and current position.

Thank you all for illustrating functional utility of specific AC4P principles in the real world. You have given readers specific direction for effectively teaching, implementing, and/or evaluating AC4P interventions to address the human dynamics of critical large-scale issues affecting quality of life.

While your intervention plans targeted distinct settings and circumstances, many aspects of your methods can be adapted for different situations. Indeed, I hope readers will be inspired to customize and apply exemplars for problem domains beyond those addressed in your chapters. I also hope the success stories from these innovations and extensions will be sent to the Actively Caring for People Foundation, Inc. for possible inclusion in a subsequent edition of this book.

Five individuals contributed generously and extensively to preparing this book, Shane McCarty assisted throughout preparation of the first edition, from soliciting potential authors and recommending topics to helping me edit and refine several chapters, including my own.

I received valuable advice from Joanne Dean Geller with regard to the practicality of ideas and concepts. With unique experiences as a high-school teacher, public relations agent, sales representative, and safety director, Joanne offered invaluable feedback regarding the relevance of particular intervention plans and the selection of words to describe principles, applications, and ramifications.

Jenna McCutchen, current coordinator of the research and scholarship in our Center for Applied Behavior Systems (CABS), formatted the text of the entire book, including the painstaking processing of my handwritten chapters and continuous-improvement editing of every chapter.

Sophia Teie dedicated significant time and expertise preparing the first edition of this book for final processing. This required diligent proofing of the print, photos, and illustrations to assure the document sent to the printing company was the best it could be.

It's obvious the development, preparation and refinement of the information shared in this book was an interdependent team effort. Indeed, the vision of a book to teach AC4P principles and applications could not have become a reality without the valuable assistance of the individuals listed here. But there's more exceptional support to recognize.

I'm indebted to the long-term advice, alliance, and friendship of Dave Johnson, Editor of *Industrial Safety and Hygiene News (ISHN)*. Dave and I began collaborating in 1990 when I submitted my first five articles for publication in his magazine. Each time one of my articles was published, I learned something about communicating more effectively a principle or practice from behavioral or psychological science. This invaluable learning experience continued for the 19 consecutive years of my monthly *ISHN* column: *The Psychology of Safety*.

Dave was the Editor of my first safety book,[1] and two subsequent textbooks on people-based safety.[2] Plus, we co-authored a book that teaches relevant behavioral science to health-care workers.[3] In all four scholarship collaborations, including this book, Dave added his "magic" to the written expression and made it more concise, clear, and comprehensible.

Thank you, Dave Johnson, for continuing to help me make my scholarship more appreciable and appreciated by the general public. Indeed, if the contents of this book are not understood and accepted by masses of people beyond the ivory towers of university and research institutions, the applied research reported in this book has no chance of making the beneficial cultural difference it was designed to make.

Since 1990, my teaching, textbooks, and workbooks have benefitted from the artistic talents of George Wills – the creator of the instructive and entertaining illustrations interspersed throughout this book. I'm also beholden to Nancy Poes, the professional artist/illustrator who designed the cover of this book, displaying its purpose and mission so vividly and pertinently. Thanks to Nancy, you *can* judge *this* book by its cover.

I need to also acknowledge and thank a number of organizations and aggregations of individuals who believe in the mission and vision of CABS and the Actively Caring for People Foundation, Inc. They have been collaborating with us on several fronts.

Our continual partnerships with these groups will enable us to make our mutual aspirations a reality. Some of these associations of like-minded people have contributed financially to support our research Center, as well as the preparation and dissemination of this book. In particular, I'm truly grateful for the ongoing support and inspiration from:

- American Psychological Foundation (apa.org/apf)
- Angel Fund (angelfundva.org)
- Center for Peace Studies and Violence Prevention, Virginia Tech (cpsvp.vt.edu)
- Chardon Healing Fund (chardonhealingfund.com)
- Kevin R. Lawall Fellowship
- National Center for the Prevention of Community Violence (solveviolence.com)
- Safety Performance Solutions, Inc. (safetyperformance.com)
- VTV Family Outreach Foundation (vtvfamilyfoundation.org)

My 45-year teaching and research career at Virginia Tech, reflected by much of the contents of this book, has benefitted hugely from an extensive support system in both the academic and consulting worlds – professional colleagues, university students, and consumers of my books and education/training programs. All of you have offered constructive feedback to help me improve, and you've inspired me to keep on keeping on.

I thank you all very much. The synergy from your past, present, and future sustenance enables a legacy – AC4P principles and practices readers can use to enrich their lives and contribute to cultivating cultures of interpersonal compassion at work, school, home, and everywhere in between.

E. Scott Geller
May, 2014

Notes

1. Geller, E. S. (1996). *The psychology of safety: How to improve behaviors and attitudes on the job.* Radnor, PA: Chilton Book Company.

2. Geller, E. S. (2005). *People-based safety: The source.* Virginia Beach, VA: Coastal Training and Technologies Corporation; Geller, E. S. (2008). *Leading people-based safety: Enriching your culture.* Virginia Beach, VA: Coastal Training and Technologies Corporation.

3. Geller, E.S., & Johnson, D. (2008). *People-based patient safety: Enriching your culture to prevent medical error.* Virginia Beach, VA: Coastal Training and Technologies Corporation.

About the Authors

E. SCOTT GELLER, Alumni Distinguished Professor and Director of the Center for Applied Behavior Systems in the Department of Psychology at Virginia Tech, has authored or co-authored 41 books, 56 book chapters, 38 training manuals, 246 magazine articles, and over 350 research articles addressing the development and evaluation of behavior-change interventions to improve quality of life. His extramural grant funding, totaling more than $6 million, has involved the application of behavioral science for the benefit of corporations, institutions, government agencies, and communities.

He is a Fellow of the American Psychological Association, the Association of Behavior Analysis International, the Association for Psychological Science, and the World Academy of Productivity and Quality Sciences. He is past Editor of the *Journal of Applied Behavior Analysis* (1989-1992), current Associate Editor of *Environment and Behavior* (since 1982), and current Consulting Editor for *Behavior and Social Issues,* the *Journal of Organizational Behavior Management,* and the *Journal of Safety Research.*

Throughout his 45-year career, Dr. Geller has been honored with a number of prestigious awards, including teaching awards from the American Psychological Association, the Association for Behavior Anaylsis International, every university-wide teaching award offered at Virginia Tech, the University Alumni Award for Excellence in Research, the Alumni Outreach Award for exemplary real-world applications of behavioral science, the University Alumni Award for Graduate Student Advising,

the Virginia Outstanding Faculty Award by the State Council of Higher Education, the Award for Effective Presentation of Behavior Analysis in the Mass Media by the Society for the Advancement of Behavior Analysis, and Lifetime Achievement Awards from the American Psychological Foundation and the International Organizational Behavior Management Network.

In 2010, Scott Geller was awarded an Applied Research Award from the American Psychological Association and in 2011, The College of Wooster, Dr. Geller's alma mater, awarded him the honorary degree: Doctor of Humane Letters.

Dr. Geller is a Co-Founder and Senior Partner of Safety Performance Solutions, Inc., a leading-edge organization specializing in people-based safety training and consulting since 1995 (safetyperformance.com).

Joseph E. Bolduc, M.B.A. from Thomas College in Waterville ME; previously Division Manager Environmental, Health and Safety at Shaw Industries in Dalton, GA; currently Director of Health and Safety for Masco Contractor Services in Daytona, FL.

Wray A. Carvelas, M.B.A. from University of Johannesburg; President and CEO of DRA Americas, and Director of DRA Mineral Projects in South Africa; pioneered the implementation of People-Based Safety and AC4P for DRA in South Africa.

Joseph C. Dean, B.S. in Psychology from Virginia Tech, where he conducted research for the Center for Applied Behavior Systems; currently Environmental, Health and Safety Manager at the Aiken, SC location of Shaw Industries Group, Inc.

Joanne Dean Geller, B.A. in Elementary and Secondary Physical Education from Elon University; formerly a high-school teacher, and Director of Safety for a construction company in New Jersey; currently a professional caterer and fitness instructor.

Christopher Downing, B.S. in Psychology from Delaware State University; M.S. in Industrial/Organizational Psychology from Virginia Tech; currently conducting Ph.D. dissertation research in the Center for Applied Behavior Systems.

Mike Doyle, graduate of the Royal Canadian Armed Forces, University of Alberta's Occupational Health & Safety program, Behavior Modification from Okanogan University College. Designated Canadian Registered Safety Professional (CRSP). Presently EHS Manager for Suncor Energy Inc.

Chris S. Dula, Ph.D. in Clinical Psychology from Virginia Tech; currently Associate Professor of Psychology at East Tennessee State University in Johnson City, TN and a Licensed Clinical Psychologist, H.S.P.

Connie Engelbrecht, B.A. in Psychology from the University of South Africa; People-Based Safety (PBS) Manager for DRA Mineral Projects since 2006. Responsible for developing and implementng PBS intervention for DRA Mineral Projects in Africa.

Matthew J. Foy, B.S. in Psychology from Virginia Tech; formerly a Coordinator for the Center for Applied Behavior Systems; currently College Recruiter for Shaw Industries Group, Inc., Dalton, GA.

Cory B. Furrow, B.S. in Psychology from Virginia Tech; currently an M.S. student in Forest Resources and Environmental Conservation at Virginia Tech.

Justin Graves, B.S. in Sociology from Virginia Tech; currently pursuing an M.A.Ed. in Higher Education Administration at Virginia Tech.

Douglas Russell Hole, B.A. in Physical Education from the College of Wooster, Wooster, OH; M.A. in Political Science from Auburn University at Montgomery; 28 years in the U.S. Air Force rising to the rank of Colonel; worldwide duties in Intelligence.

Dave Johnson, B.S. in Journalism from Ohio University, Athens, OH; Chief Editor of the magazine *Industrial Safety & Hygiene News* (established 1967, circulation 71,400 subscribers) since 1980.

Bobby Kipper, Director of National Center for the Prevention of Community Violence. Former Newport News police officer and Director of Virginia's Gang Reduction Program.

Timothy Ludwig, Ph.D. in Applied Experimental Psychology from Virginia Tech; currently Professor of Psychology at Appalachian State University, and senior consultant with Safety Performance Solutions, Inc.

Benjamin Martin, B.S. in Psychology and an M.A. in Sociology from East Tennessee State University, Johnson City, TN.

Shane M. McCarty, B.S. in Marketing from Virginia Tech; currently a Ph.D. Student in Industrial/Organizational Psychology at Virginia Tech; research assistant in the Center for Applied Behavior Systems and the Center for Peace Studies and Violence Prevention at Virginia Tech.

Molly McClintock, B.S. in Communication from Cornell University; Co-Founder and currently an External Consultant with Safety Performance Solutions, Inc.

David M. McHugh, Maintenance and Safety Auditor for Nabors Completion and Production Services; Safety Facilitator and District People-Based Safety Facilitator from 2004 to present; pursuing a B.S. in Psychology and Photography at Long Beach City College.

Martin Mudryk, graduate of the University of Alberta's Occupational Health & Safety program and a 2015 MBA candidate. Designated Canadian Registered Safety Professional (CRSP) and Certified Safety Professional (CSP).

Chuck Pettinger, B.S. in Psychology from University of Florida; M.S. in Psychology from Rensselaer Polytechnic Institute; Ph.D. in Applied/Experimental Psychology from Virginia Tech; currently Process Change Leader at Predictive Solutions, Inc.

Turner Plunkett, B.S. in Chemical Engineering from Georgia Institute of Technology; M.B.A. from University of Richmond; currently Group Director of Manufacturing at Shaw Industries Group, Inc.

Corrine Picht, Graduated from Stillwater Area High School, Withrow, MN; currently an hourly employee leader for the Andersen Bayport People-Based Safety process.

Martin Ralph, B.S. in Environmental Science from Murdoch University (Western Australia) in Environmental Science and a post-graduate certificate in Organisational Human Resources and Safety, a Chartered Radiation Protection professional, and a member of the Australian Institute of Company Directors. He has been the Managing Director of the Industrial Foundation for Accident Prevention (IFAP) since 2001.

Steve Roberts, M.S. in Industrial/Organizational Psychology from West Chester University and a M.S. and Ph.D. in Applied/Experimental Psychology from Virginia Tech; Co-Founder and Senior Partner at Safety Performance Solutions, Inc.

Ryan C. Smith, B.S. in Psychology at Virginia Tech; B.A.s in Political Science and Sociology at Virginia Tech; M.S. and Ph.D. in Industrial/Organizational Psychology from Virginia Tech; Awarded Virginia Tech "Graduate Student of the Year" in 2013.

Adam C. Tucker, B.S. in Geology from Kent State University; currently the Director of Health Safety and Environment for the Distributions Business Unit of Cummins, Inc.

Bob Veazie, B.S. in Financial Management from California Polytechnic University of San Luis Obispo; M.B.A. from Long Beach State University; President of People-Powered Leadership, Inc.

Deborah Verdugo-Williams, B.S. in Music Education from the University of Alabama; M.A. from California State University in Liberal Studies; M.A. in School Administration from Cal Lutheran University; currently Vice Principal/Magnet Specialist at Mt. Vernon Creative & Performing Arts Magnet School in Bakersfield, CA.

Eric C. Williams, District People-Based Safety Facilitator at Nabors Completing Production Services; research assistant at the Gold Coast Recovery Center in Ventura, CA on substance abuse rehabilitation.

Index

Symbols

Other books by E. Scott Geller reflecting AC4P:

Actively Caring at Your School: How to Make it Happen (2014)

When No One's Watching: Living and leading self-motivation (2010)
(co-authored with Bob Veazie)

The Courage Factor: Leading people-based culture change (2009)
(co-authored with Bob Veazie)

Leading People-Based Safety: Enriching your culture (2008)

People-Based Patient Safety: Enriching your culture to prevent medical error (2007)
(co-authored with Dave Johnson)

People-Based Safety: The source (2005)

The Participation Factor: How to increase involvement in occupational safety (2002)

The Psychology of Safety Handbook (2001)

Intervening to Improve the Safety of Occupational Driving (2000)
(co-authored with Timothy D. Ludwig)

What Can Behavior-Based Safety Do for Me? (1999)

Understanding Behavior-Based Safety (1998)

Beyond Safety Accountability: How to increase personal responsibility (1998)

Building Successful Safety Teams: Together Everyone Achieves More (1998)

Working Safe: How to help people actively care for health and safety (1996)

The Psychology of Safety: Improving behaviors and attitudes on the job (1996)

Motivating Health Behavior (1994)
(co-authored by John P. Elder, Mel F. Hovell, & Joni A. Mayer)

Behavior Analysis Training for Occupational Safety (1987)
(co-authored by Galen R. Lehman & Michael R. Kalsher)

Preserving the Environment: New strategies for behavior change (1982)
(co-authored by Richard A. Winett & Peter B. Everett)

CPSIA information can be obtained
at www.ICGtesting.com
Printed in the USA
LVHW061921270819
629114LV00010B/302/P